DERBY PORCELAIN FIGURES, 1750–1848

THE FABER MONOGRAPHS ON POTTERY AND PORCELAIN

Present Editors: R. J. CHARLESTON *and* MARGARET MEDLEY
Former Editors: W. B. HONEY, ARTHUR LANE
and SIR HARRY GARNER

DERBY PORCELAIN FIGURES 1750–1848 *by* Peter Bradshaw

ROCKINGHAM POTTERY AND PORCELAIN 1745–1842 *by* Alwyn *and* Angela Cox

SÈVRES PORCELAIN *by* Svend Eriksen *and* Sir Geoffrey de Bellaigue

ORIENTAL BLUE AND WHITE *by* Sir Harry Garner

CHINESE CELADON WARES *by* G. St. G. M. Gompertz

SUNG PORCELAIN AND STONEWARE *by* Basil Gray

MASON PORCELAIN AND IRONSTONE *by* Reginald Haggar *and* Elizabeth Adams

NEW HALL *by* David Holgate

JAPANESE POTTERY *by* Soame Jenyns

MING POTTERY AND PORCELAIN *by* Soame Jenyns

YÜAN PORCELAIN AND STONEWARE *by* Margaret Medley

T'ANG POTTERY AND PORCELAIN *by* Margaret Medley

ENGLISH BROWN STONEWARE
by Adrian Oswald, R. J. C. Hildyard *and* R. G. Hughes

ENGLISH BLUE AND WHITE PORCELAIN OF THE EIGHTEENTH CENTURY
by Bernard Watney

PERSIAN LUSTRE WARE *by* Oliver Watson

ENGLISH TRANSFER-PRINTED POTTERY AND PORCELAIN
by Cyril Williams-Wood

Derby Porcelain Figures
1750–1848

Peter Bradshaw

ff
faber and faber
LONDON · BOSTON

First published in 1990
by Faber and Faber Limited
3 Queen Square London WC1N 3AU

Printed in Great Britain by
Butler & Tanner Ltd, Frome and London

CIP data for this book is available from the British Library

ISBN 0-571-15332-1

Publication of this book has been
assisted by a generous subsidy from
the Ceramica-Stiftung, Basel

Foreword

The Faber Monographs on Pottery and Porcelain have hitherto not included an individual volume devoted to the figures and groups of a single factory. When *Derby Porcelain* was published in 1971 the authors, Franklin A. Barrett and Arthur L. Thorpe, were constrained to deal with both tablewares and figures within the confines of a single pair of covers. In consequence, discussion of the figure production was restricted to some forty-five pages. The subject had already been given proportionate treatment in Arthur Lane's pioneering work *English Porcelain Figures of the 18th Century* (1961), where Derby figures received sixteen pages of penetrating analysis. Behind all these three authors lay a mass of documentary material, mostly gathered and published by John Haslem, W. Bemrose and J. E. Nightingale in the halcyon days of late-Victorian scholarship when material abounded and interpretation often seemed deceptively straightforward. We live in a more rigorous climate, and in Dr Peter Bradshaw's present book the English factory with incomparably the largest output of figures is subjected to minute scrutiny. Nor is it to be assumed that, because Derby's output of figures and groups was so large, it was stereotyped and unimportant. The figures of the earliest period often show a diversity of style and a freshness and strength of modelling which earn them a high place among the incunabula of European porcelain modelling anywhere. Later, Derby's figure-making in the biscuit had probably the greatest extension and the most successful development of that in any European factory, with the possible exception of Sèvres. In its middle period the factory richly earned the title which it bestowed upon itself of 'The Second Dresden'. Dr Bradshaw has chronicled all these developments with a thoroughness and insight which are unrivalled. His book is unlikely to be superseded, and offers essential reading to anyone wishing to be well informed on his subject.

R. J. CHARLESTON

Contents

Foreword by R. J. Charleston v
List of Colour Plates ix
List of Black and White Plates xi
Acknowledgements xxiii
Preface xxv

PART I

1 The Derby Factory, 1750–1848 3
2 Derby Porcelain Models, 1750–6 15
Experimental Derby Models, 1750–3 15
Dry-edge Derby Models, 1750–5 21
Transitional Derby Models, 1755–6 53
3 Derby Porcelain Models, 1756–69 58
Pale Family Derby Models, 1756–9 58
Patch-marked Derby Models, 1759–69 95

PART II

4 Derby Porcelain Models, 1770–96 131
5 The Derby Factory Lists 144
6 Sources of Derby Models, 1770–96 151
The Influence of Meissen 151
The Influence of French Factories on Soft-paste Biscuit Models 155
Other Sources 159

PART III

7 The Revised Derby Factory List 165

PART IV

8 The Last Derby Soft-paste Models, 1796–1810 405
9 Bone China Derby Models, 1810–48 407

APPENDICES

A Sculptors, Modellers and Craftsmen, 1770–96 443
B Modellers and Other Craftsmen, 1796–1848 462

Bibliography 466
Index 470

Colour Plates

Between pages 100 and 101

I B33. Chinoiserie group emblematic of *Taste*, from a set representing *The Five Senses*
II B30. *Venus with Cupid* group
III No. 256. *The Alpine Shepherdess*
IV B11. *Dancing Girl*, possibly *Columbine*
V B17. *Dancing Shepherdess*
VI C10. *Neptune* seated upon the stern-castle of an archaic ship
VII D26. *Cybele with a Lion*
VIII D22. Pair of *Grape-sellers*
IX E17. Pair of *Ranelagh Dancers*

Between pages 324 and 325

X E18. Pair of *Minuet Dancers*
XI E19. Group of *Tyrolean Dancers*
XII E7. *David Garrick as Tancred*
XIII E23. The *Garland Shepherds*
XIV F10. *George III in Van Dyck dress*
XV B34. *Lady with Parrot*, emblematic of *Feeling*, from a set representing *The Five Senses*
XVI No. 53. Pair of *Grimacing Dwarfs*
XVII No. 395. *Lady Feeding a Sheep with Hay*
XVIII Nos. 81 and 84. The *Shoe-black* and *Hair-dresser* groups
XIX G50. *Sleeping Nymph*

Black and White Plates

All examples are enamelled unless designated white or biscuit.

1 A1, A2 and A3. *Astrology*, *Literature* and *Music* (white)
2 A8. *Harlequin* seated with bagpipes (white)
3 A8. Facial features of *Harlequin*
4 A8. *Harlequin*'s spidery webbed fingers
5 A9. *Kitty Clive as Mrs Riot* (white)
6 A12. *Pug Dog Scratching* (white)
7 B11. Under-surface of base of *Dancing Girl*, showing a screw-hole
8 B34. The exposed rim of paste on the mound base of *Gallant Taking Snuff*, known as a dry-edge
9 B34. A circular aperture penetrating model from the back
10 B1. Pair of *Wild Boars* (white)
11 B3. Pair of *Ewe and Ram*, standing (white)
12 B6. *Male Goat*, standing (white)
13 B6. Companion *Female Goat*, suckling a kid
14 B9. Pair of *Recumbent Lion and Lioness* (white)
15 B10. Standing *Actor* striking an histrionic pose (white)
16 B11. *Dancer* wearing a Pierrot costume
17 B11. *Dancing Girl*, possibly *Columbine*
18 B13. *Harlequin* and *Columbine* (white)
19 B14. Group of *Huntsman Flautist and Reclining Lady*
20 B16. Male *Absinthe-seller*
21 B17. Pair of *Boy Shepherd Piper* and *Dancing Shepherdess* (white)
22 B19. *Map-seller* (white)
23 B21. *Apollo*, representing The Arts
24 B24. *Mars* (white)
25 B28. *St Philip*
26 B29. *St Thomas* (white)

27 B31. *The Four Infant Seasons* (white)
28 B32. Pair of *Street Vendors* (biscuit)
29 B32. Male harvester emblematic of *Summer* (white)
30 B32. Woman holding bird's nest, emblematic of *Summer*
31 B32. Rustic carrying grapes, emblematic of *Autumn*
32 B33. Chinoiserie groups emblematic of *Smell* and *Taste*
33 B33. Chinoiserie group emblematic of *Feeling* (white)
34 B34. Lady stroking a parrot, emblematic of *Feeling*
35 Gallant with a bird-cage, emblematic of *Hearing*, an example of erroneous restoration, and lady representing *Feeling*
36 B34. Gallant taking snuff, emblematic of *Smell*
37 B34. Gallant looking at his own reflection, emblematic of *Sight*
38 B34. Lady seated eating fruit, emblematic of *Taste* (white, glazed)
39 B37. Chinoiserie group of *Chinese Mother and Child* (white, glazed)
40 B38. Chinoiserie watch-stand
41 C2. *Crested Pheasant*, taperstick
42 C5. *Dancing Beribboned Youth*
43 C6 and C8. *Seated Lady* fondling a lamb, and *Seated Gentleman* with bird and dog
44 C10. *Neptune* seated upon a ship
45 D1. *Male Dancer* in Pierrot costume
46 D2. *Gentleman Flautist*
47 D4. Group of *Harlequin and Columbine*
48 D5. *Punch* holding a lantern
49 D6. *Lady Seated Playing a Mandoline*
50 D7. *Lady Seated Holding a Musical Score*, possibly emblematic of *Hearing*
51 D8. Group of *Two Lovers with a Clown*
52 D14. *Boy Shepherd and Dancing Shepherdess in Scottish Dress*
53 D15. *Youth and Girl Seated*, each with a posy
54 D16. *Youth and Girl Seated*, stiffly posed
55 D17. *The Dresden Shepherds*
56 D17. Alternative model of *Dresden Shepherdess*
57 D18. *Farmer* and his *Wife* standing bareheaded with flowers
58 D19. *Farmer's Wife* wearing a hat, adapted from D18
59 D20. *Farmer* wearing a hat and playing a reed-pipe
60 D20. *Farmer's Wife*, adapted to symbolize *Autumn*
61 D21. Seated boy and girl emblematic of *Spring* and *Summer*
62 D22. Seated pair of *Grape-sellers*

63 D24. *The Four Classical Seasons*, after Eberlein
64 D25. Girl with flowers emblematic of *Spring*
65 D25. Youth with axe and brazier emblematic of *Winter*
66 D25. Companion girl wearing a cloak warming her hands over a brazier, emblematic of *Winter*
67 D26. *Cybele with a Lion*
68 D31. *St Philip*
69 D32. *St Thomas*
70 D33. *Putto* decked with flowers
71 D45. *Unidentified* yellow- and purple-splashed *Bird*
72 E71. Patch-marks upon the under-surface of a model emblematic of *Africa*, c. 1760
73 E9. *Man with Flageolet and Tabor*
74 E13. *Mandoline and Bagpipe Players*
75 E17. *The Ranelagh Dancers*
76 E18. Pair of *Minuet Dancers*, after Watteau
77 E20. Group representing *The Dancing Lesson*
78 E22. *Gallant and Lady attired as Shepherd and Shepherdess*
79 E25. *Huntsman and Lady*
80 E26. *Italian Farmers*, c. 1760
81 E26. *Italian Farmers* before bocages, c. 1765
82 E29. *Shepherd* and *Shepherdess with Fruit and Flowers*
83 E30. *Shepherd* playing a recorder on scrolled base, before a bocage
84 E30. Companion *Shepherdess* with flowers
85 E31. *Basket Shepherds* (pair)
86 E33. *Dancing Shepherdess* with restyled dress
87 E33. *Shepherd Piper* and dog, new companion to the above
88 E35. Pair of *Jewish Pedlars*
89 E36. *Map-seller* and *Companion*
90 E37. *Negress* and *Abyssinian Archer*
91 E42 and E45. *Field Marshal Sir Henry Seymour Conway* and *John Wilkes, MP*
92 E50. *Diana with a Hunting-dog*
93 E52. Group of *Europa and the Bull*
94 E54 and E55. *Juno and a Peacock* and *Jupiter and an Eagle*, each in a chariot
95 E57. *Justice* with sword and scales
96 E59 and E60. *Mars* and *Minerva*, c. 1760
97 E59 and E67. *Mars* and *Venus with Cupid*, candlesticks
98 E60. *Minerva*, holding a spear and shield

99 *Neptune with a Dolphin*
100 E48, E61 and E66. *Britannia with a Lion, Neptune with a Dolphin* and *Venus and Cupid Seated upon a Dolphin*
101 E62. *Pluto and Cerberus*
102 E71. *Africa* and *Asia*
103 E76. Seated boy and girl representing *Spring* and *Autumn*
104 E77. *Putto* with flowers
105 E81. *Bull, Recumbent* before a small bocage
106 E84. *Ewe and Ram, Recumbent*
107 E85. *Fox, Seated*
108 E88. *Hound, Seated*
109 E92. *Pug Dog, Seated*
110 E98. Pair of *Red Squirrels* eating nuts
111 E99. *Stag and Doe at Lodge*
112 E100. *Doe at Lodge* before a bocage
113 E101. Pair of *Tigers*, prowling
114 E102. *Blue Tit*
115 E104. Candlestick groups of nesting *Buntings*
116 E109. *Goldfinch*
117 E119. *Unidentified Birds* watched by two dogs
118 F2. *General John Drinkwater*
119 F5. *William Pitt, the Lord Chatham*
120 F13. *Crucifixion Group*
121 F17. *The Four Elements*
122 F25. *Cock and Jewel Candlestick*
123 F26. *Vain Jackdaw Candlestick*
124 No. 3. Under-surface showing incised 'No. 3. Second', three patch-marks and flat glazed surface perforated by intermediate-sized hole
125 ?No. 1. Group of *Minerva Crowning Constancy and Hercules Killing the Hydra*
126 No. 3. *Air, Water* and *Earth*, from set of *The Four Elements*, c. 1772
127 No. 3. Complete set of *The Four Elements*, c. 1820
128 ?No. 4. *Pastoral Group*
129 No. 6. *The Four Infant Seasons*
130 No. 7. *Gardener and Companion*
131 No. 8. *Seated Boy and Girl with Fruit and Flowers*, biscuit examples
132 No. 9. *Boy with French Horn*
133 No. 9. Companion *Girl with Guitar*
134 No. 10. *Boy with Flute* (missing) and *Girl with Hurdy-gurdy*

135 No. 11. *Seated Gentleman with Flute and Lady with Lute*
136 No. 12. *Pastoral Group by a Fountain*
137 No. 13. *Cupid Riding a Goat* (one of a pair)
138 No. 14. *Sacrifice Figure*
139 No. 15. *Prudence* and *Discretion*
140 No. 16. *Dancing Couple*
141 No. 17. *Dancing Couple*
142 ?No. 19. *Child with Basket of Fruit*
143 No. 20. *Standing Boy and Girl with Fruit and Flowers*
144 No. 21. *David Garrick* and *Edmund Kean*, each as Richard III
145 Mezzotint of *David Garrick as Richard III* by J. Dixon after Nathaniel Dance
146 No. 25. *Calliope* (biscuit)
147 No. 35. Girl holding a cornsheaf, emblematic of *Summer* from a set of *The Four Rustic Seasons*
148 No. 36. *Seated Boy and Girl, Each with Flowers*
149 No. 37. Group of *Jason and Medea at the Altar of Diana*
150 No. 40. Group of two putti representing *Music*
151 Nos. 41, 43 and 44. Groups, each of two putti, representing *Commerce, Astronomy and Geometry*, and *Arithmetic*
152 No. 45. Group of two putti representing *Literature*
153 No. 46. *Boy and Girl Dancing a Reel*
154 No. 47. *Spring* and *Summer* from *The Four Grotesque Seasons*
155 No. 47. *Autumn* and *Winter* from *The Four Grotesque Seasons*
156 No. 48. Group of two putti representing *Air*
157 No. 48. Two groups, each of two putti representing *Water* and *Earth*
158 No. 48. Group of two putti representing *Fire*
159 No. 49. *Boy and Girl with Macaroni Dog and Cat*
160 No. 50. *Huntsman* with gun and dog
161 No. 50. *Lady* with gun and falcon
162 No. 51. *Gentleman and Lady with Dog and Cat*
163 No. 53. *Pair of Grimacing Dwarfs*
164 No. 55. Male member of *The Dresden Shepherds*
165 No. 55. Female member of *The Dresden Shepherds*
166 No. 56. *The Garland Shepherds*
167 No. 57. *The French Shepherds*
168 No. 58. *Shepherd Playing a Reed-pipe* (missing) with his dog
169 No. 59. Seated lady with Cupid, emblematic of *Feeling*
170 No. 59. Seated lady with mandoline, emblematic of *Hearing*

171 No. 59. Seated youth with a spy-glass and eagle, emblematic of *Sight*
172 No. 59. Seated youth with a posy and hound, emblematic of *Smell*
173 No. 59. Seated youth eating grapes beside a panther, emblematic of *Taste*
174 No. 60. Male *Singing Shepherd*
175 No. 60. Female *Singing Shepherd*
176 No. 61. Three seated girls emblematic of *Spring, Summer* and *Autumn*
177 No. 62. *The Welch Tailor and his Family*
178 No. 63. *Boy and Girl in Turkish Costumes*
179 No. 65. *Diana with a Hunting-dog*
180 No. 66. *Venus and Cupid* group
181 No. 68. Two biscuit groups representing *Autumn and Summer*, and *Spring and Winter*
182 No. 71. *Boy Seated with Cat*
183 No. 71. *Girl Seated with Dog*
184 No. 72. *Pastoral Group with Dog*
185 No. 73. *Pastoral Group with Dog and Lamb*
186 No. 75 and No. 76. Two groups: *Procris and Cephalus* and *Renaldo and Armida*
187 No. 77. *Stocking-mender Group*, c. 1815
188 No. 78. *Shoe-maker Group*, c. 1820
189 No. 78. *Shoe-maker Group*, c. 1775
190 No. 81. *Shoe-black Group*, c. 1820
191 No. 83. *Fury Group with Broken Chair*
192 No. 84. *Hairdresser Group*, c. 1815
193 No. 88. *Mrs Catherine Macaulay* (biscuit with parcel enamel and gilt)
194 No. 89. *The Unfaithful Husband* group, biscuit
195 No. 90. *A Cook*
196 No. 91. Group of *Two Female Macaronis*
197 No. 92. Group of *Three Figures Learning Music*
198 The Chelsea group of *The Music Lesson*
199 Sèvres group of *La Leçon Agréable*
200 No. 93. Group of *Children Playing Hazard*
201 No. 94. Group of *Children at a Peep-show*, c. 1775
202 No. 94. *Three Children at a Peep-show* c. 1820
203 No. 99. *Aesculapius*
204 No. 100. *Andromache Weeping over the Ashes of Hector*
205 No. 101. *Boy Eating an Apple and Girl Curds-and-Whey*
206 No. 105. Seated *Monk* and *Nun*, each reading a book
207 ?No. 109. *Monk* standing, holding a skull

208 ?No. 111. *Confessional Group with Monk and Nun*
209 No. 114. *Mars*
210 Chelsea version of *Mars*
211 No. 115. *Venus and Cupid* group
212 *Bronze Group of Aphrodite with a Child Centaur*
213 No. 117. *Jupiter and an Eagle*
214 No. 119. *Juno with a Peacock*
215 No. 120. *Diana*
216 No. 123. *The French Seasons*, c. 1790, enamelled
217 No. 123. *Spring* and *Summer*, biscuit
218 No. 123. *Autumn* and *Winter*, biscuit
219 No. 124. Group of *Time Clipping the Wings of Love*
220 No. 125. Sportsman, emblematic of *Autumn*, from *The Chelsea Seasons*
221 No. 126. *John Wilkes, MP* (biscuit and parcel gilt)
222 No. 137. *The Prudent Mother* group
223 No. 138. *Madonna and Child* group
224 No. 139. *Musical Group of Two Figures*
225 No. 140. *Musical Group of Two Figures*
226 No. 142. *Boy Riding a Dolphin*
227 No. 146 and 147. Busts of *Addison* and *Virgil* (biscuit)
228 No. 156. *Bust of Zingara*
229 Nos. 159 and 160. Busts of a *Philosopher Laughing* and a *Philosopher Crying*
230 Nos. 161 and 162. *Antique Figures of Wisdom* and *Justice*
231 No. 163. *Antique Figure of Plenty* (biscuit)
232 No. 164. *Antique Figure of Peace*
233 No. 176. Group of *Grape-gatherers*
234 No. 178. Group of the *Alpine Shepherdess*
235 No. 179. Group of *Four Children Playing Music* (biscuit)
236 No. 182. *Cupid Riding a Buck* (one of a pair)
237 No. 184. *Boy Reading a Book*
238 No. 184. Companion *Girl Tatting*
239 No. 192. *Man and Woman Standing beside Hampers*
240 No. 193. *Bacchus* (biscuit)
241 No. 194. *Ariadne* (biscuit)
242 No. 194. *Ariadne*
243 No. 195. Group of *Two Virgins Awakening Cupid* (biscuit)
244 No. 196. Group of *Two Bacchantes Adorning a Bust of Pan* (biscuit)
245 No. 198. Male figure of a *Haymaker*

246 No. 198. Female *Haymaker's Companion*
247 No. 199. *Harlequin and Columbine* (biscuit)
248 No. 199. *Harlequin* (enamelled)
249 No. 200. *The Four Quarters of the Globe*
250 Nos. 202 and 205. *Cupid* with gun and hound, companion with hunting-horn (biscuit)
251 No. 204. *Gardener* with a pannier of flowers
252 No. 204. *Gardener's Companion* with a watering-can
253 No. 213. *Cupid Seated with a Dog* (biscuit)
254 No. 214. Companion *Cupid with a Falcon*
255 No. 216. Group emblematic of *Poetry* (biscuit)
256 No. 217. Group emblematic of *Music* (biscuit)
257 No. 222. *Winged Time*
258 No. 227. The Mansion House *Dwarfs*
259 Etching by Callot of a Dwarf with a big belly
260 Etching by Callot of a Dwarf with a tall hat
261 No. 231. *James Quinn as Sir John Falstaff*
262 No. 234. Group of *Four Cupids Bird's-Nesting* (biscuit)
263 No. 235. Group of *Three Graces Distressing Cupid* (biscuit)
264 No. 235. Group of *Three Graces Distressing Cupid*
265 No. 243. *Apollo*
266 No. 245. *Charlotte Weeping for Werther*
267 No. 248. Group of *The Antique Seasons* (biscuit)
268 No. 251. Group of *Four Cupids Hunting* (biscuit)
269 No. 252. Group of *Three Cupids* (biscuit)
270 Nos. 255 and 256. Two groups: *The Knot in the Cravat* and the *Alpine Shepherdess*
271 No. 259. *Britannia*
272 No. 260. *Girl Laughing*, holding her brother's ball
273 No. 260. Companion *Boy Crying*, reaching out for his ball
274 Nos. 262–78. Five *Cupids in Disguise*
275 Nos. 262–78. *Cupid Disguised as a Money-lender*
276 Nos. 262–78. *Cupid Disguised as a Hurdy-gurdy Girl*
277 *Cupid Disguised as a Hurdy-gurdy Girl*, red anchor Chelsea version
278 No. 280. *Seated Musicians with Bagpipes and Guitar*, candlesticks
279 ?No. 281. Possibly a pair of *Spring Candlesticks*
280 ?No. 281. Possibly a pair of *Spring Candlesticks*
281 ?No. 283. Possibly *Gardener Candlesticks*

282 No. 288. *Mars and Venus* candlesticks
283 No. 292. Pair of *Dessert Gardeners*
284 No. 293. *Tithe Pig Group*
285 No. 294. Group of *The Four Seasons* about an obelisk
286 No. 295. Group of *The Four Quarters of the Globe* about an obelisk
287 No. 296. Biscuit figure of *The Haymaker's Companion* (one of a pair)
288 Nos. 297 and 305. *John Milton* and *William Shakespeare*
289 No. 298. *Minerva*
290 No. 299. *Neptune with a Dolphin* on a tall shell-encrusted base
291 No. 302. *Fame and Mercury* candlesticks
292 No. 307. *Seated Bagpiper and Lady with a Lute*
293 No. 311. *Male Musician*, standing with flageolet and tabor
294 No. 311. *Companion Female Musician* with a triangle
295 No. 316. *Sailor and his Lass*
296 No. 317. *Pair of Dancing Figures*
297 No. 323. *Cupid Candlestick* (biscuit)
298 No. 332. *The Four Quarters of the Globe*
299 No. 333. Group of *Four Boys Playing Music* (biscuit)
300 No. 334. Group of *Four Boys with Pets*
301 No. 334. Reverse view of *Four Boys with Pets*
302 No. 358. Group of *Cupid Disarmed by Euphrosyne* (biscuit)
303 No. 359. *Gardener* leaning upon a spade (missing) by Coffee (biscuit)
304 No. 359. *Gardener's Companion* (biscuit)
305 No. 359. *Gardener* by Spengler (biscuit)
306 No. 361. *Gardener*
307 No. 362. *Seated Boy with Macaroni Dog and Girl with Cat*
308 No. 363. *Two Figures Burying a Dead Bird* (biscuit)
309 No. 364. Group of *Gallant and Lady Waltzing* (biscuit)
310 No. 365. *Boy Piping as He Dances*
311 No. 365. *Boy Piping* (biscuit)
312 No. 365. *Companion Girl Dancing with Cymbals* (biscuit)
313 No. 366. Group of *Palemon and Lavinia* (biscuit)
314 No. 369. *Shepherd Playing Flute* (biscuit)
315 No. 369. *Companion Shepherdess Playing Flute* (biscuit)
316 No. 370. Group of *Belisarius and his Daughter* (biscuit)
317 No. 372. Pair of figures known as *The Proposal* (biscuit)
318 No. 373. Biscuit group of *Four Figures, Subject Unidentified*
319 No. 376. Biscuit group of *Bacchus with Nymphs on Mount Nysa*

320 No. 378. *Scotsman and his Lass*
321 No. 379. Group emblematic of *Music* (biscuit)
322 No. 380. Group of *Art, Literature* and *Astrology*
323 No. 380. Reverse view of above
324 No. 384. *Admiral Lord Howe* (biscuit)
325 No. 385. *Aesculapius and Hygeia*
326 No. 388. Group of four putti emblematic of *The Four Seasons* (biscuit)
327 No. 388. Reverse view of above
328 No. 389. *The Alpine Shepherds* (biscuit pair)
329 No. 390 (ii). *Flora* (biscuit)
330 No. 391. *Prince Frederick Augustus, Duke of York*
331 No. 393. Group of *The Russian Shepherds* (biscuit)
332 No. 394. *Seated Piper* (biscuit). May be part of *The Russian Shepherds* group or a single model
333 No. 395. *Lady Feeding a Sheep with Hay* (biscuit)
334 No. 396. *Shepherd with his Dog* (biscuit)
335 *Bronze, after the antique, of Hermes*
336 No. 397. *Cupid Entreating a Virgin* (damaged biscuit group)
337 G2. *Maria Foote as Arinette*
338 G3. *Grimaldi the Clown*
339 G5. *John Liston as Paul Pry*
340 G8. *Three Tyrolese Singers*
341 G9. *Madam Vestris as a Bavarian Peasant Woman*
342 G9. *Madam Vestris* in a slightly different version
343 G10. *Billy Waters*, the one-legged negro fiddler
344 G11. *Dr Syntax Retiring to Bed*
345 G12. *Dr Syntax Sketching*
346 G15. *Dr Syntax Playing a Violin*
347 G16. *Dr Syntax Reciting in the Green Room*
348 G17. *Dr Syntax at York Races*
349 G18. *Dr Syntax Chased by a Bull*
350 G22. *Dr Syntax Astride his Horse Grizzle*
351 G23. *Dr Syntax Landing at Calais*
352 G26. *Napoleon Bonaparte*
353 G28. *George IV* (biscuit)
354 G29. *Mazeppa* group (biscuit)
355 G30. The young *Queen Victoria* (biscuit)
356 G31. *The Duke of Wellington* (biscuit)

357 G34. *Industrious Girl* (one of a pair)
358 G35. *Man and Woman with Milk Churns*
359 G39. *Toper*
360 G39. Companion *Toper*
361 G40. *Romantic Boy and Girl* (biscuit)
362 G41. *A Warden* and *A Vicar*
363 G50. *Sleeping Nymph* (biscuit)
364 G50. *Nymph Asleep Amidst Flowers*
365 G59. *Monkey Orchestra*
366 G60. Pair of *Cats* on cushions
367 G66. *Cow and Calf* group
368 G70. Group of two *Hounds* (biscuit)
369 G72. Seated *Poodle Dog*
370 G73. Another *Poodle Dog*
371 G74. Pair of seated *Pug Dogs*
372 G76. *Pointer* or *Setter, Prowling*
373 G79. *Elephant without Mahout*
374 G85. *Leopard Prowling* (one of a pair)
375 G90. *Ewe, Recumbent*
376 G90. *Ram, Recumbent*
377 G91. Group of *Sheep*
378 G92. *Squirrel* seated with a nut (one of a pair)
379 G94. *Peacock amongst Flowers*

Acknowledgements

It is a pleasure to thank Miss Judith Anderson for allowing me to examine and photograph items in her charge in the Derby Museums and Art Gallery and for showing me memoranda made by past members of the museum staff. I am especially grateful also to Peter and Shirley Neve for their photographs of models in private collections, to Peter Williams for locating examples of rare figures, and to David Thorn who permitted me unlimited access to his private collection, stock and library. I wish to record my sincere thanks to the following who supplied the photographs: Miss Emmeline Leary, Birmingham Museum and Art Gallery; David Garlick, Bowes Museum, Barnard Castle; Miss Aileen Dawson, British Museum; Miss Pamela Wood, Castle Museum, Nottingham; Miss J. Clarke, Cecil Higgins Museum, Bedford; Miss Judith Anderson, Derby Museums and Art Gallery; Miss Julia Poole, Fitzwilliam Museum, Cambridge; Thomas Garnon, Hanbury Hall, Droitwich; Miss Maureen Atrill, Plymouth Museum and Art Gallery; Miss Natalia Wiecozovek, Royal Crown Derby Museum; A. J. Finlinson, Upton House, near Bambury; J. V. G. Mallet, Victoria and Albert Museum; Miss Molly Pearce and David Siers, Weston Park Museum, Sheffield; Mrs Susanna van Langenberg, National Magazine Co. Ltd; A. J. Finlison, Regional Director, The National Trust; Eric Knowles, W. and F. C. Bonham and Son Ltd; Hugo Morley-Fletcher and Anton Gabszewicz, Christie, Manson and Woods Ltd; John Sandon, Phillips, London; Peter Williams and Peter Waldron, Sotheby's, London; Mrs Letitia Roberts, Sotheby's, New York; Mrs Pamela Rowan; Aldbury Antiques, Blockley; Mrs E. Falik, Burnley Antiques, Burnley; Stafford Lorie, Grosvenor Antiques, Holland Street, London; Timothy Kendrew, T. Kendrew Antiques, Stamford, Lincs.; Mrs Betty Klaber, Klaber and Klaber, Kensington Church Street, London; David Love, David Love Antiques, Harrogate, Yorks.; Mrs Pearl Manheim, D. M. and P. Manheim Ltd, London; Springfield Antiques, Kensington Church Street, London; David Thorn, B. and T. Thorn, Budleigh Salterton, Devon; R. H. Thornton, Thornton's of Harrogate, Yorks.; Mrs Sheila Davis, Venner's Antiques, New Cavendish Street, London; W. W. Warber, Warber's Antiques, Brasted,

Kent; Robert Williams, Winifred Williams, late of Bury Street, London, now at Eastbourne, Sussex; Norman C. Ashton; Mrs Robin Barkla; Major and Mrs D. R. Baxter; Dr H. M. E. Edwards; Colonel A. E. Dodson; Raymond Shingler; Miss Phyllis Winterton.

Lastly, but by no means least, this work was generously sponsored by Ceramica-Stiftung, Basel, Switzerland, by a grant without which publication in its present form would not have been possible.

Preface

English soft-paste porcelain figures possess an elegance and charm that have endeared them to generations of connoisseurs and collectors and once prompted the late W. B. Honey to refer to them as 'delightful nonsense'. They made their début about 1745 at Chelsea and, within less than five years, appeared also at Bow, Longton Hall and Derby. The earliest examples were derived from a variety of two- and three-dimensional sources, but after about 1752 the majority were based on Meissen prototypes. During the early 1740s the fashion had been introduced at the Electoral Court in Saxony of decorating the festive board with up to two or three hundred porcelain figures arranged about a centre-piece depicting a theme appropriate to the occasion. In England, during the 1750s and 1760s, the display was more modest with perhaps twenty or thirty models laid out down the centre of the dining-table, sometimes upon a patterned carpet of coloured marble chips contained in shallow silver trays. The interval between the creation of a Meissen prototype and the appearance of its English copy was initially six to eight years so that the Baroque style was reflected long after it had yielded to the Rococo on the Continent. However, by about 1756 the time-gap had narrowed to little more than twelve months and this was associated with the influence of the more exuberant decorative style. The years 1752–8 were the Golden Age of English porcelain figures, manifest in products bearing the red anchor mark of Chelsea, and including dry-edge Derby and middle period Bow models and groups.

During the autumn of 1756 Dresden was occupied by the Prussian troops of Frederick the Great at the commencement of the Seven Years War. The export of new Meissen models virtually came to an end although old stock continued to reach this country, albeit in steadily diminishing amounts, until about 1764. English modellers turned increasingly to Sèvres for fresh sources of inspiration but for technical reasons were unable to copy the white biscuit favoured by the French factory and instead employed the lavish enamelled and gilt decoration evident on their table ware. After 1760, the English figures became progressively debased to fulfil only a minor role in what had become a purely decorative ensemble. The stiffly posed figures stare vacantly into space, clad in sumptuous garments adorned with enamel and gold, mounted on sculptured bases before arbours of leaves and flowers, known as bocages. These were often surmounted by a tulip candle-holder or flanked with swan-necked candle-sconces and were obviously better suited for display upon the mantelpiece or library shelf than on the dining-table. Chelsea set the fashion, while Derby and Bow were content to follow.

A charge of provincialism has been levelled against Derby, for aping a London style and wearily maintaining it long after it became obsolete. Such an untutored narrowness and failure to reflect contemporary taste may possibly explain the failure of the Bow factory in 1776 but is manifestly untrue of Derby. There, following the acquisition of the Chelsea works in 1770, the former fripperies of the High Rococo were shed as the importance of the figure was reasserted by a fresh generation of sculptor-modellers recruited from North-west Europe. Their work was perfectly adapted to portray the more disciplined Louis Seize style and was salted by occasional contributions made by young sculptors resident in London. Further, by April 1771, William Duesbury had evolved a paste sufficiently refined to allow biscuit figures (without coverage by glaze) to be issued which were invariably left white to simulate the finest Italian marble. This medium permitted the reproduction of crisp, moulded detail and a greater severity of form and line imposed after 1785 with the rising tide of Neo-Classicism. Although some exquisite work was created, the larger scale that was now favoured, coupled with the absence of glaze and colour, transformed what had once been a charming toy into miniature sculpture; and, in this metamorphosis, most of the magic was lost.

The demand in London for porcelain figures began to decline by 1786 and accordingly production of new models was curtailed. The closing years of the eighteenth century witnessed the departure from Derby of the last of the great sculptor-modellers and thereafter humbler craftsmen with more modest talent staffed the figure department. Between about 1810 and 1815 the sensuous soft paste was abandoned in favour of a bone china body clad in a feldspathic glaze. Now, as the Industrial Revolution gained momentum, an entirely new clientele arose with tastes that were very different from those enjoyed by both the aristocracy and landed gentry who hitherto had comprised the bulk of the market. The new patrons demanded more robust models, at times amounting almost to lampoons, of their favourite stage personalities, public figures or characters derived from contemporary literature. Others included children portrayed in sentimental vein or models that illustrated either the work ethic or the wages of sin. These were mostly presented in strong enamel colours enlivened with lavish gilding or, less often, in a dry hard-paste biscuit. Very little of artistic merit was created and, after entering a period of decline, the factory failed in 1848.

Although much has been written about old Derby porcelain, most of this relates to cabinet pieces and table wares, while individual figures, which probably made up nearly half the output, have not received adequate attention. Here, figure models and groups of the several phases of production are considered in depth and the factory list covering approximately the years 1772–96, has been revised, extended and liberally illustrated. Two earlier versions, one published by John Haslem in 1876, the other by William Bemrose in 1898, both contain many errors, blanks and ambiguities and after nearly a century the time seemed ripe for complete reappraisal. The lives of modellers and others concerned with the modelling department at Derby between 1770 and 1796 are summarized in Appendix A, and those of the succeeding period, 1797–1848, in Appendix B.

Part I

1 · The Derby Factory, 1750–1848

The origins of the Derby porcelain factory remain to this day shrouded in mystery. Llewellynn Jewitt[1] relates the account written by Samuel Keys in 1837 from his past recollections:

> China was first made at Derby I believe by a man in a very humble way (but his name I cannot recollect). He resided in Lodge Lane in some old premises up a yard by the (now Brown Bear) public house. When he first began, he fired his articles in a small pipe kiln very near, till he had constructed a small kiln in a fireplace in the old premises he lived in. He had only small animals and birds, laying-down lambs, etc. Mr. William Duesbury the first, got his knowledge firstly from that man and improved on it. I never knew much of Mr. Duesbury's origin, but believe he came from Walsall, or the neighbourhood. Mr. Duesbury was on friendly terms with Mr. Heath, the banker and the proprietor of the Pot Works on Cockpit-Hill, and which I well remember. Mr. Duesbury had improved on his small experience with small china toy making, and Mr. Heath assisted him in the most liberal and friendly manner, with money and other means to carry on, which he did with credit to himself and benefit to others.

William Chaffers[2] recorded a similar story, although he ascribes it to William Locker, who was the factory clerk between 1809 and 1848:

> About 1745 a man, said to be a foreigner in very poor circumstances living in Lodge Lane made small articles in china such as birds, cats, dogs, sheep, and other ornamental toys, which he fired in a kiln in the neighbourhood belonging to a pipe maker named Woodward. Mr. Duesbury frequently visited this

1 Llewellynn Jewitt, *The Ceramic Art of Great Britain*, London, 1878, II, p. 63.

2 William Chaffers, *Marks and Monograms on European and Oriental Pottery and Porcelain*, London, 15th rev. ed., 1965, II, p. 189.

image maker in his small factory, and becoming desirous of improving the art, he engaged his services on his own account . . .

It is scarcely credible that the porcelain models which today are considered to represent the first products of the Derby factory could have been fired in a pipe-clay oven and it would seem that Samuel Keys and William Locker have repeated stories which both derive from a common and fallible source. Nevertheless, in 1898 William Bemrose[3] announced the discovery of an oven-kiln in Lodge Lane, supposedly one which once had belonged to Woodward. However, in 1927 Williamson[4] demonstrated that this was constructed with bricks baked in the nineteenth century and that the building in which it was located had not been erected before 1795, although this does not preclude the possibilty of an earlier kiln on the same site.

Jewitt[5] and Mrs Donald MacAlister[6] have identified the 'foreigner' as André Planché (1727–1809), the son of Paul Planché, coffee-man, and his wife, née Marie-Anne Fournier, Huguenot refugees who separately fled France after the revocation of the Edict of Nantes to meet and marry in London. André, of the parish of St Anne's, Westminster, was apprenticed jeweller to Edward Mounteney of Foster's Lane, London, on 3 July 1740. Normally he would have been free of this bond after seven years and, on 28 September 1747, he wed Sarah Stone in St Pancras Church. Probably within months he migrated to Derby, then the centre of a thriving jewellery trade. We have no inkling as to why he chose to exchange the security afforded by his guild for the uncertainties attached to the then novel ceramic industry, although two other Huguenots, Nicholas Sprimont, silversmith, and Charles Gouyn, goldsmith, followed a similar course and became proprietors, respectively, of the Chelsea and Girl-in-a-Swing porcelain factories. Nor is it known where Planché acquired the expertise necessary for such a career, although Jewitt[7] wrote: 'I believe he went into Saxony and there learned the art of making porcelain at Dresden.' The Derby frit porcelain is, however, totally dissimilar from the Meissen hard paste and it is scarcely credible that Planché was taught to model in wax or clay by J. J. Kändler or his associates. Twitchett[8] noted that a potter at Chantilly was named Fournier; he may possibly have been a kinsman of Planché's mother and helped to create a similar soft paste at Derby. Twitchett also recalls the legend that an illegitimate son of the proprietor of Chantilly, Louis-Henri de

3 William Bemrose, *Bow, Chelsea and Derby Porcelain*, London, 1898, pp. 104 and 105.

4 F. Williamson, *Connoisseur*, 77, 1927, pp. 228–9.

5 Jewitt, op. cit., pp. 57–66.

6 Mrs Donald MacAlister, 'The Early Work of Planché and Duesbury', *Trans. EPC*, no. 2, 1929, pp. 45–59.

7 Jewitt, op. cit., pp. 57–66.

8 John Twitchett, 'William Duesbury, A Man of Achievement', *Ceramics*, August 1987, pp. 72–80.

Bourbon, Prince de Condé, was sent during the early 1750s to work at the Derby manufactory. In any event, there must have been several men, both Huguenot émigrés and Englishmen, who had acquired the arcanum and had experience of modelling figures. A possible candidate was James Marchant, about whom more will be said later. Jewitt wrote of André's brother, Jacques: 'He made his way to Geneva where he learned the business of watch making.' Subsequently he was associated with the London atelier of Benjamin Vulliamy, clockmaker to George III.

The date when porcelain was first made in the town of Derby remains uncertain. On 1 January 1775, Josiah Wedgwood wrote a letter to his partner, Thomas Bentley,[9] in which he intimated that he had been interrupted at work 'by a man from the Derby China works, who wants to be hired – he is a Derby man and has a wife and family there, and has worked at the manufactory twenty-eight years. His name is Holmes ...' Taken literally, this presupposes the presence in Derby of a porcelain factory as early as 1747, most probably the year when Planché arrived in the town. Although porcelain may have been made there around 1748, the first documentary pieces are three creamers incised, respectively, 'D. 1750',[10] 'D',[11] and 'Derby'.[12] These are made from a non-phosphatic glassy paste containing 4.6–6 per cent of lead oxide, and are sprigged with strawberry flowers that have four or five concave petals, clumsy-looking stems and thick leaves. Interestingly enough, Dr Bernard Watney[13] has described a small group of figures displaying some unusual modelling traits, slip-cast from a similar paste and bearing some identical sprigging. These may represent the first attempts to model in porcelain at Derby, and are here referred to as Experimental Derby, listed on pp. 17–21 (List A).

The registers of St Alkmund's Church, Derby, once situated upon the road leading down to St Mary's Bridge but now demolished, contain entries under the name 'Andrew Planche, china maker'. They include the baptisms of his first-born son, Paul Edmund, on 21 September 1751; his second son, James, on 12 October 1754; his third but illegitimate son by Margaret Burrows, William, on 4 March 1756; and of his fourth and legitimate son, William, on 3 July 1756. Also recorded is the burial of his infant son James, on 11 December 1754. The absence of later entries suggests that Planché left Derby in the autumn of 1756.

The unusually fine quality of the seventy-odd models made at Derby c. 1750–55,

9 W. H. Tapp, 'The History of Derby Porcelain Figures', *Apollo*, December 1934, p. 1.
10 Victoria and Albert Museum.
11 British Museum.
12 Colonial Williamsburg Foundation, USA.
13 Bernard Watney, 'A Hare, a Ram, Two Putti and Associated Figures', *Transactions of the English Ceramic Circle* (hereinafter *Trans. ECC*), 8, 1972, pt. 2, pp. 224–7.

here called 'Dry-edge' and listed on pp. 32–52 (List B), has led some to suggest that their master models were created by sculptors resident in London and dispatched to Derby for translation into porcelain. However, as will later be shown, some of the relevant moulds that survive are incised 'A. P.' while, after the departure of Planché, the quality of both paste and glaze were debased and a marked deterioration of modelling standards ensued. There may of course have been more than one modeller, and a candidate for this role must be James Marchant, a potter, who possibly met Planché when the two men both lived in the parish of St Anne's, Westminster between 1740 and 1746. In 1752 Marchant married Mary Oldfield in St Alkmund's Church, so that his association with the china works at St Mary's Bridge seems assured.

The link between dry-edge models and the Derby factory seems certain. The glassy non-phosphatic paste is similar to that from which the three marked Derby creamers are made, while several later Derby models of the 'Pale Family' and 'patch-marked' periods, listed on pp. 65–81 and 95–128, (Lists D and E) were either copied or adapted from the dry-edge prototypes. Lastly, several moulds sold when the Derby factory failed in 1848 relate to these early products. A notable example is the mould for the head of a Chinese lady wearing a head-dress resembling an inverted egg-cup from the chinoiserie group emblematic of *Sight* (B33).

It was once believed that the dry-edge models were made at the Pot Works on Cockpit Hill, although no porcelain sherds have been recovered from the site. On 26 January 1753, the *Derby Mercury* announced:

> We heard that yesterday morning the body of a man who appeared to have lain a considerable time in the water, was taken from the river [Derwent] near Borrowash. 'Tis said he was one of the workmen belonging to the China Works near Mary Bridge, and had been missing since Christmas Eve, at which time the waters being much out 'tis thought he fell accidentally near the said Bridge and was drowned.

This could not refer to the Pot Works which was situated some three miles downstream from where the corpse was found. An advertisement in the *Derby Mercury* of 30 July 1756 describes as for sale a property owned by a Charles Shepherdson of King's Newton, near Derby. This was 'Near St Mary's Bridge' . . . 'occupied by Mr. Heath & Co.' and 'let at £10 per annum'. On 25 October it was readvertised and, according to information supplied in a later document, was purchased on 19 November 1756 by the sitting tenant, John Heath. These facts suggest that Planché worked in a china works financed by Heath and that following his departure Heath and Duesbury bought the property and there expanded the old factory. This was close to St Mary's Bridge, on the east bank of the river Derwent, upon the Nottingham Road within the parish of St Alkmund's.

The Pot Works was, from about 1751, run by John Heath, banker and twice Mayor of Derby in 1763 and 1772, Thomas Rivet, MP, William Butts, potter, and Ralph Stean; Heath's brother, Christopher, was taken into partnership in 1770. Towards autumn 1755, Heath evidently resolved to expand and diversify production at the China Works and on 6 January 1756, Articles of Agreement were drawn up between the parties: 'John Heath of Derby in ye County of Derby Gentleman, Andrew Planche of ye same place China Maker and Wm. Duesbury in ye County of Stafford Enameller . . .' The full text of this unsigned document, or a contemporary copy, is in the Victoria and Albert Museum and has been reproduced by Twitchett.[14] Possibly the extra-marital adventures of Planché with Margaret Burrows offended the Non-Conformist consciences of such worthies as Heath and Duesbury, for the draft does not appear to have been ratified and Planché disappeared from the Derby ceramic scene. Many Huguenots residing in England in those days used to hyphenate their name with its English translation, and a number were engaged in the dyer's trade. A Planché-Floor, who was a dyer, died in 1809 in Bath.[15] Though some have doubted whether this was the same person as the Derby china-man, because his occupation was so far removed from the jewellery and ceramic trades, it should be recalled that the articles of agreement had laid down: 'Ye sd. Copartners shall not at any time hereafter use or Follow ye Trade aforesaid [porcelain manufacture] or any other Trade what so ever during ye sd. Term to their private Benefit.'

William Duesbury (1725–86) was born at Longton in Staffordshire, the son of a leather trader, or currier, of Cannock, bearing the same name. Dennis Rice[16] suggests that Duesbury (*fils*) may have been apprenticed to Thomas Hughes of Clerkenwell as early as 1742,[17] before establishing his own atelier for the decoration of ceramics in London. His *London Account Book*,[18] covering the period November 1751 to August 1753, survives. Entries written in several different hands employ a strange phonetic spelling. Duesbury employed both 'hinammeld' (enamel) and unfired pigments for the decoration of wares and figures from 'Chelsee', 'Bogh',

14 John Twitchett, *Derby Porcelain*, London, 1980, p. 25.

15 MacAlister, op. cit., pp. 51–2.

16 Dennis Rice, *Derby Porcelain, the Golden Years 1750–70*, London, 1983, p. 9.

17 W. H. Tapp, 'Thomas Hughes, the First Enameller of English China of Clerkenwell', *Trans. EEC*, 2, no. 6, 1939, pp. 53–65.

18 Mrs Donald MacAlister, *William Duesbury's London Account Book, 1751–3*, London, 1931 (special ECC publication).

'Darbey' and 'Staffartshire'. Jewitt[19] ascertained that Duesbury married Sarah James of Shrewsbury, and Major Tapp[20] found the baptismal record of their eldest daughter, Mary, in the registers of St James's Church, Westminster, dated 18 February 1753. Jewitt[21] also discovered that their second daughter, Anne, was born at Longton on 3 October 1754. Duesbury may, of course, have worked in London prior to November 1751, but he must have left at some date between August 1753 and October 1754 for Longton, where he may have been employed decorating porcelain made at the factory of William Littler, although no examples of his work from this period have so far been identified.

Most porcelain manufactories in England were, at this time, appointing enamellers to their staff, and William Duesbury probably felt constrained to secure his own future by purchasing a share in one of them. The limitations of Longton Hall must have been apparent almost as soon as he arrived there and he would naturally have turned his attention to nearby Derby. His lack of liquid assets necessary for such a venture was made good by a loan from his father. In an Article of Agreement, dated 27 September 1755,[22] William Duesbury (*père*) surrendered to his son 'all his money, goods and chattles', in return for the solemn undertaking by William Duesbury (*fils*), 'to provide during the term of his natural life, good and sufficient meat, drink, washing and Lodging, wearing apparel, and all other necessities whatsoever'. By this means Duesbury was able to purchase a share in the Derby porcelain company in which John Heath had already invested some £1,000 of his own fortune.

The departure of Planché must have created a hiatus that was difficult to fill, and one might expect to find a few models and wares that bridge the gap between this event and the establishment of subsequent production under Duesbury. Arthur Lane[23] has identified just such a group of figures, which he named 'Transitional Derby', examples of which are here listed on pp. 55–7 (List C). Dennis Rice,[24] however, believes that they form a group *sui generis* and chooses to call the unknown factory of their origin after one of the models, the Girl-on-a-Horse Factory. Evidence in support of Lane's contention will later be presented.

William Duesbury became part-proprietor and the manager of the Derby manufactory during the first quarter of 1756, when dwelling houses adjacent to the old factory site 'were converted into and then continued to be workshops and employ'd

19 Jewitt, op. cit., p. 68.

20 Cited by MacAlister, op. cit., 1931, p. xi.

21 Jewitt, op. cit., p. 68.

22 F. Severne MacKenna, *Chelsea Porcelain, the Gold Anchor Wares*, Leigh-on-Sea, 1952, p. 36.

23 Arthur Lane, *English Porcelain Figures of the Eighteenth Century*, London, 1961, p. 100.

24 Dennis Rice, op. cit., pp. 33–7.

by sd. W. Duesbury and Company as such in the making of China'.[25] The occupation of Meissen by the Prussians in the autumn of the same year disrupted production there which, for the next seven years, was mostly geared to meet the requirements of the conqueror. Duesbury resolved to fill thc vacuum thereby created and to capture the market for porcelain figures. However, despite his detailed instructions to craftsmen it proved impossible to reproduce the devilry and *élan* of Meissen models, and attempts to simulate the cold glitter of hard paste by inclusion of cobalt in the glaze were artistically unsuccessful. In May 1757 the *Public Advertiser*[26] reported the sale of a china dealer named Thomas Williams:

> At the Large Auction Room facing Craig's Court, near the Admiralty, Whitehall, there were numbers of the Quality and Gentry, who expressed great satisfaction at seeing the extensive number of foreign, and a Great Variety of English Manufactories; and admired at the Great Perfection of Derby Figures in particular, are arrived to, that many Good Judges could not distinguish them from real Dresden.

This eulogy may be discounted as little more than sales promotion, for no one who was familiar with the dramatically sculpted Meissen figures clad in brilliant enamel colours could have mistaken them for the stiffly posed and pale-coloured counterparts from Derby.

Nevertheless, despite many shortcomings, the Derby factory thrived and, on 28 January 1758, the *Public Advertiser*[27] announced:

> The Proprietors of the Derby China Factory beg leave to acquaint the Nobility and Gentry that they have fix'd their Porcelain to be sold by their Factor, Mr. Williams, at his Large Foreign Warehouse up one Pair of Stairs, formerly known by the name of Oliver Cromwell's Drawing Room, facing Craigg's Court, near the Admiralty, consisting of a Great Variety of Figures, the nearest the Dresden ... the Great Demand there is for them, has encouraged the Proprietors to enlarge their Manufactory, and they have engaged double the Number of Hands they used to employ, which will enable them to sent to the said Warehouse every week a Great Variety of Goods.

Later, in April 1758, Craigg's Court was demolished to allow road-widening and Mr Williams transferred his premises to Pall Mall.

25 *The Duesbury Manuscripts*, including the *Bemrose Papers*. Housed in the Department of Medieval and Later Antiquities, British Museum.

26 J. E. Nightingale, *Contributions towards the History of Early English Porcelain*, Salisbury, 1881, appendix, p. 69.

27 *Ibid.*, appendix, pp. lxx–lxxi.

In 1763 forty-two boxes of assorted porcelain items were dispatched to London from Derby for sale. The following models were included:

Bird-catchers	Neptunes
Boys, second size	Quarters, large [of the Globe]
Britannias, large	Shakespeares
Dianas	Shepherds, garland
Elements, sets of	Shepherds, Spanish
Europas [Europa and the Bull]	Tumblers
Hussars, second size	Bucks and Does, on pedestals
Jupetors [sic] and Junos	Pidgeons [sic]
Ledas [Leda & the Swan]	Chickens
Mars and Minervas	Rabbets [sic], small
Muses	Sheep, feeding and standing

Sprimont had been trying to sell the Chelsea factory since 1763 and, in August 1769, it was purchased by James Cox for £600. The new proprietor made mechanical toys and automata and, since he knew little about porcelain manufacture, he must have intended to rely upon the factory clerk, Francis Thomas, to run the works. However, shortly after the transaction had been finalized, Thomas died and Cox resold the factory to William Duesbury for £840. The lease had been secured in 1759 for fourteen years but, in 1770, it was renegotiated to run for a further ten years and this was subsequently extended for two further periods each of two years. Thus the Chelsea–Derby era extended from 1770–84, although nothing was produced at Chelsea after 1783. Llewellynn Jewitt[28] tells us that Richard Barton was placed in charge and that he, assisted by Robert Boyer, carried out most of the skilled work including potting, repairing and glazing, each at a daily rate of 3s 6d. They were supported by Roberts, whose duties included grinding the case clay, Inglefield, who cleaned the biscuit to be glazed, both also paid 3s 6d daily, and Piggot, whose function is not stated and who received a mere 1s 9d per day. After October 1770 three new workmen were engaged to make small seals, including Jenks, who 'laid grounds', Snowdon, and Wolloms who was probably the brother of Joseph Willems, chief modeller at Chelsea, who died at Tournai in 1766. In February 1772, the most highly paid employee was Gauron, who received 8s 9d a day, a great deal more than the 5s 3d allowed to Zachariah Boreman. The London site seems to have been reserved for manufacture of étuis, scent-bottles, patch-boxes and seals, together with the decorative vases that had proved to be so popular in the previous decade. Probably all figure moulds were transferred to Derby,

28 Jewitt, op. cit., pp. 68–9.

although it remains possible that those models marked by a gilt anchor intersecting a script letter 'D' may have been decorated at Chelsea.

The Chelsea–Derby period was associated with important technical advances and stylistic changes in which the Rococo was displaced first by a more disciplined Louis Seize style and ultimately by a muted Neo-Classicism. Skilled sculptors/modellers recruited from North-West Europe immeasurably improved the modelling; the lives and works of these and other artists are summarized in Appendix A. In June 1773 Duesbury opened London showrooms at 1 Bedford Street, Covent Garden, previously the Old Castle Tavern. William Wood was installed as manager and, not long afterwards, was honoured by a visit from George III.[29] Later, in July 1776, Wood wrote:[30]

> On Friday last Her Majesty accompanied by the Duchess of Ancaster was pleased to honour with her presence Mr. Duesbury's Rooms in Bedford Street, Covent Garden. Condescended to express great approbation of those Beautiful Articles of Derby and Chelsea Porcelain and Paintings and Encouraged the same by making some purchases . . .

In 1775, according to Joseph Lygo, who succeeded Wood, Duesbury obtained a royal appointment. The factory was also visited in 1777 by Dr Samuel Johnson who pronounced: 'The China is beautiful, but it is too dear; for that I could have vessels in silver of the same size as cheap as what here was made of porcelain.' In 1779, following the bankruptcy of the brothers John and Christopher Heath, Duesbury became the sole proprietor of the Derby factory. He also took the opportunity of purchasing a large quantity of earthenware from the Cockpit Hill works which he sold advantageously in Ireland.

Shortly before the Chelsea lease expired, a sale took place between 11 and 13 December 1783[31] of: 'The Remaining Finished and Unfinished Stock of the Chelsea Porcelain Manufactory in Lawrence Street, near the Church, Chelsea, with all Buildings and Fixtures thereto belonging.' On 18 February 1784, Richard Bower, who had been entrusted with the clearance of the site, wrote to his employer:[32] 'We are pretty forward in pulling down the buildings at Chelsea . . .' Within a few months all those items remaining over from the sale were either transferred to Derby or destroyed, and the site abandoned.

Joseph Lygo, who was a loyal and devoted agent of the Duesbury family (including Richard Egan who had married Anne, the sister of William Duesbury II),

29 John Haslem, *The Old Derby China Factory*, London, 1876, p. 25.
30 F. A. Barrett and A. L. Thorpe, *Derby Porcelain*, London, 1971, p. 138.
31 Nightingale, op. cit., appendix, p. 79.
32 Barrett and Thorpe, op. cit., p. 36.

established himself in October 1792 as a china dealer in Bath. Lygo wrote almost weekly letters to his employer from London, many of which survive and are distributed between the British and Victoria and Albert Museums, and the Derby Local Studies Library. Most relate to the years 1786 to 1797, and have been abstracted by Brayshaw Gilhespy,[33] John Twitchett[34] and others. This correspondence provides information about modellers, their products and sources of inspiration, other craftsmen, patterns employed on useful ware, clients and the day-to-day business of the factory. One of the more notable customers was Mr Williams, who ordered several hundred dozen 'Small Boys at 10 d each', in 1784 and again in 1787. Benjamin Vulliamy (1747–1812) was an even more illustrious client. He was the son of Justin Vulliamy, who had come to London from Switzerland to be apprenticed to Benjamin Gray. Justin married Gray's daughter, Mary, and on his father-in-law's death inherited the business. He was honoured by a royal appointment and his son Benjamin followed in the same trade. Between 1780 and 1796, Benjamin Vulliamy made decorative clocks and barometers in the Louis Seize style, examples of which are now in Buckingham Palace, the Bank of England and the Victoria and Albert Museum. Many of these are embellished with ceramic figures, including a number in Derby biscuit. In 1790 Vulliamy complained to Duesbury that the figures he supplied were too small for the metalwork that had been prepared and, the following year, the entire production of figures had to be suspended to facilitate fulfilment of Vulliamy's huge order. Both Lygo and Vulliamy often engaged the services of young sculptors residing in London, whose master models were dispatched to Derby for translation into porcelain.

The independent porcelain decorator James Giles, who worked in Kentish Town (c. 1756–63), Cockspur Street (1763–76), and Berwick Street (1776–78), had received financial assistance from Duesbury since about 1777.[35] According to Jewitt[36] Duesbury took over the whole concern in 1778. Duesbury had already purchased the Chelsea factory (1770) and the ailing Bow factory (1776),[37] and had weathered the storm created by the bankruptcy of his partner, John Heath. In addition he owned sizeable interests in quarries, mines and canals and must have been among the most successful industrialists of the eighteenth century. In 1785 he took his son, also named William, into partnership but the following year suffered a stroke and, after a long illness, died on 30 October 1786.

33 F. Brayshaw Gilhespy, 'Joseph Lygo's Letters to Derby', *Trans. ECC*, 5, 1955, pp. 203–16.
34 Twitchett, op. cit., pp. 305–7.
35 H. R. Marshall, 'James Giles, Enameller', *Trans. ECC*, 3, 1969, pt. 1, pp. 1–9.
36 Jewitt, op. cit., p. 215.
37 Frank Hurlbutt, *Bow Porcelain*, London, 1926, p. 30.

William Duesbury II did not enjoy robust health but he soon proved himself to be an efficient, skilled and industrious proprietor. During his first year in office, Lygo wrote informing him that the demand for figures in London had declined, and perusal of contemporary sale catalogues shows how this led to a reduction in the number of new models issued. Nevertheless, in 1790 one further accomplished modeller, possibly the greatest ever to work at Derby, arrived in England. He was the highly gifted, though troublesome, French-speaking Swiss, Jean-Jacques Spengler. He did not stay long and departed in the autumn of 1795. This, for practical purposes, marks the end of the tradition of sculptor/modellers working in soft paste at Derby and, in 1796, William Duesbury II died, leaving a son then only ten years old.

Michael Kean, an Irish miniature painter, had been engaged as manager by William Duesbury II and, in 1798, he married his late employer's widow, when the firm traded as Duesbury and Kean. William Duesbury III was dispatched to a boarding school and played no part in the further business of the manufactory. Kean has been credited with the invention of the process known as smear-glazing, by which the satin-like surface sheen upon Derby biscuit was assured, although judging from surviving examples of Spengler's work it must have been in routine use not later than 1790. The factory prospered and new buildings were erected upon Calver Close, which became known as the New Works. All hollow wares formed from soft paste were liable to crack when filled with hot liquids and, as early as 1790, Duesbury II had been constrained to issue prepared instructions to purchasers:

> To prevent Accidents with Tea Pots – Let about a Tea Cupful of Cold Water be sent up in the Tea Pot, and just before you wish to make Tea pour about 2 Tea Cupfulls of boiling water to the cold in the Pot and give it a shake round. This will gradually expand the Pot and prepare it for the Reception of boiling water to make the Tea. It being the expansion of Tea Pots, etc. by means of boiling water suddenly thrown in that rends them.[38]

In face of mounting competition from other manufactories making wares of more durable materials including stoneware, creamware, hard-paste porcelain and bone china, the Derby management abandoned soft paste in favour of bone china about 1810–15 and thereafter all figures and groups were issued in the new medium.

The marriage of convenience between Michael Kean and Elizabeth Duesbury proved to be unhappy and, by 1811, Kean had disposed of all his shares in the factory to William Sheffield, the father-in-law of William Duesbury III. Robert

38 Barrett and Thorpe, op. cit., p. 141.

Bloor, whom Michael Kean had appointed manager in 1809, leased the New Works in Calver Close in 1811 and, in 1815, in addition rented the Old Works on the Nottingham Road for £110 per annum. When during that same year Sheffield withdrew, Bloor purchased the entire factory, equipment, stock and good will, for £5,000. In addition, as a condition of purchase, he had to invest a further £5,000 to buy annuities for surviving members of the Duesbury family. Faced with the need to raise what then amounted to a huge capital sum, Bloor ordered the decoration and sale of defective stock remaining in his warehouses. Blemishes were concealed beneath dark opaque enamel colours enlivened with brash gilding, a procedure which explains the occasional appearance today of soft-paste Derby models decorated in the style of the late Regency. Although Bloor has been condemned for this action that led inevitably to a general lowering of standards, had he done otherwise, the factory would have failed in 1815, whereas it continued to prosper and survived for more than thirty years. One of these sales took place in September 1822 and evidently the proceeds enabled Bloor to pay off his loan capital of £3,544 12s 8d, including interest, as the final instalment on 30 December of that year. Bloor was a fine potter who was honoured by a royal appointment, and although the golden age of porcelain figures had long since passed, under his proprietorship many splendid vases, decorative urns, tea-, dessert- and dinner-services were made. In 1828 he began to exhibit signs of mental incapacity resulting in his admission to an asylum where he remained until his death in 1846. During this period, James Thomason took over the management. He was the uncle of John Haslem who, after being employed as a travelling salesman for Messrs Davenport, had been confidential manager at Derby for thirty years. Meanwhile, Bloor's granddaughter and sole heir had married Thomas Clarke, a corn-factor and maltster who, in 1844, took out a Statute of Lunacy upon his father-in-law which enabled him to assume proprietorship of the manufactory. He lacked any experience of the ceramic industry, and after only a few years marked by falling standards and diminishing sales, the factory failed in 1848.

Some of the old hands, including Samuel Fearn, John Henson and Samuel Sharp (potters), Sampson Hancock (enameller), and James Locker (gilder), formed a consortium under the leadership of William Locker (factory clerk). After purchasing some of the old moulds, stock and equipment, they established a small porcelain works in King Street, Derby. Several of the models first made on the Nottingham Road site were reissued, though often in debased forms. William Locker died in 1859 and was succeeded by the ex-draper, Stevenson, who survived until 1866. In 1935 the factory was merged with the Royal Crown Derby Porcelain Company on the Osmaston Road.

2 · Derby Porcelain Models, 1750–6

EXPERIMENTAL DERBY MODELS, 1750–3

Dr Bernard Watney[1] has presented a small group of slip-cast soft-paste models that may possibly represent the first Derby venture into the field of modelling during the early 1750s. They share some features with Derby and others with the so-called Girl-in-a-Swing Factory which, it is believed, operated between about 1749 and 1754 somewhere in the Chelsea area.

PASTE AND GLAZE

The paste is glassy, containing between 4.8 and 6.3 per cent of lead oxide, and its lack of stability in the kiln and poor plasticity must have created great difficulty in handling the material. Evidence of this is provided by fire-cracks and sagging of figures out of alignment. The thick glaze presents a greyish cast and is usually crazed. In some figures the glaze terminates above the lower circumference of the base leaving a rim of exposed paste known as a 'dry-edge', which is a constant finding on models known to have been made at Derby from about 1750 and 1755.

BASES

Some bases are square or rectangular with their sides sloping downwards and outwards, while the model of *Harlequin* (A8) is mounted upon a cube-shaped base. Others are like flat hexagonal plates with the circumference scalloped, while portrait figures of *Kitty Clive* and *Henry Woodward* are mounted upon star-like structures. The under-surface may be wiped free of glaze, ground, or exhibit a dry-edge. Shallow crescentic incisions, resembling finger-nail parings[2] may be seen upon the upper surface, in common with Girl-in-a-Swing figures. Ventilation holes are medium to small and may taper slightly as they approach the central cavity. Many bases are sprigged with strawberry flowers which have four or five concave petals,

1 Bernard Watney, 'A Hare, a Ram, Two Putti and Associated figures', *Trans. ECC* 8, 1972, pt. 2, pp. 224–7.
2 Arthur Lane and R. J. Charleston, 'Girl-in-a-Swing Porcelain and Chelsea', Ibid., 5, 1962, pt. 3, pp. 111–44.

thick leaves and clumsy stems, and similar decoration also appears on three early Derby creamers.[3]

ENAMEL COLOURS

All examples so far identified are uncoloured.

MODELLING

The quality of the modelling is less elegant than that of Girl-in-a-Swing figures and there is also greater obscuration of moulded detail by the thick glaze. Eyes are represented by small perforated discs applied below carefully delineated eyelids, noses are short and straight but look sharp in profile, while lips seem to be pursed. Long, spidery fingers look as if they are webbed, owing to insufficient separation between them compounded by pooling of glaze.

MODELS

Fourteen different models have been identified so far of which no fewer than six are putti. Three representing the *Arts and Sciences* are each seated upon an octagonal plinth: *Astrology* (A1) supports a celestial globe, *Literature* (A2) holds a parchment scroll, while *Music* (A3) plays a lyre. Three other putti, seated with knees apart and legs obliquely placed, represent *The Four Seasons: Spring* (A4) wears a floral chaplet and holds posies, *Summer* (A5) dispenses fruits, and *Winter* (A6), wrapped in a cloak, warms his hands over a brazier. The model emblematic of *Autumn* has not yet been identified. The different sizes and varying styles of the bases suggest that the models described do not comprise an incomplete set.

Primitive models of a standing *Turk and Levantine Lady* (A11) appear on flat bases with scalloped octagonal sides. The figure of an *Actor* (A7) lacks a head. Kitty Clive (née Rafter, 1711–85) is portrayed as *Mrs Riot* (A9) in Garrick's farce *Lethe*, and was adapted from Charles Moseley's engraving of a watercolour by Thomas Worlidge. The comedienne wears a lace cap, laced-trimmed dress with pagoda sleeves and hooped skirt, and carries a spaniel. The companion model of Henry Woodward as *The Fine Gentleman* (A10) in the same play was based on James McArdell's mezzotint after the portrait by Francis Hayman.[4] He stands, feet apart, hands thrust into his pockets, clad in a huge tricorn hat and contemporary dress including a foppish waistcoat. Both are mounted on star-shaped bases, unlike

3 Creamers respectively incised 'D. 1750', 'Derby 1750' and 'D' in the British Museum, Victoria and Albert Museum, and Colonial Williamsburg Foundation.

4 Hugh G. Tait, 'Some Consequences of the Bow Special Exhibition' *Apollo*, 71, no. 705, 1960, pt. 1, pp. 40–4.

the more familiar Bow versions which have square bases and detachable stands.[5] Although *Lethe* opened on 15 April 1740, Kitty Clive did not join the cast until 1749. Bow examples of both figures survive that are incised '1750'[6] and it is improbable that Derby examples are earlier.

The model of *Harlequin* (A8), seated cross-legged playing bagpipes, echoes one of many possible originals made by J. J. Kändler during the mid-1740s. It is extremely heavy for a slip-cast figure and the cause is to be found in the construction of the cube base. Utilizing a radiological technique known as tomography,[7] it is evident that the model is slip-cast but the base is made from two squares of paste, placed one on top of the other, perforated only by a small ventilation hole that narrows slightly as it approaches the central cavity. The model of a *Pug Dog Scratching* (A12) exists also in a Bow version, and most probably both were inspired by Kändler's portrait replica of Count Heinrich von Brühl's favourite pet. Dr Watney has pointed out that some models of *Finches* (A13), perched upon tree-stumps with one leg raised, may belong to this supposedly Derby group, although there are others that stem from Chelsea[8] or the Girl-in-a-Swing manufactories.[9]

LIST A. EXPERIMENTAL DERBY MODELS, 1750–3

ARTS & SCIENCES

A1 *Astrology*. A scantily draped putto seated upon an octagonal plinth holding a celestial globe.

A2 *Literature*. A similar putto holding a parchment scroll.

A3 *Music*. A similar putto holding a lyre. All 4 in (10.2 cm). Sotheby's, *Sale Catalogue*, 11 December, 1982, lot 103; *Trans. ECC*, 8, 1972, pt. 2, pl. 182b.

THE FOUR SEASONS

A4 *Spring*. 4½ in (11.4 cm). A naked winged putto wearing a floral chaplet and holding flowers, mounted on a square chamfered base. *Trans. ECC*, 8, 1972, pt. 2, pl. 181a.

A5 *Summer*. 5⅝ in (14.1 cm). A similar putto holding fruits, mounted on a flat octagonal base. Ibid.

5 Yvonne Hackenbroch, *Chelsea and Other English Porcelain, Pottery and Enamel in the Irwin Untermyer Collection*, Cambridge, Mass., 1957, fig. 241, pls. 76 and 77.

6 Ibid., pl. 76, Henry Woodward, incised '1750'. Fitzwilliam Museum, Cambridge, Kitty Clive, incised '1750'.

7 Peter Bradshaw and Ronald Grainger, 'Evidence that a few Bow Figures were Cast Solid,' *Northern Ceramic Society Journal*, I, 1973–4, pp. 41–4. Includes description of radiological technique.

8 Arthur Lane and R. J. Charleston, op. cit., pls. 132c, 133a and 133b. Girl-in-a-Swing models of *Finches*.

9 Ibid., pl. 132a. Chelsea model of *Finch*.

1 A1. *Astrology* (left). A2. *Literature* (centre). A3. *Music* (right). All 4 in (10.2 cm). *Sotheby's*

A6 *Winter*. $4\frac{3}{4}$ in (12.2 cm). A similar putto wrapped in a cloak warming his hands over a brazier. Sigmund Katz Collection, Boston Museum of Fine Arts; ibid.

THEATRICAL

A7 *Actor* (lacking a head). 6 in (15.2 cm). He stands wearing contemporary dress and a cloak with his left hand upon his heart. Synge Hutchinson Collection; ibid., pl. 183d.

A8 *Harlequin*. $5\frac{1}{4}$ in (13.3 cm). Seated upon a mound playing bagpipes. Author's Collection.

A9 *Kitty Clive as Mrs Riot in 'Lethe'*. $9\frac{3}{4}$ in (24.8 cm). She stands wearing a lace cap, bodice and a hooped skirt, and holds a pug under her arm. Mounted on a star-shaped base sprigged with strawberry flowers. William Deacon Collection; *Trans. ECC*, 8, 1972, pl. 183c; Delomosne, Rice, 1983, pl. 21.

A10 *Henry Woodward as the Fine Gentleman in 'Lethe'*. $10\frac{3}{4}$ in (27.3 cm). He stands legs separated, hands in pockets, wearing a foppish tricorn hat and waistcoat, jacket and breeches; in some versions he carries a sword. Rice, 1983, pl. 21.

A11 *Turk and Levantine Lady* (pair). 6 in (15.2 cm). He wears a turban and she a soft head-dress, over loose robes. Rous Lench Court, *Trans. ECC*, 8, 1972, pl. 182.

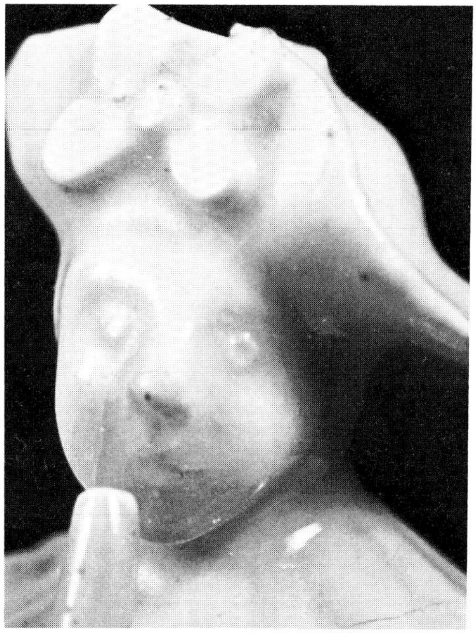

2 A8. *Harlequin* seated with bagpipes. $5\frac{1}{4}$ in (13.3 cm). Author's Collection

3 A8. Facial features of *Harlequin* with seemingly pursed lips and eyes represented with applied perforated discs.

4 A8. *Harlequin*'s long, spidery fingers which appear to be webbed.

5 A9. *Kitty Clive as Mrs Riot in 'Lethe'.* $9\frac{3}{4}$ in (24.8 cm). *Sotheby's*

A12 *Pug Dog Scratching.* $5\frac{3}{4}$ in (14.6 cm). Victoria and Albert Museum; *Trans. ECC*, 8, 1972, pl. 181; Private Collection.

A13 *Finch.* $5\frac{1}{2}$ in (14 cm). Perched upon a tree-stump with one leg raised. Sigmund Katz Collection, Boston Museum of Fine Arts; *Trans. ECC*, 5, 1962, pt. 3, pl. 133.

DRY-EDGE DERBY MODELS, 1750–5

Approximately seventy different models of both human and animal subjects, issued between about 1750 and 1755, have been attributed to the Derby manufactory, and are among the finest ever to have been made in England.

PASTE AND GLAZE

The paste is non-phosphatic, glassy and relatively short. Analysis shows 70 per cent silica, 20.5 per cent lime, 5.5 per cent alumina, and about 2 per cent lead oxide. The poor plasticity accounts for the surface tearing of the paste and full-thickness fire-cracks that may be encountered. The relative instability in the kiln sometimes led to sideways drooping of the models. Slip-casting was employed although some items are thick-walled and hence heavy in the hand. The quality of the glaze at its

6 A12. *Pug Dog Scratching.* $5\frac{3}{4}$ in (14.6 cm). Private Collection

best is thin, tight-fitting, glossy and faintly blued, but it varies a great deal between specimens and may be either thick, warm in tone and creamy or, at its worst, may resemble candle-grease. Glazing was effected by dipping the inverted once-fired figure into a vat of the material and great care was taken to prevent it from flowing over the under-surface of the base. This usually left around the lower circumference a rim of unglazed paste, known as a dry edge, which has over the years absorbed grime and become discoloured (see Plate 8). The lower edge of the glaze is often heaped up like treacle in a manner not evident when the lower surface has been ground, while this area of exposed paste feels slightly rough to the touch and is slightly uneven.

BASES

Most of the bases are either steep mounds or irregular pads that are unadorned, although a few are sprigged with sharply moulded thin leaves and one or two tightly rolled flower-heads. Other decoration may be employed when this is more appropriate, for example acorns are encrusted upon the bases of a *Pair of Wild Boars* (B1). The figures of *St Philip* (B28) and *St Thomas* (B29) show the instruments of their martyrdom in addition to the asymmetrical arrangement of moulded scrolls, reflecting perhaps the first manifestation of the Rococo style at Derby. These were probably issued about 1755. The ventilation hole may take one of three forms. A

7 Under-surface of the base of a *Dancing Girl* (B11) (Plate 17), showing a screw-hole.

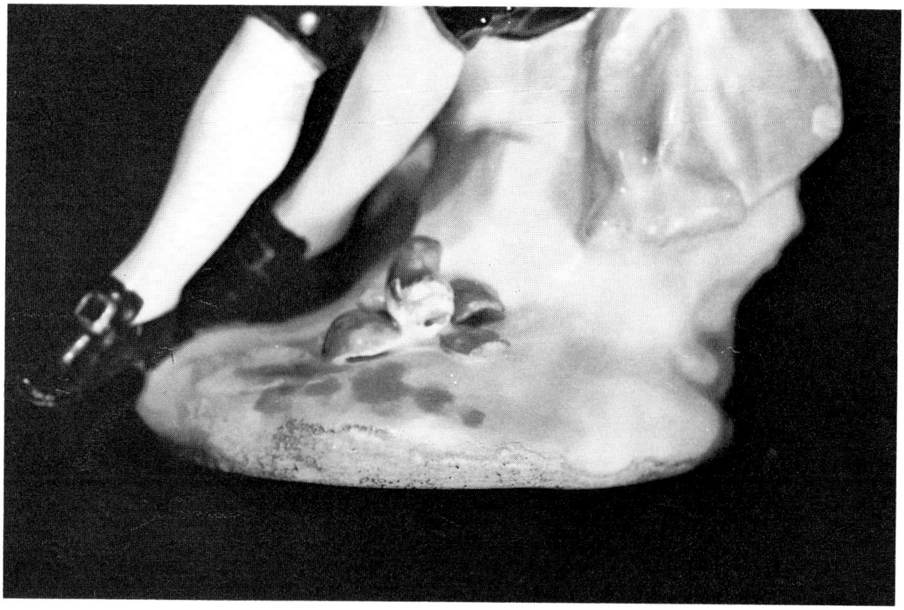

8 Mound base of *Gallant Taking Snuff* (B34), displaying a dry-edge.

few are medium in size and cylindrical, others originate from an oval depression with a vertical circumference, while the last are akin to those made by a carpenter with a countersink to accept the head of a screw, and are known as screw-holes (see Plate 7). A few models have a second aperture that penetrates the back of the figure or its support to enter the central cavity horizontally (see Plate 9). This was intended to accept a brass fitment attached to a candle-sconce or to metal leaves and stems terminating in porcelain flower-heads, a few of which have survived. Rare examples are *Air* and *Water* (B35) in Geoffrey Godden's collection.[10]

ENAMEL DECORATION

About three-quarters of all dry-edge models are white, although in a few, traces of oil paint and gold leaf deep in crevices indicate they were decorated in cold colours. Enamelled examples may show a glaze that lacks lustre, in association with myriads of small air bubbles best seen with a magnifying-glass. This suggests that enamels were applied months or years after a figure's emerging from the glost kiln, and when associated with at least three different styles of decoration, that this was effected outside the factory. Certainly three independent decorators are known who

10 Dennis Rice, *Derby Porcelain, the Golden Years, 1750–70*, London, 1983, pl. 14.

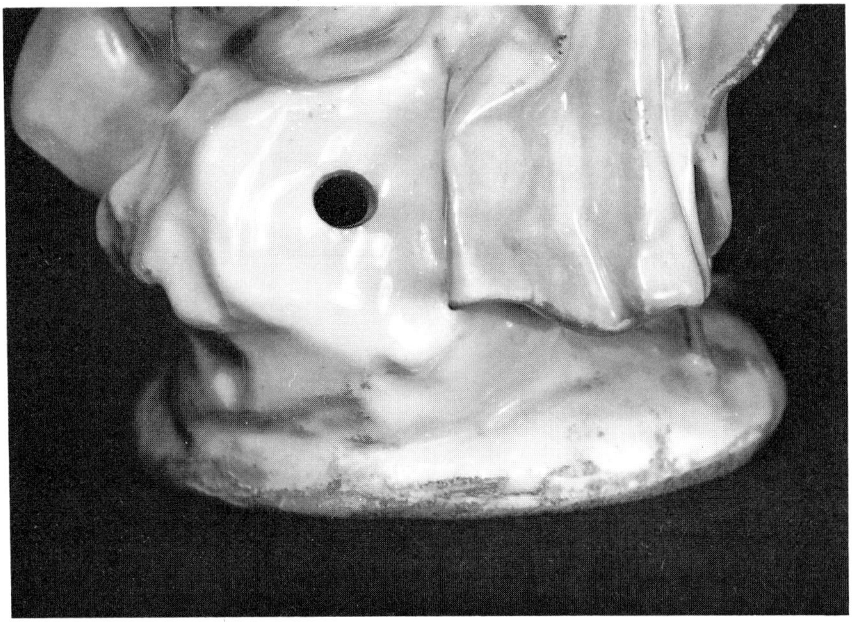

9 Reverse view of *Gallant Taking Snuff*, revealing a circular aperture intended for acceptance of a metal fitment.

may have been responsible. The *London Account Book* of William Duesbury, covering the period November 1751 to August 1753,[11] survives, and entries relating to Derby figures include: '1 Darbyshire Sesen 1s. ... 1 Darbyshire sitting Sesen 1s. ... 2 prs. dansing Darby figs. 6s. ... 1 pr. Darby figures 4s 6d. ... 1 pr. Darby figars large 8s.' Other items not stated to be Derby but which are known in Derby examples include: 'Chinese men ... Wild Boors ... and Staggs'. Although it is thought that most of Duesbury's work was effected in cold colours, he certainly used enamels, for which he charged almost double. His style may include large open flowers with heavy-looking leaves executed in a palette predominantly of yellow, yellow-green, and puce, of no great artistic merit (see Plate II). A memorandum in his account book reads: 'How to colour group, gentleman Busing a lade – gentlm a gold trim'd cote, a pink waistcot and trim'd with gold and black Breeches and socs, the lade a flowr'd sack with yellow robings, a black stomegar, her hare black his wig powder'd'. Similar black breeches may be seen on seated gallants emblematic of *Smell* and *Taste* (B34). The star-cross motif, composed of

11 Mrs Donald MacAlister, *William Duesbury's London Account Book, 1751–3*, London, 1931 (special ECC publication).

four trifid symbols resembling bird's feet arranged pointing outwards about a small circle as a cross (see Plate I), has been attributed to Duesbury, but occurs on several models issued after he vacated his London studio.

Dr Bernard Watney[12] has described two further styles of enamel decoration. Type A (see Plate III), found also on a London painted Meissen figure emblematic of *Winter*, an English decorated Chinese teapot, a raised anchor Chelsea *Bird*, and several Chaffers' Liverpool models, consists of rather spiky-looking floral sprays outlined in purple or black, effected in a seemingly dry palette. Bouquets are centred on either a tightly rolled cabbage-rose or an anemone in semi-profile above which arches a sketchy trail of Michaelmas daisies. Other flowers include a yellow harebell and a whiskered heart's-ease as well as an unidentified blossom which has almost rectangular petals. Leaves may be both lanceolate and broad, often with the tip curled upwards. A less sophisticated variant has a central flower facing downwards against a thick curved stem and was ascribed to the same artist while he was still inexperienced. The same floral sprays may also be found painted in either a light blue (see Plate IV) or a puce monochrome.[13] Dr Watney tentatively ascribed all of this work to John Bolton of Kentish Town, about 1755–6.[14]

Type B (see Plate V) occurs also upon an English decorated Chinese teapot stand, a Worcester coffee-can, several Girl-in-a-Swing scent bottles, and Chaffers' Liverpool models. Decoration is effected in a more brilliant palette including an orange-red, yellow-green, deep yellow and pink. A greyish-purple used for shading appears black beneath the green of leaves and brown on yellow flowers. The device of a double cherry is usually interspersed between sprays or placed adjacent to the hems of dresses which are often edged with a double pink line or a broad band of purple.[15] Dr Watney believes this style was developed in the atelier of James Giles.

Types A and B may both be associated with painted insects on service wares but these are omitted from figures. Models in both also have rather pale buff flesh tints, heightened with a faint orange blush on their cheeks; mouths are large, untidily painted and seem to be smudged, while eyelids and lashes are depicted in brown pencilling which in some examples, though not all, forms a continuous ellipse around the eyeball. There are at least two instances where the irises are painted a violet-blue, namely the gallant taking snuff emblematic of *Smell* in the author's collection, and a lady with a parrot representing *Feeling* (B34), also in a private

12 Bernard Watney, *The King, the Nun and Other Figures, Trans. ECC*, 7, 1968, pt. 1, pp. 48–58, pls. 56–60.

13 Peter Bradshaw, *Eighteenth-century English Porcelain Figures*, 1745–95, Woodbridge, 1981, col. pl. L.

14 Watney, op. cit., p. 57.

15 Bradshaw, op cit., col. pl. I.

collection. They serve to refute the assertion sometimes made that English eighteenth-century figures never have blue eyes.[16]

Gilding is sometimes employed in association with Type B decoration. The hem of the dress of a lady emblematic of *Taste* in the Broderip Collection is embellished with pale watery gold, while the turret-crown and edges of the garments worn by *Cybele* in the Victoria and Albert Museum are similarly decorated. The superior gilding on the buttons, shoe-buckles, garters, snuffbox and edges of the tricorn hat of the model portraying *Smell* are illustrated (see Plate 36). Throughout this period extending up to about 1800 the honey-gilding process was employed and is described in a later section.

MODELLING

Reference has already been made to the superbly sculpted features of the dry-edge Derby models, which compare favourably with all but the very best red anchor Chelsea figures. In some, this may simply reflect the excellence of a Meissen prototype, although equal competence in execution and artistic merit is also evident in those based on other sources including prints and engravings. They possess magnificent sculptural qualities with the elimination of all superfluous detail and a broad handling of mass and form that enshrine, as it were, all the dynamic force and turbulence of the Baroque style. Human faces are oval with high, wide cheekbones, a rather large mouth and a short, straight nose, often with the tip turned downwards. Heads are rotated and inclined to one side and the gaze seemingly directed above or below the horizontal. Folds in drapery, necessarily simplified, are arranged in deeply moulded triangular patterns and portrayed in a manner that is at once attractive and realistic. Animal models, most of which were based on Meissen prototypes, reflect much of the essential spirit and brutishness that had been so brilliantly portrayed by Kändler and his associates.

MODELS

Probably the most familiar of all dry-edge models is the pair of *Wild Boars* (B1), the one seated, the other trotting. The former is the more successful and, according to tradition, was based on Pietro Tacca's marble after the antique, now in the Uffizi Gallery. It is likely that one of many small ormolu or bronze replicas then available provided an intermediate source or, perhaps, the stone statue in the forecourt of Chatsworth House which was not far from the factory. A pair of spirited charging

16 Peter Bradshaw, 'Some Eighteenth-century Porcelain Figures with Blue Eyes', *Journal of the Northern Ceramic Society*, 2, 1975, pp. 93–8.

Bulls (B2) echo Peter Reinicke's models adapted from an engraving by Elias Riedinger,[17] *Auer Ochse im Zorm* (Bulls in a rage). Derby models of a standing *Ewe* and companion *Ram* (B3) have broad backs and heads turned in mirror poses, and were made in two sizes. These, together with a group depicting a *Ewe Suckling a Lamb* (B4), known also in a Bow version,[18] follow Meissen originals.[19] A pair of standing *Goats* (B6), the female suckling a kid, and recumbent *Goats* (B7), as well as the dog-like *Lion and Lioness* (B9) also follow Meissen prototypes. However, the dry-edge versions of the *Stag and Doe at Lodge* (B8) appear to have been adapted from a different source despite the existence of several possible Meissen models. Here it may be recalled that the stag is the crest of the town of Derby, so that engravings of the beasts would have been plentiful.

There is a rare model of an *Actor* (B10) striking an histrionic pose, and a pair of *Dancers* (B11) feature a man clad in Pierrot's costume and a lady wearing a panniered skirt holding aloft a mask. They might pass for characters from the Italian Comedy, although the male figure seems to have been based on one of a pair by F. E. Meyer,[20] unaccountably described as *Dancing Shepherds*. A *Seated Bagpiper* (B15), once in the Wallace Elliot collection, is now ascribed to the Bow manufactory, but *Harlequin and Columbine* dancing (B13) echo Meissen prototypes. The source of the standing *Gentleman Playing a Reed-pipe* (B12) is not known although he reappeared with minor alterations (D2) upon a high base during the years 1756–8. An exquisite group of a *Huntsman Flautist and Reclining Lady* (B14), who holds a musical score and rests her right hand upon her companion's sleeve, calls to mind one of the pairs of lovers in Watteau's *fêtes galantes*.

The *Map-seller* (B19) wears a brimmed hat and bears upon his back a pack secured by crossed belts; he holds a rolled chart and an open map in either hand. He was copied from one of the *Cris de Paris*[21] issued between 1745 and 1747 by Kändler, Eberlein and Reinicke. Their first series of models were loosely based on engravings made by Ann-Claude-Philippe de Tubières, Comte de Caylus, after sixty red chalk drawings by Edmé Bouchardon. These appeared in five sets, each of twelve engravings, entitled *Etudes prises dans le bas peuple, ou les cris de Paris*.[22]

17 Yvonne Hackenbroch, 'English Porcelain and Enamel from the Collection of Judge Untermyer', *Connoisseur*, 138, 1956, p. 108: fig. 10, engraving by E. Riedinger; fig. 11, Derby models of *Bulls*.

18 Frank Hurlbutt, *Bow Porcelain*, London, 1926, pl. 1A.

19 S. Ducret, *Meissner Porzellan 1710–1810*, Berne, 1952, nos. 1150 and 1151, Meissen models of *Standing Ewe and Ram*, and ibid., no. 116, Meissen group of *Ewe Suckling a Lamb*.

20 K. Berling, *Festive Publication to Commemorate the 200th Jubilee of the Oldest European China Factory, Meissen*, Meissen, 1910, table 17, no. 2, *Meissen Dancing Shepherd*.

21 Cleo M. and G. Ryland Scott, *Antique Porcelain Digest*, Newport, 1961, pl. 71, fig. 264.

22 British Museum. Folio of sixty red chalk drawings by Edmé Bouchardon, interleaved with engravings by the Comte de Caylus.

The *Map-seller* is known also in both triangle[23] and red anchor[24] marked Chelsea versions. The Derby model was later reissued with a companion *Woman Pedlar* (E36) adapted from Kändler's *Trinket-seller* of about 1748, both mounted on scrolled bases before low bocages. Kändler and his associates created a second series of Paris Cries between 1752–1754, based upon watercolour sketches made by Christophe Huet, brother of Charles-François Huet, the Paris art dealer. The models were less dramatically posed, paler in colouring, and mounted upon bases adorned with scrolls picked out in gilt and enamel in the Rococo taste. Two were copied at this period by Derby, including the *Absinthe-seller* (B16) bearing a tray of bottles before him, and a female *Vegetable-seller* (B20). The Derby *Cobbler* (B18), seated before his bench holding an awl and a shoe, may have been inspired by a lost Meissen model in Kändler's small Artisan series.[25]

A delightful *Boy Shepherd Piper* and companion *Dancing Shepherdess* (B17) are known too in Bow versions. The female figure was evidently cast from the mould of *Columbine* (B13) after the Meissen original by Peter Reinicke in a set made for the Duke of Weissenfels.[26] The source of the male figure is uncertain but the couple reappear during the period 1756–9 in Scottish dress (G14), while in a later patch-mark issue the lady's dress is brought into line with the current fashion (E33) and she acquires a new partner.

Classical mythology is well represented. *Venus with Cupid* (B30) depicts the scantily clad goddess holding aloft an apple and restraining her son with her left hand as he reaches up to gather the forbidden fruit. This may possibly have been adapted from a bronze, after the antique, of Aphrodite holding aloft castanets which a child centaur attempts to grasp.[27] *Mars* (B24) is attired as a Roman centurion in a manner befitting the god of war and the symbol of the militaristic State of Rome, and echoes Kändler's Meissen original.[28] The companion figure of *Minerva* (B25), resplendent in a plumed helmet, ankle-length skirt and sandals, holds a spear and with her left hand leans upon an oval shield, in the centre of which is the severed head of the gorgon Medusa. Later versions provide the goddess with a cuirass, and all seem to have been based on John Cheere's lead garden statue.[29] *Neptune* (B26), his mantle blown out by the wind, holds a trident in his upraised hand and stands

23 Nathaniel Harris, *Porcelain Figurines,* Maidenhead, 1975, p. 47, first period Chelsea *Map-seller.*

24 Ibid., p. 49, red anchor Chelsea *Map-seller.*

25 Erica Pauls-Eisenbeiss, *German Porcelain of the Eighteenth Century,* London, 1972, I, p. 93, examples of Meissen 'Small Artisan' series by J. J. Kändler.

26 Ibid., pp. 302–21, Italian Comedy models by Kändler and Reinicke.

27 See Plate 212, Bronze after the Antique of Aphrodite with a Child Centaur.

28 K. Berling, *Königlich, Sächsische Porzellan Manufaktur Meissen 1710–1910,* Dresden, 1911, pl. 9, fig. 4.

29 M. Whinney, *Sculpture in Britain 1530–1830,* London, 1964, pl. 107b.

beside a dolphin. Dr Bernard Watney[30] identified the source of this fine group as a small bronze by Michel Anguier (1612–68), though the pagan nudity of the bronze was draped and the hippocampus replaced by a dolphin. Dr Watney noticed also an affinity between another of Anguier's bronzes, *Neptune Calming the Waves*, and the Derby *Pluto and Cerberus* (B27) in which the Lord of Tartarus, wearing a crown and mantle, stands beside Cerberus, the three-headed dog that guarded the entrance to his domain.

Models of mythological subjects include *Apollo* (B21). The model known as *Cybele with a Lion* (B22) wears the turret-crown of a mother goddess and holds a cornucopia. She should, more properly, be named Ceres, for Cybele was the Phrygian goddess of earth, as contrasted to fertile soil, who was worshipped in deep caverns and upon the barren hilltops. The ancient calendar included only three seasons represented by a lion, a bull or a goat, and a serpent which might be incorporated in a chimera. Thus Cybele's attendant lion represents spring and does not imply any African connection. The dry-edge model appears upon a low mound but, about 1756, the model was reissued on a tall base resembling an inverted bowler-hat encrusted with leaves, fruits and flowers (D26). Some have remarked upon the facial resemblance of the Derby Cybele to both the Bow version[31] and the Muse Melpomene.[32]

Although many people believe porcelain to be a medium unsuited to portray more serious religious subjects, two fine devotional images were made at Derby about 1755. *St Philip* (B28) is portrayed as an elderly bearded man, wearing a soft cap, trousers and mantle, who stands regarding a crucifix; the basket at his feet contains loaves of bread, recalling the miraculous feeding of the five thousand. A metal staff surmounted by a Roman cross may once have been in his hand. *St Thomas* (B29) stands bareheaded and barefoot, his cloak gathered about him, and may once have held a metal spear which was the instrument of his martyrdom. The orb and broken sword at his feet bear witness that his death was contrived without due process of Roman law. Some enamelled versions show the saint attired inappropriately in sumptuous garments such as a robe decorated with fleur-de-lys or a cloak edged with ermine, and this has prompted some to afford him the title of

30 Bernard Watney, *Some Parallels and Proto-types in Ceramics, Trans ECC*, 10, 1980, pt. 4, pp. 350–6: pls. 148a and 148b, Derby models of *Neptune*; pls. 148c and 148d, bronze group by M. Anguier.

31 Anton Gabszewicz and Geoffrey Freeman, *Bow Porcelain, The Collection Formed by Geoffrey Freeman*, London, 1982, pl. 228.

32 Elizabeth Adams and David Redstone, *Bow Porcelain*, London, 1981, p. 142.

King Lear. A set of pottery *Saints and Apostles* in the Earle Collection[33] includes both St Thomas and St Philip whose names appear upon ceramic labels, so their identity cannot be in doubt. It would seem likely that the enamelled examples were decorated outside the factory when the artist responsible was unfamiliar with the subjects.

During both the seventeenth and eighteenth centuries great interest was aroused in the Middle and Far East, which led to the occidental fantasies known as *chinoiseries* and *japonaiseries*. Life in these distant lands was idealized by elegant ladies playing in beautiful gardens with happy children and wise sages deliberating or playing chequers in stately pavilions. Gabriel Huquier's folio of engravings by J. J. Baléchou after Boucher was published in 1740 entitled *Livres de six feuilles représentant les cinq sens par différents amusements chinois sur les dessins de F. Boucher*.[34] These may have provided the inspiration of the set of *chinoiserie Senses* (B33). *Sight* is represented by a Chinese lady who holds aloft a bird in her left hand while gesticulating with her right to a seated chinaman. The other four senses are each portrayed by an adult Chinese with a child. The two figures in the group of *Sight* were also reissued separately to provide a *Chinese Lady Drummer* and a *Chinaman with a guitar* (B36). This has caused some doubt concerning the identity of the group which, it is held, may more properly be emblematic of *Hearing*. There are, of course, many instances when models taken from a group are adapted to represent an entirely different theme, such as the two children taken from the groups of *Feeling* and *Smell* that were adapted to portray the elements of *Air* and *Water* (B35). Further, one other group has already been identified as *Hearing* while no other is known for *Sight*.

The Five Senses (B34) are also represented by a set of seated adults wearing European dress. Two of them, *Smell* and *Taste*, portrayed respectively by a gallant taking a pinch of snuff, and by a lady eating fruit from a basket upon her lap, were adapted from a Meissen group, *An Actor Offers a Lady Snuff, the Two Seated upon a Green Sward*, created about 1745 by J. J. Kändler.[35] In addition, *Sight* and *Feeling*, represented respectively by a gallant wearing a nightcap and dressing-gown regarding his reflection in a hand-mirror, and by a lady holding a parrot that pecks her fingers, were also adapted from a Meissen group, *Two Lovers upon a Green Sward*, about 1745, by Kändler.[36] In both, minor alterations were effected because

33 C. Earle, *The Earle Collection of Early Staffordshire Pottery*, London, 1915, no. 133, model of *St Thomas*; no. 136, model of *St Philip*. Victoria and Albert Museum.

34 Mentioned in the *Mercure* of 1740.

35 Peter Bradshaw, 'A Beggar, a Snuff-taker and a Lady', *Trans. ECC*, 12, 1984, pt. 1, pp. 26–8: pl. 34a, Derby model of *Smell*; pl. 34b, Derby model of *Taste*; pl. 34c, Meissen group of an *Actor and Lady*.

36 Ibid: pl. 35a, Derby model of *Feeling*; pl. 35b, Derby model of *Sight*; pl. 35c, Meissen group of *Two Lovers*.

of the more upright postures of the Derby figures. The missing model of *Hearing* has not been identified, although there exists a slightly smaller model of a *Lady Seated Holding a Musical Score* (D7). Despite the presence of a dry-edge upon one example in the Royal Crown Derby Museum, the primitive modelling of the facial features and pale colouring indicate manufacture about 1756–7, and it is interesting to note that another example in a private collection does not have a dry edge. A spurious contender for the title is a seated *Gallant Holding a Birdcage,*[37] which is, in fact, no more than a damaged snuff-taker erroneously repaired.

The Four Infant Seasons (B31) comprise four scantily draped seated putti holding appropriate attributes. Most probably they follow one of several similar sets created at Meissen by F. E. Meyer. The figure representing *Autumn* later reappeared incorporated into a candlestick (D39). *The Four Rustic Seasons* (B32) are among the most successful of all dry-edge sets. Each Season is portrayed by two standing peasants in the genre of David Teniers, the elder. *Spring* is depicted by a gardener with a basket of flowers over his arm, proffering a posy, and by a woman with blossoms in a fold of her apron holding out a nosegay; *Summer* is a harvester holding in both hands a cornsheaf, and a woman holding a bird's nest to which she points; *Autumn* is a yokel with a square basket of grapes attached to a stave over his shoulder, and a woman holding grapes in a fold of her apron, with a bunch in her upraised hand; *Winter* consists of a man and woman in mirror poses, one hand held over a brazier, the other in a muff. The gardener and woman with grapes were also issued separately as a pair of *Street Vendors*[38] and one example in the Norman C. Ashton Collection was evidently issued in smear-glazed biscuit (see Plate 27).

Chinese Mother and Child (B37), in a private collection, and a Rococo-styled chinoiserie *Watch-stand* (B38) are also known. Recently Dr Bernard Watney has reported a model of a seated *Pug* and there is a recumbent *Lowing Cow*, later reissued in the Bloor period (G65) which Mrs Robin Barkla kindly brought to my notice.

When the Derby factory failed in 1848, many master models, clay squeezes and moulds were purchased, according to Haslem, by a Mr Boyle. It is unclear whether this person was Samuel Boyle, who was proprietor of an ironstone works that was closed in 1852, or John Boyle of Minton. In any event, the material was purchased in 1849 by Alderman William Taylor Copeland. During transportation in barges or while off-loading, many items fell into the canal and were lost, but the remainder is stored to this day in a room in the manufactory, known as 'the morgue'. In the

37 John Twitchett, *Derby Porcelain*, London, 1980, pl. 22.

38 Sotheby's *Sale Catalogue*, 6 July 1981, lot 158. Derby biscuit models of *Street Vendors*, about 1754.

autumn of 1923, at the request of Ronald Copeland, it was inspected by the brothers Frank and William Stoner, whose incomplete study was published.[39] A shelf contained wax master models supposedly mostly from Chelsea including several *Cupids in Disguise,* a *Shepherd* piper with his dog and companion *Shepherdess* with a mandoline and a lamb, all of which are known in Derby versions of about 1780–5. No items relating to the Bow factory were identified. The author saw the contents of the 'morgue' in 1984. It was then thick with black dust and included many thousands of arms, legs and torsos as clay squeezes, lead and terracotta master models and mould sections all mingled pell-mell. During the last three years, Pamela Rowan has resumed the previous cursory study with diligence and application and in a preliminary communication has revealed valuable fresh information. Terracotta models, albeit disarticulated, were found representing the dry-edge Derby *Boars, Bulls,* and a recumbent *Lowing Cow.* Human figures or moulds related to *St Philip,* a seated lady emblematic of *Taste,* and *Neptune.* A more complete and detailed report is eagerly expected. Interestingly enough, two of these moulds were incised 'A.P.', which suggests a link with André Planché. Moulds of one of the *Mansion House Dwarfs* and other figures, some as yet unidentified, were also discovered. The information was presented at a meeting of the Derby Porcelain International Society, held on 14 November 1987, in the Derby Museums and Art Gallery.

39 Frank Stoner, 'Chelsea Moulds: an Important Discovery', *Connoisseur,* LXIX, 1924, pp. 3–10. See *The Cheyne Book of Chelsea China and Pottery,* ed. Reginald Blunt, London, 1924, chapter by Frank Stoner entitled 'Chelsea Moulds and Models', pp. 104–8. Also Frank Stoner, *Chelsea, Bow and Derby Porcelain Figures,* Newport, 1955, pp. 14 and 15.

LIST B. DRY-EDGE DERBY MODELS, 1750–5

ANIMALS AND BIRDS

B1 *Wild Boars* (pair). $4\frac{1}{2}$ in (11.4 cm). One seated, the other trotting. Victoria and Albert Museum, Barrett and Thorpe, pl. 18; British Museum, Rice, 1983, pl. 27; N. C. Ashton Collection, Bradshaw, pl. 171.

B2 *Bulls* (pair). $5\frac{1}{2}$ in (14 cms). They are in mirror poses, charging. Derby Museums and Art Gallery, Twitchett, pl. 12. Smaller versions, $2\frac{3}{4}$ in (7 cm) are in the Royal Crown Derby Museum, Twitchett, pl. 12.

B3 *Ewe and Ram,* standing (pair). 4 and $4\frac{1}{2}$ in (10.2 and 11.4 cm). Christie's, Rice, 1983, pl. 31; N. C. Ashton Collection, Bradshaw, pl. 85.

B4 *Ewe Suckling a Lamb* (group). $4\frac{7}{8}$ in (12.3 cm). Derby Museums and Art Gallery.

B5 *Finches,* two amongst a leafing branch (group). $4\frac{7}{8}$ in (12.3 cm). Gilhespy, 1951, pl. 104, fig. 190; Victoria and Albert Museum, Rice, 1983, pl. 35.

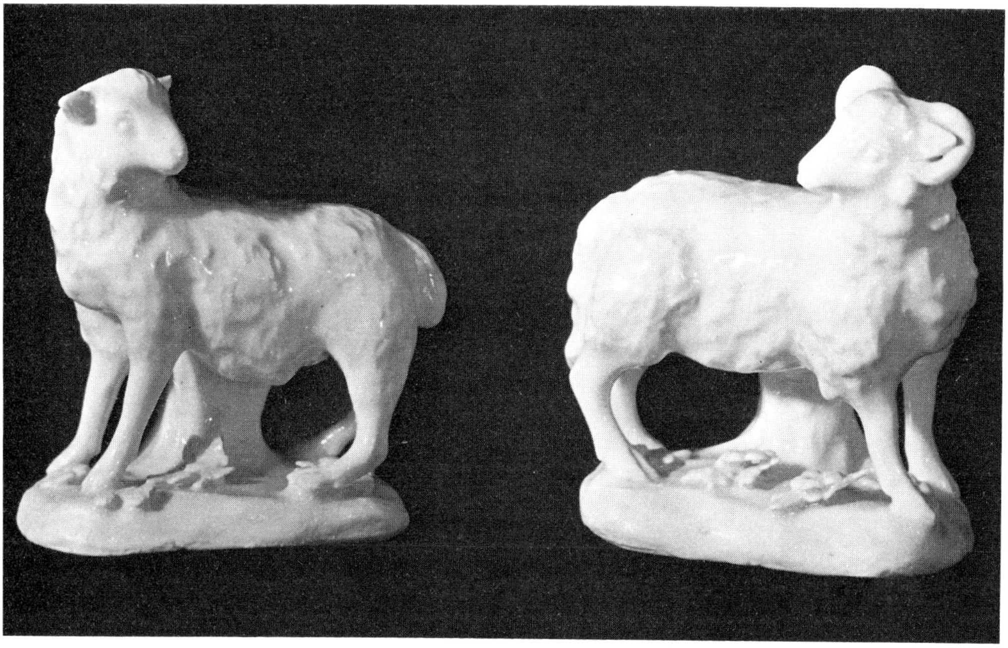

10 B1. *Wild Boars* (pair). 4½ in (11.3 cm). *N. C. Ashton Collection*
11 B3. *Ewe and Ram*, standing 4 and 4½ in (10.2 and 11.4 cm). *N. C. Ashton Collection*

12 B6. *Male Goat,* standing. $6\frac{1}{2}$ in (16.5 cm). *N. C. Ashton Collection*

13 B6. *Companion Female Goat,* suckling a kid. $6\frac{1}{2}$ in (16.5 cm). *N. C. Ashton Collection*

14 B9. *Lion and Lioness, Recumbent.* $3\frac{1}{2}$ in (8.9 cm). *N. C. Ashton Collection*

B6 *Goats*, standing (pair). 6½ in (16.5 cm). Male animal with head turned, female suckling a kid. Victoria and Albert Museum, Twitchett, pl. 5; N. C. Ashton Collection, Bradshaw, pls. 175 and 176.

B7 *Goats*, recumbent (pair). 4 in (11.4 cm). Sotheby's, *Sale Catalogue*, 13 October 1970, lot 213.

B8 *Stag and Doe at Lodge* (pair). 5 in (12.7 cm). Derby Museums and Art Gallery, Barrett and Thorpe, pl. 21; British Museum, Rice, 1983, pls. 28 and 29.

B9 *Lion and Lioness*, recumbent (pair). 3½ in (8.9 cm). Sotheby's, Rice, 1983, pl. 32; N. C. Ashton Collection, Bradshaw, pl. 86.

The following items have elsewhere been designated as dry-edge Derby, but here are assigned to other phases of production:

A12 *Pug Dog Scratching*.
A13 *Finch*.
C1 *Cat and Dog Candlesticks*.
C3 *Crested Pheasant*.

Further, the group depicting a *Boy Milking a Goat* (Rice, 1983, pl. 44) is in the author's opinion not of Derby manufacture.

Finally, Dr Bernard Watney informs me that he has identified a pair of *Pugs Seated*, and Mrs Robin Barkla has found a pair of *Cow and Bull*, both recumbent, which are dry-edge Derby.

THEATRE, MUSIC AND DANCE

B10 *Actor*. 6¾ in (17.1 cm). He wears a brimmed hat, falling ruffle, tunic, breeches and cloak, and stands with left hand on hip and right upraised. N. C. Ashton Collection, Bradshaw, pl. 88; Sotheby's, Rice 1983, pl. 11a.

B11 *Dancers* (pair). 6½ in (16.5 cm). The male wears a cockaded hat, falling ruffle, jacket with a flounce and breeches, and dances with his left arm elevated. His companion wears a full skirt and holds a mask aloft in her right hand. British Museum, Rice, 1983, pl. 22; Metropolitan Museum, New York, Untermyer, fig. 271; Stoner, pl. 48.

B12 *Gentleman Playing a Reed-pipe*. 6¼ in (15.9 cm). He stands bareheaded. Gilhespy, 1961, pl. 15.

B13 *Harlequin and Columbine* (pair). 4¾ in (12.1 cm). Klaber and Klaber, Rice, 1983, pl. 26.

B14 *Huntsman Flautist and Lady Reclining* (group). 6¼ in (15.9 cm). The huntsman plays a flute to a recumbent lady who holds a musical score and has her hand upon his sleeve. Statham Collection, Lane, pl. 56b; N. C. Ashton Collection, Bradshaw, col. pl. P.

B15 *Seated Bagpipers* 6 in (15.2 cm). Late Wallace Elliot collection, *Connoisseur* (1927), vol. LXXIX, col. pl., p. 10. Now reallocated to the Bow factory.

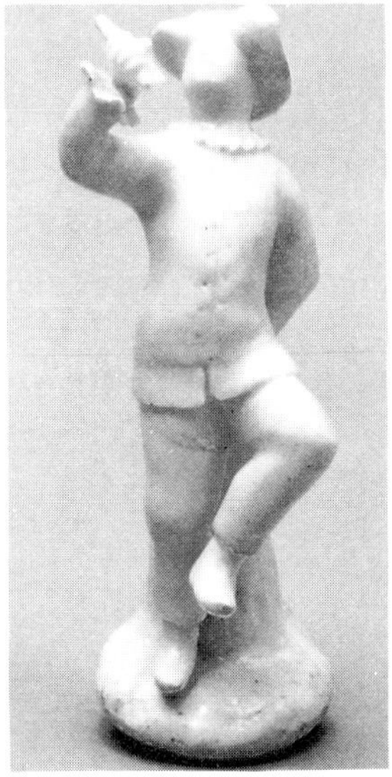

15 B10. *Actor* striking an histrionic pose. $6\frac{3}{4}$in (17.1 cm). *N. C. Ashton Collection*
18 B13. *Harlequin* and *Columbine*. $4\frac{3}{4}$in (12.1 cm). *Klaber and Klaber*

16 B11. *Dancer* wearing a Pierrot costume. $6\frac{1}{2}$ in (16.5 cm). *Sotheby's*

17 B11. *Dancing Girl,* possibly *Columbine.* $6\frac{1}{2}$ in (16.5 cm). Plate IV. See also *David Thorn Collection*

19 B14. *Huntsman Flautist and Reclining Lady* who holds a musical score. $6\frac{1}{4}$ in (15.9 cm).
N. C. Ashton Collection

PASTORAL AND PEASANT

B16 *Absinthe-seller*. $7\frac{1}{8}$ in (18.1 cm). Victoria and Albert Museum, Lane, pl. 61c; Rice, 1983, pl. 20.

B17 *Boy Shepherd Piper* and *Dancing Shepherdess*. 7 in (17.8 cm). The youth plays bagpipes and stands beside his dog, his companion lifts her skirts as if about to dance, with a lamb at her feet. Sotheby's, Rice, 1983, pl. 19; N. C. Ashton Collection, Bradshaw, col. pl. i; Victoria and Albert Museum, Gilhespy, 1961, pl. 16.

20 B16. *Absinthe-seller* $7\frac{1}{8}$ in (18.1 cm). *Victoria and Albert Museum*

21 B17. *Boy Shepherd Piper* and *Dancing Shepherdess*. 7 in (17.8 cm). See also Plate v.
N. C. Ashton Collection

B18 *Cobbler*. $6\frac{7}{8}$ in (17.3 cm). He sits, wearing a soft cap, shirt, breeches and apron, with a shoe and an awl in either hand. Victoria and Albert Museum, Rice, 1983, pl. 25.

B19 *Map-seller*. $6\frac{1}{4}$ in (15.9 cm). He stands, a pack of samples upon his back and a chart in either hand. N. C. Ashton Collection, Bradshaw, pl. 90.

B20 *Vegetable-seller*. $7\frac{1}{8}$ in (18.2 cm). A woman wearing a linen cap, bodice, skirt and apron, stands with right hand on hip, supporting a basket of vegetables with her left. Victoria and Albert Museum, Rice, 1983, pl. 67; Lane, pl. 61b.

22 B19. *Map-seller*. $6\frac{1}{4}$ in (15.9 cm). *N. C. Ashton Collection*

23 B21. *Apollo*, standing amidst trophies of the Arts. $6\frac{1}{4}$ in (15.9 cm). *N. C. Ashton Collection*

24 B24. *Mars*, attired as a Roman centurion. $5\frac{5}{8}$ in (14.3 cm). *N. C. Ashton Collection*

MYTHOLOGICAL AND RELIGIOUS

B21 *Apollo,* standing amidst trophies of the Arts. 6¼ in (15.9 cm). Victoria and Albert Museum, Barrett and Thorpe, pl. 10; N. C. Ashton Collection, Bradshaw, pl. 94.

B22 *Cybele with a Lion.* 6 in (15.2 cm). The goddess stands holding a cornucopia and proffering fruits beside a lion, upon a low mound base. Winifred Williams, *Trans. ECC,* 7, 1968, pt. 1, pl. 57d. For a later version see D26 (Plate 67).

B23 *Jupiter.* 6 in (15.2 cm). Crowned, he holds thunderbolts in either hand and stands beside an eagle. *Connoisseur,* September 1927, p. 3, pl. vi.

B24 *Mars,* attired as a Roman centurion. 5⅝ in (14.3 cm). Gilhespy, 1961, pl. 5; N. C. Ashton Collection, Bradshaw, pl. 95.

25 B28. *St Philip.* 9½ in (24.1 cm). *Victoria and Albert Museum*

26 B29. *St Thomas.* 9½ in (24.1 cm). *N. C. Ashton Collection*

B25 *Minerva*. 7 in (17.8 cm). She stands wearing a plumed helmet, bodice, thonged skirt and sandals, holding a spear in her right hand and leaning upon a shield with her left. Christie's, *Sale Catalogue*, 1 June 1987, lot 250.

B26 *Neptune with a Dolphin*. $6\frac{3}{4}$ in (17.1 cm). The god stands crowned, his mantle blown out by the wind, holding a trident, beside a dolphin. Gilhespy, 1961, pl. 3.

B27 *Pluto and Cerberus*. $6\frac{5}{8}$ in (16.8 cm). The god stands crowned and scantily draped beside the three-headed Cerberus. Victoria and Albert Museum, Lane, pl. 60a.

B28 *St Philip*. $9\frac{1}{2}$ in (24.1 cm). The saint is shown as a bearded man clad in a soft cap and tattered cloak, standing barefoot, regarding a crucifix. At his feet lie scattered either stones or loaves of bread. Victoria and Albert Museum, Lane, pl. 59; Rice, 1983, pl. 67.

B29 *St Thomas*. $9\frac{1}{2}$ in (24.1 cm). A bearded, bareheaded man in Roman attire gathers a mantle about him; an orb and a broken sword lie at his feet. Schreiber, no. 287, pl. 10; N. C. Ashton Collection, Bradshaw, col. pl. K; Sotheby's, Rice, 1983, pl. 23.

B30 *Venus with Cupid* (group). $7\frac{1}{2}$ in (19.1 cm). The goddess stands bareheaded and barefoot holding aloft an apple in her right hand while with her left she restrains Cupid from grasping the forbidden fruit. N. C. Ashton Collection, Bradshaw, col. pl. K; Sotheby's, Rice, 1983, pl. 17. See Plate 11.

27 B31. *The Four Infant Seasons*. 4–$5\frac{1}{4}$ in (10.2–13.3 cm). *N. C. Ashton Collection*

ALLEGORICAL

B31 *The Four Infant Seasons.* 4–5¼ in (10.2–13.3 cm). Represented by four scantily draped seated putti:

Spring, wearing a floral chaplet holding a basket of flowers.

Summer, with a diadem made from cornstalks, holding a cornsheaf.

Autumn, seated upon a pannier of grapes, crowned with vine leaves and grapes and holding aloft a bunch of grapes.

Winter, wrapped in a mantle, warming his hands over a brazier.

Victoria and Albert Museum, Lane, pls. 56a and 57a; Twitchett, pl. 17; N. C. Ashton Collection.

B32 *The Four Rustic Seasons.* 6¼–7 in (15.9–17.7 cm). Represented by four pairs of standing figures:

Spring: a woman wearing a brimmed hat over a mob-cap, laced bodice, apron and skirt, securing blossoms in her apron while proffering a posy with her left hand. Also a gardener clad in a brimmed hat, jacket and breeches, with a basket of flowers over his left arm and proffering a posy with his right.

28 B32. A biscuit pair of *Street Vendors.* 6¼ and 7 in (16.5 and 17.8 cm). Taken from the *Four Rustic Seasons* representing *Spring* (right) and *Autumn* (left). *N. C. Ashton Collection*

29 B32. *Summer,* represented by a harvester with a cornsheaf
30 B32. and a woman holding a bird's nest. Both $6\frac{1}{4}$in (15.9 cm). *N. C. Ashton Collection*

Summer: a woman attired in a rustic dress holding a nest in her left hand containing birds' eggs to which she points with her right forefinger. Also a rustic wearing a hat who holds a cornsheaf with both hands.

Autumn: a woman wearing a brimmed hat over a mob-cap, long jacket, apron and skirt, holding aloft a bunch of grapes and securing grapes in a fold of her apron. Also a yokel wearing a hat, jacket and breeches who carries over his shoulder a pole to which is attached a square basket of grapes.

Winter: a woman wearing a headscarf, dress and coat, with one hand in a muff and the other held over a brazier. Also a man wearing a hat and overcoat in mirror pose.

N. C. Ashton Collection, Bradshaw, col. pl. J. illustrates *Spring* (female), *Summer* (male and female) and *Winter* (male); ibid., pls. 96–9, *Summer* (male and female), *Autumn* (male) and *Winter* (female); Fitzwilliam Museum, Barrett and Thorpe, pls. 14 and 15, *Summer* (male and female); R. W. Raven Collection, Twitchett, pl. 4, *Autumn* (female); Twitchett, pl. 10, *Spring and Winter* (female).

31 B32. *Autumn,* represented by a rustic carrying grapes. $6\frac{1}{2}$ in (16.5 cm). *N. C. Ashton Collection*

B33 *The Five Chinoiserie Senses.* $7\frac{3}{4}$–$9\frac{3}{4}$ in (19.7–24.7 cm). Represented by five groups, each of two figures:

Feeling: a Chinaman, wearing a conical hat, standing with his right fist raised about to strike a boy at his side.

Hearing: a Chinese lady, playing a lyre to a child seated upon a chair.

Sight: A Chinese lady, wearing a head-dress like an inverted egg-cup, holds her left hand (which may once have held a bird) aloft while gesticulating with her right to a seated Chinaman.

Smell: a Chinese youth wearing a conical hat holds a posy to his nose and a small child reaches up to grasp it.

Taste: a Chinaman clad in a conical hat and wide-sleeved robe holds a bottle in his left hand and a glass in his right, while a boy leans over a basket lying upon its side containing bottles.

British Museum, Twitchett, pl. 19, *Feeling*; Victoria and Albert Museum, *Sight, Taste* and *Smell*; N.C. Ashton Collection, Bradshaw, pl. 100, *Feeling*, pl. 101, *Smell.*

32 B33. Two chinoiserie groups representing *Smell* (left) *and Taste* (right). $7\frac{3}{4}$ and 8 in (19.7 and 20.3 cm). *Late N. Rockefeller Collection, Christie's*

33 B33. Chinoiserie group emblematic of *Feeling*. $9\frac{3}{4}$ in (24.8 cm). *N. C. Ashton Collection*

B34 *The Five Senses*. $6\frac{1}{4}$–$6\frac{1}{2}$ in (15.9–16.5 cm), represented by seated adult figures in contemporary European dress:

Feeling: a lady seated with a parrot in her lap that pecks her fingers as she strokes it.

Hearing: unidentified, although D7 may be a later version.

Smell: a gallant taking snuff from a snuffbox.

Sight: a gallant regarding his reflection in a hand-mirror (missing).

Taste: a lady eating fruit from a basket upon her lap.

Fitzwilliam Museum, Barrett and Thorpe, pl. 8, *Feeling and Taste;* Victoria and Albert Museum, Twitchett, pl. 18, *Taste;* Woollett and Son, Gilhespy, 1961, pl. 14, *Feeling, Sight, Smell* and *Taste;* N. C. Ashton Collection, Bradshaw, col. pls. L and M, *Feeling, Sight* and *Smell.*

34 B34. *Feeling*, portrayed by a lady stroking a parrot that pecks her fingers. 6½ in (16.5 cm). See also Plate III. *Private Collection*

35 B34. Another example of *Feeling* (bottom left). 6½ in (16.5 cm). A gallant holding a bird-cage (bottom right), purporting to represent *Hearing*, but in fact a wrongly restored damaged snuff-taker. 6½ in (16.5 cm), *Sotheby's*

36 B34. *Smell*, portrayed by a gallant taking snuff (top right). 6¼ in (15.9 cm). *Author's Collection*

37 B34. *Sight*, represented by a gallant looking at his own reflection in a hand-mirror (missing). $6\frac{1}{4}$ in (15.9 cm). *David Thorn Collection*

38 B34. *Taste*, shown as a lady eating fruit. $6\frac{1}{2}$ in (16.5 cm). *Victoria and Albert Museum*

B35 *The Four Elements*. 3 in (7.6 cm). Only two, represented by seated children, have been identified:

Air: a Chinese boy with shaven head, clad in a jacket with falling ruffle and trousers, seated with his right arm upraised, which may once have held a bird. Adapted from the child in the group emblematic of *Smell* (B33).

Water: a Chinese boy seated cross-legged with both arms elevated before him, which may once have held a fishing rod or net. Adapted from the child in B37.

Christie's, Rice, 1983, pl. 13; H. J. Hyams Collection, Barrett and Thorpe, pl. 13.

B36 *Chinese Musicians.* $5\frac{1}{2}$ in (14 cm). These are adapted from the two figures in the chinoiserie group *Sight*: a seated Chinaman playing a guitar, and companion Lady beating a pair of small drums. Indianapolis Museum of Art, Twitchett, pl. 24.

B37 *Chinese Mother and Child* (group), possibly representing *Hearing.* $9\frac{1}{4}$ in (23.5 cm). Private Collection.

B38 *Chinaman and Boy*, incorporated into a Rococo watch-stand. $9\frac{1}{2}$ in (24.1 cm). Winifred Williams, Bradshaw, pl. 92. A recent variation in which a Chinese lady faces the Chinaman has been reported.

39 B37. *Chinese Mother and Child,* possibly representing *Hearing.* $9\frac{1}{4}$ in (23.5 cm). *Private Collection*

40 B38. *Chinaman and Boy*, incorporated into a Rococo chinoiserie watch-stand. $9\frac{1}{2}$in (24.1 cm).
Winifred Williams

TRANSITIONAL DERBY MODELS, 1755–6

Arthur Lane[40] described a small group of about a dozen slip-cast soft-paste models that he called 'Transitional Derby', in the belief they had been made between the departure of Planché and the advent of fresh modelling staff under William Duesbury. Dennis Rice,[41] however, failed to identify any feature shared between this group and either the preceding or subsequent Derby models, and in the absence of any assured source of origin he chose to describe them as Girl-on-a-Horse Factory figures, after one equestrian example.

PASTE AND GLAZE

The paste is coarse in texture, grey in appearance and, when held up before a powerful source of light, is only faintly translucent. Models are thickly potted and accordingly heavy in the hand and may show fire-cracks due to the shortness of the paste. There may also be evidence of instability in the kiln as exemplified by the figure of a *Chinese Boy Climbing a Creeper-like Tree* (C4), in the Fitzwilliam Museum, which has sagged out of alignment whilst a foot that became detached lies on the top of the base. The glaze has a greenish cast, is often heavily sanded, and by reason of its thickness obscures much of the moulded detail and has usually formed droplets upon the under-surface.

ENAMEL COLOURS

The spectrum of colours in the enamel palette is restricted to include a streaky puce, deep yellow, orange-red, yellow-green, a purplish dark blue, a cold dark brown and buff. Human flesh tints are either pale or omitted altogether, as may be seen in the figure of *Neptune* (C10). Eyes are oval, almost round, with dark brown pupils that impart the semblance of a piercing stare. Garments are left with large passages of white adorned with rather clumsily painted floral sprays which generally include a rose. Overall colours are used sparingly and gilding is not employed.

BASES

Many of the bases are deeply moulded with a central shell-like concavity flanked by scrolls accented in puce enamel, and a few show comma-shaped fenestrations which in others are suggested with placements of puce enamel. Under-surfaces are

40 Arthur Lane, *English Porcelain Figures of the Eighteenth Century*, London, 1961, p. 100.
41 Dennis Rice, *Derby Porcelain, the Golden Years 1750–70*, London, 1983, pp. 33–7.

frequently flat but uneven and unglazed apart from accumulated droplets around the periphery. Ventilation holes are large and oval, some being several inches in diameter. Some models have an incised mark, seemingly a letter 'Y', contained within a triangle inside a circle drawn with the aid of a compass.

MODELLING

Three models of seated adults (C7, C8 and C9) are crudely fashioned with egg-shaped heads, wide, round eyes, button noses, and slot-like mouths. They are stiffly posed in clothing devoid of realistic folds and creases and resemble Staffordshire salt glaze *Pew Groups*. A *Dancing Beribboned Youth* (C5) shows an improved standard of modelling with a commendable sense of animation, while the rare figure of *Neptune* (C10) has fine sculptural features which may possibly have been copied from a small bronze.

MODELS

Three crudely fashioned zoological groups possess a naïve charm. A *Cat and Dog Candlestick* showing a dog chasing a cat up a tree (C1) is known in only one example lacking the dog, whose original presence may be inferred from paw-marks in the glaze. A *Crested Pheasant* (C2) may be adapted as a taperstick while a pair of *Rabbit Candlesticks* (C3) do not appear to have been illustrated.

A *Lady* and bareheaded *Gentleman* (C6 and C7) are seated in mirror poses upon heavily scrolled bases; the man pats a dog at his left side and the lady caresses a lamb. The male figure is also known adapted to wear a hat and with a strange stork-like bird added beneath his right arm (C8). The *Dancing Youth* (C5) is encrusted with moulded flowers and ribbons. *Neptune* (C10) sits upon the stern-castle of an archaic ship, his left arm elevated and a hippocampus swimming in the ocean at his feet. A *Chinese Boy Climbing a Creeper-like Tree* (C4), and a *Lady Riding Side-saddle upon a Prancing Horse* (C9) complete this rare group.

The primitive modelling of facial features mentioned above may also be seen in early Derby figures of the Pale Family, while decorative rosettes upon the prancing charger of C9 are echoed upon the dress of the lady in the Pale Family version of *Two Lovers with a Clown* (D8). Further, moulded flowers applied to the *Dancing Beribboned Youth* (C5) are similar to those on a Pale Family *Shepherdess* (D17), while a few later Derby groups, including the *Four Addorsed Blackamoors* (E38), are mounted upon deeply sculpted scrolled bases. Lastly, the bare-headed seated *Lady and Gentleman* (C6 and C7) seem to have been adapted to serve either as shell salts or sweetmeat containers (D35) and may also have provided the basis for the *Lady*

Seated Holding a Musical Score (D7) of about 1756/7. These considerations favour retention of the term 'Transitional Derby' and obviate the need for any descriptive title such as 'Girl-on-a-Horse Factory'.

LIST C. TRANSITIONAL DERBY MODELS, 1755–6

ANIMALS AND BIRDS

C1 *Cat and Dog Candlesticks.* $6\frac{7}{8}$ in (17.3 cm). A cat in the branches of a tree, with footprints suggesting it was being chased by a dog. Victoria and Albert Museum, Rice, 1983, pl. 43.

C2 *Crested Pheasant* (taperstick). 7 in (17.8 cm). The bird stands with one leg raised, supported by a tree-stump, on a scrolled base. Winifred Williams, Rice, 1983, pl. 42; Eckstein and Fodden Collection, Barrett and Thorpe pl. 23; Untermyer, fig. 280.

41 C2. *Crested Pheasant* adapted as a taperstick. 7 in (17.8 cm). *Victoria and Albert Museum*

42 C5. *Dancing Beribboned Youth.* $7\frac{1}{4}$ in (18.4 cm). *Victoria and Albert Museum*

C3 *Rabbit Candlesticks.* Cited by Rice, 1983, p.36, but not illustrated and no measurements quoted.

HUMAN SUBJECTS

C4 *Chinese Boy Climbing a Creeper-like Tree.* $8\frac{3}{4}$ in (22.2 cm). Fitzwilliam Museum, Barrett and Thorpe, pl. 25.

C5 *Dancing Beribboned Youth.* $7\frac{1}{4}$ in (18.4 cm). Victoria and Albert Museum, Rice, 1983, pl. 41; Lane, pl. 62c.

C6 *Seated Lady* fondling a lamb. $5\frac{1}{2}$ in (14 cm). British Museum, Lane, pl. 62b. See Plate 43.

C7 *Seated Gentleman* caressing a dog. 6 in (15.2 cm). He is bareheaded. Fitzwilliam Museum, Rice, 1983, col. pl. B.

C8 *Seated Gentleman* caressing a dog. $5\frac{1}{2}$ in (14 cm). Adapted from C7, he wears a hat and carries a stork-like bird beneath his right arm. British Museum, Lane, pl. 62; Rice, 1983, pl. 40. See Plate 43.

adorned with rosettes and the group mounted on a scrolled base. Rice, 1983, col. pl. A.

C10 *Neptune.* $10\frac{1}{2}$ in (26.7 cm). The god is seated on the stern-castle of an archaic ship, his left arm upraised, and with a hippocampus swimming at his feet. Author's Collection. See also Plate VI.

43 C6. *Seated Lady* fondling a lamb (right). $5\frac{1}{2}$ in (14 cm). C8. *Seated Gentleman* caressing a dog with a stork-like bird under his arm (left). $5\frac{1}{2}$ in (14 cm). *British Museum*

44 C10. *Neptune* seated upon the stern-castle of an archaic ship with a Hippocampus swimming at his feet. $10\frac{1}{2}$ in (26.7 cm).
Author's Collection

3 · Derby Porcelain Models, 1756–69

PALE FAMILY DERBY MODELS, 1756–9

William Duesbury appears to have become joint proprietor and manager of the Derby porcelain factory during the first quarter of 1756 and at about the same time Planché withdrew from the business.

PASTE AND GLAZE

The paste is light in weight, dry to the touch and chalky-white in appearance. A sample taken from a model of a *Lady Seated Playing a Mandoline* (D6) contains silica, 70 per cent, lime, 20 per cent, alumina, 5 per cent and lead oxide, 2 per cent. The relatively high lead content indicates the inclusion of fragments of broken glass, or cullet, leading to lack of stability in the kiln so that some models sag out of alignment. The low alumina content implies lack of plasticity, or shortness, accounting for surface tearing of the paste and fire-cracks, and making it impossible to reproduce crisply moulded edges. The lead glaze was opacified with tin oxide and blued by inclusion of a pinch of smalt. This served to conceal underlying blemishes of the body after firing and transformed an otherwise warm appearance to a cold glitter hopefully resembling that of Meissen hard paste. The thickness of the glaze also tended to collect in crevices to obscure moulded detail. Models were inverted and dipped into a vat of liquid glaze which was now allowed to cover the inferior surface so that the dry edge is rarely encountered.

BASES

The earlier rather steep mounds were now mostly replaced by flatter, wider structures edged with C- and S-shaped scrolls and with the upper surface encrusted with leaves and flowers. The under-surface of many bases are concave and glazed apart from those areas where scrolls come into contact with the table-top. Others give the semblance of being elevated upon three legs when viewed from the front, an illusion created by inverted U-shaped excisions into the base upon which the model stands, leaving the central and also sometimes the posterior portion flat. Alternatively mounds may be adorned with scrolls usually picked out in pale green, yellow and puce. After about 1757 most bases have flat glazed under-surfaces with three or four oval areas resembling thumb-prints (see Plate 72) where the paste is exposed and discoloured. These were produced by the attachment of clay pads to prevent adherence of the model that had been dipped in glaze to the floor of the saggar; these were later removed. Ventilation holes are small to intermediate in size and cylindrical in shape, although in rare instances a screw-hole may be encountered. A second aperture may sometimes be evident piercing the back of the figure or its support to enter the central cavity horizontally. This is most often circular and hence dissimilar from the square or triangular holes found upon contemporary Bow models; they were probably intended to accept metal fitments attached either to a candle-sconce or to additional ornament.

Moulded flowers laid upon the upper surfaces of bases of Derby figures are large in scale; those adorning the model of *Cybele* (D26) are, for example, larger than the head of the attendant lion. Most of them appear to have been individually modelled and resemble full-blown cabbages. Leaves are proportionately big, flat with serpentiform circumferences, and are coloured a light or medium green. Many have branching dorsal veins pencilled in purplish-black. After about 1757 flowers and leaves become smaller and were cast in pitcher-moulds.

MARKS

Prior to about 1784 Derby products, including figures, were mostly left unmarked although there are a few examples where different letters were incised upon the underside of the base. These include a *Gardener* in the Derby Museums and Art Gallery, incised 'New D', paired with an unmarked companion *Woman*; a *Putto* garlanded with flowers and holding posies in the author's collection, marked either with a script 'H' or with the initials 'J.C.'; a *Sportsman and Lady* in the British Museum incised 'TxT' and another model bearing 'TTL'.

ENAMEL COLOURS

The almost pastel colouring of Derby models issued between 1756 and 1759 has earned for them the descriptive title Pale Family. The palette includes both lemon and straw-yellow, a streaky manganese which when thickly applied also provided puce, a watery turquoise, a dry brownish-red, an opaque yellow-green, dark brown and purplish-black. These enamels, derived from metallic ores, were costly to produce and were applied sparingly. They also sank deeply into the lead glaze in the muffle-kiln and produced overall the appearance of oil paint mixed with an excess of turpentine in which individual brush-strokes remained visible. Flesh tints are extremely pale and may at times consist of little more than a faint orange-red blush upon the cheeks and mouth which is smaller and more tidily pencilled than formerly obtained. Eyelids and eyelashes are suggested with elliptical lines drawn in a warm brown whilst the irises may be orange-pink following the style introduced at Meissen, or either grey or brown. Pupils are dark brown or black and eyebrows are pencilled in a similar colour. Human hair is invariably blond or light brown unless a powdered wig is depicted.

The plain washes of pale colour laid upon garments may often be embellished with motifs, such as the star-cross or *œil de perdrix* (peacock's eye) (see Plate VIII) which had been favoured at Sèvres. However, the most attractive form of decoration was provided by floral sprays executed in the European manner (*deutsche Blumen*) and in a scale rather large for the model. This was most often employed upon garments that were either white or pale in hue, and at least two distinct styles have been recognized. One (Plate IX) is painted in a seemingly dry palette and stands out in slight relief upon the surface of the glaze, embracing iron-red, deep yellow, yellow-green and brown. A flower outlined in red but left partly uncoloured, as well as half-open anemones, is invariably included in bouquets which have thread-like stems. This last feature has prompted the cognomen 'Cotton-stem Painter', to identify the unknown artist. A second style (Plate VII) is executed in a far more brilliant palette including rose-pink, clear yellow, yellow-green, and some attractive purples and mauves which have sunk into the glaze to assume a glossy and sumptuous form of decoration. Enamel painting after the Oriental manner (Plate X) (*indianische Blumen*) is not common during this period at Derby and, accordingly, will be described in a later section.

MODELLING

About twelve dry-edge models were refurbished to reappear in pale colouring upon scrolled bases in accord with the Rococo taste. Most are less sharply moulded and are slightly smaller than their originals but nevertheless are among the most attractive of Pale Family products. The majority echo Meissen prototypes but, owing to the restrictions imposed by materials they fall far short of the originals. Most are between 5–7 inches (12.7–17.8 cm) tall although a few exceptions like *Cybele* (D26) and *Diana* (D27) stand 10 or 11 inches (25 or 28 cm) in height. Human heads are often egg-shaped and faces lack normal furrows; eyes seem to stare vacantly into space and drapery is insufficiently detailed to be convincing. Poses are usually stiff and doll-like and the relative scale of human forms, animals and flora may be completely ignored. Thus, for example, in one candlestick group (D38) puppet-like figures are dwarfed by a huge bird and enormous flowers.

MODELS

The dry-edge *Male Dancer* (B11) in Pierrot costume was now reissued (D1), paired with a fresh companion wearing a long, slim-fitting dress and holding out her apron with her left hand. Similar Meissen models by F. E. Meyer[1] are unaccountably designated *Shepherds.* The Derby group of *Harlequin and Columbine* (D4) showing them standing hand-in-hand on a wide and flat scrolled base is known in a much finer Chelsea version.[2] *Harlequin's Family* (D3) echoes Kändler's original group[3] and portrays Harlequin making playful gestures to a child clad in motley held by Columbine. The addition of a tree to the soft-paste copy was required to minimize the risk of collapse in the kiln. *Two Lovers with a Clown* (D8) follows another Kändler group entitled *The Invalid Duped*,[4] in which a gallant wearing an invalid's hat kisses a lady who helps herself to refreshments passed behind his back by a clown; a fourth figure behind the gallant makes derogatory gestures. The gentler idiom of the English version omits both the trappings of illness together with the fourth figure of the derisive clown. Applied rosettes decorating the lady's dress call to mind those upon the harness of the Transitional Derby *Lady Riding Side-saddle on a Prancing Horse* (C19). The pair of *Harlequin and Punch Candlesticks* (D5) were probably adapted from one of many Meissen examples.

The *Lady Seated Playing a Mandoline* (D6), adapted from the dry-edge model emblematic of *Taste* (B34), is slightly smaller and mounted on a scrolled base. Another model of a *Lady Seated Holding a Musical Score* (D7) may have been adapted from the missing dry-edge figure emblematic of *Hearing* (B34); she too is smaller than other members of the set of *Senses.* A *Gentleman Flautist* (D2) also follows a dry-edge predecessor (B12) but has acquired a hat and exchanged his recorder for a flute and also stands upon a base fashioned to suggest it is elevated on legs. Small models of a pair of *New Dancers* (D9) are only 4½ in (11.4 cm) tall and exist also in contemporary Longton Hall versions.[5] They seem to have been the source of inspiration for the Bow pair, also known as the *New Dancers*,[6] which were

1 K. Berling, *Festive Publication To Commemorate the 200th Jubilee of the Oldest European China Factory, Meissen*, Meissen, 1910, table 17, nos. 1 and 2.

2 Nathaniel Harris, *Porcelain Figurines*, London, 1975, pp. 24, 25.

3 Erica Pauls-Eisenbeiss, *Eighteenth-Century German Porcelain*, London, 1972, I, p. 271.

4 Ibid., p. 277.

5 Sotheby's, *Sale Catalogue*, 22 May 1984, lot 134.

6 Peter Bradshaw, *Eighteenth-Century English Porcelain Figures 1745–95*, Woodbridge, 1981, pl. 66.

reissued with several modifications between 1760 and 1770. Two other rather banal small models are of a *Youth Standing Playing a Reed-pipe* (D10) and a similar *Youth Standing with Flageolet and Tabor* (D11).

The portrait model of *Shakespeare* (D13) was inspired by Peter Scheemakers' marble in Westminster Abbey. The Bard stands in traditional attire, leaning his elbow upon a pile of books resting on a plinth decorated with the busts of four monarchs that provide the titles to some of his historical dramas. The early examples are mounted on scrolled bases. The companion model of *Milton* (D12) was probably adapted from a maquette issued from the studio of Scheemakers or possibly provided by John Cheere. One plaster model, painted to simulate bronze, is incised 'John Cheere fecit'.[7] The Poet is portrayed in Van Dyck dress, leaning upon a pedestal decorated in relief with a scene from *Paradise Lost*.

The *Boy Shepherd Piper* and *Dancing Shepherdess*, first seen in dry-edge examples (B17) were now reissued wearing Scottish dress (D14). Other representatives of the idyllic pastoral scene are provided by two pairs of seated figures. One of them (D15) portrays the man holding a nosegay with his legs positioned to suggest movement, while his companion sits with her brimmed hat upon her lap; the other pair are stiffly posed sitting demurely with both feet together (D16). A standing pair *Shepherd with a Dog and Shepherdess with a Lamb* (D17), follow Meissen prototypes and are among the earliest English versions of the *Dresden Shepherds*. The man, clad in brimmed hat and cloak, holds a basket of fruit to his breast with his left hand and proffers an apple in his right. His more usual companion in mirror pose secures flowers in her apron and extends a nosegay in her left outstretched hand. Sometimes, however, the same male is paired with a different shepherdess who may hold a crook and in some versions wears a flower-encrusted dress.

Rather primitively modelled figures of a *Farmer* and his *Wife* (D18–D20) are known in several variations. Most often the man is bareheaded and his companion wears a floral chaplet, but both are sometimes depicted wearing hats and carrying baskets which contain respectively fruits and flowers (D19). Again, the farmer may be portrayed playing a reed-pipe and his wife be clad in a dress adorned with vine leaves and grapes, and both free-standing and candlestick examples survive. Rather similar, but seated, models of a youth and girl wear coronets formed from flowers and corn and also hold additional blossoms or corn in their laps to represent *Spring and Summer* (D21). They display a tranquil beauty that is also evident in Longton Hall examples.[8] A pair of seated *Grape-sellers* (D22) wear hats and hold baskets of

7 City Art Gallery, New York. Plaster model of *Milton*, painted to simulate bronze and signed 'John Cheere fecit'.

8 Bernard Watney, *Longton Hall Porcelain*, London, 1957, pl. 34.

grapes before them in both hands. However, at least one example shows the woman holding flowers instead of grapes so that the couple represent *Autumn* and *Spring*. The same *Seasons* are portrayed by two groups usually called *Lovers* (D23) in which the male wears a brimmed hat and secures either flowers or grapes in his apron with his left hand while his right arm is about the shoulders of his female companion, who also holds either a posy or fruit. These are copies of Meissen *Seasons*[9] by J. J. Kändler and the group emblematic of *Spring* was also issued at Chelsea.[10]

The Four Classical Seasons (D24) echo Eberlein's Meissen originals.[11] Each Season is represented by an appropriate standing divinity, accompanied by a putto bearing suitable emblems: Flora stands by a putto bearing a pannier of flowers; Cere's attendant carries a cornsheaf; Bacchus, decked with grapes and vine leaves, a bunch of grapes and a goblet in either hand, is escorted by a putto bearing fruit; Vulcan, wrapped in a mantle, warms his hands over a brazier at his feet as a putto splits logs with an axe. The Irwin Untermyer Collection contains a pair of identical *Summer, or Harvester, Candlesticks* (D42), each incorporating a bored-looking harvester seated with his chin resting in his cupped hand, holding with the other a cornsheaf and regarding a rustic maid who peeps at him around the Rococo scrolled stick.

Most models of classical divinities echo dry-edge precursors. Thus, *Cybele with a Lion* (B22 and D26), first issued on a low mound, reappeared upon a tall base shaped like a bowler-hat encrusted with leaves, fruits and flowers. Most of the refurbished versions are larger, more elaborate both in the manner of their modelling and their enamel decoration, and display asymmetrically scrolled bases after the current Rococo taste. Some examples include *Mars* (B24 and D28), *Minerva* (B25 and D29), and *Neptune* (B26 and D30). *Diana with a Hunting-dog* (D27), however, was a new arrival from Mount Olympus. She was shown in the act of selecting an arrow from a quiver slung behind her right shoulder, with a long-bow in her left hand, and a hunting-dog at her left side. This was copied from J. F. Eberlein's Meissen model which had been adapted from a seventeenth-century French bronze, after an archaic Greek marble of Artemis. The devotional figures of *St Philip* (B28 and D31) and *St Thomas* (B29 and D32) were also reissued, although the Pale Family versions lack something of the verve of their originals.

Recently a fine pair of *Turkish Dancers* (D37) have come to light. Numerous models of standing *Putti* (D33) garlanded with flowers were made, most of them stiffly posed and unpleasing, although early Pale Family examples are often charm-

9 Berling, op. cit., table 13, nos. 8 and 10.

10 J. V. G. Mallet, *Upton House, the Bearsted Collection: Porcelain*, Plaistow, 1964, pl. 4B.

11 F. Brayshaw Gilhespy, *Derby Porcelain*, London, 1961, pls. 19 and 20.

ing, with individually hand-modelled flowers and clear, pale colours. A model of a *Putto Seated Naked Beside a Vase* (D34) is only 3 in (7.6 cm) tall but unexpectedly echoes a Meissen prototype. A *Candlestick* group (D38) of a man, woman and dog regarding a huge bird perched in the fork of a branching tree-trunk, and *Dogs and Squirrel Candlestick* (D40) both exemplify the disregard for any proper scale relative to human beings, fauna and flora. There are several representations of ewe with lamb, and ram, as in the *Sheep Candlesticks* (D41) in which anatomical proportions are well preserved, although reference here is made only to a single example. Lastly, the putto emblematic of *Autumn* (B31) was incorporated into a single-light *Candlestick* (D39).

45 D1. *Male Dancer* in Pierrot costume. 6¾ in (17.1 cm). A reissue of B11 (Plate 16). *Author's Collection*

46 D2. *Gentleman Flautist*. 7 in (17.8 cm). Adapted from B12. *Sotheby's*

LIST D. PALE FAMILY DERBY MODELS, 1756–9

DANCERS AND MUSICIANS

D1 *Male Dancer*. $6\frac{3}{4}$ in (17.1 cm). A reissue of B11. Acquires a different *Companion Lady* who has plumes in her hair and wears a long dress and apron that she holds out in her right hand. Christie's, Twitchett, pl. 92; Derby Museums and Art Gallery, Barrett and Thorpe, fig. 51.

D2 *Gentleman Flautist*. 7 in (17.8 cm). Adapted from B12, by the addition of a hat and acquisition of a flute in place of a reed-pipe. Gilhespy, 1961, fig. 15.

D3 *Harlequin's Family*. (group). $6\frac{1}{2}$ in (16.5 cm). Harlequin makes playful gestures to a baby dressed in motley held by Columbine, before a leafing tree. Fitz-william Museum, Barrett and Thorpe frontispiece.

D4 *Harlequin and Columbine* (group). $6\frac{1}{2}$ in (16.5 cm). Private Collection, Gilhespy, 1961, fig. 26; Barrett and Thorpe, pl. 64; Sotheby's, New York.

47 D4. *Harlequin and Columbine* (group). $6\frac{1}{2}$ in (16.5 cm). *Sotheby's, New York*

48 D5. *Punch* holding a lantern mounted before a candlestick. $9\frac{1}{2}$ in (24.1 cm). *Sotheby's, New York*

D5 *Harlequin and Punch Candlesticks.* $9\frac{1}{2}$ in (24.1 cm). Harlequin dancing with slap-sticks and Punch holding a lantern. Private Collection, Gilhespy, 1961, pl. 25; Victoria and Albert Museum, Rice, 1983, pl. 60; Sotheby's, New York.

D6 *Lady Seated Playing a Mandoline.* $5\frac{1}{2}$ in (14 cm). Adapted from a model emblematic of *Taste* (B34). Victoria and Albert Museum; Private Collection.

D7 *Lady Seated Holding a Musical Score.* $5\frac{1}{2}$ in (14 cm). Possibly a reissue of the missing model emblematic of *Hearing* (B34). Royal Crown Derby Museum; Private Collection.

D8 *Two Lovers with a Clown.* $5\frac{1}{4}$ in (13.3 cm). A seated lady takes refreshments from a tray passed by a clown behind the back of her lover. Winifred Williams, Twitchett, pl. 30; Sotheby's, New York.

49 D6. *Lady Seated Playing a Mandoline.* $5\frac{1}{2}$ in (14 cm). Adapted from *Taste,* shown as a lady eating fruit (B34 (Plate 38)). *Private Collection*

50 D7. *Lady Seated Holding a Musical Score.* $5\frac{1}{2}$ in (14 cm). Possibly adapted from the missing model emblematic of *Hearing* (B33). *Private Collection*

51 D8. *Two Lovers with a Clown.* $5\frac{1}{4}$ in (13.3 cm). *Sotheby's, New York*

D9 *New Dancers.* (pair). $4\frac{1}{2}$–$4\frac{3}{4}$ in (11.4–12.1 cm). A boy and companion girl stand with arms extended forwards, as if dancing. George Wood Collection, Twitchett, col. pl. 4.

D10 *Youth Standing Playing a Reed-pipe.* $5\frac{1}{2}$ in (14 cm). Christie's, Morley-Fletcher, p. 107; Ronald Raven Collection, Twitchett, pl. 45.

D11 *Youth Standing with Flageolet and Tabor.* $5\frac{1}{2}$ in (14.1 cm). Derby Museums and Art Gallery, Barrett and Thorpe, pl. 49.

NOTABLES

D12 *Milton.* $11\frac{1}{2}$ in (29.2 cm). He wears Van Dyck dress under a cloak and stands leaning upon a plinth decorated in relief with scenes from *Paradise Lost.* Knoblock Collection, Lane, pl. 64.

D13 *Shakespeare.* $11\frac{1}{2}$ in (29.2 cm). The Bard stands cross-legged leaning upon a pile of books placed on a plinth decorated with the masks of monarchs representing some of his historical dramas. Knoblock Collection, Lane, pl. 64.

52 D14. *Boy Shepherd and Dancing Shepherdess in Scottish Dress.* 7 in (17.8 cm). *Aldbury Antiques*

53 D15. *Youth and Girl Seated.* $5\frac{1}{4}$ in (13.3 cm). *Winifred Williams*

54 D16. *Youth and Girl Seated.* $5\frac{1}{4}$ in (13.3 cm). *Private Collection*

PASTORAL AND PEASANT

D14 *Boy Shepherd and Dancing Shepherdess in Scottish Dress.* 7 in (17.8 cm). Adapted from B17. Barry Waiting Collection, Twitchett, pl. 95; Morley-Fletcher, p. 136; Aldbury Antiques.

D15 *Youth and Girl Seated.* $5\frac{1}{4}$ in (13.3 cm). The youth holds a nosegay and kicks out his legs, his companion has her hat on her lap. Winifred Williams, Bradshaw, pl. 106; Victoria and Albert Museum, Rice, 1983, pls. 52 and 53.

D16 *Youth and Girl Seated.* $5\frac{1}{4}$ in (13.3 cm). Similar to D15, but in less animated poses. Late Brayshaw Gilhespy Collection, Gilhespy, 1961, col. pl. vii.

D17 *Shepherd with a Dog* and *Shepherdess with a Lamb.* $10\frac{1}{2}$ in (26.7 cm). Known as the *Dresden Shepherds*, the male holds a basket of fruit and proffers an apple, while his companion holds flowers in her apron and tenders a nosegay. D. M. and P. Manheim at the Grosvenor House Antiques Fair, 1985, see handbook, p. 111; Victoria and Albert Museum, Twitchett, pl. 90; Sotheby's.

Sometimes the female partner is different and either wears a flower-encrusted dress, or holds a crook. Delomosne, Rice, 1983, pl. 48; B. and T. Thorn Antiques.

55 D17. *Shepherd with a Dog* and *Shepherdess with a Lamb,* known as *The Dresden Shepherds.* $10\frac{1}{2}$ in (26.7 cm). *Sotheby's*

55 D17. *Shepherd with a Dog* and *Shepherdess with a Lamb,* known as *The Dresden Shepherds.* $10\frac{1}{2}$ in (26.7 cm). *Sotheby's*

57 D18. *Farmer* standing bare-headed with flowers and companion *Wife* wearing a floral chaplet. 6 and $6\frac{1}{2}$ in (15.2 and 16.5 cm). *Sotheby's*

D18 *Farmer* and *Wife*. 6–6½ in (15.2–16.5 cm). The male is bareheaded and holds grapes; his companion wears a chaplet and stands holding flowers. Sotheby's, Rice, 1983, pl. 90.

D19 *Farmer's Wife*. 6 in (15.2 cm). Adapted from D18, she wears a hat. Delomosne, Rice, 1983, pl. 91.

D20 *Farmer* and *Wife*. 9¾ in (24.8 cm). He wears a hat and plays a reed-pipe, whilst she is encrusted with grapes. Sotheby's. The same two figures may appear mounted before candlesticks 9¾ in (24.8 cm). Delomosne, Rice, 1983, pl. 51.

58 D19. *Farmer's Wife* wearing a hat. 6 in (15.2 cm). Adapted from D18 (Plate 57). *Sotheby's*

59 D20. *Farmer* wearing a hat and playing a reed-pipe. 9¾ in (24.8 cm). Adapted from D18 (Plate 57). *Sotheby's*

60 D20. Companion *Farmer's Wife* with grapes. 9¾ in (24.8 cm). *Sotheby's*

61 D21. *Spring* (left) and *Summer* (right), represented by a girl wearing a floral chaplet and a boy with a diadem of corn-stalks. Both $5\frac{3}{4}$ in (14.6 cm). *Derby Museums and Art Gallery*

D21 *Spring and Summer*. $5\frac{3}{4}$ in (14.6 cm). Represented by a seated Girl and Boy wearing chaplets and holding respectively flowers and corn. Christie's, Rice, 1983, pl. 88; Derby Museums and Art Gallery, Barrett and Thorpe pl. 48.

D22 *Grape-sellers*. (pair). $5\frac{1}{4}$–$5\frac{1}{2}$ in (13.3–14 cm). Seated adult figures holding baskets of grapes in both hands. Author's Collection. Similar figures but with the woman's basket filled with flowers. Sotheby's, Rice, 1983, pl. 89.

D23 *Spring and Autumn*. (two groups). $5\frac{1}{4}$–$5\frac{1}{2}$ in (13.3–14 cm). *Spring*: a man wearing a cocked hat holding flowers stands with his right arm about the shoulders of a woman who secures flowers in her apron. Christie's, *Sale Catalogue*, 10 February 1986, lot 277.

Autumn: a similar couple with grapes substituted for flowers. Sotheby's, Rice, 1983, pl. 89; Royal Crown Derby Museum, Twitchett, pl. 40.

D24 *The Four Classical Seasons*. 9 in (22.9 cm). Represented by four standing divinities each attended by a putto:

Spring: Flora and a putto bearing a basket of flowers upon his head.

Summer: Ceres with a putto holding a cornsheaf.

Autumn: Bacchus bedecked with vine leaves holding a bunch of grapes and a goblet in either hand attended by a putto carrying grapes.

Winter: Vulcan wrapped in a mantle warming his hands over a brazier, while a putto chops logs with an axe.
Antique Porcelain Co., Gilhespy, 1961, fig. 19; Christie's, Rice, 1983, pl. 87; Private Collection, Bradshaw, pl. 114.

D25 *The Four Rustic Seasons.* 5–5½ in (12.7–14 cm). Adapted from B32:
Spring: a man with a basket of flowers proffering a posy. Derby Museums and Art Gallery, Barrett and Thorpe, pl. 51. Also a woman with flowers in her apron tendering a nosegay. Private Collection.
Summer: a woman holding her apron containing corn with her right hand. Derby Museums and Art Gallery, Barrett and Thorpe, pl. 51. Male figure unknown to author.
Autumn: examples unknown to author.
Winter: a woman wearing a cloak, one hand in a muff, warming herself before a brazier. Also a man holding an axe beside a brazier. Private Collection.

RELIGIOUS AND MYTHOLOGICAL

D26 *Cybele with a Lion.* 9¼ in (23.5 cm). Adapted from B22, and mounted upon a tall flower and fruit-encrusted base. Victoria and Albert Museum, Barrett and Thorpe, pl. 24; Bradshaw, Plate VII.

62 D22. *Grape-sellers* (pair). 5¼ and 5½ in (13.3 and 14 cm). See also Plate VIII.
Author's Collection

63 D24. *The Four Classical Seasons*. 9 in (22.9 cm). *Christie's*

64 D25. *Spring,* represented by a woman holding a posy in her hand while securing blossoms in her apron. 5 in (12.7 cm). Adapted from B32 (Plate 28). *Private Collection*

65 D25. *Winter,* portrayed by a man holding an axe standing beside a brazier. 5 in (12.7 cm). *Private Collection*

66 D25. Companion girl emblematic of *Winter*, wearing a cloak and warming her hands over a brazier. $5\frac{1}{4}$ in (13.3 cm). *Private Collection*

67 D26. *Cybele with a Lion.* $9\frac{1}{4}$ in (23.5 cm). Adapted from B22. See also Plate VII. *Author's Collection*

D27 *Diana with a Hunting-dog.* 10 in (25.4 cm). She stands with a long-bow in her left hand, selecting an arrow from a quiver beside her hound. Godden Reserve Collection; late B. and T. Thorn Antiques; J. Dixon, pl. 38.

D28 *Mars.* Sizes ranging between 8–$13\frac{1}{2}$ in (20.2–34.4 cm). Adapted from B24, mounted on a scroll base. Private Collection, Bradley, no. 9.

D29 *Minerva.* Sizes ranging between 8–$13\frac{1}{2}$ in (20.3–34.3 cm). Adapted from B25. Acquires a cuirass. Private Collection, Bradley, no. 10.

D30 *Neptune with a Dolphin.* $8\frac{1}{2}$ in (21.6 cm). Adapted from B26, upon a tall base encrusted with marine life. *Antique Dealer and Collector's Guide*, June 1985, p. 8 (advertisement by Simon Spero).

68 D31. *St Philip.* 10 in (25.4 cm). Adapted from B28 (Plate 25). *Private Collection*
69 D32. *St Thomas.* 10 in (25.4 cm). Adapted from B29 (Plate 26). *Private Collection*

D31 *St Philip.* 10 in (25.4 cm). Adapted from B28. Private Collection.

D32 *St Thomas.* 10 in (25.4 cm). Adapted from B29. Royal Crown Derby Museum, Twitchett, pl. 78; Private Collection.

MISCELLANEOUS

D33 *Putti* (various). $4\frac{1}{4}$–5 in (10.8–12.7 cm). Stiffly posed standing putti, decked with chaplets and garlands and holding posies. Author's Collection.

D34 *Putto Seated Naked Beside a Vase.* 3 in (7.6 cm). Winifred Williams, *Exhibition Catalogue*, 9–18 January 1973, fig. 3.

D35 *Sweetmeat Containers.* 7 in (17.8 cm). A gallant seated with a dog, and companion lady with a sheep, each holding shell containers. Private Collection.

70 D33. *Putto* decked with flowers. $4\frac{3}{4}$ in (12.1 cm). *Author's Collection*

D36 *Sweetmeat Containers.* $7\frac{1}{2}$ in (19.1 cm). A gallant and companion lady each seated and holding open the lids of rectangular hampers. Burnley Antiques, Northern Antique Dealers' Fair, 18–25 September 1980, *Catalogue*, p. 25.

D37 *Turkish Dancers.* 9 in (22.9 cm). The male wears a turban and the female is bareheaded, and both dance with arms outstretched. Burnley Antiques, Northern Antique Dealers' Fair, 20–26 September, 1984, *Catalogue*, p. 49 (col. pl.).

CANDLESTICK FIGURES AND GROUPS

D38 *A Gallant and Lady Candlestick.* 9 in (22.9 cm). The couple, accompanied by a dog, regard a huge bird in a forked flower-encrusted candlestick. Derby Museums and Art Gallery.

D39 *Autumn Candlestick.* 7¾ in (19.7 cm). Incorporates a putto with grapes after the figure B31 in the *Four Infant Seasons.* Derby Museums and Art Gallery.

D40 *Dogs and Squirrel Candlestick.* 9 in (22.9 cm). A seated and a begging dog regard a squirrel in a flower-encrusted single candlestick. Derby Museums and Art Gallery, Barrett and Thorpe, pl. 58.

D41 *Sheep Candlesticks.* 8½ in (21.6 cm). Two candlesticks, one with a ram, the other with a ewe and a lamb, before flower-encrusted candlesticks. B. and T. Thorn Antiques; Thornton's of Harrogate. There are several versions of these items.

D42 *Summer,* or *Harvester, Candlesticks.* 11½ in (29.2 cm). Each includes a youth seated with chin resting in his cupped left hand, holding a cornsheaf, regarding a rustic maid who peeps at him round a Rococo candlestick. Christie's, Rice, 1983, pl. 92.

D43 *Rococo Chinoiserie Candlesticks* (pair). 10 in (25.4 cm). Two Chinese boys face one another from either side of a Rococo candlestick. Untermyer, pl. 107, fig. 289; Stoner, pl. 49.

71 D45. *Unidentified Bird,* yellow with purple splashes. 4 in (10.2 cm). *Private Collection*

BIRDS

Few models of birds can with certainty be allocated to the Pale Family and many possible examples are included in List E.

D44 *Finch.* $4\frac{3}{4}$ in (12.1 cm). Perched upon a tree-stump encrusted with flowers, with upturned tail and wings unfurled. Rice, 1983, col. pl. D.

D45 *Unidentified Bird.* 4 in (10.2 cm). Yellow with splashes of purple. Private Collection.

PATCH-MARKED DERBY MODELS, 1759–69

PASTE AND GLAZE

Between 1758 and 1759 the porcelain body became closer-grained, heavier, whiter and more stable in the kiln. Analysis of material taken from a model of *Diana* in the Victoria and Albert Museum, dated to the period 1760–5, reveals silica, 74 per cent, lime, 22 per cent, alumina, 5 per cent, and only a trace of lead. The virtual elimination of lead indicates that cullet was no longer included in the mix, and the augmentation of alumina reflects enhanced plasticity. These qualities reduced surface-tearing of the paste and fire-cracks, facilitated the adoption of a larger scale and greater sharpness of moulded detail, and permitted modellers to employ more ambitious poses with less need to support the figures by ceramic props that had been thinly disguised as tree-stumps.

Glaze continued to be applied by dipping the inverted figure into a vat of liquid and then standing it upon three pads of clay to prevent adherence to the floor of the saggar. Thus patch-marks remained a constant feature of Derby models until well into the nineteenth century. The inclusion of smalt appears to have been abandoned about 1758, although opacification with tin oxide continued to be used, albeit on a steadily diminishing number of models, until about 1765. The remainder have a clear but faintly straw-coloured glaze. Dry patches may be evident where the glaze failed to adhere to the body, but pin-hole defects, crazing and smoke-staining are uncommon.

BASES

Many of the earlier bases retain a mound shape but are less steep and smaller than obtained during the dry-edge period and, in a few instances, these may be trimmed by four vertical slices. Most of them are embellished with moulded leaves and flowers cast from pitcher-moulds. Others are adorned with scrolls in low relief arranged asymmetrically and accented with enamel colour or gilt. During the mid-

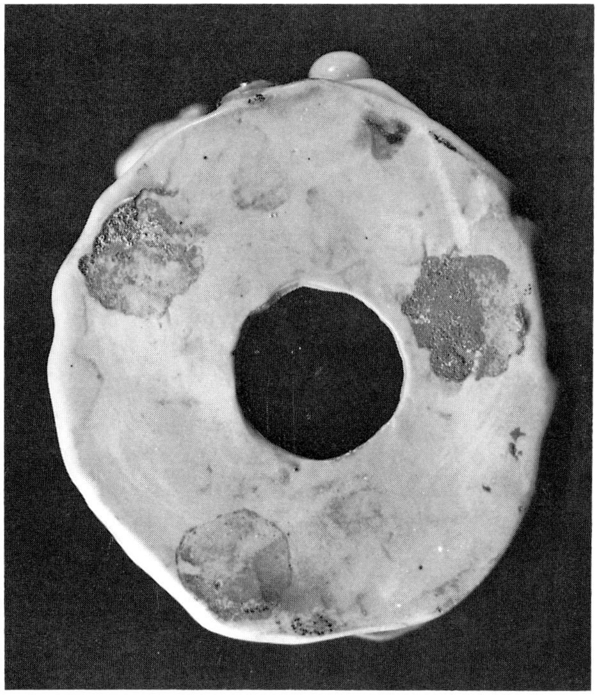

72 Under-surface of the base of *Africa* (E71 (Plate 102)), showing three oval patch-marks and a large ventilation hole.

and later 1760s, increasingly elaborate forms were adopted with short, curved, cabriole legs between which dependent scrolls may be seen. These replaced the former bases that had been undercut to give the appearance of being elevated upon legs whereas, in fact, the central area had always remained in contact with the table-top. The Derby bases rarely assume the elaborate forms encountered in contemporary Bow models. The asymmetrical arrangement of C- and S-shaped scrolls that had reflected the Rococo style were replaced after about 1765 by the more disciplined symmetry of the Louis Seize taste, although for a while some bases remained complex with alternating concave and convex surfaces, sometimes fenestrated, edged with light blue and accented by gilt. There are a few models, including *Jupiter* and *Juno*, each riding in a chariot, and the reclining muses, *Clio* and *Erato*, in which the bases were fashioned to resemble billowing clouds.

Most soft-paste models were supported with ceramic props, thinly disguised as tree-stumps, to reduce the risks of collapse in the kiln. After about 1758 these were sparsely decorated with leaves and flowers that subsequently enlarged to form initially fans of foliage on either side of the figure and subsequently large arbours known as bocages. These may have been prompted by the practice adopted at Sèvres of mounting French, Meissen and Oriental porcelain upon ormolu bases to which were attached metal leaves and stems terminating in flower-heads made of Vincennes porcelain. Some early Derby models have similar brass fitments with porcelain flower-heads,[12] few of which have survived.

The moulded leaves employed for decoration of the upper surface of bases or within bocages are small, flat and thin, with serrated edges, and may display a pin-hole upon their under-surface where they had been pricked out of a pitcher-mould by a sharp instrument. Neither painted nor moulded dorsal veins are usually seen, although such are common on Bow leaves which are generally larger, thicker and often also twisted. The Chelsea foliage is composed of small, thick leaves that are variegated in colour and usually display purplish branching dorsal veins. Derby flowers are also small, resembling either flat cog-wheels, trumpets or diminutive hot cross buns; a few have four or five concave petals arranged about a raised centre and included among them there may be one or two that have been modelled by hand. Flat blossoms may be painted with concentric circles of red, puce and yellow; others have the edges of petals touched with blue, red, yellow or puce. Centres may be dark brown or yellow though few have any surrounding ring of dots that are commonly seen on Chelsea blossoms. Flowers contained in Derby bocages show a preponderance of blue and white.

ENAMEL COLOURS

The quality of enamel colours improved and the range extended between 1760 and 1770. Enamels were more generously applied with the elimination of visible brush-strokes that had earlier been apparent. However, the Derby palette never achieved the richness of Chelsea. Inevitably the nature of the decoration reflected the increasing influence of the Rococo style, and the plain washes of pale colour that had been so pleasing were now broken by irregular-shaped reserves containing stylized leaves and stems intended to simulate brocade patterns. These were sometimes trefoil or quatrefoil in form and edged with gilt arabesques. At other times garments were adorned with patterns composed of geometrical shapes, lines, circles and dots (see Plate XI), or by floral sprays in the manner of *indianische Blumen* (see Plate X). This usually eschewed shading and perspective drawing and portrayed flowers with flat washes of brownish-red, yellow, purplish-blue and green, sometimes accented with touches of gilt.

Between about 1760 and 1765 salmon-pink patches appeared upon the cheeks of

12 Dennis Rice, *Derby Porcelain, the Golden Years, 1750–70*, London, 1983, pl. 14.

human subjects though later this gave place to a buff flesh tint heightened with orange-red. The use of a warm brown to represent eyelashes and lids, as well as the manner of painting the eyes, remained unaltered from former days. Mouths were touched with pale vermilion while hair, usually blonde or light brown, was suggested by irregular fine pencilling laid on a wash of a paler hue. Gold was applied by the process of honey-gilding whereby a mixture of powdered gold leaf and honey was painted on to the appropriate area and heated in a muffle-kiln to about 600°C. This emerged from the firing as a dull-brown, but when burnished with an agate provided a sumptuous gold.

MODELLING

The average height of models that had been $5\frac{1}{2}$–7 in (14–17.8 cm) now increased to 10–12 in (25.4–30.5 cm), although in this metamorphosis much of the toy-like charm was lost. The little people with their egg-shaped heads, button noses and wide, staring eyes were replaced by a new generation with narrow faces, long, thin noses and stylized mouths. They lack the finely chiselled features of Chelsea characterized by oval visages, widely spaced eyes and retroussé noses, and are also dissimilar from their less sophisticated cousins from Bow which have an impudent appearance and a magnificent sense of animation. The drapery of Derby models after 1760 was more detailed and realistic in presentation. However, when the full effects of the Rococo became evident, less attention was paid to the modelling of the figure as embellishments like bocages, attached candle-sconces and lavish enamel and gilt decoration were developed.

MODELS

The large number of models and groups created at Derby between 1760 and 1769 renders it impracticable to mention more than some representative examples here. Notable among portrait models of stage personalities is David Garrick as *Tancred* (E7), in the title role of the play *Tancred and Sigismunda*, by James Thomson, that opened in London in 1745. Tancred, attired in shako, pelisse and dolman, stands striking a dramatic pose. The companion model of a *Street Vendor* wears a headscarf, dress and apron and carries before her a tray of bottles. Some have identified her, without supporting evidence, as Susannah Cibber in the guise of a *vivandière*, although, whatever her identity, she must surely represent an actress who appeared with Garrick. James Quinn was depicted as the wine-bibbing, corpulent knight, *Falstaff* (E4) who appears in Shakespeare's *Henry IV*. Attired in a brimmed and plumed hat, doublet, baggy breeches, cloak and boots, he holds an oval shield and a sword in either hand; the model was later reissued in five sizes (No. 291.) and was adapted from a mezzotint by James McArdell after Francis Hayman.[13] The Bow version is different and portrays David Garrick in the role based on an engraving by Truchy.[14] Interest in the Italian Comedy had, by this time, begun to wane and only one Derby model of *Harlequin* (E5) appears to have been issued, although a pair, *Boy and Girl as Harlequin and Columbine* (E2), both with and without bocages, were made. The Pale Family original of *Two Lovers with a Clown* (D8) was reissued upon a scrolled base before a bocage with minor alterations (E6).

The Derby orchestra is smaller than that of Bow although in both the instrumentalists are loosely based on Meissen originals. Artistically the most pleasing are those decorated with plain washes of pale colour and mounted on mound bases. They include a *Gentleman Cellist* (E8), and *Violinist* (E15), a lady *Hurdy-gurdy Player* (E11) and a *Man with Flageolet and Drum* (E10). The last-mentioned recalls the Meissen *Savoyard Drummer*,[15] one of the *Cris de Paris* adapted from a watercolour sketch by Christophe Huet. Somewhat similar is a *Man with Flageolet and Tabor* paired by a *Lady Playing a Triangle* (E9). These are known also in Bow versions[16] and may be called the *Idyllic Musicians*, or *Flambé Musicians* on account of the flame-like plumes they wear. Seated *Mandoline and Bagpipe Players* (E13) are among the most common of all Derby models and their sumptuous attire betrays them as members of the aristocracy in masquerade. Rare examples of about 1765 in the Derby Museums and Art Gallery appear in chinoiserie gazebos, each surmounted by a cupola, but simpler versions both free-standing and before bocages survive, while Chelsea–Derby reissues are entitled *Sitting Pipe and Guitar* (Nos. 301 and 307).

The *Tyrolean Dancers* (E19) echo Eberlein's Meissen group of about 1735 conceived in the Baroque style.[17] Similar Bow versions[18] are known, though at Chelsea[19] embellishments of the Rococo were added, and there is also a strange Chinese example.[20] They depict a rustic swain dancing a wild gavotte with a peasant maid. The end of the seventeenth century saw the emergence in France of the *noblesse de robe* who, unlike members of the *ancien régime*, no longer commissioned huge canvases depicting scenes from ancient classical mythology, or portraits of them-

13 Raymond Mander and Joe Mitchenson, 'The China Statuettes of Quin as Falstaff', *Theatre Notebook*, XII, no. 2, 1958, p. 54, pls. 8–10.

14 Aubrey J. Toppin, 'The Origin of Some Ceramic Designs', *Trans ECC*, no. 10, vol. 2, 1948, pp. 266–76, pls. CIc and CId.

15 K. Berling, *Festive Publication to Commemorate the 200th. Jubilee of the Oldest European China Factory, Meissen*, Meissen, 1910, fig. 130, no. 5.

16 Frank Hurlbutt, *Bow Porcelain*, London, 1926, p. 131. pl. 62.

17 Erica Pauls-Eisenbeiss, *German Porcelain of the Eighteenth Century*, London, 1972, I, p. 81.

18 Hurlbutt, op. cit., pl. 85.

19 Hugo Morley-Fletcher, *Investing in Pottery and Porcelain*, London, 1968, col. pl. facing p. 55.

20 Fitzwilliam Museum, Cambridge.

selves attired as heroes in grandiose settings. The *fêtes galantes* of Antoine Watteau (1684–1721) and his successors Pater and Lancret, came as a breath of fresh air portraying gallants and their paramours elegantly clad in seventeenth-century theatrical dress, playing music, dancing, or in romantic dalliance in parks or gardens. These delightful works influenced, *inter alia*, the ceramic modelling scene. The *Dutch Dancers* (E16) are in this genre, the male sporting a plumed cap and cloak and his partner a fine silken gown. Their admirable sense of animation suggests the intermediate source of a Meissen pair of models. The *Minuet Dancers* (E18) were adapted from Laurent Cars's engraving after Watteau's *Fête Venitienne*.[21] The gallant, clad in turban, sash and baggy breeches, is thought to represent Nicholas Vleughels, an artist and friend of Watteau. His companion is an elegant lady whose hair is decked with ribbons, leaning slightly backwards holding out the skirts of her satin dress awaiting the beat upon which to enter the dance. Smaller and far more attractive versions were made at Frankenthal.[22]

On 24 May 1759, a masked ball was held in Ranelagh Gardens, Vauxhall, to commemorate the birthday of Frederick George, Prince of Wales. The colourful and often bizarre costumes of the guests prompted several contemporary engravings and one of these probably inspired some dozen Chelsea models that were made.[23] Only two *Ranelagh Dancers* (E17) were created at Derby – a gallant wearing a tricorn hat, cloak and theatrical costume holding a letter inscribed 'Domine Lucretia' in his outstretched hand, and a lady clad in a mantle and Court dress with plumes in her hair; the cameo suspended on a ribbon from her shoulder is believed to have been the token of admission to the festivities. Aubrey Toppin[24] suggested that the female figure had been adapted from a mezzotint by James McArdell of the portrait painted in 1757 by Thomas Hudson of Mary, Duchess of Ancaster, although the resemblance is anything but striking. Two rather unprepossessing groups follow compositions of about 1765 by Carle Vanloo. Both incorporate an adolescent couple with a dog. In *The Dancing Lesson* (E20) the young lady holds a dog wearing motley upon its hind-legs on a pedestal while her companion plays dance music upon a hurdy-gurdy; in *The Singing Lesson* (E21) the girl supports an unclad dog upon a plinth as her partner holds a song-sheet before the wretched animal's eyes and attempts to force open its mouth to sing.

The ethereal *fêtes galantes* almost inevitably led to the more sensuous idyllic

21 E. Dacier and A. Vuaflart, *Jean de Julienne et les graveurs de Watteau au XVIIIe siècle*, Paris, 1929, no. 6. Painting by Watteau now in the National Gallery, Edinburgh.

22 Winifred Williams, 3 Bury Street, St James's, London.

23 John C. Austin, *Chelsea Porcelain at Williamsburg*, Virginia, USA, 1977, col. pls. 130–8.

24 Aubrey J. Toppin, 'Francis Place, Holdship and the Ranelagh Figures', *Trans ECC*, 3, 1951, pt. 1, p. 70.

pastorals of Nicolas Lancret (1690–1743), François Boucher (1703–70) and their contemporaries. They portrayed members of the nobility and royal family as shepherds and shepherdesses lingering with faithful dogs and their flocks in an Arcadian setting. Their rustic garments were incongruously fashioned with silks, satins, brocades and velvets; upon their heads were powdered wigs, while their gold buttons were matched by the buckles upon their scarlet lacquered shoes. It was intended to be a fancy-dress without any pretence to represent real pastoral folk. Indeed, the title of one of Boucher's paintings confirms this: *Berger et la Bergère représentant Louis XV et Madame de Pompadour*. Most pastoral subjects echo Meissen models adapted from French engravings. One pair, *Gallant and Lady Attired as Shepherd and Shepherdess* (E22), the male with a ewe beneath his arm and his lady holding a basket of flowers, has erroneously been designated the *Dresden Shepherds* although here this title has been afforded as it was used by Haslem. In the *Garland Shepherds* (E23) the man stands with right hand on hip reading a letter while his companion stoops to garland a sheep. The *Piping Shepherds* (E30) comprise a youth standing cross-legged beside his dog, playing a recorder, while his partner gathers flowers in her apron and proffers a posy. They follow Meissen prototypes[25] and are also known in bocaged Derby and Chelsea[26] versions. The *Basket Shepherds* (E31) both carry panniers of blossoms and most surviving examples are mounted before candlesticks. The *Dancing Shepherds* (E33) are adapted from dry-edge precursors (B19). The lady's dress is, however, altered by provision of pagoda sleeves and a triple flounce added to the skirt to conform to *haut ton*! She is also given a new partner, a youth wearing a brimmed hat playing a reed-pipe, to the evident disapproval of a seated hound who regards his master with a doleful expression. In the so-called *Italian Farmers* (E26) the farmer is depicted clad in a plumed hat, jacket and trousers, holding a cockerel, his partner a woman who stands barefoot with a hen in her arms. They were so named because it was once thought they had been adapted from Doccia prototypes,[27] although it is now known that both these and the Derby versions were copied from Meissen.[28]

Also depicting the pastoral scene is a pair of *Harvesters* (E24) showing a rustic sharpening his scythe and a woman with a wine-flask hanging from her belt holding their luncheon wrapped in a handkerchief; these closely resemble a Chelsea couple. There is also a splendid pair of *Huntsman and Lady* (E25); here the male wears a

25 *Catalogue of the C. H. Fischer Collection*, 1906, nos. 488 and 489, fig. p. 70.

26 Peter Bradshaw, *Eighteenth-Century English Porcelain Figures, 1745–95*, Woodbridge, 1981, pl. 109; bocaged Derby models, pl. 47, Chelsea versions.

27 Arthur Lane, *Italian Porcelain*, London, 1954, col. pl. C.

28 M. Sauerlandt, 'Eine Wachsfigur nach Meissner Modell', *Der Kunstwanderer, VII*, 1925, pp. 430–1, figs. 1–3.

hat, long coat, breeches and boots, and stands holding a dangerous flint-lock gun, while his elegant companion, wearing a jacket over her gown, holds a game bird in one hand and caresses a hound with the other. Late versions of both have plumes added to their hats. The *Tithe Pig Group* (E34) was adapted from an engraving by J. S. Muller about 1751, after Boitard.[29] The farmer stands grasping the tithe pig watching his wife who proffers their tenth child to the astonished parson. The subject is also portrayed by a set of three separate models, issued *en suite*, in two different sizes. This rather gentle dig at the establishment must have been popular, for both porcelain and pottery models and groups continued to be made well into the nineteenth century. The seemingly irreconcilable estates of liberty and matrimony were satirized by many artists including Nicolas Lancret, whose painting shows a bareheaded gallant, a gun and a ram beside him, holding aloft a bird, while his lady companion opens the door of an empty bird-cage. These Freudian connotations prompted a fine pair of Meissen models[30] that were copied at Bow about 1752. Derby variations on this theme are, by comparison, emasculated. One version of *Liberty and Matrimony* (E27) consists of a youth bearing before him with both hands a nest of fledglings, and a girl holding a lantern-like bird-cage. In another (E28) similar figures recline holding respectively a bird and a bird-cage on their knees, mounted upon elaborately scrolled bases before bocages flanked by swan-necked candle-sconces. This same pair are also known holding cups or beakers when they represent *Topers* (E28b).

Kändler's model of a female *Trinket-seller* of about 1748[31] was adapted by replacement of her hat by a lace cap and the suspension of a map at her left side, to provide a companion to a refurbished *Map-seller* (E36). Both were mounted on scrolled bases before waist-high bocages. The red anchor Chelsea *Jewish Pedlar*,[32] is supposed to have been adapted from Kändler's male *Trinket-seller*, although this figure is clean-shaven, hatless and wears a coat devoid of any fur trim buttoned up in front. This, together with the Meissen female *Trinket-seller*, formed the basis of the Derby pair of *Jewish Pedlars* (E35), although both were greatly simplified and the Jew's casket of gewgaws was replaced by an open tray of bottles.

During the seventeenth and eighteenth centuries new interest in the Middle and Far East was awakened by travellers' tales. The inhabitants of these regions were known collectively as Indians, which explains the term *indianische Blumen* used to

29 H. Boswell Lancaster, 'The Origins of the Tithe Pig Pottery Group', *Connoisseur*, 105, 1940, pp. 253–5.

30 K. Berling, *Das Meissner Porzellan und seine Geschichte*, Leipzig, 1900, p. 131, fig. 195.

31 Berling, op. cit., fig. 40, no. 2785.

32 Yvonne Hackenbroch, *Chelsea and Other English Porcelain, Pottery and Enamels in the Irwin Untermyer Collection*, Cambridge, Mass., 1957, pl. 27, fig. 43.

describe floral painting after the manner of the Orient. In 1714 Monsieur Ferriole, French Ambassador to the Sublime Port, commissioned a folio of engravings by G. Scotin and others depicting Negroes, Turks, Levantines and other nationalities extant in the streets of Constantinople. This was entitled: *Recueil de cent estampes représentant les différentes Nations du Levant tiré sur les tableaux peints d'après Nature en 1707–8, par ordres de Monsieur Ferriole.*[33] This material provided sources of inspiration to Meissen modellers including Kändler who based his models of *Six Orientals*[34] on them. One of these, the *Abyssinian Archer* (E37), a tall, black-skinned man holding a bunch of arrows in his upraised right hand, was copied at Derby. The companion Derby *Negress*, attired in a cloak and a feathered head-dress, was adapted from the unrelated Meissen model of an *African Queen*.[35] Later Derby versions of the archer portray him with a white skin.[36] The pair *Blackamoor and Negress* (E39), one wearing a turban, the other a toque, also echo Meissen prototypes and suffered a similar metamorphosis to become white-skinned *Turks* (E40). During the eighteenth century slavery was accepted as a necessary part of civilized society and porcelain models reflected this hypothesis. Thus there are the pairs *Blackamoor and Negress* (E39 and E40), kneeling in mirror positions holding shell containers for sweetmeats, and a group of *Four Seated Africans* (E38) addorsed about an open receptacle.

The idea of portraying monkeys in human clothing most probably originated in China. In Europe such *singeries* depicted the animals drinking tea, smoking, out hunting or playing on musical instruments, and were painted by artists like Claude Audran (1658–1734) for adornment of the royal palaces of Marley and La Muette, and by Christophe Huet in the *salon des singes* in the château at Chantilly belonging to Henri de Bourbon, Prince de Condé. An undated folio, *Singeries ou Différentes Actions De La Vie Humaine Représentees Par Des Singes Dediée Au Public. Gravée sur les desseins de C. Huet par J. Guelard* (Paris), survives. The engravings probably provided the basis for Kändler's *Affenkapelle* of about 1752 that includes a conductor, two chanteuses and eighteen instrumentalists. Two of these, a *Monkey Violinist* and *Monkey with a French Horn* (E90) were copied in both soft paste and bone china at Derby.

A number of Derby models of about 1764 relate to the scandal of John Wilkes (1727–97), although the versions of the 1770s are better known. John Wilkes was

33 J. I. Smith, 'An Eighteenth-Century Turkish Delight', *Connoisseur*, 156, 1964, no. 705, pp. 215–19.

34 Berling, op. cit., p. 28, fig. 36.

35 Cleo M. and G. Ryland Scott, *Antique Porcelain Digest*, Newport, 1961, pl. 4, no. 12.

36 B. and T. Thorn Antiques, Budleigh-Salterton, Devon.

born at Clerkenwell, the son of a distiller.[37] He married the daughter of Dr Mead, a wealthy physician, in accord with his parents' wishes. The lady was ten years his senior and, after the birth of a daughter, the ill-matched couple separated. Wilkes was elected Member of Parliament for Aylesbury in 1757 but was a profligate adventurer and one of the notorious 'Monks of Medmenham'. The refusal of Lord Bute to appoint him Governor of Quebec or Ambassador to the Sublime Port prompted Wilkes to attack the administration in his weekly journal, *North Briton*. Then, after fighting a duel with Lord Talbot, he roundly condemned the illiberal programme set out in the King's Speech in No. 45 of the paper. The Secretary of State, Lord Halifax, ordered his immediate arrest on a common warrant but, when he was brought before Charles Pratt, then Chief Justice of Common Pleas, his detention was declared illegal and he was set free amongst general rejoicing. Earlier, Wilkes had composed a parody of Pope's *Essay on Man*, entitled *Essay on Woman*, that had been printed privately, doubtless for the Monks of Medmenham. This was read out in the House of Lords, deemed to be seditious libel, and a copy was burned by the Public Hangman. Wilkes was expelled from the House of Commons and, fearing imprisonment for debt, fled to the Continent when he was dubbed an outlaw. In 1768 he returned to England where, after paying a fine of £1,000, he submitted to twenty-two months' imprisonment. This proved to be a nominal sentence during which he was afforded every luxury and he actually contested the vacant parliamentary seat of Middlesex from the gaol. Three times he topped the poll and thrice his election was deemed to be invalid. After his release he became first an alderman and, in 1774, Lord Mayor of the City of London. His election to Parliament the following year was accepted though he made little impact upon the legislature and, when he spoke against the Lord George Gordon riots, his popular image as the champion of liberty was somewhat tarnished. He retired to Bath where he died in 1797.

The first models of *John Wilkes* (E45) were issued about 1764, based upon the portrait by Nathaniel Dance, posed beside a plinth after the manner of Scheemaker's marble of Shakespeare. He stands left hand on hip, his right resting upon the plinth from which two scrolls hang inscribed 'Magna Charta' and 'Bill of Rights', while at his feet sits a putto holding the 'Cap of Liberty', and supporting a tome entitled 'Lock on Govt'. Models reissued after he became Lord Mayor in 1774 (No. 126) have the mace of his office appended to the upper surface of the base. The companion model is of *Field Marshal Conway* (E42) and depicts him with right hand on hip and his left resting on the barrel of a cannon; at his feet sits a putto holding a shield

37 Horace Bleakley, *The Life of John Wilkes*, London, 1918.

emblazoned with the Saracen's Head, which was the family crest. General Sir Henry Seymour Conway (1721–95) criticized in the House of Commons the government's handling of the affair and, for his temerity, was dismissed as Gentleman of the Royal Bedchamber and deprived of his command. Subsequently reinstated, he was promoted to Field Marshal, as the baton held by the model signifies. Charles Pratt (1713–94) had been called to the Bar in 1738 and rapidly rose in his profession to become Lord Chancellor, and in 1786 was ennobled as Baron Camden. The model (E44) was based on Ravenet's engraving made in 1766 after the portrait by Sir Joshua Reynolds. He stands in a full-bottomed wig and robes of office complete with gold chain, hand on heart; his left hand holds a scroll and rests on a legal tome 'Coke Vol. I', placed on a plinth moulded with a relief of Justice.

William Pitt, the elder (1708–78), entered Parliament in 1735 to pursue a long and distinguished career, becoming Paymaster General, Secretary of State and Prime Minister, in opposition to Walpole. He was ennobled as Lord Chatham in 1766 but was compelled by ill-health to resign the premiership two years afterwards. He waged successful wars against both France and Spain but opposed the harsh policies enacted for the American Colonies, wherever possible favouring honourable compromise. The model (E43) portrays him wearing Court dress, standing beside a pedestal, an alligator at his feet and a Red Indian girl kneeling before him.

During the eighteenth century most gentlemen of quality made the Grand Tour and were conversant with the myths of ancient Greece and Rome. Contemporary porcelain factories, including Derby, served this interest with a veritable Pantheon of figures of gods and goddesses. Most of the Derby examples follow Meissen prototypes which had been based on bronzes, marbles, or illustrations in books. The engravings in Cesare Ripa's *Iconologia* of 1593 portrayed the traditional attire and accessories appropriate to each of the classical divinities. Derby versions include a large and ugly *Jupiter* (E56), nearly 17 in (43.2 cm) tall, wearing a crown and regal robes, holding thunderbolts, and companion *Juno* (E53) standing beside a peacock. Another pair of *Jupiter* (E55) and *Juno* (E54), each riding a chariot, are mounted on bases simulating billowing clouds and reflect something of the slender elegance of Eberlein's Meissen originals. Many other models follow either dry-edge or Pale Family examples but are larger, more elaborate and are mounted on scrolled bases. They include *Mars* (B24 and E59), *Minerva* (B25 and E60), *Pluto and Cerberus* (B27 and E62), *Neptune with a Dolphin* (B27 and E61), and *Diana with a Hunting-dog* (D27 and E50). The earlier examples modelled in the manner of the Baroque received more sympathetic treatment than later versions that were influenced by the succeeding Rococo taste. The grace and dignity of the first model of Diana as the virgin huntress of the forests were sadly displaced by a lewd-looking woman with rouged cheeks wearing a décolleté dress that is garishly decorated. Some new replicas of deities include *Venus Standing beside a Dolphin* (E65) adapted from Eberlein's original that had comprised a third figure of Cupid,[38] and *Venus and Cupid Seated on a Dolphin* (E66), which also echoes a Meissen prototype.

Two Derby groups illustrate Jupiter's seductions of mortal women, *Europa and the Bull* (E52) portrays a rather ugly princess seated beside a diminutive animal that she decks with flowers. Legends tell how Jupiter disguised as a white bull waylaid the lady when she was walking in the water-meadows and knelt before her. Europa was so charmed by this homage that she garlanded the beast with flowers, whereupon it reared up, bore her away upon its back over the oceans and ravished her. *Leda and the Swan* (E58) shows the lady seated bareheaded and barefoot beside an aggressive cob, supporting its breast with one hand as she caresses it with the other. The myth relates how Jupiter in the guise of a swan seduced Leda who, that same night, coupled with her husband. The progeny of this double union were two sets of twins: Hellen and Pollux who were divine, and Clytemnestra and Castor who were human. Dr Bernard Watney[39] has suggested that *Europa and the Bull* may have been adapted, somewhat unexpectedly, from a bronze replica of *Leda and the Swan* by Jean Thierry (1669–1739), while the Derby *Leda Group* may have been a copy of a lost second bronze, also by Thierry.

Among the contents of boxes of porcelain dispatched from Derby to London in 1763, were two models of Muses. *Clio* (E49), the Muse of history, is depicted reclining, a quill in her hand and a lyre by her side, attended by Cupid who bears a parchment and wags his forefinger at the goddess. The companion model of *Erato* (E51), the muse of love poetry, reclines in mirror pose, holding a tambourine, while an attendant Cupid stoops forward carrying flowers. Both are mounted on bases that simulate billowing clouds and were probably adapted from Jean Daullé's engraving after Boucher,[40] although biscuit Sèvres groups by Etienne-Maurice Falconet may have been the intermediate sources.

A large model of *Britannia* (E48) stands beside a lion supporting a shield emblazoned with the superimposed crosses of St George and St Patrick. She would readily pass for a busy housewife with the hem of her skirt hitched up to her waist and her sleeves rolled, were it not for her plumed helmet. *Justice* (E57), portrayed as a bareheaded woman standing barefoot with her eyes closed, holds a short sword with upturned point and scales in either hand. A youth clad in doublet, mantle and

38 Berling, op. cit., fig. 70, no. 998.

39 Bernard Watney, 'The Origin of Design for English Ceramics of the Eighteenth Century', *Burlington Magazine*, 144, 1972, no. 837, pp. 818–26.

40 Hugh Tait, *Porcelain*, London, 1962, fig. 29, engraving of *La Muse Erato*, by J. Daullé after Boucher.

boots, standing beside a flaming urn and a cannon, represents *War* (E70); he was later to be adapted to be emblematic of *Fire* (F17) in a set of *The Four Elements. The Four Quarters of the Globe* (E71), or *The Four Continents*, as Australasia had not then been discovered, follow Meissen originals by F. E. Meyer, although they may have been cast from moulds taken from Chelsea copies of about 1758.[41] They comprise four standing children, which were later to be reissued (Nos. 200 and 332) and adapted to provide a group (No. 295). These, together with a set of *The Five Senses* (E72), also reissued during the Chelsea–Derby period (No. 59), are described in Part III.

The Derby factory, like most others, issued several different sets of figures representing *The Four Seasons. The Infant Seasons* (E75) follow Meissen prototypes by F. E. Meyer[42] and consist of scantily draped seated putti; *Spring* wears a chaplet of flowers and holds posies, *Summer* is crowned with corn and supports a sheaf, *Autumn* in a wreath of vine leaves carries grapes, whilst *Winter*, wrapped in a cloak, precariously balances a brazier upon one knee. *The Adolescent Seasons* (E76) employ children wearing contemporary clothes and similar chaplets. *The Antique Seasons* (E73) consist of the four standing divinities, Flora, Ceres, Bacchus and Saturn, each beside a Rococo urn from which respectively emerge flowers, corn, grapes and flames. These also follow originals by F. E. Meyer.[43] *The Classical Seasons* (E74) after J. F. Eberlein[44] are refurbished Pale Family models (D24) upon scrolled, instead of square, bases.

Models of either seated or standing figures holding open hampers or shells, issued in pairs, were intended to contain sweetmeats (E78). Sometimes these were far too small for the purpose and were intended for comfits, aromatic for men and scented for women. Such breath-sweeteners must have been welcome when dental hygiene left much to be desired and guests lingered for hours at the dining-table in heavily curtained rooms. Other miscellaneous items include stiffly modelled standing *Putti* (E77), wearing diagonal garlands and crowns of flowers, some carrying flowers, others plants, while a few hold a puppy. Girls may be distinguished from boys by their narrower faces, a queue of hair at the back, and by the manner in which their drapes about their left hips point downwards and to the right, which is reversed for boys.

41 Arthur Lane, *English Porcelain Figures of the Eighteenth Century*, London, 1961, pls. 22B and 23B.

42 Berling, op. cit., table 11, nos 2, 4 and 5. *Infant Seasons* by F. E. Meyer, standing but similar to seated models in a private collection.

43 Hurlbutt, op. cit., pl. 51B. Meissen *Antique Seasons*, by F. E. Meyer.

44 F. Brayshaw Gilhespy, *Derby Porcelain*, London, 1961, pl. 19, The *Classical Seasons*, Derby; pl. 20, Meissen originals by J. F. Eberlein.

The spirited modelling of wild animals during the period 1750–5 gave promise of even greater excellence to come, but sadly this was not to be realized. Many banal replicas of farmyard beasts and pets were made which are included in List E. A few others are worthy of special mention. A small pair of *Bulls, Charging* (E80) appear to have been cast from moulds made from clay squeezes taken from their dry-edge predecessors (B2). A *Fox, Seated* (E85) was probably included with flocks of sheep and dogs to accompany models of shepherds and shepherdesses on the festive board. Two magnificent *Leopards, Prowling* (E89) show fine modelling and have a commendable sense of animation; a rare pair of small *Tigers* (E101) were probably adapted from them. A pair of *Red Squirrels* (E98), wearing blue collars and eating nuts, may have been copied directly from Meissen,[45] or indirectly via Chelsea versions.[46] The *Stag and Doe at Lodge* (E99 and E100), unlike their dry-edge ancestors, follow Meissen originals,[47] and are known with and without bocages. *Pug Dogs* (E92), seated with cropped ears, some with studded collars (E93), others upon tasselled cushions (E94) appear to have been made in large numbers and most follow Meissen prototypes.[48] In 1736 Pope Clement XII excommunicated all Catholics who continued to be Freemasons, but permitted the faithful to join a superficially similar organization known as the *Mopsorden* (Order of the Pug). Thus the pug became the symbol of an aristocratic secret society and was incorporated into masonic groups depicting men and women in their regalia, as well as appearing in an infinite variety of poses singly or in pairs in Meissen porcelain. The Derby *Pointer* (E91) also proved a popular model and on account of its doleful expression was often known as a *Dismal Hound*. It continued to be issued until the first quarter of the nineteenth century.

The Derby aviary is relatively small when compared to that of Bow. The models are quite small, stiffly posed and pale in hue. These features contrast with the larger Bow birds which have a twisted appearance and unnatural, abnormally brilliant plumage. Most Derby birds lack the sense of animation and attention to fine details evident upon their Chelsea counterparts, although a pair of *Bullfinches* (E105) provide a notable exception. The best include a *Peacock and Peahen* (E113), a *Woodpecker* (E118) and two *Titmice* (E115), all of them based on Meissen originals. There are, too, some charming bocaged groups of nesting birds (E103, 107 and

45 R. J. Charleston and John Ayers, *Meissen and Other European and Oriental Porcelain, from the James A. de Rothschild Collections at Waddesdon Manor*, London, 1971, p. 165.

46 John C. Austin, *Chelsea Porcelain at Williamsburg*, Virginia, USA, 1977, no. 104, *Squirrel*, first period Chelsea.

47 S. Ducret, *Meissner Porzellan*, Berne, 1952, nos. 1150 and 1151.

48 Ayers and Charleston, op. cit., no. 55, Meissen pair of *Roquets* (pugs).

119), some adapted as chamber candlesticks, but the majority of the remainder consist of a selection of *Tits*, *Buntings*, and others of doubtful identity.

LIST E. PATCH-MARKED DERBY MODELS, 1759–69

THEATRICAL

E1 *Actress*. 8½ in (21.6 cm). Possibly Susannah Cibber as a *vivandière*, she wears a headscarf, jacket and dress, and has a tray of bottles suspended by a strap about her neck. A pair to E7. Victoria and Albert Museum, Hughes pl. 11b; Cushion, col. pl. 121; Lane, pl. 69; Twitchett, pl. 47.

E2 *Boy and Girl as Harlequin and Columbine* (pair). 4 in (10.2 cm). Versions both with and without bocages are known. Gilhespy, 1951, pl. 82.

E3 *Columbine, Harlequin and Punch* (addorsed). 9¾ in (24.8 cm). Each holds a shell container. Stoner, pl. 59.

E4 *Falstaff, played by James Quinn*. 5¼ in (13.3 cm). He wears a plumed brimmed hat, doublet, coat, breeches and boots, and holds a shield and sword in either hand. Royal Crown Derby Museum, Barrett and Thorpe, pl. 62.

E5 *Harlequin in Motley*. 7 in (17.8 cm). He stands, right hand on his breast, with slap-sticks under his left arm. Twitchett, pl. 59; Sotheby's *Sale Catalogue*, 12 May 1974, lot 157.

E6 *Two Lovers with a Clown* (group). 12 in (30.5 cm). A larger version of D8 on a scrolled base before a bocage; here the clown proffers refreshment to the lover who ignores it. Sotheby's, Rice, 1983, pl. 63; Royal Crown Derby Museum, Twitchett, col. pl. 13; Stoner, pl. 58.

E7 *Tancred, Played by David Garrick*. 9 in (22.6 cm). He stands clad in a fur hat, pelisse, dolman and boots, with his right hand upon his stomach. Derby Museum, Barrett and Thorpe, pl. 63; Victoria and Albert Museum. See Plate XII.

MUSICIANS

E8 *Gentleman Cellist*. 6½ in (16.5 cm). Stoner, pl. 56.

E9 *Man with Flageolet and Tabor*, paired by *Lady Playing a Triangle*, female companion. Both 7¼ in (18.4 cm). Later versions No. 311. Fitzwilliam Museum, ref. nos. C64 and C65; Plymouth Museum, male figure only.

E10 *Man with Flageolet and Drum*. 7½ in (19.1 cm). Sotheby's, Twitchett, pl. 52.

E11 *Hurdy-Gurdy Player*. 6¼ in (15.9 cm). A seated female. Stoner, pl. 56.

E12 *Mandoline and Bagpipe Players* (pair). 12 in (30.5 cm). A lady sits clad in a fine gown with plumes in her hair playing a mandoline; her companion wears

73 E9. *Man with Flageolet and Tabor.* $7\frac{1}{4}$ in (18.4 cm). *Sotheby's*

74 E13. *Mandoline and Bagpipe Players* (pair), seated before bocages. $9\frac{1}{2}$ in (24.1 cm). *Sotheby's*

75 E17. *The Ranelagh Dancers.* 11½ in (29.2 cm). See also Plate IX. *Sotheby's*

a plumed hat, jacket and knickerbockers secured with ribbons, and plays bagpipes. A lamb and a dog respectively lie at their feet and each is placed in a trellised gazebo surmounted by a cupola. Derby Museums and Art Gallery, Barrett and Thorpe, pl. 72; Morley-Fletcher, p. 138.

E13 *Mandoline and Bagpipe Players* (pair). 7½–9½ in (19.1–24.1 cm). Similar figures to E12, mounted both with and without bocages. Sotheby's, *Sale Catalogue*, 20 November 1979, lot 122 (no bocage); *ibid.*, 20 November 1979, lot 110 (with bocage).

E14 *Huntsman and Lady* (group). 7½ in (19.1 cm). A larger version of B14. with added bocage and scrolled base. Christie's, Rice, 1983, pl. 50.

E15 *Gentleman Violinist.* 5¼ in (13.3 cm). Untermyer, pl. 96, fig. 273.

DANCERS

E16 *Dutch Dancers* (pair). 9½ in (24.1 cm). A gallant clad in plumed hat, cloak and suit stands with his left hand behind his back and right upraised. The lady with plumes in hair holds out the skirt of her fine dress with her left hand and holds her right elevated. Stoner, pl. 55.

76 E18. *Minuet Dancers*, after Antoine Watteau. 10¼ and 11 in (27.3 and 27.9 cm). See also Plate X. *Sotheby's*

E17 *The Ranelagh Dancers.* 11½ in (29.2 cm). A gallant attired in a tricorn hat, doublet, hose and cloak, stands right hand on hip and holds a letter in his outstretched left. His companion wears plumes in her hair, a gown and cloak, and stands in mirror pose; a medallion is suspended by a ribbon from her shoulder. Stoner, pl. 57; Sotheby's. Variations with figures adapted as candlesticks. Royal Crown Derby Museum, Twitchett, pl. 66 show bocaged versions.

E18 *Minuet Dancers.* 10¼–11 in (27.3–27.9 cm). A gallant wearing a turban, short-sleeved coat and breeches stands leaning backwards, his left hand on hip and right behind his back. His lady has her hair bedecked with ribbons and holds out the skirt of her gown to dance. Victoria and Albert Museum, Rice, 1983, pl. 56; King, col. pl. II; Sotheby's.

E19 *Tyrolean Dancers* (group). 7½ in (19.1 cm). A peasant youth dances a wild gavotte with a rustic maid. Fitzwilliam Museum. See Plate XI.

E20 *The Dancing Lesson* (group). 11 in (27.9 cm). An adolescent girl supports a macaroni dog upon its hind-legs on a plinth while her companion plays dance music upon a hurdy-gurdy. Victoria and Albert Museum, Honey, pl. 15a.

77 E20. *The Dancing Lesson*, after Vanloo. 11 in (27.9 cm). *Victoria and Albert Museum*

78 E22. *Gallant and Lady Attired as Shepherd and Shepherdess.* 9 in (22.9 cm). *David Love Antiques*

E21 *The Singing Lesson* (group). 11 in (27.9 cm). An adolescent girl supports a dog upon a pedestal and forces its mouth open to sing while her companion holds a song-sheet before the wretched animal's eyes. Metropolitan Museum, Lane, pl. 67.

PASTORAL AND PEASANT

E22 *Gallant and Lady Attired as Shepherd and Shepherdess* (pair). 9 in (22.9 cm). The man holds a lamb under his right arm and a basket of flowers lies at his feet; his companion carries a pannier of eggs and secures flowers in her apron. Victoria and Albert Museum, Twitchett, pl. 49; David Love Antiques, Bradshaw, pl. 108.

1 Chinoiserie group emblematic of *Taste*, from a set representing *The Five Senses* (B33), c. 1752/3. $7\frac{3}{4}$ in (19.7 cm). The Chinaman's robe shows the star-cross decorative motif (see pp. 24–5). *Victoria and Albert Museum*

11 *Venus with Cupid* group (B30), c. 1752/3. $7\frac{1}{2}$ in (19.1 cm). The restricted palette and heavy appearance of the floral sprays suggests decoration by William Duesbury (see p. 24). *N. C. Ashton Collection*

III *Lady with a Parrot*, emblematic of *Feeling*, from a set representing *The Five Senses* (B34), c. 1752/3. $6\frac{3}{8}$ in (16.2 cm). The floral sprays are painted in the manner of Type A (see p. 25) and may be from the hand of John Bolton of Kentish Town. See also Plate 34. *Fitzwilliam Museum*

IV *Dancing Girl*, possibly *Columbine* (B11), c. 1752/3. $6\frac{1}{2}$ in (16.5 cm). Decorative floral sprays in the manner of Type A are effected in blue monochrome (see pp. 25–6). See also Plate 17.
David Thorn Collection

v *Dancing Shepherdess* (B17), c. 1754/5. $6\frac{1}{2}$ in (16.5 cm). The double pink hemlines, the device of a double cherry, and the painted floral sprays are after the manner of Type B (see p. 25) and probably stem from the studio of James Giles. See also Plate 21. *N. C. Ashton Collection*

VI *Neptune* seated upon the stern-castle of an archaic ship, with a hippocampus swimming at his feet (C10), c. 1755/6. $10\frac{1}{2}$ in (26.7 cm). The limited range of enamel colours and sanded glaze suggests this is a Transitional Derby piece. *Author's Collection*

VII *Cybele with a Lion* (D26), c. 1756/7. $9\frac{1}{4}$ in (23.4 cm). Floral sprays are painted in soft enamels that have sunk below the surface of the glaze, giving a sumptuous glossy effect (see p. 59). The disproportionately large moulded flowers are typical of the Pale Family models. See also Plate 67.
Author's Collection

VIII Pair of *Grape-sellers* (D22), c. 1758. $5\frac{1}{4}$ in (13.3 cm). The figures are stiffly posed and mounted on wide flat bases edged with scrolls. The pale colouring includes the use of the *œil de perdrix* upon the lady's skirt. See also Plate 62.
Author's Collection

IX Pair of *Ranelagh Dancers* (E17), c. 1760. $11\frac{1}{2}$ in (29.2 cm). Enamelled floral sprays include a red blossom left partially uncoloured and the style is that of the *Cotton-stem Painter* (see p. 60). See also Plate 75. *Aldbury Antiques*

E23 *Garland Shepherds*. $7\frac{3}{4}$ in (19.7 cm). The man stands with right hand on hip with a letter in his outstretched left; his companion places a garland about the neck of a sheep. Victoria and Albert Museum, Herbert Allen, pl. 13 no. 39; Aldbury Antiques, see Plate XIII.

E24 *Harvesters* (pair). 9 in (22.9 cm). A rustic stands before a barrel sharpening a scythe; his companion has a wine-flask hanging from her belt and holds a package wrapped in a handkerchief. Both mounted before bocages on scrolled bases. Sotheby's, *Sale Catalogue*, 16 March 1982, lot 123.

E25 *Huntsman and Lady* (pair). $7\frac{1}{2}$ in (19.1 cm). The man, wearing a hat, coat, breeches and boots, stands holding a gun; his companion is clad in hat, jacket and gown and caresses a hound while holding game in her left hand. Victoria and Albert Museum, Twitchett, pl. 105.

79 E25. *Huntsman and Lady* (pair). $7\frac{1}{2}$ in (19.1 cm). *Victoria and Albert Museum*

80 E26. *Italian Farmers* (pair), c. 1760. 6 and $6\frac{1}{2}$ in (15.2 and 16.5 cm). *Private Collection*

81 E26. *Italian Farmers* mounted before bocages, c. 1765. $8\frac{3}{4}$ in (22.2 cm). *Sotheby's*

82 E29. *Shepherd* and *Shepherdess with Fruit and Flowers* (pair). 9½ in (24.1 cm). *Sotheby's*

E26 *Italian Farmers* (pair). 8¾ in (22.2 cm). The farmer wears a hat, jacket, trousers and shoes and stands holding a cockerel; his wife in dress and apron stands barefoot holding a hen. Early versions 6–6½ in (15.2–16.5 cm), Private Collection; David Thorn Collection, Bradshaw col. pl. Q. Later versions with bocages, Sotheby's, *Sale Catalogue*, March 1982, lot 128.

E27 *Liberty* and *Matrimony* (pair). 9 in (22.9 cm). A youth wearing a brimmed hat and contemporary clothes stands bearing in both hands a nest of fledglings; his companion carries a lantern-like bird-cage. Rice, 1983, col. pl. K.

E28 *Liberty* and *Matrimony* (pair). 11½ in (29.2 cm). A shepherd reclines supporting a bird upon his knee, a dog at his feet; his companion in a mirror pose holds a bird-cage. Both mounted before bocages upon scrolled bases flanked by candle-sconces. Victoria and Albert Museum, Stoner, pl. 62; Sotheby's, *Sale Catalogue*, 20 October 1981, lot 128.

The same pair may appear in the guise of *Topers* when each figure holds a beaker or wine glass in an outstretched hand. Sotheby's, *Sale Catalogue*, 2 February 1982, lot 159.

E29 *Shepherd* and *Shepherdess with Fruit and Flowers* (pair). 9½ in (24.1 cm). A shepherd stands holding fruit in his left hand and with his right grasping a flower-encrusted candle-holder; his companion secures flowers in her apron and grasps a sconce with her left hand. Sotheby's, *Sale Catalogue*, 24 July 1984, lot 186. For models without candle-sconces Barrett and Thorpe, pl. 70, female only. See Plate 82.

83 E30. *Shepherd* standing cross-legged playing a recorder beside his dog, mounted before a bocage. 8 in (20.3 cm).

84 E30. Companion *Shepherdess* with flowers in her apron proffering a posy. 8 in (20.3 cm). *Sotheby's*

E30 *Piping Shepherds* (pair). 8 in (20.3 cm). The shepherd stands cross-legged playing a recorder, a dog at his feet; his companion holds flowers in her apron and tenders a posy in her right hand, a sheep lies at her feet. Bradshaw, pl. 109; Sotheby's, *Sale Catalogue*, 31 July 1979, lot 56a. Examples mounted on tall bases 9½ in (24.1 cm), Sotheby's, *Sale Catalogue*, 20 November 1979, lot 107.

E31 *Basket Shepherds* (pair). 11⅜ (28.9 cm). A shepherd stands with a basket of flowers in his right hand and a posy in his left; his companion secures blossoms in a fold of her apron with her left hand and has a pannier of flowers over her right arm. Both mounted on scrolled bases before small bocages and candlesticks. Royal Crown Derby Museum, Twitchett, col. pl. 12; Sotheby's.

E32 *Singing Shepherds*. 8¾–9 in (22.2–22.9 cm). A bareheaded man and woman, each wearing a short cape, stand in mirror positions with one hand on hip

85 E31. *Basket Shepherds* (pair), adapted as candlesticks (sconces missing). $11\frac{3}{8}$ in (28.9 cm). *Sotheby's*

and holding in the other a song-sheet. Derby Museums and Art Gallery, Barrett and Thorpe, pl. 68.

E33 *Dancing Shepherds*. 6–$6\frac{1}{4}$ in (15.2–15.9 cm). The shepherd stands playing a reed-pipe regarded by a large mournful dog; his companion is adapted from B17 (Plate 21) with a triple flounce added to the dress and pagoda sleeves appended to the bodice. Private Collection, Bradley, nos. 11 and 12; Victoria and Albert Museum.

E34 *The Tithe Pig* (three figures). 6–$8\frac{1}{2}$ in (15.2–21.6 cm). A farmer holding the tithe pig under his arm; his wife proffering her tenth child in swaddling bands; an astonished parson dressed in black. Samson Selig Collection, Gilhespy, 1961, fig. 154; Burnley Antiques for large versions. *The Tithe Pig Group*. $6\frac{1}{2}$ in (16.5 cm). Same figures married upon a mound base beneath a flowering tree. Bradshaw, pl. 120. For Chelsea–Derby version, Derby Museums and Art Gallery, Barrett and Thorpe, pl. 67.

86 E33. *Dancing Shepherdess*, adapted from B17 (Plate 21), with a triple flounce added to her skirt. 6 in (15.2 cm). *Sotheby's*

87 E33. A new young *Shepherd Piper* as a companion for the *Dancing Shepherdess*. $6\frac{1}{4}$ in (15.9 cm). *Victoria and Albert Museum*

STREET VENDORS

E35 *Jewish Pedlars* (pair). $7\frac{1}{2}$–$10\frac{1}{2}$ in (19.1–26.7 cm). The Jew wears a fur-lined hat and coat, a waistcoat and breeches, and supports a tray of bottles; his companion is clad in lace cap and dress and carries a casket of baubles. Untermyer, pl. 98, fig. 276; Victoria and Albert Museum, Rice, 1983, pl. 82. For small versions, Private Collection.

E36 *Map-seller* and *Companion*. $6\frac{1}{4}$ in (15.9 cm). The male figure is adapted from B19 (Plate 22); the companion woman wears a brimmed hat, blouse and skirt and supports a casket of trinkets, at her left side hangs a map. Adapted from the *Jewish Pedlar*'s companion (E35). Both stand on scrolled bases before waist-tall bocages. Derby Museums and Art Gallery, Barrett and Thorpe, pl. 69; Christie's Twitchett, pl. 85; Christie's, Bradshaw, pls. 111 and 112.

88 E35. *Jewish Pedlars* (pair). $7\frac{1}{2}$ in (19.1 cm). *Private Collection*

89 E36. *Map-seller*, adapted from B19 (Plate 22). $6\frac{1}{4}$ in (15.9 cm). *Map-seller's Companion*. $6\frac{1}{8}$ in (15.6 cm). *Christie's*

FOREIGN PERSONAGES

E37 *Abyssinian Archer* and *Negress.* $12\frac{1}{2}$ in (31.8 cm). A black-skinned archer wearing a robe gathered by a sash stands holding a bunch of arrows in his right hand. The companion negress is clad in a feathered head-dress, a cape and skirt, and stands barefoot holding aloft an apple. Victoria and Albert Museum, Rice, 1983, pl. 94. A white-skinned version of *Archer*, B. and T. Thorn Antiques.

E38 *Four Seated Africans*, addorsed. 9 in (22.9 cm). Two bare-headed negroes and two negresses, respectively in jackets and trousers or dresses, sit each holding a shell container. Sotheby's, Twitchett, pl. 52; *Antique Dealer and Collector's Guide*, June 1971, p. 83, pl. 3.

E39 *Blackamoor* and *Negress* (pair). $7\frac{3}{4}$ in (19.7 cm). Shown in mirror positions upon one knee holding shell containers with both hands. Victoria and Albert Museum, Twitchett, pl. 46.

E40 *Blackamoor* and *Negress* (pair). $8\frac{1}{4}$ in (21 cm). A black-skinned man clad in a turban, cloak, jacket, trousers and boots, stands left hand on hip; his companion, wearing a tall head-dress, coat, tunic and skirt, stands in mirror pose. Derby Museum, Barrett and Thorpe, pls. 65 and 66. Identical models with white skins, presumably *Turks*, also exist. Royal Crown Derby Museum, Twitchett, pl. 42; Stoner, pl. 51.

E41 *Turks Dancing* (pair). $8\frac{3}{4}$ in (22.2 cm). A beturbaned Turk, clad in a long cloak, singlet and baggy trousers, dances with his right arm upraised. The companion Levantine lady, wearing a tall head-dress, mantle and dress, dances in mirror position. Honey, pls. 44a and 44b.

NOTABLES

E42 *Field Marshal Sir Henry Seymour Conway.* $12\frac{1}{2}$ in (31.8 cm). He stands in military uniform with his right hand grasping a baton and resting upon a cannon. A putto at his feet holds a shield bearing the device of a Saracen's Head. Private Collection, Charleston, pl. 149; Victoria and Albert Museum, Barrett and Thorpe, col. pl. D.

E43 *William Pitt, the Lord Chatham.* $14\frac{1}{2}$ in (36.8 cm). A Red Indian girl kneels before Lord Chatham who wears Court dress; his right arm rests upon a plinth inscribed 'Viscount Pitt of Barton Pynsent, Earl of Chatm. Lord Keeper of His Majesty's Privy Seal'. Victoria and Albert Museum, Twitchett, pl. 117.

90 E37. *Negress* (left) and *Abyssinian Archer* (right). Both $12\frac{1}{2}$in (31.8 cm). *Victoria and Albert Museum*

91 E42. *Field Marshal Sir Henry Seymour Conway* (left). E45. *John Wilkes, MP* (right). Both $12\frac{1}{2}$in (31.8 cm). *Victoria and Albert Museum*

E44 *Charles Pratt, the Lord Chancellor.* $12\frac{1}{2}$ in (31.8 cm). The noble Lord Camden wears the wig, ermine, gold chain and scarlet robes of office and stands leaning upon a tome placed upon a plinth sculpted in low relief with the figure of 'Justice'. Victoria and Albert Museum, Lane, pl. 72; Fitzwilliam Museum, Charleston, pl. 150; Blunt, no. 241, pl. 19, wrongly ascribed to Chelsea.

E45 *John Wilkes, MP.* $12\frac{1}{2}$ in (31.8 cm). He wears a cloak over contemporary dress and stands leaning upon a pedestal from which hangs a scroll inscribed 'Bill of Rights'. A putto at his feet supports a tome entitled 'Lock on Govt.', and holds the cap of Liberty. A plaque attached to the plinth reads 'Ino Wilkes Esq.' Victoria and Albert Museum, Barrett and Thorpe, col. pl. D; Charleston, pl. 149.

E46 *Milton.* $11\frac{1}{2}$ in (29.2 cm). Reissue of D12.

E47 *Shakespeare.* $11\frac{1}{2}$ in (29.2 cm). Reissue of D13.

RELIGIOUS AND MYTHOLOGICAL

E48 *Britannia.* $10\frac{1}{4}$ in (26 cm). She stands wearing a plumed helmet, blouse with sleeves rolled up, and dress with the hem looped to her waist beside a lion couchant. Her right hand is upraised and holds a spear while with her left she leans upon a shield emblazoned with the superimposed crosses of St George and St Patrick. Sotheby's, Bradshaw, pl. 118 for smaller version.

E49 *Clio and Cupid* (group). $8\frac{3}{4}$ in (22.2 cm). The reclining Muse has a lyre at her side and holds a quill pen; Cupid holding a scroll wags his forefinger at her (usually paired with E51). British Museum, Tait, pl. 45; Lane, pl. 68.

E50 *Diana with a Hunting-dog.* $10\frac{1}{4}$ in (26 cm). Reissue of D27. Royal Crown Derby Museum.

E51 *Erato and Cupid* (group). $8\frac{3}{4}$ in (22.2 cm). The reclining Muse plays a tambourine while an attendant Cupid brings her flowers (usually paired with E49). British Museum, Tait, fig. 30.

E52 *Europa and the Bull.* 11 in (27.9 cm). The scantily clad princess garlands a small white bull. British Museum, Twitchett, pl. 73; Victoria and Albert Museum, Lane, pl. 66.

E53 *Juno and a Peacock.* $10\frac{3}{4}$ in (27.3 cm). The goddess, crowned and wearing royal apparel, stands caressing the neck of a peacock. King, fig. 45.

E54 *Juno and a Peacock* riding in a chariot. $10\frac{3}{4}$ in (27.3 cm). Depicted with her hair streaming out behind her, accompanied by a peacock. Mounted on a base simulating billowing clouds. Sotheby's, Twitchett, pl. 70.

92 E50. *Diana with a Hunting-dog*, adapted from D27. $10\frac{1}{4}$ in (26 cm). *Sotheby's*
93 E52. *Europa and the Bull* (group). 11 in (27.9 cm). *Victoria and Albert Museum*

94 E54. *Juno and a Peacock* riding in a chariot (left) and E55. *Jupiter and an Eagle* likewise, mounted upon bases simulating billowing clouds. Both 10¾ in (27.3 cm). *Sotheby's*

E55 *Jupiter and an Eagle* riding in a chariot. 10¾ in (27.3 cm). The god is accompanied by an eagle. Companion to E54. Sotheby's, Twitchett, pl. 70.

E56 *Jupiter and an Eagle*. 8½–19 in (21.6–48.3 cm). The god stands crowned in royal robes holding thunderbolts in either hand, an eagle at his side. Derby Museums and Art Gallery, King, fig. 46; Royal Crown Derby Museum, Twitchett, col. pl. 7.

E57 *Justice*. 10 in (25.4 cm). A bareheaded lady wearing classical robes, standing with her eyes closed holding the sword and the scales of the Law. Private Collection; Victoria and Albert Museum, Hughes, pl. 9.

E58 *Leda and the Swan*. 11½ in (29.2 cm). Leda sits bareheaded and barefoot, supporting the breast of a cob with her left hand as it squats upon a reed-bed, and stroking its neck. Derby Museums and Art Gallery, Barrett and Thorpe, pl. 59.

E59 *Mars*. $7\frac{1}{2}$–14 in (19.1–35.6 cm). Adapted from B24, he may appear on a mound or scrolled base, free-standing or before a bocage. David Thorn Collection; Sotheby's; and for a bocaged version, Bradshaw, pl. 118. Candlestick version, see Plate 97.

E60 *Minerva*. 7–14 in (17.8–35.6 cm). Adapted from B25. Variations as per Mars. Sotheby's; Private Collection, Bradley, no. 10; B. and T. Thorn Antiques.

E61 *Neptune with a Dolphin*. $8\frac{1}{2}$–11 in (21.6–27.9 cm). Adapted from B26, and usually issued upon a tall shell-encrusted base. Sotheby's; Derby Museums and Art Gallery, Barrett and Thorpe, pl. 96 for a later version.

E62 *Pluto and Cerberus*. 7 in (17.8 cm). Adapted from B27. Derby Museums and Art Gallery, Barrett and Thorpe, pl. 47; Private Collection, Bradshaw, pl. 117.

E63 *Sentimental Lesson* (group). 9 in (22.9 cm). Three young ladies are lectured by a winged Cupid; one stands reading a love-letter, another holds a scent-bottle while the third sits regarding her reflection in a mirror. King, fig. 52.

95 E57. *Justice*, holding the sword and scales of the Law. 10 in (25.4 cm). *Private Collection*

96 E59. *Mars,* attired as a Roman centurion (right), and E60. *Minerva* (left). Both $13\frac{1}{4}$ in (33.7 cm). *Sotheby's*

97 E59. *Mars* candlestick (right) and companion E67. *Venus with Cupid* (left). Both 8 in (20.3 cm). *B. and T. Thorn Antiques*

98 E60. *Minerva,* holding a spear and shield. $10\frac{1}{2}$ in (26.7 cm). *B. and T. Thorn Antiques*

99 E61. *Neptune with a Dolphin,* on a tall shell-encrusted base. 10 in (25.4 cm).

100 E48. *Britannia with a Lion* (centre), $10\frac{1}{4}$ in (26.0 cm). E61. *Neptune with a Dolphin* (right). $8\frac{3}{4}$ in (22.2 cm). E66. *Venus and Cupid Seated upon a Dolphin* (left). $8\frac{3}{4}$ in (22.2 cm). *Sotheby's*

E64 *Time Clipping the Wings of Love* (group). $12\frac{1}{4}$ in (31.1 cm). Winged Time holds Cupid across his knee and clips his wings with shears. Rice, 1983, pl. 79. Later example, No. 124.

E65 *Venus Standing Beside a Dolphin.* $10\frac{1}{2}$ in (26.7 cm). The tail of the creature preserves the modesty of the goddess. Stoner, pl. 53.

E66 *Venus and Cupid Seated on a Dolphin* (group). $8\frac{3}{4}$ in (22.2 cm). The goddess holds Cupid before her in both hands as she sits upon a dolphin. Derby Museums and Art Gallery, Barrett and Thorpe, pl. 60; Sotheby's.

E67 *Venus and Cupid* (group). 8 in (22.2 cm). Venus, wearing a simple dress, holds an apple level with her right breast and with her left hand restrains Cupid; a dolphin is at her right side. British Museum, King, fig. 51; Private Collection, Bradley, no. 26.

A similar group omitting the dolphin is adapted from B30. 8 in (20.3 cm). Ludlow Collection, pl. 190, no. 100; Bradshaw, pl. 118, for a bocaged version.

E68 *Venus and Cupid Mounted before a Vase.* 12 in (30.5 cm). The seated goddess leans with her left hand upon a flower-encrusted Rococo vase and holds a bouquet in her right. Cupid faces her in a mirror pose. Private Collection, Rice, 1983, pl. 139.

E69 *Vulcan*. 15 in (38.1 cm). The god, represented by an effeminate-looking youth, supports a flaming urn upon a plinth and stands beside a swan. King, fig. 44.

E70 *War*. $8\frac{1}{2}$ in (21.6 cm). Represented by a bareheaded youth clad in falling ruffle, doublet, boots and a cloak, standing beside a flaming urn placed upon a plinth before a cannon. Cecil Higgins Museum, Barrett and Thorpe, pl. 61.

ALLEGORICAL

E71 *The Four Quarters of the Globe* (four figures). $7\frac{1}{4}$–$8\frac{1}{2}$ in (18.4–21.6 cm). Represented by four standing children:

Africa: a blackamoor wearing an elephant head-dress and cloak, holding a crab and a cornucopia, stepping over a lion.

101 E62. *Pluto and Cerberus*. 7 in (17.8 cm). *Sotheby's*

Asia: a Levantine girl, wearing a toque, dress and cloak, holding a perfume-burner and feeding a recumbent camel with leaves and berries.

America: a Red Indian girl wearing a feathered skirt and head-dress, holding a long-bow, standing beside an alligator.

Europe: a white girl, crowned and clad in regal robes, holding an orb and sceptre in either hand.

Christie's, Rice, 1983, pl. 86; Derby Museums and Art Gallery, Twitchett, pl. 104; Bradshaw, pl. 113; *Africa* and *Asia* only.

E72 *The Five Senses* (five seated groups). $9\frac{1}{2}$ in (24.1 cm). Nearly all surviving examples date to the Chelsea–Derby era and are incised 'No. 59'.

E73 *The Four Antique Seasons* (four figures). $9\frac{1}{2}$ in (24.1 cm). Represented by four standing divinities, each beside a Rococo vase:

Spring: Flora with flowers in her hair and scantily draped, beside a vase from which fruits and flowers emerge.

Summer: Ceres clad in a loose robe bedecked with ears of corn, beside a vase from which corn sprouts.

Autumn: Bacchus adorned with vine leaves beside an urn from which grapes grow.

Winter: Vulcan shown as an effeminate youth standing beside a flaming urn.

Derby Museums and Art Gallery, Barrett and Thorpe, pl. 56, *Spring* only; Temple Newsam House, Leeds, *Autumn* only; Private Collection, *Winter*. Example of *Summer* unknown to author.

E74 *The Four Classical Seasons* (four figures). $10\frac{1}{4}$ in (26.0 cm). These are later versions of D24, and differ only by their colouring and scrolled bases. Christie's, *Sale Catalogue*, 15 February 1988, lot 248.

E75 *The Four Infant Seasons* (four figures). $5\frac{1}{4}$ in (13.3 cm). Represented by scantily draped seated putti:

Spring: wearing a floral chaplet, holding a basket of flowers and proffering a posy.

Summer: similar but with corn replacing flowers.

Autumn: crowned with vine leaves and grapes, supporting a pannier of grapes and holding a bunch in his hand.

Winter: wrapped in a mantle warming both hands over a brazier precariously balanced upon one knee.

Sotheby's, Twitchett, pl. 122; Constance Chiswell Antiques, Cushion, pl. 11.

E76 *The Four Adolescent Seasons* (four figures). 6 in (15.2 cm). Represented by seated children in contemporary dress, on scrolled bases before small bocages:

Spring: a youth wearing a floral chaplet holding flowers.

102 E71. *Africa* (right) and *Asia* (left), from the *Four Quarters of the Globe*. $7\frac{1}{4}$ in (18.4 cm). *Author's Collection*

103 E76. *Spring* (right) and *Autumn* (left), portrayed by a seated boy with flowers and a girl with grapes, from *The Four Infant Seasons*. 6 in (15.2 cm). *Private Collection*

Autumn: a girl crowned with vine leaves holding grapes.

Winter: a youth wearing a hat with ear-muffs, with a muff on one hand and a brazier at his feet.

Example of *Summer* unknown to author. Holburne-Menstrie Museum, Gilhespy, 1951, pl. 81, *Spring* only; Private Collection, *Winter* only.

MISCELLANEOUS

E77 *Putti* (various). $4\frac{1}{2}$–$5\frac{3}{4}$ in (11.4–14.6 cm). Stiffly posed standing putti wearing floral chaplets and garlands; some hold baskets of flowers, others pot plants or posies, a few have puppies. Private Collections, Scott and Scott, pls. 623–5.

E78 *Sweetmeat Containers* (pair). $9\frac{3}{4}$ in (24.8 cm). Adapted from D35. A bare-headed gallant sits cross-legged holding a shell container in both hands, a dog lies at his feet. The companion lady sits likewise beside two lambs. Christie's, Rice, 1983, pl. 45.

E79 *The Welch Tailor and his Family* (two groups). $9\frac{1}{2}$ in (24.1 cm). These are more familiar as Chelsea–Derby models and are described in Part III. No. 62 (page 221).

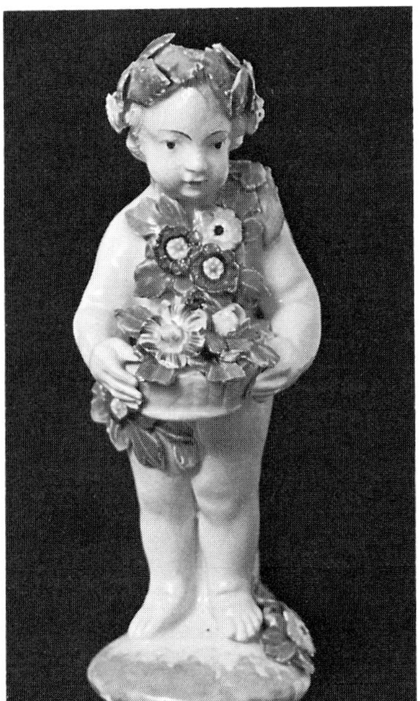

104 E77. *Putto* with flowers. $4\frac{3}{4}$ in (12.1 cm). *Private Collection*

105 E81. *Bull, Recumbent* before a small bocage. $3\frac{1}{2}$ in (8.9 cm). *Private Collection*

106 E84. *Horned Ewe and Ram, Recumbent* (pair). 4¾ in (12.1 cm) long. *Sotheby's*

ANIMAL SUBJECTS

E80 *Bulls, Charging* (pair). 2¾ in (7 cm). Reissue of B2. Royal Crown Derby Museum, Twitchett, pl. 12.

E81 *Bull, Recumbent* before a small bocage. 3½ in (8.9 cm). Gilhespy, 1961, fig. 151.

E82 *Bull and Cow suckling a Calf* (pair). 5½ in (14 cm). Sotheby's, *Sale Catalogue*, 25 March 1974, lot 193.

E83 *Ram and Ewe Suckling a Lamb* (pair). 5 in (12.7 cm). Winifred Williams, *Exhibition Catalogue*, fig. 58.

E84 *A Horned Ewe and Ram, Recumbent* (pair). 4¾ in (12.1 cm) long. Sotheby's, *Sale Catalogue* 5 May 1980, lot 101.

E85 *Fox, Seated.* 3 in (7.6 cm). David Thorn Collection.

107 E85. *Fox, Seated.* 3 in (7.6 cm). *David Thorn Collection*

108 E88. *Hound, Seated.* 2¾ in (7 cm). *David Thorn Collection*

109 E92. *Pug Dog, Seated.* $2\frac{3}{4}$ in (7 cm). *Private Collection*

E86 *Goats, Recumbent* (pair). $4\frac{3}{4}$ in (12.1 cm). Savage, 1958, pl. 68.

E87 *Goats, Standing* (pair). $3\frac{3}{4}$–$4\frac{1}{4}$ in (9.5–10.8 cm). Sotheby's, *Sale Catalogue*, 25 March 1974, lot 192.

E88 *Hound, Seated.* $2\frac{3}{4}$ in (7.0 cm). David Thorn Collection.

E89 *Leopards, Prowling* (pair). $3\frac{1}{2}$ in (8.9 cm). Victoria and Albert Museum, Rice, 1983, pl. 76.

E90 *Monkey Musicians, Standing* (pair). 7 in (17.8 cm). They wear tricorn hats, jackets and breeches: one has a violin, the other a French horn. Sotheby's *Sale Catalogue*, 22 October 1968, lots 81 and 82.

E91 *Pointer* (or Setter). $4\frac{1}{2}$ in (11.4 cm). Schreiber, pl. 41, no. 433 (old no.).

E92 *Pug Dogs, Seated* (pair). $2\frac{3}{4}$ in (7.0 cm). Sotheby's, Twitchett, pl. 69; Private Collection.

E93 *Pug Dogs* with studded collars, seated (pair). $3\frac{1}{2}$ in (8.9 cm). Christie's, Rice, 1983, pl. 77.

E94 *Pug Dogs,* seated on tasselled cushions (pair). $2\frac{3}{4}$ in (7 cm). Savage, 1958, pl. 89b.

E95 *Ram with Lambs* (group). $5\frac{1}{2}$ in (14 cm). Sotheby's, *Sale Catalogue*, 25 March 1974, lot 190.

E96 *Sheep, Recumbent* (pair). $2\frac{1}{2}$ in (6.3 cm). Ibid.

E97 *Sheep Candlesticks* (pair), 9 in (22.8 cm). Ram and group of ewe with a lamb, each mounted before a bocaged candlestick. Thornton's of Harrogate.

110 E98. *Red Squirrels* eating nuts (pair). $3\frac{1}{2}$ in (8.9 cm). *Author's Collection*

111 E99. *Stag and Doe at Lodge* (pair). $4\frac{1}{2}$ and $2\frac{3}{4}$ in (11.4 and 7 cm). *Winifred Williams*

113 E101. *Tigers, Prowling* (pair). $2\frac{1}{2}$ in (6.3 cm). *Private Collection*

112 E100. *Doe at Lodge* before a bocage. $8\frac{1}{2}$ in (21.6 cm). *Sotheby's*

114 E102. *Blue Tit*. 5 in (12.7 cm). *Sotheby's*

115 E104. *Buntings*, in bocaged candlesticks. 10½ in (26.7 cm). *Sotheby's*

E98 *Red Squirrels* with blue collars eating nuts (pair). 3½ in (8.9 cm). Twitchett, pl. 72; Author's Collection.

E99 *Stag and Doe at Lodge* (pair), 4½ in (11.4 cm). Winifred Williams, *Exhibition Catalogue*, fig. 58.

E100 *Stag and Doe at Lodge* before a bocage (pair). 8½ in (21.6 cm). Sotheby's, *Sale Catalogue*, 12 July 1983, lot 49; Twitchett, pl. 71.

E101 *Tigers, Prowling* (pair). 2½ in (6.3 cm). Probably adapted from *Leopards* (E89). Private Collection.

BIRDS

E102 *Blue Tits* (pair). 5 in (12.7 cm). Sotheby's, *Sale Catalogue*, 18 April 1973, lot 72; ibid., 14 April 1967, lot 30, small examples 2¾ in (7 cm).

E103 *Buntings* (pair). 3¾ in (9.5 cm). Untermyer, pl. 110, fig. 28.

E104 *Buntings* (two groups). 10½ in (26.7 cm). Two bocaged candlesticks, each with a pair of birds and a nest. Sotheby's, *Sale Catalogue*, 21 July 1964, lot 70.

116 E109. *Goldfinch*, perched on a tree-stump. 5 in (12.7 cm). *Sotheby's*

E105 *Bullfinches* (pair). 4¼ in (11.4 cm). Stoner, pl. 61; also 6 in (15.2 cm). Winifred Williams, *Exhibition Catalogue*, fig. 56.

E106 *Dove*. 3 in (7.6 cm). Victoria and Albert Museum, Barrett and Thorpe, pl. 54.

E107 *Finches, Nesting* (pair). 9¾ in (24.8 cm). Two birds nesting in each of two bocaged candlesticks. Royal Crown Derby Museum, Twitchett, pl. 63; Sotheby's, *Sale Catalogue*, 12 July 1983, lot 47.

E108 *Finches* on a Y-shaped tree-stump (group). 7 in (17.8 cm). Sotheby's, *Sale Catalogue*, 12 July 1983, lot 48.

E109 *Goldfinches* (pair). 5 in (12.7 cm). Sotheby's, Rice, 1983, pl. 69; also 4 in (10.2 cm) ECC, *Exhibition Catalogue*, 1948, pl. 67, nos. 312 and 313.

E110 *Great Tits* (pair). 4¾ in (12.1 cm). Stoner, pl. 60.

E111 *Owl*. 2½ in (6.3 cm). Sotheby's, *Sale Catalogue*, 22 March 1974, lot 186.

E112 *Parrots* (pair). 8⅞ in (22.6 cm). Victoria and Albert Museum, Rice, 1983, pl. 71. For versions 3½ in (8.9 cm), Sotheby's, *Sale Catalogue*, 18 April 1974, lot 29.

117 E119. *Unidentified Birds* watched by two dogs, in a bocaged candlestick. $8\frac{1}{4}$ in (20.9 cm). *Sotheby's*

E113 *Peacock and Peahen* (pair). $3\frac{1}{2}$ in (8.9 cm). Sotheby's, *Sale Catalogue*, 25 March 1974, lot 46. For versions $6\frac{1}{2}$ (16.5 cm). *Antique Dealer and Collector's Guide*, September 1969, p. 80.

E114 *Song Bird*. 5 in (12.7 cm). Untermyer, pl. 110. fig. 286.

E115 *Titmice* (pair). 4 in (10.2 cm). Ibid., fig. 285.

E116 *Tomtits* (pair). $4\frac{3}{4}$ in (12.1 cm). Victoria and Albert Museum, Barrett and Thorpe, pl. 54.

E117 *Warblers* (pair). $4\frac{1}{2}$ in (11.4 cm). Untermyer, pl. 105, fig. 287.

E118 *Woodpecker*. $6\frac{1}{2}$ in (16.5 cm). Untermyer, pl. 110, fig. 70.

E119 *Unidentified Birds*, possibly Buntings, nesting. $8\frac{1}{4}$ in (20.9 cm). The pair nest in a candlestick bocage, watched by two dogs. Victoria and Albert Museum, Gilhespy, 1951, fig. 145; Rice, 1983, pl. 75a.

E120 *Unidentified Yellow and Green Bird*. $5\frac{1}{2}$ in (14 cm). Rice, 1983, pl. 73b.

E121 *Unidentified Bird, Possibly a Finch*. 6 in (15.3 cm). Sotheby's, Rice, 1983, pl. 72.

Part II

4 · Derby Porcelain Models, 1770–96

PASTE AND GLAZE

When William Duesbury purchased the Chelsea factory in 1770, he became privy to Nicholas Sprimont's secret formulae for paste, glaze and enamel colours. Bone ash, which greatly enhances stability in the kiln, had been included in the Bow paste not later than 1749[1] and some years before 1759 had been adopted also at Chelsea.[2] The Derby Factory Accounts for the period March to July, 1770[3] contain an entry: 'Mr. William Johnson, for ten bags of Bone Ash from London . . .' Analysis of the Derby soft paste made between 1770 and 1796 reveals:[4]

Silica	41.94 per cent
Lead oxide	0.36 per cent
Alumina	15.97 per cent
Lime	24.28 per cent
Phosphoric acid	14.96 per cent
Soda	1.06 per cent
Potash	0.90 per cent
Magnesia	0.20 per cent

The level of phosphoric acid indicates the inclusion of about 40 per cent of calcined cattle bones in the mix which must have reduced the proportion of wasters emerging from the kiln. The high alumina content reflects increased plasticity that may have eliminated surface-tearing of the paste and fire-cracks, and allowed larger models to be constructed with sharper reproduction of moulded details. The new ceramic is close-grained, very white and semi-translucent.

Between 1745 and about 1754 the Chelsea glaze had been opacified by the

1 William Chaffers, *Marks and Monograms on European and Oriental Pottery and Porcelain*, London, 1965 (15th rev. edn), II, p. 271.

2 George Savage, personal communication, 1979.

3 F.A. Barrett and A.L. Thorpe, *Derby Porcelain*, London, 1971, p. 32.

4 Herbert Eccles and Bernard Rackham, *Analysed Specimens of English Porcelain*, London, 1922, p. 31.

inclusion of tin oxide but then became tight-fitting, transparent and faintly straw-coloured. Following the incorporation of bone ash in the paste, there followed an increase in the difference in coefficients of expansion between paste and glaze. This led to the appearance of multiple small fissures in the glaze known as crazing. The same fault became evident after 1770 at Derby, although by about 1775–80 a well-nigh perfect lead glaze had been evolved.[5]

BASES

During the late 1760s the ebullience of the high Rococo had been muted to provide a more disciplined Louis Seize style in which asymmetry was eschewed. After 1770 this influence continued to be reflected in a few of the figure-bases in fairly complex forms that combined both concave and convex surfaces, sometimes fenestrated, edged with light blue enamel and accented by gilding. Increasingly, however, simpler shapes were favoured such as shallow mounds edged with moulded scrolls, or irregular pads covered in a transparent light green, encrusted with leaves and flowers. These were relatively small in scale, the leaves being thin with smooth serpentiform contours, the flowers resembling flat cog-wheels, trumpet-shaped, or stellate. Often there might also be included a light blue lover's knot or bow, or alternatively trophies appropriate to the subject. The bases on which Greek and Roman divinities were mounted were frequently plain rectangles or squares, although some, such as *Apollo and the Nine Muses* (Nos. 25–34), were also provided with detachable stands composed of pierced scrollwork.

The influence of Neo-Classicism became increasingly manifest between 1785 and 1795, and bases assumed geometrical shapes. Some were oval or round, like shallow cylinders, often adorned with a circumferential gilt band; others were octagonal, embellished with the Greek key-fret pattern in low relief; a few were square with chamfered corners and decorated with vertical fluting. Many biscuit groups displaying figures arranged about either an obelisk or a leafing tree, were given rock-like bases. Some of the most imposing groups, like the *Russian Shepherds* (No. 393) have bases constructed in separate sections. These might include two semi-mounds, contained by a circular collar, which slotted into an elaborate stand decorated with fluted pilasters between which there are dependent swags.

The under-surfaces of most of the bases are flat, glazed and patch-marked. Prior to 1785 the ventilation holes are usually large enough to admit the tip of a finger but later become progressively smaller. Bocages were uncommon, being generally reserved for gardening and pastoral themes, rarely extending much above waist-

5 Barrett and Thorpe, op. cit., p. 120.

height. The attachment of swan-necked candle-sconces was abandoned, although some models were adapted as chamber candlesticks with loop handles and floral thumb-rests, or were mounted upon the bases of candlesticks.

ENAMEL COLOURS

Sprimont had endeavoured to emulate the Sèvres palette in a spectrum of colours that included 'claret' or 'crimson' (*rose Pompadour*), 'pea green' (*bleu céleste*), a bluish-green (*vert de mer*), deep yellow (*jaune jonquille*), chocolate-brown and a delectable range of purples and mauves. These were employed in association with an inky underglaze 'Mazarine blue' (*gros bleu*). In the *Sale Catalogue* of 17–20 April 1771,[6] William Duesbury offered his clients: 'Useful and Ornamental Articles: many of which are much admired. Mazarine Blue and Gold, Pea Green and Crimson ... also a few Select Pieces of Rich Ultramarine and Blue Celeste, which Mr. Duesbury has with Great Labour and Expense brought to a State of Perfection equal to that of the French.' However, just as Chelsea had failed to recreate the sumptuous enamel palette of Sèvres, now Derby too was to fall short of the magnificence that Chelsea had achieved.

Hitherto the Derby green had been unpredictable and this was now superseded by a translucent light colour used liberally upon irregular mound bases, leaves and garments. Its lack of any tonal variation engenders a certain monotony when sets of figures so decorated are viewed together. The uneven, streaky manganese was replaced by an opaque, glossy but rather pale pink that, beside the Chelsea claret, looks insipid. An opaque Cambridge blue was substituted for the turquoise that formerly had often had a muddy appearance, while a fresh vermilion was introduced to supplement the existing dry orange-red. A warm chocolate, some fine purples and exquisite mauves completed the new colour range. During the early 1770s, Constantine Smith introduced a dark blue enamel with a purplish cast which bears his name. This was intended as a substitute for the blue used to decorate service ware which had proved difficult to control and rarely appears on figures. This may be seen on the two chamber candlesticks: the *Cock and Jewel* (F25) and the *Vain Jackdaw* (F26), adapted from *Aesop's Fables*. Smith's Blue resembles the *bleu de roi* of Sèvres.

DECORATIVE STYLES

During the preceding decade at Chelsea, Bow and Derby, the garments of rustic folk had been painted to simulate silks, satins, velvets and brocades, while both

6 A. E. Nightingale, *Contributions towards the History of Early English Porcelain*, Salisbury, 1881, p. 15.

their buttons and shoe-buckles had been gilded. After 1770 this masquerade became *démodé* and a simpler and more natural decoration was chosen. Rather pale washes of colour were laid upon items of attire with a preference for pale yellow, light green, Cambridge blue, mauve and pink; stronger passages of dark blue and red are exceptional, while black was reserved to accent hats, belts and shoes. Floral sprays in the European style, and small in scale, were often laid upon a pale ground wash either in a darker shade or in a contrasting hue. Thus purple roses may decorate a pale mauve dress, while blue daisies may appear upon yellow breeches. Less frequently, floral sprays executed in the Oriental manner are painted in polychrome on a larger scale. Bouquets usually then contain daisy-like blossoms in blue and yellow grouped about a brownish-red flower-head which is either lobed in form or has flame-shaped petals arranged about a small circle. This may be further embellished with gilt.

The striking salmon-pink cheeks of Derby figures created in the years 1755–65, gave place to buff flesh tints that after 1770 became a uniform mawkish pink. The manner in which human hair, eyelids and eyelashes were represented continued largely unaltered, but the mouths of children and adolescents became stylized to resemble a Cupid's bow with upturned corners, often creating the semblance of a smirk.

MODELLING

Although up to 1770 very little is known about the modellers and other craftsmen working at Derby, after that year a great deal of information is available in letters and documents that have not yet been fully examined. Especially relevant are the letters written by Joseph Lygo and Benjamin Vulliamy to William Duesbury I and II, now distributed between the Victoria and Albert and British Museums, and the Derby Local Studies Library. These allow some tentative attributions of models to men like Nicolas-Joseph-François Gauron, Pierre Stephan, William Coffee and Jean-Jacques Spengler. Summaries of the lives of other craftsmen concerned with the production of figures at Derby between 1770 and 1796 are provided in Appendix A.

MODELS

The vast majority of models issued between 1770 and 1796 are included in the Factory List presented in Part III. Also included are items that bear no incised numbers but correspond with titles provided in the list. Thus, *Minerva Crowning Constancy and Hercules killing the Hydra* has been identified tentatively as No. 1, a *Pastoral Group* as No. 4, and three groups portraying the *Royal Family* as Nos. 22, 23 and 24.

Other figures and groups which appear to be unrelated to the Factory List are here described and detailed on pp. 135–42 (List F). These include a pair of busts, one of *Jean-Jacques Rousseau* (F7), inspired by J. H. Tarval's portrait based on a bronze medal struck about 1761, and *Alexander Pope* (F9), adapted from J. Smith's engraving after a portrait painted in 1716 by Sir Godfrey Kneller. The source of a *Crucifixion Group* (F13) is undetermined but shows St John standing beside the Blessed Virgin Mary and St Mary Magdalene with long undressed blonde hair, seated upon a grassy mound. This has erroneously been identified as *The Three Maries*, but a square socket behind the figures was probably made to accept the foot of a detachable cross or crucifix.

A biscuit group, emblematic of *Astronomy* (F12), incorporated into a barometer, may be the trial model given in 1790 to Spengler. Far less successful is the set of large standing models representing *The Four Elements* (F17); the figure emblematic of *Fire* was adapted from the earlier one portraying *War* (E70), and *Water* may have been based upon the Bow model *Venus with Doves*. More pleasing are four small busts of *The Four Seasons* (F18) which call to mind a delightful set of similar red anchor Chelsea busts of pagan gods. The group called a *Lesson in Love* (F19) shows three young ladies being instructed by a winged Cupid. It is a copy of a Sèvres biscuit group of about 1763, by Étienne-Maurice Falconet,[7] based on a lost drawing by François Boucher. It is an example of a composition that, although successful in larger sculpture, is far too detailed to permit a successful translation into porcelain.

Most of the models of animals issued between 1770 and 1796 were to reappear in bone china versions after 1815, and in order to avoid repetition they are listed only once on pp. 417–39 (List G) with the following few exceptions. There are two bocaged chamber candlesticks portraying the *Cock and Jewel* on a dungheap (F25), and the *Vain Jackdaw* (F26), which were adapted from illustrative engravings for *Fables I* and *XLVII*, in the 1687 edition of *Aesop's Fables*. A melancholy model of a *Pointer* (F28) was made in several variations and has earlier been mentioned together with two *Monkey Musicians* (F27).

LIST F. DERBY MODELS, 1770–1810, WITHOUT INCISED NUMBERS AND OMITTED FROM THE FACTORY LIST

NOTABLES

F1 *Field Marshal Sir Henry Seymour Conway*. $12\frac{1}{2}$ in (31.8 cm). Reissue of E42.

F2 *John Drinkwater*. 12 in (30.5 cm). British Museum.

7 George Levitine, *The Sculpture of Falconet*, New York, 1972, pls. 43 and 44.

118 F2. *General John Drinkwater.* Biscuit, 12 in (30.5 cm). *British Museum*

F3 *Admiral Sir Adam Duncan.* 11¼ in (28.6 cm). He stands in naval uniform, his hair *en queue*, holding a baton in his right hand, while resting his left upon his hip; two putti bearing trophies are at his feet. Upton House, *Catalogue of the Bearsted Collection,* no. 59. *Note:* some doubt has been expressed concerning the correct identity of this model.

F4 *Admiral Lord Hood.* 12 in (30.5 cm). He stands wearing a cocked hat and uniform, a sword in his right hand and a telescope in his left, with trophies scattered at his feet. 'Ceramic Americana of the Eighteenth Century', *Art in America,* V, 1916, pp. 55–6, fig. 10. A black basaltes version.

F5 *William Pitt, the Lord Chatham.* 13¼ in (33.7 cm). Reissue of E43.

119 F5. *William Pitt, the Lord Chatham,* in court dress, with Red Indian girl kneeling before him. $13\frac{1}{4}$ in (33.7 cm). *Victoria and Albert Museum*

F6 *Charles Pratt, Baron Camden.* $12\frac{1}{4}$ in (31.1 cm). Reissue of E44.

F7 *Jean-Jacques Rousseau* (a small bust). $6\frac{1}{4}$ in (15.9 cm). Victoria and Albert Museum, Twitchett, pl. 124.

F8 *Admiral Lord Rodney.* $11\frac{1}{4}$ in (28.6 cm). He stands wearing a cocked hat and uniform, turned to sinister, with a sword in his right hand resting upon the barrel of a cannon, and points with his left forefinger. 'Ceramic Americana of the Eighteenth Century', pp. 55–6, fig. 11, Derby biscuit model; fig. 12, black basaltes version.

F9 *Alexander Pope* (a small bust). $6\frac{1}{4}$ in (15.9 cm). Usually paired with F7. Victoria and Albert Museum, Schreiber, pl. 41, no. 360.

F10 *The Royal family* (three groups). $14\frac{1}{2}$ in (36.8 cm). These are detailed in Part III, Nos. 22, 23 and 24.

F11 *John Wilkes, MP.* $12\frac{1}{4}$ in (31.1 cm). Mounted upon a scrolled base, a reissue of E45; later version including the mace of the Lord Mayor of London (No. 126).

120 F13. *Crucifixion Group.* St John comforts the Blessed Virgin while St Mary Magdalene is shown with long hair seated upon the grass. A socket behind the figures was designed to hold a crucifix. $10\frac{1}{4}$ in (26 cm). *Victoria and Albert Museum*

121 F17. *The Four Elements*. 9–9¾ in (22.9–24.1 cm). Left to right: *Fire, Water, Air and Earth*. *Sotheby's*

MYTHOLOGICAL AND RELIGIOUS

F12 *Astronomy*, measurement unknown to author. Represented by a lady who stands bareheaded wearing a classical robe, attended by a putto holding a sextant. Biscuit mounted upon an ornamental clock. Barrett and Thorpe, pl. 102.

F13 *Crucifixion Group*. 10¼ in (26 cm). St John stands comforting the Blessed Virgin Mary while St Mary Magdalene with long hair sits upon a grassy mound. There is a square socket behind the three figures, presumably intended to accept a crucifix. Victoria and Albert Museum, Twitchett, pl. 96.

F14 *Minerva Crowning Constancy and Hercules killing the Hydra* (double composite group). 11 in (27.9 cm). This is described in Part III (No. 1). Birmingham Museum and Art Gallery, Gilhespy, 1951, figs. 156 and 157.

F15 *Neptune with a Dolphin*. 9¾ in (24.8 cm). Reissue of E61 on a pierced mound base encrusted with shells and seaweed; marked with a gold anchor, but bearing patch-marks. Upton House, *Catalogue of the Bearsted Collection*, no. 64.

F16 *Putti* (various). 4½–5¼ in (11.4–13.3 cm). Reissues of E72.

ALLEGORICAL

F17 *The Four Elements* (four figures). 9–9½ in (22.9–24.1 cm).
Air: a bareheaded lady holding a bird-cage.
Earth: a gardener leaning upon a spade with fruits and flowers.
Fire: a youth standing beside a flaming urn beside a cannon. Adapted from the figure representing *War* (E70).
Water: a bareheaded lady stands with a creel at her feet, and holds a fish. Adapted from a Bow model, *Venus with Doves*.
Sotheby's, New York.

F18 *The Four Seasons,* represented by four small busts. 3¼ in (8.3 cm):
Spring: female head and shoulders decked with flowers.
Summer: female head and shoulders decked with corn-ears and stems.
Autumn: head and shoulders of a youth decked with vine leaves and grapes.
Winter: head and shoulders of a bearded man with a cowl over his head, wrapped in a cloak.
Schreiber, pl. 41, nos. 359 and 360, for *Spring* and *Winter;* Grosvenor Antiques for *Summer* and *Autumn*.

F19 *Lesson in Love* (group). 9½ in (24.1 cm). Reissue of E63 in biscuit. Private Collection.

PASTORAL AND PEASANT

F20 *Gardening Group*. 8 in (20.3 cm). A bareheaded gardener and companion woman wearing a hat stand facing away from one another amid garden implements, fruits and flowers. Private Collection, Barrett and Thorpe, pl. 100.

F21 *Gardener*. Measurements unknown to author. He stands wearing a tricorn hat, shirt, waistcoat and breeches, holding a posy and leaning on his spade. Late Hurlbutt Collection, Mackenna, 1951, pl. 63, fig. 124.

MISCELLANEOUS

F22 *Sweetmeat Containers* (pair). 9¾ in (24.8 cm). A gallant seated cross-legged and bareheaded holds a shell in both hands, and has two dogs at his feet. Companion lady seated likewise with a ewe and lamb at her feet. Mounted on pierced scrolled bases. Christie's, Rice, 1983, pl. 45, male model only.

F23 *Sweetmeat Containers* (pair). 9½ in (24.1 cm). A peasant wearing a tricorn hat, jacket and breeches, stands holding open the lid of a rectangular hamper. The companion woman is clad in a headscarf, blouse, skirt and apron, and is portrayed in mirror position. Grosvenor Antiques.

122 F25. *Cock and Jewel Candlestick.* 12½ in (31.8 cm). *Weston Park Museum*

ANIMALS

F24 *Bolognese Dog.* 6¾ in (17.1 cm). Private Collection.

F25 *Cock and Jewel Candlestick.* 12½ in (31.8 cm). A cock and hen scratch upon a dungheap ignoring a jewel. Adapted as a bocaged chamber candlestick. Weston Park Museum, Sheffield.

F26 *Vain Jackdaw Candlestick.* 12½ in (31.8 cm). A jackdaw wearing borrowed plumage struts amongst peacocks. Pair to F25. Weston Park Museum, Sheffield.

F27 *Monkey Musicians* (two figures). 4 in–7 in (10.2–17.8 cm). Monkey wearing tricorn hat, jacket and breeches stands on a scrolled base playing a violin. David Goldblatt Collection, Gilhespy, 1961, fig. 148. Another with musical instrument missing. Private Collection.

F28 *Pointer.* 6½ in (16.5 cm). Victoria and Albert Museum, Schreiber, pl. 41, no. 433.

Several other animal models which are known in both soft- and hard-paste examples are listed only on pp. 432–7 (List G).

123 F26. *Vain Jackdaw Candlestick.* $12\frac{1}{2}$ in (31.8 cm). *Weston Park Museum*

ADDENDA

F29 *Calliope and three Naiads* (group). 10 in (25.0 cm). The muse Calliope carrying three books and three naiads playing musical instruments stand barefoot and bareheaded about a pedestal on which an urn rests, mounted on a base resembling a rocky mound. Incised with a star but no other marks, biscuit. *Journal of the Derby Porcelain International Society*, vol. I, colour pl. IV and pl. 17.

F30 *The Music Lesson* (group). $5\frac{1}{2}$ in (14 cm). A replica of the Sèvres biscuit group (see Plate 197) after Boucher, incised with crown, crossed batons and script D but no incised No. Recently brought by a member of the public to the Derby Museums and Art Gallery for appraisal.

SUPPLEMENTARY LIST

DRINKING CUPS

Bacchus Heads. $3\frac{1}{2}$ in (8.9 cm). Gilhespy, 1961, col. pl. x.
Fox Heads, issued in three sizes, priced at 4s 6d, 4s and 3s 6d. *Antique Collector,* March 1967, p. xxi.
Goat Heads. 7 in (17.8 cm). Gilhespy, 1961, pl. 155.
Hare Heads, priced at 7s. Derby examples unknown to author.
Neptune Heads. $3\frac{1}{2}$ in (8.9 cm). Gilhespy, 1951, pl. 100.
Satyr Heads. 4 in (10.1 cm). Private Collection.
Trout Heads with mottos, in three sizes priced at 6s, 5s and 3s 6d. *Antique Collector,* March 1967, p. xxi.

MISCELLANEOUS ITEMS

Duck sauce-boats with gold dentil, two sizes priced at 3s and 2s. Sotheby's, *Sale Catalogue,* 16 June 1981, lot 148.
Inkstands on Cats priced at 18s. Unknown to author.
Pigeon sauce-boats priced at 12s 6d. Unknown to author.
Tulip Eggcups priced at 4s. Unknown to author.

VASES

The following only are mentioned by J. Haslem:
Season Vase. 15 in (38.1 cm). This may possibly be one decorated with a scene including Celadon and Amelia, based on an engraving by F. Bartolozzi in *The Seasons*, Book II, by James Thomson, after Angelica Kauffmann. Victoria and Albert Museum, ref. no. 825–1882, Twitchett, pl. 152.
Fountain Vase. $16\frac{1}{4}$ in (41.3 cm). Described by William Bemrose as: 'A trunkated vase in lapis lazuli blue veined with gold scollop'd and leaved pediment zone and top; round the vase are four Cupids, two holding a festoon in gold, fixed to two gold faces of satyrs, and two riding on dolphins forming the anses. On the cover is a genius vanquished by Cupid. The body of the vase is supported by two naiades, or sea gods, the pedestal answering the vase has four sphynxes for its supporters, the emblem of Wisdom.' Delomosne, Twitchett, pl. 137.
Vases with Common Festoons. Possibly copies of Sèvres original. 9 in (22.9 cm). Gilhespy, 1961, fig. 75.
Vases with Best Festoons. An example may be a biscuit vase in the Victoria and Albert Museum, ref. no. C294–A–1935, Twitchett, pl. 146.

5 · The Derby Factory Lists

John Haslem (1808–84) was born at Carrington in Cheshire and as a boy came to live in Derby with his uncle James Thomason. In 1822 he was apprenticed enameller to the Derby porcelain factory, then under the proprietorship of Robert Bloor. There he gained access to a collection of plaster casts and terracottas that had once been the property of Joseph Wright (1734–97), the 'Candle-light Painter of Derby'. These had been purchased after the artist's death by Michael Kean for the instruction of craftsmen. Haslem became interested in drawing the human form and abandoned his original aim of becoming a painter of flowers on porcelain. In 1835 he moved to London and for a while worked in the studio of the artist E. T. Parris. Not long afterwards he came to appreciate that higher remuneration might be gained by enamelling upon metal after the manner of the French and, accordingly, he left to acquire the specialized skills requisite for a career in this field. He achieved considerable proficiency and in 1844 was honoured by royal patronage, executing many commissions for both Queen Victoria and Prince Albert. Indeed, he became something of a fashionable artist so that it was an unpleasant surprise when the work he submitted to the Great Exhibition of 1851 failed to win high commendation. Probably as a result of this, public demand for his services declined and in 1857 he returned to Derby. There he occupied himself producing a folio volume of his earlier royal commissions and became interested in photography. He also wrote a series of articles in the *Derby Reporter* in which he recorded his recollections of the Derby porcelain manufactory. In 1876, these memoirs were expanded into a book entitled *The Old Derby China Factory*.[1] Haslem was a founder member of the Corporation Art Gallery, later to be renamed the Derby Museums and Art Gallery and, shortly before his death in 1884, he donated to the museum items from his personal collection of Derby porcelain including the famous *Thistle Dish*, painted by Quaker Pegg, which has remained on public display to the present day.

The Old Derby China Factory supplies a great deal of information concerning the

1 John Haslem, *The Old Derby China Factory*, London, 1876.

factory management and staff, the patterns painted upon useful wares, the different models produced and other sundry matters. 'The writer', he intimates, 'is fortunate in being able to afford collector's means of identifying figures made at Derby by a careful list drawn up at the works early in the present nineteenth century.' He continues: 'This list distinguishes many of those which had their origins at Chelsea and Bow, and in numerous instances the modellers' names are identified with their productions. This latter information has been extended from personal knowledge and from facts gleaned from some of the old hands.'[2] Here it should be recalled that Haslem commenced his apprenticeship at Derby nearly a quarter of a century after the numbered list had ceased to be used, while much of the information presented was not gathered until 1857 and relied upon the fallible memories of retired craftsmen and elderly people. It is scarcely surprising, therefore, that Haslem's accounts of modellers who ceased to be active before 1800 should often be inaccurate or totally erroneous, although his comments about the staff and work people engaged after that time are likely to be completely reliable.

Haslem's Factory List[3] numbers 390 items but leaves 120 of them blank. About seventy of the 272 descriptive titles provided have not so far been matched with a model bearing the appropriate incised numeral, while in six others the identification is wrong. Two different models are known, both incised 'No. 390', and the numbers of *The Prudent Mother* (No. 137) and the *Madonna and Child* (No. 138) are erroneously transposed. However, the main defect of the list is that many of the titles provided, such as *Dancing Group, Group of Four Boys,* and *Pastoral Group,* are insufficiently precise to afford the means of identification and are repeated several times in connection with entirely dissimilar figures. Further, other titles, such as *Spanish Group, Johnny Wapstraw and Companion,* and *Christie*, provide scarcely a clue as to their identity. Here, some twenty-seven blanks have been filled and the nature of many other models, previously obscure, has been established.

William Bemrose[4] provided another version of the Factory List which 'was made out, and a valuation put thereon, in 1810 by four workmen named Soar, Longdon, Farnsworth and Hardenburg, for the purpose of a Chancery suit, *Duesbury versus Kean*'. This includes 397 items of which 186 are either left blank or relate to vases, tripods and urns, omitted by Haslem. Some forty of the titles have not so far been matched with models incised with the appropriate number, and a further thirty are erroneous. There are eighteen items that are designated differently in the two lists where the existence of an incised specimen affords verification, and of these the

2 Ibid., p. 149.

3 Ibid., pp. 170–8.

4 William Bemrose, *Bow, Chelsea and Derby Porcelain,* London, 1898.

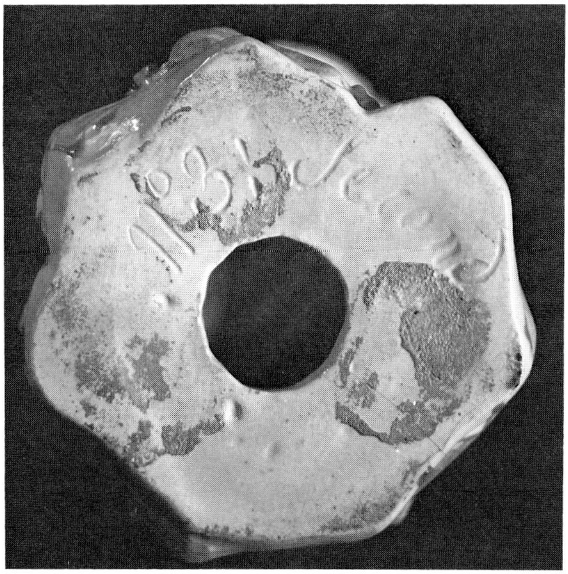

124 Under-surface of the *Water Girl,* from the set of *Four Elements,* c. 1772. Three patch-marks and a large ventilation hole are evident; also incised marks 'No. 3' and 'Second', corresponding to the Factory List number and the size.

Haslem title is correct in fifteen and the Bemrose in only three. Despite areas of divergence there is a broad spectrum of agreement, although it is clear that neither compiler had access either to an original factory inventory or to a comprehensive range of stock.

The precise date when the Factory List became implemented is unknown, although it is unlikely to have been as early as 1770: several surviving models and groups which for technical and stylistic reasons must have been made afer the acquisition of the Chelsea factory are omitted. Clearly a numbered catalogue would be an important business asset for a provincial factory with London showrooms and the idea probably came to William Wood some time before the opening of the Covent Garden premises in 1773. It is usually possible to match descriptions of lots in contemporary sale catalogues with titles in the Factory List and, when this is done, no less than seven (possibly eight) of the first fifteen items appear in the *Catalogue of the Last Year's Produce of the Chelsea and Derby Factories,*[5] of 17–21 April 1771:

5 J. E. Nightingale, *Contributions towards the History of Early English Porcelain,* Salisbury, 1881.

Antique Seasons, on pedestals, large & small.	No. 5.
French Seasons, large & small.	No. 6. (?)
Gardener & Companion [also 'New Gardener'].	No. 7.
Pair of Sitting Figures with fruit & flowers.	No. 8.
Gentleman with flute & Lady singing.	No. 10.
Bacchus & Cupid riding a goat & a panther.	No. 13.
Two Curious Figures with an altar-piece.	No. 14.
Prudence & Discretion, with urns.	No. 15.

This suggests that the Factory List might have come into use as early as the spring of 1771, although a date in 1772 is more probable. Also included in the same catalogue are five models which appear to have unexpectedly high serial numbers, viz:

Dresden Shepherds, large & small.	No. 55.
Welch taylor & family.	No. 62.
Cupid & Flora [possibly Venus & Cupid].	No. 66 (?)
Time clipping the wings of Love.	No. 124.
Gentleman reading & Lady knotting.	No. 184.

The first four of these were first issued prior to 1770 and so may represent old stock still available for purchase in 1771. The last-mentioned item was, however, created after 1770 and we must look for some other explanation. There are several instances of models and groups being reissued after an interval of years when they were allocated different serial numbers. It seems likely that the first numbers provided for the *Gentleman Reading* and the *Lady Knotting*, when they were issued in April 1771, were much lower and are now among those left blank in the Factory List, while No. 184 relates to a later version of the pair. Another minor difficulty is created by the three groups representing the Royal Family,[6] after Zoffany, which according to William Wood[7] were not available until 1773, and bear no incised numbers. The Bemrose version of the Factory List includes, however, 'No. 23. Fragments of the Royal Family' and this number is approximately compatible with the date of issue. The only complete set to survive is in the royal collection and is unmarked. This may have been a special order from Queen Charlotte herself or have constituted a presentation to King George III when in 1773 he visited Duesbury's London showrooms.[8]

6 Bellamy Gardner, 'English China Collections of the Past', *Trans. ECC*, 4, 1937, pp. 23–7, pl. IXd.
7 Haslem, op. cit., p. 22.
8 Ibid., p. 23.

Attention has already been drawn to the high serial numbers allocated to models first issued during the 1760s and to the lower ones appended to others created after 1770. For example, *Milton* and *Shakespeare* are, respectively, Nos. 297 and 305, despite the fact that they were first issued about 1758, while the *Pastoral Group by a Fountain* (No. 12) and *The Antique Seasons* (No. 5) were not made until 1771. This has prompted some to suggest the items were not arranged in chronological order, although in what other way the Factory List could have been compiled has never been suggested. Any efficient business management would seek to sell off old stock before new products bearing the latest catalogue number. This is evident from a letter dated 19 August 1786, written by Joseph Lygo and addressed to William Duesbury: 'Regarding the Great Stock of enamelled figures in the Warehouse, these must be sold first owing to the body being altered and the new figures of different size.' It would appear that when old stocks of a particular model were exhausted the new version that replaced it was allocated the next vacant number. When models first issued before 1770 are disregarded, those that remain are in chronological sequence.

Pairs of models, like *Prudence and Discretion* (No. 15) and sets, such as *The Four Quarters of the Globe* (No. 200) usually share the same number, although there are a few exceptions, including the *Boy and Girl Riding a Dolphin and a Swan* (Nos. 142 and 143). Some others that relate to one another although they are not pairs, such as *Milton* (No. 297) and *Shakespeare* (No. 305) rather surprisingly bear numbers that are not in sequence. Only a handful of models very rarely bear incised numerals, of which *Monks and Nuns* (Nos. 102–13) and *Cupids in Disguise* (Nos. 262–78) afford examples. The more popular figures were issued in between two and six different sizes indicated with incised marks, in diminishing order of height, '1st Size', '2nd Size', '3rd Size', etc., or simply by 'First', 'Second', 'Third', etc. Similar models of different sizes generally share the same serial number, although there are a few exceptions, which include the pair of *Haymakers*; No. 198 is $6\frac{1}{2}$ in (16.5 cm) and No. 296 $9\frac{3}{4}$ in (24.8 cm) tall. Likewise two otherwise identical versions of *Neptune and a Dolphin* (Nos. 299 and 300) are mounted respectively upon a tall base encrusted with marine life and a low mound.

The device of a script letter 'D' intersected by an anchor, pencilled in gilt in several variations, may be found on a few models issued about 1770–4, and these may have been decorated at Chelsea. A script letter 'N', either incised or in blue enamel, Arabic numerals lacking the prefix 'No.', as well as capital letters drawn in red may also be found, and relate to painters, gilders and repairers. The device of a jewelled crown over crossed batons surmounting the script letter 'D' was introduced in red or blue enamel about 1784.

Haslem considered that No. 300 had been reached by 1780 and, if this is correct, some 300 different items were issued in the nine years 1771–80, while in the subsequent fifteen years 1781–96, only another ninety-seven were added. The matter could readily be determined by reference to contemporary sale catalogues although many are incomplete or lost. However, it is usually possible to match lots with titles in the Factory List and to append the appropriate number. When the lowest and the highest numbers so obtained are charted, the following pattern emerges:

Date(s) of Sale Catalogue(s)	*Lowest and Highest Numbers*
April 1771	Nos. 5–66
February and March 1773	Nos. 12–51
February 1778	Nos. 52–199
May 1779 and April 1780	Nos. 88–231
May 1782	Nos. 55–235

Although the data is incomplete the results suggest that a figure nearer to No. 250 than No. 300 had been reached in the year 1780.

Joseph Lygo wrote in 1794 to William Duesbury:[9] 'Mr. Latiefiere brought me a print of Lord Howe [on] July 2, 1794 ... A drawing of the Duke of York is going to be engraved.' Both these portrait models must have been available in 1794 or 1795 and are incised respectively 'No. 384' and 'No. 391'. Also, it is known that J. J. Spengler, who modelled the *Lady Feeding a Sheep with Hay* (No. 395) left the Derby factory for the last time in the autumn of 1795. Since the Haslem and Bemrose versions of the Factory List finish with items No. 390 and No. 397, it is virtually certain that the list ceased to be operational about 1795/6.

The prices cited by Haslem do not accord with those quoted in contemporary sale catalogues, which presumably must be correct. Since we do not know either the source or the date of Haslem's information it can have very little significance today, except perhaps to indicate that biscuit figures cost between one fifth and one quarter more than their enamelled counterparts. Nor can we accept Haslem's attributions of Derby models cast from Chelsea moulds. For example, neither the *Huntsman* and companion *Lady* (No. 50) nor *The Four Chelsea Seasons* (No. 125) can be matched with a red or gold anchor marked Chelsea original. The *Venus, Chelsea Model* (No. 67) appears to have no Chelsea prototype, although it does recall the Bow figure of *Venus with Doves*.[10] Conversely, Haslem does not relate any of the

9 F. Gilhespy and J. Brayshaw, (B), *Derby Porcelain*, London, 1961, p. 70.

10 Arthur Lane, *English Porcelain Figures of the Eighteenth Century*, London, 1961, col. pl. B.

numerous *Cupids in Disguise* (Nos. 262–78) to the London manufactory although most were cast from gold anchor moulds. Some of these still remain in Copeland's manufactory to which reference will be made later. Here one should note that there exist other Derby Cupids which are derived from a completely different source that has not yet been identified. These were issued in pairs and were also incorporated into two groups, each of *Four Cupids Hunting* (Nos. 251 and 257).

6 · Sources of Derby Models, 1770–96

THE INFLUENCE OF MEISSEN

The influence of Meissen on English porcelain figures was negligible until 1751 when Nicholas Sprimont, proprietor of the Chelsea manufactory, wrote to Sir Everard Fawkener asking him to purchase through the good offices of the British Ambassador some Meissen models that he might copy. The diplomat in question was Sir Charles Hanbury Williams, who had already formed a collection of Meissen porcelain which included 166 figures. During his sojourn abroad, this was stored in Holland House.[1] He loaned it to Sprimont and, between the autumn of 1751 and spring of 1752, Chelsea copies began to appear, many bearing the raised-anchor mark. Other English factories, including Derby, were not slow to follow this lead, although the sources of their Meissen prototypes have not yet been determined.

Although the processes by which true, or hard-paste, porcelain is made were known to the Chinese by the eleventh century, it was not until 1709 that the arcanum was rediscovered in Europe by Graf Ehrenfried Walther von Tschirnhaus (1651–1708) and Johann Friedrich Böttger (1682–1719) at Albrechtsburg Castle in Saxony. The Elector of Saxony and King of Poland, Augustus the Strong, established the Royal Meissen Porcelain Manufactory in the suburbs of Dresden in 1710.[2] Most of the early models followed Oriental originals or were adapted from designs provided by Jakob Irminger, the Court goldsmith, although a few puppet-like figures were created by wood and ivory carvers. Augustus was determined to furnish his 'Japanese palace' with both Oriental and Meissen porcelain and ordered almost life-sized models of animals and birds.[3] The sculptor Johann Göttlieb Kirchner (1706–63) was appointed in 1727 to expedite this work, but enormous technical problems arose and progress was agonizingly slow. In 1731 Johann

1 The Earl of Ilchester, 'A Notable Service of Meissen Porcelain', *Burlington Magazine*, LV, 1929, p. 188.

2 K. Berling, *Festive Publication to Commemorate the 200th Jubilee of the Oldest European China Factory, Meissen*, Meissen, 1910, pp. 4–6.

3 Hugo Morley-Fletcher, 'Meissen Beasts for Augustus the Strong', *Connoisseur*, 189, no. 760, 1975, pp. 95–9.

Joachim Kändler (1706–75) was engaged as Kirchner's assistant[4] but, within two years, the king died, Kirchner left Meissen and Kändler became *Modellmeister*. For a while he was fully occupied with the plastic designs of the great Baroque dinner-services, culminating with the *Swan Service* comprising some 2,200 items,[5] and with completion of the large zoological models. Then, in 1735, he refocussed his genius on the small scale *Porzellanfiguren*, or *Puppen*.

Kändler perceived that the new material required novel treatment in the handling of mass and form and that it was not enough simply to create conventional sculpture in miniature. Accordingly he eliminated much of the detail that hitherto had been portrayed in the round and suggested many features by applications of enamel colour. The medium was stretched to its limits to create knife-sharp edges, the angular projection of limbs, and unsupported trailing drapery. He chose a scale of between 5–8 in (12.7–20.8 cm), which seems to be exactly appropriate for the material, and mounted his models upon simple mound bases sparsely encrusted with leaves and flowers to avoid distraction from the subject. Kändler preferred the dramatic poses beloved by Mannerist sculptors and was at his best modelling the characters from the Italian Comedy in their colourful costumes and histrionic poses, or sturdy street criers, artisans and peasants. He was able, in a few cubic inches of paste, to depict fear, anger, violent movement or satire, but rarely chose to reflect elegance, tenderness or beauty, while his small animals and birds seem to recapture the essential spirit, or *Gestalt*, of the creature, in a manner that must have involved hours of personal observation. In short, his work was fully in accord with all the turbulent force of the Baroque style and was intended to be viewed from any angle as a complete entity in itself. Close collaboration between Kändler and the *Obermaler*, Johann Gregor Höroldt, ensured the optimum artistic effect by employing a palette of strong colours with a preponderance of bright red, deep yellow, dark blue and black. Small passages of these enamels were laid between large areas left white, to exploit fully the reflections between interfaces covered with a brilliant mirror-like feldspathic glaze. Floral sprays painted either upon ground washes or uncoloured areas were executed without perspective drawing or shading after the manner favoured in the Orient which came to be known as *indianische Blumen*.[6]

Kändler was assisted by Johann Friedrich Eberlein after 1735 and by Peter Reinicke after 1743, in which year he came to Meissen. Reinicke's style closely resembles that of Kändler and probably much of his work has been wrongly

4 Berling, op. cit., pp. 22 *et seq.*
5 Hugo Morley-Fletcher, *Meissen*, London, 1971, p. 65.
6 Berling, op. cit., pp. 14–18.

accredited to his master. Eberlein[7] gave his models almond-shaped eyes, thin, downward-drooping noses, and overall a slender elegance that is immediately identifiable. He is rightly famed for his allegorical subjects as well as for Turks, Levantines and divinities from Greek and Roman mythology. A fourth modeller, Johann Gottlieb Ehder, also worked at the factory between 1739 and 1750.

During the late 1740s modelling at Meissen was increasingly influenced by the French Rococo style. This arose essentially as a reaction to the ponderous grandeur of the Baroque, seeking to replace monumental solidity with lightness and movement, and majesty by elegance and wit. Hulst, the artistic director of Sèvres, formulated the requirements for his staff: 'Gentilesse, nouveauté, variété doivent être sa devise. Qui dit gentilesse dit choses légères. On ne lui demande que éternuements de sa génie, sembles à ceaux d'une jolie femme, c'est à dire riante et agréable.' Meissen models became more slender, less dramatically posed, and were mounted upon bases decorated with asymmetrical patterns composed of C- and S-shaped scrolls. Colouring became almost pastel with a predominance of light yellow, pale green, mauves and pinks; very little was left white and gilding which hitherto had been restrained was now liberally applied. Floral sprays painted upon white or coloured grounds were executed in the naturalistic European taste known as *deutsche Blumen*.

The harsh satire that had earlier been favoured now yielded to a gentler idiom in which shepherds and shepherdesses depicted in romantic dalliance, *après* Boucher, children in the guise of artisans, or sophisticated adaptations of ancient Greek and Roman divinities appeared. *Singeries* and Cupids in Disguise made their debut. In 1748 Frederick Elias Meyer (1723–85) was engaged as modeller to replace the ailing Eberlein, who died the following year. He chose to create unnaturally elongated figures with small heads and overhanging brows[8] reminiscent of the human subjects painted by El Greco, and enhanced the effect by use of tall bases. Inevitably his style led to disagreements with Kändler.

The halcyon days of Meissen came to an abrupt end during the Seven Years War, when the Prussian soldiery of Frederick the Great occupied the factory in the autumn of 1756. The flow of new models to England ceased, but old stock, given in lieu of payment for military supplies provided by Carl Heinrich Schimmelmann,[9] was first moved to Hamburg in 1758, and there sold at carefully stage-managed auctions, when much of it reached this country. In 1763 peace was signed and the Prussian yoke lifted, but Meissen was never again able to re-establish the hegemony

7 Ibid., pp. 40–44.

8 Ibid., p. 45.

9 Erica Pauls-Eisenbeiss, *German Porcelain of the Eighteenth Century*, London, 1972, I, *Meissen*, pp. 27–8.

she had once enjoyed. The Rococo style was by then *démodé* and Neo-Classicism all the rage. Kändler and those associates who had remained with him at Meissen were either unable or unwilling to adapt their work to the new style. Michel-Victor Acier was appointed *Modellmeister* to be co-equal with Kändler, under the management of Count Camillo Marcolini. Acier created sentimental idealizations of domestic and pastoral subjects and numerous models of children, many of them based on drawing made by Johann Elias Zeissig. Henceforth, the influence of Meissen on the English modelling scene was negligible. Derby copies of Meissen figures, many first issued in the 1760s and 1770s, include the following:

No.	*Derby Model or Group*	*Modeller of Meissen Original*
6	*The Four Infant Seasons*	F. E. Meyer
8	*Seated Boy and Girl with Fruit and Flowers*	M. V. Acier
13	*Cupid and Bacchus Riding*	J. J. Kändler
16	*Dancing Couple*	J. J. Kändler
17	*Dancing Couple*	J. J. Kändler
39–45	*The Arts and Sciences* (7 groups)	M. V. Acier
51	*Gentleman and Lady with Dog and Cat*	J. J. Kändler
55	*The Dresden Shepherds*	J. J. Kändler and P. Reinicke
61	*The Four Seasons*	F. E. Meyer
62	*The Welch Tailor and his Family*	J. J. Kändler and J. F. Eberlein
66	*Venus and Cupid* (group)	J. F. Eberlein
90	*Cook*	P. Reinicke
105	*Seated Monk and Nun Reading*	J. J. Kändler and P. Reinicke
114	*Mars*	J. J. Kändler
117	*Jupiter and an Eagle*	J. J. Kändler and P. Reinicke
182	*Cupids Riding Bucks*	J. J. Kändler
198	*Pair of Haymakers*	J. F. Eberlein
199	*Harlequin and Columbine*	J. J. Kändler and P. Reinicke
200	*The Four Quarters of the Globe*	F. E. Meyer
262–78	*Cupids in Disguise*	J. J. Kändler
295	*The Four Quarters of the Globe*	Adapted from No. 200
296	*Pair of Haymakers*	Larger versions of No. 198
301	*Shepherd Bagpiper and Lady with a Guitar*	J. J. Kändler and P. Reinicke
307	*Bagpiper and Lady with a Lute*	Adapted from No. 301

311	*The Idyllic Musicians*	J. F. Eberlein
332	*The Four Quarters of the Globe*	Adapted from No. 200
362	*Boy with a Macaroni Dog and Girl with a Cat*	J. J. Kändler

THE INFLUENCE OF FRENCH FACTORIES ON SOFT-PASTE BISCUIT MODELS

Jean-Jacques Bachelier (1724–1805), who had been appointed Director of Studios at the Vincennes porcelain factory in 1747, claimed that biscuit models, that is, without glaze, had been made as early as 1751, although it is improbable that commercial production was effected much before 1753.[10] In 1754 Madame de Pompadour ordered biscuit versions of *Les Enfants de Boucher* to replace a set of glazed models earlier created by Blondeau.[11] After this unequivocal lead from the acknowledged arbiter of elegance and good taste, biscuit became *de rigueur* and only a few glazed and enamelled figures continued to be issued. The success of the enterprise depended largely upon the beauty of the *pâte tendre* and, although this has been credited to François Gravant, it would appear to have been invented as early as 1734 by Claude-Humbert Gérin, who had been employed for a time at the Chantilly manufactory.[12] When Gérin died in 1750, Gravant became Master of the Slip-house, a post that he retained until his death in 1768.

By 1751 an almost perfect *pâte tendre* was evolved that is warm in tone, presents a flawless surface and feels velvety to the touch. It resembles the finest Italian marble and allowed reproduction of crisp moulded detail unobscured by glaze. Flowers of tinted biscuit were an early speciality. In 1749 the Dauphine, Marie-Josèphe, sent 480 biscuit blossoms attached to metal stems contained in two white glazed ormolu-mounted vases, as a birthday present to her father, Augustus III, King of Poland and Elector of Saxony.[13] Some years later Madame de Pompadour delighted her royal lover by a display of flowers during January in her conservatory at Bellevue – all fashioned in tinted Vincennes biscuit and appropriately scented!

Vincennes models are totally dissimilar from those created at Meissen, for they are larger in scale, devoid of glaze and are left uncoloured. The French sculptor-

10 W. B. Honey, *French Porcelain of the Eighteenth Century*, London, 1950, p. 25.

11 George Savage, *Seventeenth and Eighteenth Century French Porcelain*, London, 1960, pl. 73a, biscuit model of *Le Jeune Suppliant*; pl. 73b, white glazed model of *Le Jeune Suppliant*, both by Blondeau.

12 Antoine de Albis, *The Early Years of the Porcelain Manufactory of Vincennes*, Catalogue of the International Ceramics Fair and Seminar, London, 1986, pp. 10–23.

13 Hugh Tait, *Porcelain*, London and New York, 1962, fig. 15, ormolu-mounted white glazed vase containing biscuit flowers.

modellers strove to reflect elegance and beauty and eschewed the harsh satire that had so often characterized the Meissen *Porzellanfiguren*. Instead of modelling stocky peasants or the colourful *dramatis personae* of the Italian Comedy, they elected to portray in sentimental mood little children at their mothers' skirts or accompanied by domestic animals or attired as artisans. Examples include the eight models by Blondeau already mentioned, and some forty groups of naked putti disporting themselves with flowers or playing musical instruments made by Félix de la Rue after terracottas by François Duquesnoy.[14] In 1756 the factory was transferred to Sèvres and, in the same year, Étienne-Maurice Falconet was appointed head of the figure department. He was a sculptor of distinction who often made miniature biscuit copies of his work in marble. His models based on Greek mythology include *Pygmalion and Galatea, Cupid and Psyche, Hercules and Omphale* and *Leda and the Swan*. He also reproduced groups illustrating scenes from contemporary French drama of which *Le Baiser Donné* and *Le Baiser Rendu* are perhaps the best-known. Many of his figures and groups were based upon paintings by Boucher illustrating the idyllic pastoral such as *La Bergère des Alpes* and *Pensent-Ils au Raisins*? The rather sentimental mood of the age finds expression in two groups of children entitled *La Tournique* and *La Lanterne Magique*, while the rising bourgeois influence is reflected by four groups en suite known as *En Grande Toilette*.

Biscuit models were created in England contemporaneously with, if not before, those issued at Vincennes. Although the Bow biscuit version of Kitty Clive as *Mrs Riot*[15] lacks an arm and may be no more than a waster, the companion biscuit figure of Henry Woodward as the *Fine Gentleman*[16] also survives with little damage. There are other early biscuit models including a Bow *Sportsman and Lady*,[17] a Longton Hall *Pheasant*,[18] and two Derby *Street Vendors*,[19] all of which date to about 1750–4. Further, an entry in the Bow *Memorandum Book*, kept by John Bowcock,[20] reads: '15th May, 1756. Mrs. Whitfield to have 1 p. white biscuit candlesticks.' The paucity of examples of early English biscuit most likely reflects the public taste that preferred enamelled and gilded models after the manner of Meissen rather than to the supposedly unattractive appearance of the soft pastes.

14 Honey, op. cit., pl. 65a. group of white glazed *Putti* by Félix de la Rue.

15 British Museum.

16 Sigmund and Jessica Katz Collection, Museum of Fine Arts, Boston.

17 Private Collection, *Trans ECC*, 7, 1969, pls. 129b and 129c, biscuit models of Bow *Sportsman and Companion*.

18 Frank Tilley, 'The Rare and the Curious', *Antique Collector*, June 1964, pp. 107–12, fig. 7, biscuit Longton Hall *Pheasant*, from Rous Lench Court.

19 Sotheby's, *Sale Catalogue*, 16 June 1981, lot 158. Pair of Derby biscuit *Street Vendors*.

20 William Chaffers, *Marks and Monograms on European and Oriental Pottery and Porcelain*, 15th revised ed., London, 1964, II, p. 275.

In 1770 William Duesbury engaged two modellers from Tournai, named Nicolas-Joseph-François Gauron and Pierre Stephan, who may have given advice concerning designs suitable for issue in biscuit. However, the standard Derby soft paste does not seem to have been modified. Shortly afterwards, in the Derby *Sale Catalogue* of 18 April 1771,[21] there appeared: 'Lot 47. A group of three figures Minerva crowning Constancy with laurel and Hercules kiling [sic] the Hydra, very curiously finish'd in biscuit £5 15s od.' Also in the same catalogue: 'Lot 60. A pair of sitting figures, a gentleman reading and lady knotting, most curiously ornamented with lace £5 5s od'. Michel-Victor Acier is believed to have discovered how to reproduce lace in porcelain by dipping it into slip, attaching it to the figure, and placing it in the kiln when the material burned away leaving a perfect facsimile in porcelain.

The popularity of biscuit figures steadily increased after 1771. A sale held by Messrs Christie at the Royal Academy, Pall Mall, on 9 and 10 February 1773[22] included sixty-three lots of which twenty-one consisted of figures and groups; of these eighteen lots, including forty-four items, were biscuit and only three lots of nine items were enamelled. During the late 1780s and 1790s almost all of the best work was in biscuit, and enamel decoration seems to have been reserved for examples emerging from the kiln with unsightly blemishes that had to be concealed.

The maximum sharpness of moulded detail was ensured by the selection of the first castings from each mould which were assembled and incised 'B'.[23] Occasionally figures so marked sustained damage and became unsuitable for issue in biscuit, and this may explain why some glazed and enamelled figures are incised with 'B' instead of 'G' (to be glazed). The need for perfection also accounts for the higher prices cited for biscuit as contrasted with enamelled models. The attractive surface sheen upon biscuit models made at Derby may initially have been produced accidentally when traces of glaze left over in the kiln vaporized and were later deposited upon the surface as a fine mist. Between 1771 and 1783, the surface sheen is unevenly distributed but displays an ivory-coloured tone and feels like satin to the touch. The body is close-grained and faintly translucent when thinly potted sections are held up before a bright light. The models are lighter in the hand than their Continental counterparts owing to their construction by slip-casting contrasted with the press-moulding employed in France. They lack the whiteness of Sèvres and the bluish tinge of Tournai, while confirmation of a Derby origin may be afforded by patch-marks, serial and size numbers or the factory device. Until about

21 J. E. Nightingale, *Contributions towards the History of Early English Porcelain*, Salisbury, 1881, appendix p. 19.

22 Ibid., appendix pp. 38–42.

23 John Haslem, *The Old Derby China Factory*, London, 1876, p. 150.

1790 the surface sheen had been unpredictable but thereafter was assured by smear-glazing, whereby glaze was either painted over the inner walls of saggars or placed in a small cup beside the models. According to Haslem,[24] this was introduced by Michael Kean, although it appears to have been employed on all the surviving examples of Spengler's work.

The glory of Sèvres was made possible by huge subsidies from Louis XV prompted by Madame de Pompadour, and depended on the beauty of the *pâte tendre*, the designs provided by François Boucher, and the skill of the sculptor/modellers led by Falconet. This recipe for excellence lasted barely a decade. In 1764 Madame de Pompadour died and in September 1766 Falconet left Sèvres to create a statue of Peter the Great for the Empress Catherine II of Russia. He had for several years been dissatisfied with both his artistic status and his low remuneration. Neither Jean-Jacques Caffieri nor Louis-Simon Boizot who succeeded him proved his equal. Boucher had faced increasingly adverse criticism of his work during his declining years, orchestrated by Denis Diderot and, in 1770, he was found dead beside his easel.

Lastly, in 1768, a *pâte dure* was introduced which within a few years replaced the *pâte tendre*. Henceforth the influence of Sèvres upon Derby models was negligible.

The following Derby models echo a Sèvres original by Falconet:

No.	*Derby Model or Group*	*Sèvres Prototype*	*Date*
46	*Boy and Girl Dancing a Reel*	*La Danse Allemande*	1755
73	*Pastoral Group with Dog and Lamb*	*Le Mouton Favorite*	1754
77	*Stocking Mender* (group)	*En Grande Toilette*	1766
78	*Shoe-maker* (group)	*En Grande Toilette*	1766
81	*Shoe-black* (group)	*En Grande Toilette*	1766
84	*Hairdresser* (group)	*En Grande Toilette*	1766
93	*Children Playing Hazard* (group)	*Le Tourniquet*	1757
94	*Children at a Peep-show* (group)	*La Lanterne Magique*	1757
176	*Grape Gatherers* (group)	*Pensent-Ils au Raisins?*	1752
177	*The Knot in the Cravat* (group)	*Le Noeud de Cravate*	1766
178	*Alpine Shepherdess* (group)	*La Bergère des Alpes*	1766
247	*Grape Gatherers* (added tree)	Reissue of No. 176	
255	*Knot in the Cravat* (added tree)	Reissue of No. 177	
256	*Alpine Shepherdess* (added tree)	Reissue of No. 178	
F19	*Lesson in Love* (group)	*L'Education Sentimentale*	1754

24 Ibid., pp. 146–7.

The small soft-paste porcelain factory established by François Peterinck about 1752 at Tournai employed two modellers, Nicolas-Joseph-François Gauron, and Pierre Stephan, both of whom came to England about 1770 to work for William Duesbury. Here they reproduced some of their earlier work, although the Derby examples were cast from different moulds. Their lives and work are presented in Appendix A. The following Derby models have Tournai prototypes:

No.	*Derby Model(s)*	*Modeller of Tournai original(s)*
(?) 1	*Minerva Crowning Constancy and Hercules Killing the Hydra*	N.-J.-F. Gauron
3	*The Four Elements* (4 models)	P. Stephan
48	*The Four Elements* (4 groups)	N.-J.-F. Gauron
123	*The French Seasons* (4 models)	N.-J.-F. Gauron
249	*Fire and Water* (group)	Adapted from No. 3
250	*Earth and Air* (group)	Adapted from No. 3

Many Tournai groups portray children or putti grouped around a central feature, such as a leafing tree or an obelisk, upon an irregular-shaped base resembling a rocky mound. The following Derby groups follow this format although no Tournai prototypes have yet been identified.

No.	*Derby Group*
179	*Four Children Playing Music*
234	*Four Cupids Bird's-nesting*
251	*Four Cupids Hunting*
252	*Group of Three Cupids*
257	*Four Cupids Hunting* (different from No. 251)
333	*Four Boys Playing Music*
334	*Four Boys with Pets*
388	*The Four Seasons*

OTHER SOURCES

Three-dimensional sources, other than porcelain models made at other manufactories, inspired several Derby figures and groups. These include marbles, bronzes, garden statues of lead or artificial stone, terracottas and plaster maquettes, as follows.

No.	*Derby Model or Group*	*Source*
88	*Mrs Catherine Macaulay*	Possibly a marble by C. F. Moore
121	*Minerva*	Lead statue by J. Cheere
122	*Winged Time*	Possible adaptation from a marble Venus by Giovanni da Bologna
146	*Bust of Addison*	Mould supplied by J. Cheere
147	*Bust of Virgil*	Mould supplied by J. Cheere
156	*Bust of Zingara*	After a bronze head by N. Cordier
193	*Bacchus*	Marble by J. Sansovino
194	*Ariadne*	Probable terracotta after the antique
222	*Winged Time*	Reissue of 122
259	*Britannia*	Lead statue by J. Cheere
297	*Milton*	Plaster maquette by M. Rysbrack
299	*Neptune with a Dolphin*	Bronze by Michel Anguier
300	*Neptune with a Dolphin*	Bronze by Michel Anguier
305	*Shakespeare*	Plaster maquette by P. Scheemakers
369	*Shepherd and Shepherdess Playing Flutes*	Adaptation from the Capitoline Faun
396	*Shepherd with his dog*	Terracotta of Hermes after the antique

Other Derby figures and groups were adapted from two-dimensional sources, mostly engravings, some serving as book illustrations.

No.	*Derby Model or Group*	*Engraving or Painting*
14	*Pair of Sacrifice Figures*	C. Monnet's engraving in *Les Metamorphoses d'Ovide*, Mire et Basan
21	*Garrick as Richard III*	J. Dixon after Nathaniel Dance
37	*Jason and Medea at the Altar of Diana*	C. Monnet's engraving in *Les Metamorphoses d'Ovide*, Mire et Basan
75	*Procris and Cephalus*	C. Monnet's engraving in *Les Metamorphoses d'Ovide*, Mire et Basan
76	*Renaldo and Armida*	P. de Bailliu after A. van Dyck
100	*Andromache Weeping Over the Ashes of Hector*	T. Burke after A. Kauffmann
124	*Time Clipping the Wings of Love*	C. Phillips after A. van Dyck

126	*John Wilkes, MP*	Portrait by N. Dance
195	*Two Virgins Awakening Cupid*	F. Bartolozzi after A. Kauffmann
196	*Two Bacchantes Adorning a Bust of Pan*	F. Bartolozzi after A. Kauffmann
227	*Pair of Dwarfs*	J. Callot's *Varie Figure Gobbi*
231	*Quinn as Sir John Falstaff*	J. McArdell after F. Hayman
235	*Three Graces Distressing Cupid*	F. Bartolozzi after A. Kauffmann
291	*Quinn as Sir John Falstaff*	Reissue of No. 231
293	*Tithe Pig Group*	J. S. Muller after Boitard
316	*Sailor and His Lass*	A. L. Hobson's engraving of 'Farewell to Black-eyed Susan', by Gray
358	*Cupid with Euphrosyne*	T. Burke after A. Kauffmann
365	*Boy Piping and Girl Dancing with Cymbals*	C. White
366	*Palemon and Lavinia*	C. Le Vasseur's engraving, or Cyfflé's Lunéville group
380	*Art, Literature and Astrology*	M. Raimondi after Raphael
384	*Admiral Lord Howe*	M. Brown's portrait
389	*Alpine Shepherds*	F. Bartolozzi after A. Kauffmann
390	*Gualtieri and Griselda*	Engraving in Boccaccio's *Decameron*
390	*Flora*	G. Grignion's engraving of *An Opera Girl of Paris*
391	*Prince William, Duke of York*	C. Dixon
393	*Russian Shepherds*	J. B. Tillard after Le Prince
395	*Lady Feeding a Sheep with Hay*	J. Hogg after F. Wheatley
F7	*Bust of Rousseau*	After a portrait by Taraval
F9	*Bust of Pope*	J. Smith after G. Kneller
F10	*The Royal Family* (Three Groups)	R. Earlom after J. Zoffany
F28	*Pointer*	T. Bewick's engraving in *The General History of Quadrupeds*

Part III

125 ? No. 1. *Minerva Crowning Constancy and Hercules Killing the Hydra.* $11\frac{1}{2}$ in (29.2 cm).
Birmingham Museum and Art Gallery

7 · The Revised Derby Factory List

The following revised and extended Derby Factory List has been compiled after personal examination of many hundreds of Derby models and groups, and perusal of catalogues past and present of sales, public and private collections and other relevant literature. The title of each item is provided only when an example bearing the appropriate serial number has been seen and when none is evident it is designated 'Not Identified'. Some of the latter may tentatively be named from less certain information. Beneath, the title descriptions given by both Haslem and Bemrose are provided together with the author's description. In order to allow comparison with data from other sources, measurements are provided first in inches, and prices in old £.s.d. Background information appears when this seems appropriate, together with the locations where other examples may be seen or are illustrated.

No. 1. *Not Identified*

HASLEM 'Group of the Virtues, 2 sizes: 1st. 11½ins., enamelled £2 2s 0d. 2nd. No details provided.'

BEMROSE 'A Boy, 2 sizes.'

No Derby group is known that is incised 'No. 1'. However, the *Derby Sale Catalogue* of 17 April 1771[1] includes: 'Lot 19. A fine group of the Virtues, with Minerva crowning Constancy with a garland of flowers, and Hercules kiling [sic] the Hydra, very curiously finish'd in biscuit £5 15s 0d.' This corresponds with the title provided by Haslem and which is here illustrated. It is a double composite group with two putti attired as Minerva and Constancy, separated by a leafing tree from the third putto representing Hercules slaying the Hydra. This was based upon a Tournai original of about 1764 by N. J. F. Gauron[2] in which the two themes are divided by an obelisk instead of a tree. The two groups were evidently cast from different moulds but both are ascribed to Gauron.

Examples

A Birmingham Museum. Enamelled, $11\frac{1}{2}$ in (29.2 cm), incised '7' but without the prefix 'No.', as illustrated.
F. Brayshaw Gilhespy, *Crown Derby Porcelain*, Leigh-on-Sea, 1951, figs. 156 and 157.

B Timothy Clifford, 'Derby Biscuit', *Trans. ECC*, 7, 1969, part 2, pl. 122. Biscuit, $11\frac{1}{2}$ in (29.2 cm), no marks reported. B. N. Clifford Collection (private).

References

1 J. E. Nightingale, *Contributions Towards the History of Early English Porcelain*, Salisbury, 1881, appendix p. 21.
2 Clifford, 1969, pls. 121A and 121B.

No. 2. *Boy Holding a Basket*

HASLEM No item mentioned.
BEMROSE No item mentioned.

A bareheaded boy stands, wearing a jacket, breeches and apron, holding before him a kidney-shaped basket which he grasps with both hands. Mounted on a scrolled base.

Example

Sotheby's, *Sale Catalogue*, 24 April 1968, lot 155. Enamelled, $4\frac{1}{2}$ in (11.4 cm), incised 'No. 2', no illustration provided.

No. 3. *The Four Elements* (set of four models)

HASLEM 'The Elements, Stephan, 3 sizes: 1st. 10 ins., enamelled £3 3s 0d., biscuit £3 13s 6d. 2nd. $9\frac{1}{4}$ ins., enamelled £2 12s 6d., biscuit £3 3s 0d. 3rd. $7\frac{1}{8}$ ins., enamelled £1 12s 6d., biscuit £2 2s 0d.'
BEMROSE 'Tryangular trypod [sic].'

A set of four standing rustic figures mounted on irregular mounds.

Water A girl wearing a simple dress standing barefoot and bareheaded holding a fishing-net in her right hand and securing with her left a catch of fish in a fold of her skirt.
Earth A gardener clad in a brimmed hat and contemporary dress, removing a pot-plant from a plinth with his right hand and leaning upon a spade with his left.
Fire A bareheaded youth holding aloft in his left hand a burning-glass with which he ignites a faggot in his right.

126 No. 3. Three of *The Four Elements*, c. 1772, by Pierre Stephan. Left to right: *Air, Water* and *Earth*. $9\frac{1}{4}$ in (23.5 cm). *Sotheby's*

127 No. 3. *The Four Elements*, c. 1820, after Pierre Stephan. $7\frac{1}{2}$ in (19.1 cm). *Private Collection*

Air A girl clad in a laced bodice, apron and skirt, holding a bird in her upraised left hand and a hunting horn in her right.

The Derby models were based on Tournai originals of about 1760 made by Pierre Stephan[1] and have been ascribed to the same modeller. The *Derby Sale Catalogues* of 9–10 February, 1773[2] mention: 'Two groups of elements, Earth and Air, finely modelled in biscuit', but these almost certainly refer to the set of paired groups, No. 48 by N. J. F. Gauron. The set, No. 3, was later reissued adapted as two groups, Nos. 249 and 250.

Examples

A F. Brayshaw Gilhespy, *Derby Porcelain*, London, 1961, fig. 143. Enamelled set, 9½ in (24.1 cm), incised 'No. 3', c. 1772.

B Arthur Lane, *English Porcelain Figures of the Eighteenth Century*, London, 1961, pl. 74. Biscuit, *Water* and *Air* only, 7⅜ and 7 in (18.7 and 17.8 cm), incised 'No. 3. Size 3', on octagonal bases.

C F. A. Barrett and A. L. Thorpe, *Derby Porcelain*, London, 1971, pl. 125. Enamelled set, c. 1820, 6½–7 in (16.5–17.8 cm), incised 'No. 3'.

References

1 Mille M. Jottrand, 'Tournai Porcelain and English Ceramics', *Trans ECC*, 10, 1977, part 2, p. 135, appendix III.

2 Nightingale, op. cit., p. 38.

No. 4. *Not Identified*

HASLEM 'Pastoral Group: Size not given, enamelled £2 12s 6d., biscuit £3 3s od.'
BEMROSE No item mentioned.

No group that conforms to the above description by Haslem is known that is incised 'No. 4', though there are several unmarked groups including the one here illustrated.

No. 5. *The Antique Seasons* (set of four models)

HASLEM 'Four Antique Seasons, in a set, 3 sizes: 1st. 8 ins., enamelled £1 4s od. 2nd. 6½ ins., enamelled 16s od. 3rd. 4⅛ ins., enamelled 12s od.'
BEMROSE 'Set of Antique Seasons.'

A set of four single models mounted on tall plinths:

Spring Flora, wearing a diadem of flowers and a loose robe that she gathers with her left hand, stands proffering a posy.

128 ? No. 4. *Pastoral Group*. $7\frac{1}{2}$ in (19 cm) no incised mark. *Aldbury Antiques*

Summer Ceres, crowned with ears of corn and wearing a long robe, holds a reaping-hook in her right hand and corn in her left.

Autumn Bacchus, wearing a chaplet of vine leaves and grapes, holding a goblet in his right hand and a bunch of grapes in his left.

Winter Vulcan, clad in a soft cap and robe which he gathers about him with his left hand while warming his right over a brazier at his feet.

The *Derby Sale Catalogues* of 17–21 April 1771[1] mention *The Antique Seasons* no fewer than fifteen times: 'Lot 17. A set of Elegant antique seasons and pedestals, in biscuit £4 2s 6d.' They range in price from £1 19s 6d. up to £4 2s 6d. according to whether issued enamelled or in biscuit and according to size. They are today exceedingly rare although the same figures were later adapted to provide a single group, *No. 248*.

Examples

A B. N. Clifford Collection (private). Biscuit, size not known, incised 'No. 5'.

B Sotheby's, *Sale Catalogue*, 4 December 1962, lot 146. Biscuit $6\frac{1}{2}$ in (16.5 cm), incised 'No. 5' but not illustrated.

Reference

1 Nightingale, op. cit., appendix, pp. 16–36.

No. 6. *The Four Infant Seasons* (set of four models)

HASLEM 'Four Seasons, in a set: 4 ins., enamelled 10s 6d.'
BEMROSE No item mentioned.

Spring A boy wearing a scarf and a floral chaplet, seated with a basket of flowers upon his knee, proffering a posy.
Summer A boy scantily draped crowned with corn-ears, seated holding a cornsheaf.
Autumn A boy crowned with vine leaves and grapes, holding a pannier of fruit upon his knee whilst proffering a bunch of grapes with his right hand.
Winter A boy wrapped in an ermine-lined cloak, warming his hands over a brazier balanced upon his right knee.

The first Derby versions were issued c. 1765, based on Meissen originals of about 1750 by F. E. Meyer (E75).

129 No. 6. *The Four Infant Seasons.* $5\frac{1}{4}$ in (13.3 cm). No incised marks. *Sotheby's*

Examples

A Sotheby's, *Sale Catalogue*, 29 January 1980, lot 59. Enamelled example of *Spring*, $4\frac{1}{2}$ in (11.4 cm), incised 'No. 6'.

B Ibid., 6 November 1979, lot 177. Enamelled examples *Autumn* and *Spring*, $4\frac{1}{2}$ in (11.4 cm), incised 'No. 6'.

C Twitchett, op. cit., pl. 122. Complete set of c. 1765, enamelled, $5\frac{1}{4}$ in (13.3 cm), no marks reported.

No. 7. *Gardener and Companion* (pair)

HASLEM 'Gardening, 2 sizes: 1st. $6\frac{3}{4}$ ins., enamelled 15s 0d., biscuit 16s 0d.' '2nd. $5\frac{1}{4}$ ins., enamelled, 8s 0d., biscuit 9s 0d.

BEMROSE 'Gardening, 2 sizes.' Also: 'A vase, antique.'

A gardener stands bareheaded holding a flower-pot in his right hand and leaning with his left upon his spade. His companion wears a brimmed hat, laced bodice, apron and skirt and stands holding vegetables in a fold of her apron while leaning with her left forearm upon a watering-can that rests upon a plinth-like fountain.

130 No. 7. *Gardener and Companion*. 7 in (17.8 cm). Incised 'No. 7'. *Private Collection*

The male figure of this pair closely resembles Pierre Stephan's *Gardener*, emblematic of Earth, in his set of *The Four Elements* (No. 3). The pair is mentioned in the *Derby Sale Catalogue* of 18 April 1771:[1] 'Lot 35. A pair of fine figures. Gardener and Companion, in biscuit 18s 0d.' Also: 'Lot 63. A pair of figures, Gardener and Companion, finely enamel'd in colours and burnish'd gold £1 1s 0d.'

Examples

A Derby Museums and Art Gallery, ref. nos. 645 and 1520. Biscuit, 5 in (12.7 cm), incised 'No. 7'.

B Sotheby's, *Sale Catalogue*, 30 September 1980, lot 170. Enamelled, $5\frac{1}{4}$ in (13.3 cm), incised 'No. 7'.

C Ibid., 18 May 1982, lot 106. Enamelled, $6\frac{1}{2}$ and $6\frac{3}{4}$ in (16.5 and 17.2 cm), incised 'No. 7.'

Reference

1 Nightingale, op. cit., p. 23.

131 No. 8. *Seated Boy and Girl with Fruit and Flowers* (pair). $5\frac{3}{8}$ in (13.6 cm). Incised 'No. 8'.
Derby Museums and Art Gallery

No. 8. *Seated Boy and Girl with Fruit and Flowers* (pair)

HASLEM 'Fruit and Flowers: 5⅜ ins., enamelled 10s 6d., biscuit 12s 0d.'
BEMROSE 'Pair sitting fruit and flower.' Also: 'Pair Laying Goats.'

A bareheaded boy sits upon a rocky mound with his inverted hat filled with fruits upon his knee and proffering an apple with his right hand. His companion sits likewise, clad in a brimmed hat, laced bodice, apron and skirt, a pannier of flowers upon her lap, proffering a posy. The hem and neck opening of the girl's dress are edged with lace. Mounted on scrolled bases.

The Derby models were based on Meissen originals created by Michel-Victor Acier.[1] The *Derby Sale Catalogue* of 17 April 1771[2] mentions: 'Lot 35. A pair of sitting figures, elegantly decorated with fruit and flowers, and most curiously work'd with lace, 2 12s 6d.' They were evidently popular models for they continued to be issued during the first quarter of the nineteenth century in bone china, both as free-standing[3] figures and adapted as chamber candlesticks.[4]

Examples

A Derby Museums and Art Gallery, ref. no. 640. Biscuit, 5⅜ in (13.6 cm), incised 'No. 8'.

B William King, *English Porcelain Figures of the Eighteenth Century*, London, 1925, fig. 53. Enamelled, 5¼ in (13.3 cm), no marks reported, Collection of Mrs Radford, now dispersed.

C Clifford, 1969, pls. 124a and 124b. Biscuit, 5¾ in (14.6 cm), no marks reported. B. N. Clifford Collection (private).

References

1 Clifford, 1969, op. cit. p. 113.
2 Nightingale, op. cit., appendix, p. 18.
3 Collection of A. E. Dodson (private).
4 Twitchett, op. cit., col. pl. 73. Enamelled, candlestick version.

No. 9. *Boy and Girl with French Horn and Guitar* (pair)

HASLEM 'Music, 3 sizes: 1st. 6¼ ins., enamelled 14s 0d., biscuit 16s 0d. 2nd. 6 ins., enamelled 10s 6d., biscuit 12s 0d. 3rd. 4⅝ ins., enamelled 6s 0d. biscuit 7s 0d.'
BEMROSE 'French horn and cymbal, 3 sizes, single figures.'

A bareheaded youth stands, clad in a cravat, waistcoat, jacket and breeches, playing a French horn. The companion girl wearing a lace cap, bodice and skirt edged with lace, stands with a guitar. Mounted on scroll bases encrusted with leaves and flowers.

132 No. 9. *Boy with French Horn.* $4\frac{5}{8}$ in (11.9 cm). Incised 'No. 9'. *Derby Museums and Art Gallery*

133 No. 9. Companion *Girl with a Guitar.* $5\frac{7}{8}$ in (14.7 cm). Incised 'No. 7' and 'Size 3'. *Derby Museums and Art Gallery*

Example

Derby Museums and Art Gallery, ref. nos. 1519 and 395. Enamelled, $4\frac{5}{8}$ in (11.9 cm), incised 'No. 9.', as illustrated.

No. 10. *Boy and Girl with Flute and Hurdy-gurdy* (two models)

HASLEM 'Flute and Cymbal, 3 sizes: 1st. $6\frac{1}{4}$ ins., enamelled 14s 0d., biscuit 16s 0d. 2nd. $5\frac{5}{8}$ ins., enamelled 10s 6d., biscuit 12s 0d. 3rd. $4\frac{3}{4}$ ins., enamelled 6s 0d., biscuit 7s 0d.'

BEMROSE 'French horn and cymbal, 2 sizes, single figures.'

The *Derby Sale Catalogues* of 29–31 March 1773[1] mention: 'A pair of figures, with flute and cymbol [sic], in biscuit 8s 0d.' There are a number of small Derby models of musicians which do not bear incised numbers, and it is possible that the girl playing the hurdy-gurdy may not be the correct partner for the male flautist. Alternatively, Haslem and Bemrose may both have been mistaken in their identification of the female figure.

Examples

A Derby Museums and Art Gallery, ref. nos. 304 and 1435. Enamelled pair, $4\frac{3}{4}$ in (12.1 cm), male figure incised 'No. 10'.

B Christie's, *Sale Catalogue*, 15 November 1972. Enamelled male figure, 6 in (15.2 cm), incised 'No. 10'.

C Bernard Rackham, *Catalogue of the Herbert Allen Collection of English Porcelain*, London, 1917, pl. 26, no. 97. Enamelled, $6\frac{1}{2}$ in (15 cm), no marks reported.

Reference

1 Nightingale, op. cit., appendix, p. 44.

134 No. 10. *Boy with Flute* (missing) and *Girl with Hurdy-gurdy*. $4\frac{3}{4}$ in (12.1 cm). Male figure only incised 'No. 10'. *Derby Museums and Art Gallery*

No. 11. *Seated Gentleman with Flute and Lady with Lute* (pair)

HASLEM 'Flute and Guitar: $6\frac{3}{8}$ ins., enamelled £1 10s 0d., biscuit £1 11s 6d.'
BEMROSE 'Pair of new lace figures – Spangler.' Also: 'Cupid Candlesticks.'

A gentleman seated in a chair playing a flute with his brimmed hat hung upon the chair back, and a pile of books and a musical instrument case at his feet. The companion lady sits, likewise, playing a lute and with a cat seated upon her lap; a lute together with several books are scattered beneath the chair. Mounted upon octagonal low plinths.

The *Derby Sale Catalogues* of 17–20 April, 1780[1] includes: 'One figure of Diana, 1 pair figures Mars and Minerva, 1 pipe and guitar, and 4 birds £1 7s 0d.' Lady Charlotte Schreiber wrote in her journals:[2] 'Bought in Paris on November 11th [1880] At Jurel's we saw a lovely pair of little Chelsea-Derby figures, seated and playing on instruments which were offered to us as Saxe [Meissen] ... We called at Jurel's and concluded for the Chelsea figures at £9 0s 0d.'

135 No. 11. *Seated Gentleman with Flute and Lady with Lute.* $6\frac{1}{4}$ and 6 in (15.9 and 15.2 cm). *Victoria and Albert Museum*

Examples

A Barrett and Thorpe, op. cit., pl. 130. Enamelled, female figure only, 6 in, incised 'No. 11'.

B Sotheby's, *Sale Catalogue*, 30 September 1980, lot 180. Enamelled pair, Bloor period, 6½ in (16.5 cm), incised 'No. 11'.

C Bernard Rackham, *Catalogue of English Porcelain, Earthenware, Enamels etc:, collected by Charles Schreiber and the Lady Charlotte Elizabeth Schreiber and presented to the Museum* [Victoria and Albert] *in 1884*, London, 1915, I, pl. 41, no. 425 (new no. 357). Enamelled, 6¼ and 6⅜ in, (15.9 and 15.2 cm) incised 'No. 11'.

References

1 Nightingale, op. cit., appendix, p. 58.

2 Montague J. Guest (ed.), *The Lady Charlotte Schreiber's Journals, Confidences of a Collector of Ceramics and Antiques* ... London and New York, 1911, II, pp. 322–3.

No. 12. *Pastoral Group by a Fountain*

HASLEM 'Pastoral Group: 12½ ins., enamelled £2 12s 6d.'
BEMROSE 'Fountain group.'

A shepherdess wearing a laced bodice, panniered skirt and petticoat, reclines asleep beside a fountain. A shepherd attired in a brimmed hat and contemporary dress stands on her left playing a recorder, with a dog at his feet. The fountain is adorned with dolphin masks, from which water flows, and upon the top rests a covered urn with a detachable lid that serves as a candlestick. Mounted on an irregular pad base.

The group is executed in a style reminiscent of that seen in *The Four Elements* (No. 3). by Pierre Stephan, and has accordingly been ascribed to the same modeller. The *Derby Sale Catalogue* of 10 February 1773[1] mentions: 'Lot 47. A pastoral group finely modelled with an antique vase, enamel'd and elegantly finish'd £3 2s 6d.' The absence of the urn's cover in the example in the Derby Museum accounts for its smaller size.

Examples

A Barrett and Thorpe, op. cit., pl. 97. Enamelled, 11¾ in (29.8 cm), incised 'No. 12'. Derby Museums and Art Gallery.

B H. G. Bradley, *Ceramics of Derbyshire 1750–1975*, Tiverton, 1978, no. 25. Enamelled, 12½ in (31.2 cm), incised 'No. 12'.

C Sotheby's, *Sale Catalogue*, 3 October 1972, lot 179. Enamelled, 12½ in (31.2 cm), incised 'No. 12'.

D Twitchett, op. cit., pl. 116. Enamelled, 12½ in (31.2 cm), no marks reported.

E E. Percival Allam, 'The Artistic Modellers of the Derby Porcelain Factory, *Connoisseur*, 82, 1928, pp. 29–37, no. V. Biscuit, 12½ in (31.2 cm), no marks reported.

Reference

1 Nightingale, op. cit., appendix p. 41.

136 No. 12. *Pastoral Group by a Fountain.* 11¾ in (29.8 cm). Incised 'No. 12'. *Derby Museums and Art Gallery*

137 No. 13. *Cupid Riding a Goat* (one of a pair). 7 in (17.8 cm). Incised 'No. 13'. *Victoria and Albert Museum*

No. 13. *Cupid Riding a Goat and Bacchus on a Panther* (pair)

HASLEM 'Cupid and Bacchus riding: 7 ins., enamelled £1 1s 0d.'
BEMROSE 'Pair of boys each on a goat.'

Cupid scantily draped, a quiver suspended from his left shoulder by a diagonally placed strap, sits astride a seated goat. The companion putto, attired as Bacchus, wears a diadem of vine leaves and grapes, and holding a goblet and a bunch of grapes in either hand, sits upon a panther. Mounted on irregular pad bases encrusted with small leaves and flowers.

J. J. Kändler and his associate modellers at Meissen created a number of figures depicting satyrs, putti, Cupid, and the infant Bacchus, some of them riding goats, stags or panthers.[1] It is likely that the Derby examples are based on some of these though the precise source is not known. The *Derby Sale Catalogue* of 19 April 1771[2] includes: 'Lot 34. Two pair of Cupid and Bacchus riding on goats and panthers, and pedestals, in biscuit £3 9s 0d.' Other lots in the same sale were variously priced up to £5, suggesting that some of the more expensive may have been issued in biscuit.

Examples

A Victoria and Albert Museum, ref. no. C1291–1919. Enamelled, 7 in (17.8 cm), incised 'No. 13', as illustrated.

B David Love Antiques, Harrogate. Enamelled *Boy Astride a Panther* only, 7 in (17.8 cm), incised 'No. 13'.

References

1 K. Berling, *Festive Publication to Commemorate the 200th Jubilee of the Oldest European China Factory, Meissen*, Meissen, 1910, fig. 44, *Satyr Riding a Goat* by J. J. Kändler.

2 Nightingale, op. cit., appendix, p. 18.

No. 14. *Pair of Sacrifice Figures*

HASLEM 'Sacrifice Figures, pair: No size given, enamelled £1 0s 0d, biscuit £1 4s 0d.'
BEMROSE 'Two sacrafice [sic] figures, 3 sizes.'

A bareheaded youth clad in a tunic, stands barefoot, holding a sacrificial knife in his right hand poised over a kid that lies upon a plinth-like altar. A basin is placed below the victim to collect its blood.

The nature of the companion model is uncertain. A memorandum in the Derby Museums and Art Gallery indicates that a model incised 'No. 14.' was brought to the museum for identification by a member of the public. It was said to represent 'A girl holding a basket of flowers in her left hand and a bird in her right'.

The male model was adapted from Charles Monnet's engraving of the subject illustrating the Abbé Banier's version of *Les Métamorphoses d'Ovide*, published between 1767 and 1771 in Paris. The *Derby Sale Catalogue* of 19 April 1771[1] includes: 'Lot 25. A pair of figures, with an altar-piece, in biscuit £1 9s od.' However, this may refer to *Jason and Medea at the Altar of Diana* (No. 37). Joseph Lygo, in a letter written in 1788 to William Duesbury II, wrote: 'Mr. Rossi is modelling a female sacrifice figure from a drawing Mr. Vulliamy gave me from one of his books and suggests a male figure to match.'[2] This must clearly refer to a later pair of models.

Examples

A Gilhespy, 1951, pl. 85, fig. 154. Enamelled, $6\frac{1}{4}$ in (15.9 cm), stated to be incised 'No. 17' which appears to be a typographical error since the same example is illustrated by:

B Barrett and Thorpe, op. cit., fig. 90. Same as above, said to be incised 'No. 14'.

C Sotheby's, *Sale Catalogue*, 31 July 1979, lot 82. Enamelled, incised 'No. 14', 6 in (15.2 cm).

D Ibid., 16 March 1971, lot 388. Enamelled, 6 in (15.2 cm), incised 'No. 14'.

References

1 Nightingale, op. cit., appendix, p. 27.

2 Gilhespy, 1961, pp. 65–76. Abstracts of the Lygo letters to William Duesbury II.

No. 15. *Prudence* and *Discretion* (pair)

HASLEM 'Small Prudence and Discretion with urns: $9\frac{1}{4}$ ins., enamelled £1 8s od'.

BEMROSE 'Small dancing figure, group.'

Prudence is depicted as a scantily draped girl, standing regarding her reflection in a mirror held in her left outstretched hand, with a serpent entwined about her right forearm.

Discretion is portrayed as a winged Cupid, his quiver slung diagonally by a strap over his shoulder, holding his forefinger to his lips as if signalling for silence. Each figure is mounted on a pad base beside a festooned urn upon a plinth.

Bernard Watney[1] has reminded us that Prudence has traditionally been personified as a woman with a snake and a mirror and cites as an example the stucco statue by Rusconi in the church of St Ignazio in Rome, and also a Meissen porcelain version.[2] The source of the Derby models is unknown, though they

138 No. 14. *Sacrifice Figure*. 6 in (15.2 cm). Incised 'No. 14'. *Sotheby's*

139 No. 15. *Prudence* and *Discretion*. 8 and $8\frac{3}{8}$ in (20.3 and 21.3 cm). *Victoria and Albert Museum*

have more than a passing resemblance to the Sèvres biscuit figures of *Cupid* and *Psyche*[3] created by E. M. Falconet. The *Derby Sale Catalogue* of 17 April 1771[4] includes: 'Lot 61. A pair of figures of Prudence and Discretion, each a curious antique urn, on pedestals, in festoons of chas'd gold, and highly burnish'd gold £5 2s 6d.' Again, on the following day:[5] 'A very curious pair, Prudence and Discretion, each with antique urns on a pedestal, in biscuit £4 0s 0d.'

Examples

A Twitchett, op. cit., pl. 123. Enamelled, 8 and $8\frac{3}{8}$ in (20.3 and 21.3 cm), incised 'No. 15'. Victoria and Albert Museum, ref. nos. 414/410 and 414/410a.

B Rackham, 1915, pl. 40, no. 344. Enamelled, 8 and $8\frac{3}{8}$ in (20.3 and 21.3 cm), incised 'No. 15'.

C R. L. Hobson, *A Guide to English Pottery and Porcelain in the British Museum*, London, 1910, p. 62. Enamelled, $8\frac{1}{2}$ in (22 cm).

References

1 Bernard Watney, 'Some Parallels and Proto-types in Ceramics', *Trans ECC*, 10, 1980, pt. 5, pp. 350–6.

2 George Savage, *Eighteenth Century German Porcelain*, London, 1958, pl. 60a, Meissen model.

3 George Savage, *Seventeenth and Eighteenth Century French Porcelain*, London, 1960, pls. 71b and 71c, *Cupid and Psyche*, by E. M. Falconet.

4 Nightingale, op. cit., appendix, p. 19.

5 Ibid., appendix, p. 24.

No. 16. *Dancing Couple* (group)

HASLEM 'Dancing Group: $6\frac{5}{8}$ ins., enamelled 16s 0d.'
BEMROSE 'Large old Jupiter and Juno.'

A lady who is bareheaded and wears a dress with elbow-length sleeves and an apron, dances with a youth clad in a brimmed hat, jacket and breeches. The man's right arm is about his partner's waist and he holds her right hand in his left, while her left hand rests upon his shoulder. Mounted upon an oval mound edged with scrolls.

The Derby group is based on a Meissen original of about 1764 by J. J. Kändler and, together with No. 17, forms a pair. The *Derby Sale Catalogues* of 9 and 10 February 1773[1] mention: 'A pair of elegant dancing groups enamelled, finely modelled and finish'd with burnish'd gold £1 6s 0d.'

Examples

A Twitchett, op. cit., pl. 128. Enamelled, $7\frac{1}{4}$ in (18.4 cm), no incised marks reported.

B Bernard Hughes and Therle Hughes, *English Porcelain and Bone China*, 1955, 1743–1850, London, 1955, pl. 14b.

Reference

1 Nightingale, op. cit., appendix p. 41.

No. 17. *Dancing Couple* (group)

HASLEM 'Dancing Group: $6\frac{5}{8}$ ins., enamelled 16s 0d.'
BEMROSE 'A vase.' Also: 'A group, two figures.'

A lady wearing a blouse with elbow-length sleeves, laced bodice, apron and skirt, dances with a youth clad in a ruffle, jacket, and breeches. His right arm is around his partner's shoulders and he clasps her right hand in his left, whilst she has her

140 No. 16. *Dancing Couple.* 7 in (17.8 cm). Incised 'No. 16'. *Private Collection*

141 No. 17. *Dancing Couple.* $7\frac{1}{4}$ in (18.4 cm). Incised 'No. 17'. *Derby Museums and Art Gallery*

left arm about his waist. Mounted on an oval mound edged with scrolls.

The group follows a Meissen original of about 1764 by J. J. Kändler and forms a pair with No. 16.

Examples

A Hughes and Hughes, op. cit., pl. 14c. Enamelled, 7 in (17.8 cm), incised 'No. 17'; also bears crossed swords in blue enamel.

B Barrett and Thorpe, op. cit., pl. 129. Enamelled, 7 in (17.8 cm), incised 'No. 17'. Bloor period example.

C Derby Museum, ref. no. 1479. Enamelled, 7 in (17.8 cm), incised 'No. 17'; also bears crossed swords in blue enamel.

D Sotheby's, *Sale Catalogue*, 24 July 1984, lot 118. Enamelled, 7 in (17.8 cm), incised 'No. 17'. This shows a minor variation with the youth's arm elevated to be level with his partner's face.

No. 18. *Not Identified*

HASLEM No item mentioned
BEMROSE No item mentioned.

No. 19. *Child with Basket of Fruit*

HASLEM No item mentioned.
BEMROSE 'Large fountain vase.'

A scantily draped putto seated upon a rocky mound holds aloft with his left hand a floral garland and with his right holds a basket of fruits.

Barrett and Thorpe[1] have identified this model as No. 19, though no example incised with this number is known to the author.

142 ? No. 19. *Child with Basket of Fruit*. 5 in (12.7 cm). No incised marks.
Victoria and Albert Museum

Example

Twitchett, op. cit., pl. 112. Biscuit, 5 in (12.7 cm), no incised marks reported. Victoria and Albert Museum, ref. no. C1308–1919.

A *Fountain Vase* is also known, incised 'No. 19'. This is urn-shaped with handles formed as putti riding dolphins, decorated about the neck with putti holding swags; the gadrooned rim is embellished with satyrs' masks and the cover with Cupids fighting. The lower portion is decorated with infant mermen, the whole standing upon a plinth supported by four sphynxes. This was first described in Christie's *Sale Catalogue* of 9 and 10 February 1773[2], when one was sold for £17 17s. Bemrose ascribed the vase to John Charles Felix Rossi, though in 1773 he would have been only eleven years of age.

Example

Bradley, op. cit., p. 28, no. 29. Enamelled, incised 'No. 19'.

References

1 Barrett and Thorpe, op. cit., p. 181.

2 Nightingale, op. cit., appendix, p. 40.

143 No. 20. *Standing Boy and Girl with Fruit and Flowers.* $4\frac{1}{2}$ in (11.4 cm). Incised 'No. 20'. *Derby Museums and Art Gallery*

No. 20. *Standing Boy and Girl with Fruit and Flowers* (pair)

HASLEM 'Fruit and Flowers, 3 sizes: 1st. 6¼ ins. enamelled 14s 0d, biscuit 16s 0d. 2nd. 5¾ ins., enamelled 10s 0d., biscuit 12s 6d. 3rd. 4⅝ ins., enamelled 6s 0d., biscuit 7s 0d.'

BEMROSE 'Fruit and flower, 4 sizes.' Also: 'Vase-octagon'.

A bareheaded youth stands holding a basket of flowers beneath his left arm which he supports with his right hand. The companion girl, also bareheaded, stands grasping a pannier of fruits with both hands. Mounted on mound bases encrusted with small leaves and flowers and edged with scrolls.

The subject and manner of presentation of this pair are similar to those evident in the seated boy and girl (No. 8) and most probably stem from the same hand.

Examples

A Derby Museums and Art Gallery, ref. no. 654. Biscuit, 4½ in (11.4 cm), incised 'No. 20'.

B Sotheby's, *Sale Catalogue*, 2 June 1969, lot 119. Enamelled, 6 in (15.2 cm), incised 'No. 20'.

C Ibid., 16 March 1971, lot 388. Enamelled, 5 and 5¼ in (12.7 and 13.3 cm), incised 'No. 20'.

No. 21. *David Garrick as Richard III*

HASLEM 'Garrick as Richard III, Bacon: 9¾ ins., enamelled £1 5s 0d., biscuit £1 5s 0d.'

BEMROSE 'David Garrick, Esqre, 2 sizes.'

A portrait model of David Garrick in the title role of King Richard III, by William Shakespeare. The king wears a doublet, hose, ermine-trimmed cloak and buckled shoes, and stands with one foot advanced striking an histrionic pose with his right arm upraised. Mounted on an oval mound encrusted with small leaves and flowers.

The model was adapted from John Dixon's mezzotint after the portrait by Nathaniel Dance, exhibited at Burlington House in 1771. The scene relates to Bosworth Field where the monarch, his steed killed under him, cried out: 'A horse, a horse, my kingdom for a horse!' The model is mentioned in the *Derby Sale Catalogues* of 9 and 10 February 1773:[1] 'A fine figure of Garrick, in the character of Richard III, in biscuit £1 10s 0d.' There is no evidence to support Haslem's contention that the model was created by John Bacon. Babette Craven[2] has shown that when during the 1790s John Philip Kemble took over the role from Garrick,

144 No. 21. *David Garrick as Richard III* (left). *Edmund Kean in the same role* (right). Both $9\frac{1}{2}$ in (24.1 cm). Incised 'No. 21'. *Sotheby's*

145 Mezzotint of *David Garrick as Richard III* by J. Dixon after Nathaniel Dance.

the old porcelain model was refurbished and given a new head in his likeness. Further, when in due course Kemble yielded the part to Edmund Kean, the model of Kemble was reissued but with the head repainted to represent the features of the new incumbent.

David Garrick (1717–99) was born in Hereford and in 1737 set out for London in the company of his friend Dr Samuel Johnson. Garrick's first play, *Lethe*, opened at Drury Lane in 1741 and during that same year he made his début as the Duke of Gloucester upon the boards of a small theatre in Goodman's Fields. Never before had a reputation been established at a first performance and the public did not allow this triumph ever to be forgotten. Thomas Davies wrote: 'Mr. Garrick shone forth like a theatrical Newton; he threw new light on elocution, ease, simplicity and genuine humour ...'[3] The part of Gloucester, who became Richard III, remained in Garrick's repertoire until his farewell season of 1776. During his lifetime he became actor-manager of Drury Lane, Poet Laureate, and the acknowledged monarch of the English stage. There were fifty carriages in his funeral cortège and five of his six pall-bearers were peers of the realm. Dr Johnson stood by the graveside with tear-stained face and pronounced: 'I am disappointed by that stroke of death which eclipsed the gaiety of nations.' An epitaph in Westminster Abbey reads:

> 'Shakespeare and Garrick like twin stars shall shine
> and earth irradiate with a beam divine.'

Examples

A Twitchett, op. cit., pl. 294, model of Garrick; pl. 296, model of Kean, pl. 297, model of Kemble. All enamelled, $9\frac{1}{4}$–$9\frac{1}{2}$ in (23.5–24.1 cm), incised 'No. 21'.

B Victoria and Albert Museum, ref. no. 414.205–1885. As above.

C G. Bernard Hughes, *English Pottery and Porcelain Figures*, London, 1964, pl. 11a. Garrick, enamelled, 10 in (25.4 cm), incised 'No. 21'.

D Allam, op. cit., no. VII. Garrick, biscuit, 10 in (25.4 cm), incised 'No. 21'.

References

1 Nightingale, op. cit., appendix, p. 40.

2 Babette Craven, 'Derby Figures of Richard III', *Trans. ECC*, 10, 1977, part 2, pp. 95–8;
pl. 40a, Derby models of Garrick, Kean and Kemble as Richard III;
pl. 40b, mezzotint of Garrick by J. Dixon after N. Dance;
pl. 41a, Wax relief of Kemble;
pl. 41c, print of Kean by Cruikshank.

3 Catalogue of an exhibition held between 25 July and 22 August 1981, at Buxton Museum and Art Gallery entitled: *Thirty Different Likenesses – David Garrick in Portraiture and in Performance*.

Nos. 22, 23 and 24. *Not Identified*

HASLEM No item mentioned.
BEMROSE No. 22. No item mentioned. No. 23 'Fragments of the Royal Family.' No. 24. No item mentioned.

It is likely that Nos. 22, 23 and 24 are three groups representing the *Royal Family*, adapted from Richard Earlom's engraving[1] of Johann Zoffany's portrait.[2] These are described in the *Derby Sale Catalogue* of June 1773:[3] 'Their present majesties the king and queen, and royal family, in three grouped pieces in biscuit – the centre piece represents the king in a Vandyke dress, on a blue and gold basement, supported by four lions, leaning on an altar richly ornamented in blue and gold, with hanging trophies of the polite arts and sciences. The crown, munde, and sceptre reposing on a cushion of crimson, embroidered, fringed, and tasselled in gold, fourteen inches.' Two other groups were as follows: Queen Charlotte portrayed seated, holding the infant Princess Augusta and with Princess Charlotte standing at the queen's side. Also, the figures of George Prince of Wales and Frederick Duke of York standing beside the seated young Prince William playing with a cockatoo, and the Duke of Kent with a dog.

The only known complete set is in the royal collection in Windsor Castle and this may represent a special order placed by Queen Charlotte herself or alternatively was perhaps a special issue to commemorate the visit of George III to the London showrooms of the Derby factory in 1773. The *Derby Sale Catalogue* of 5–8 May 1778[4] includes mention only of 'A model of the King beside an altar £3 10s od.' An example in the British Museum is mounted upon a differently styled base from that in the royal collection but is also without any incised number. The subject has been reviewed by Timothy Clifford.

Examples

A Anthony Hoyte and Marilyn Swain, 'A New Look at Ceramics from Private Collections,' *Antique Dealer and Collector's Guide*, September 1985, pp. 58–60, fig. 4. Three groups portraying the *Royal Family* after Zoffany, Collection of H M The Queen, Windsor Castle. Biscuit with gold and enamel embellishments.

B Lane, op. cit., pl. 73. Model of George III only, biscuit with enamel and gilt embellishments, 14 in (35.6 cm), no incised marks. British Museum.

Barrett and Thorpe[5] have wrongly identified No. 23 as a pair, *Swiss Boy and Swiss Girl*. The pair in the Derby Museums and Art Gallery is bone china and is undoubtedly from the Rockingham manufactory.[6]

References
1 Timothy Clifford, *Chelsea–Derby Royal Family Groups*, London, 1985. Catalogue of an exhibition held in September 1985 at Burlington House, London, by the Derby Porcelain International Society. Fig. 4, mezzotint after Zoffany by Earlom.
2 Bellamy Gardner, 'English China Collections of the Past', *Trans. ECC*, 4, 1937, pp. 23–7, pl. IXd, mezzotint by Earlom; pls. IXa, b and c, three porcelain groups of the *Royal Family*.
3 William Chaffers, *Marks and Monograms on European and Oriental Pottery and Porcelain*, London, 15th rev. ed., 1974, II, pp. 194 and 195.
4 Nightingale, op. cit., appendix, p. 53.
5 Barrett and Thorpe, op. cit., p. 181.
6 D. G. Rice, *Ornamental Rockingham Porcelain*, London, 1965, p. 140, pl. 102. Rockingham models of *Swiss Boy and Girl* incised 'No. 23'.

Nos. 25–34. *Apollo and the Nine Muses* (set of ten models)

HASLEM 'Ten Figures of Apollo and the Muses: 5 ins., enamelled 5s 3d. each.'
BEMROSE No. 32. 'Fisherman and woman.' No other items mentioned.

The author has seen only four examples of Muses and one of Apollo. These are $4\frac{1}{4}$–$4\frac{3}{8}$ in (10.8–11.1 cm) and mounted on detachable stands of about 1–$1\frac{1}{4}$ in (2.5–3.2 cm) tall, formed from pierced scrolls with chamfered corners and eagles' heads in high relief.

Apollo Depicted as a youth wearing a laurel diadem and a loose robe, holding a lyre in his left hand.

Calliope A young woman clad in a laurel crown and loose robes who holds three tomes under her right arm.

Clio A woman seated and attired in loose robes who holds a quill in her right hand and supports an open book with her left.

Melpomene A woman who stands wearing a laurel chaplet and robes, holding a goblet in her left hand; a helmet lies at her feet.

Terpsichore A girl wearing a cloak and dancing.

The source of these models is unknown. They are dissimilar from the primitive early Bow versions as well as the sophisticated gold anchor Chelsea Muses. They are also entirely distinct from the reclining models issued at Derby about 1763. They are mentioned in the *Derby Sale Catalogues* of 9 and 10 February 1773:[1] 'Apollo and four Muses, Calliope and Terpsichore, Urania and Melpomene, finely modelled in biscuit £1 10s od:[2] 'Apollo, Erato, Clio, Urania and Calliope, in biscuit £1 10s od.' Surviving examples appear to be very rare and to have been issued both enamelled and in biscuit. The incised 'Size 3' on one indicates they were made in at least three sizes.

After Jupiter had quelled the revolt of the Giants, the gods implored him to

146 No. 25. Biscuit figure of the muse *Calliope* upon a detachable stand. 6 in (15.2 cm). Incised 'No. 25'. *Derby Museums and Art Gallery*

enliven their feasts with the Arts. Jupiter coupled with the Titaness Mnemosyne, who in the fullness of time bore him the Nine Muses. They were: Calliope (Epic Poetry), Clio (History), Erato (Love Poetry), Euterpe (Lyric Poetry), Melpomene (Tragedy), Polyhymnia (Sacred Music), Terpsichore (Dance), Thalia (Comedy) and Urania (Astrology). They dwelt on Mount Helicon but attended the feasting on Mount Olympus. Initially they were most zealous of their chastity and, when King Pyreneos attempted to ravish them when they were his guests, they sprouted wings and flew away, while the wretched monarch who attempted to follow them fell to his death upon the rocks below. Later, however, they took lovers among both gods and men. Apollo, who shared their patronage of the Arts, took the title of Musagetes, and sired the Corybantes by Thalia. They were formidable creatures with whom it was folly to trifle. The daughters of the Emanthian king, named the Pierides, challenged the Muses to a musical contest and for their temerity were transformed into magpies. The Thracian bard, Thamyris, boasted that he excelled the Muses in playing his lyre and in song, and was instantly struck deaf, blind and dumb for his presumption.

Examples

A Apollo. Enamelled, $4\frac{1}{2}$ in (11.4 cm), no marks.

B Calliope. Derby Museums and Art Gallery. See Barrett and Thorpe, op. cit., pl. 95. Biscuit, 6 in (15.2 cm) (including stand), incised 'No. 25'.

C Clio. Graham and Oxley, Kensington Church Street, London. Enamel, $4\frac{3}{4}$ in (12.1 cm), no marks reported.

D Melpomene and Terpsichore. Sotheby's, *Sale Catalogue*, 29 July 1980, lot 159. Both enamelled, $4\frac{1}{2}$ in (11.4 cm), incised respectively 'No. 27 and No. 31, Size 3'.

References

1 Nightingale, op. cit., appendix p. 38.

2 Ibid., appendix p. 39.

No. 35. *The Four Rustic Seasons* (*set of 4 models*)

HASLEM 'Four Seasons: 6 ins., enamelled £1 1s od., biscuit £1 4s od.'

BEMROSE 'Four Seasons.'

Four models of standing men and women with accessories appropriate to the season, mounted on mound bases encrusted with leaves and flowers:

Spring A bareheaded girl, wearing a laced bodice, apron and skirt, with a basket of flowers over her right arm and a posy in her left hand.

Summer A girl attired in a brimmed hat, bodice, apron and skirt, with a corn sheaf beneath her left arm.

Autumn A bareheaded youth, clad in a scarf, long jacket and breeches, holding in his upraised left hand a bunch of grapes and with his right securing his inverted hat filled with fruit.

Winter A youth attired in a brimmed hat, scarf, jacket, breeches and boots, holding a branch of holly in his left hand.

The source of these models is undetermined. Minor variations may be encountered so that, for example, the lady emblematic of Spring may have the basket of flowers at her feet instead of over one arm. A rare variant of Winter may hold a leashed hound. Later, the four models were adapted to provide two groups, *Spring and*

147 No. 35. Girl holding a cornsheaf, emblematic of *Summer* from the set of *The Four Rustic Seasons*. 6 in (15.2 cm). Incised 'No. 35'. *Victoria and Albert Museum*

Autumn and *Summer and Winter* (No. 68) and finally were formed into a single group, when the models were arranged about an obelisk (No. 294).

Examples

A Rackham, 1917, pl. 26, no. 101. Enamelled example of *Spring*, 6 in (15.2 cm), incised 'No. 35'.

B Sotheby's, *Sale Catalogue,* 18 May 1982, lot 110. Enamelled example of *Autumn,* 6 in (15.2 cm), incised 'No. 35'.

C Ibid., 29 June 1971, lot 48. Enamelled example of *Winter,* holding a leashed hound, 6½ in (16.5 cm), incised 'No. 35'.

148 No. 36. *Seated Boy and Girl, Each with Flowers.* $5\frac{3}{8}$ in (13.8 cm). Incised 'No. 36'.
Victoria and Albert Museum

No. 36. *Seated Boy and Girl, Each with Flowers* (pair)

HASLEM 'Sitting Fruit: 5 ins., enamelled 10s 6d., biscuit 12s 0d.'
BEMROSE No item mentioned.

A bareheaded boy and girl seated in mirror positions upon, respectively, an upturned basket and a rocky mound. The boy holds his inverted hat filled with blossoms in his lap and proffers a posy in his left hand; the girl secures flowers in a fold of her apron and proffers a bunch of flowers with her right hand. Mounted upon mound bases edged with scrolls.

Examples

A Rackham (A), op. cit., pl. 33, no. 126. Enamelled, $5\frac{3}{8}$ in, incised 'No. 36', as illustrated.

B Sotheby's, *Sale Catalogue,* 29 July 1980, lot 154. Enamelled, $5\frac{5}{8}$ in (13.8 cm), incised 'No. 36'.

No. 37. *Jason and Medea at the Altar of Diana* (group)

HASLEM 'Jason and Medea, 3 sizes: 1st. no size given, enamelled £3 3s 0d., biscuit £3 13s 6d. 2nd. $12\frac{3}{4}$ ins., enamelled £2 2s 0d., biscuit £3 3s 0d., 3rd. no size given, enamelled £1 11s 6d., biscuit £2 12s 6d.'
BEMROSE 'Large group Jason and Midia [sic].'

The goddess Diana stands bareheaded and barefoot attired in loose robes upon an altar, her left hand upon her breast. Jason clad in Roman armour kneels before her with his right hand on his heart and his left upraised. Medea stands facing Jason, her right arm also elevated. Mounted on an oval mound encrusted with leaves and flowers.

149 No. 37. *Jason and Medea at the Altar of Diana.* 13 in (33 cm). Incised 'No. 37'. *Derby Museums and Art Gallery*

The group was adapted from Charles Monnet's engraving of 'Jason and Medea at the Altar of Diana', illustrating the Abbé Banier's edition of *Les Métamorphoses d'Ovide*, published in Paris 1767–71.[1] The *Derby Sale Catalogues* of 9 and 10 February 1973[2] mention: 'A large group, Jason and Medea, vowing before the altar of Diana, enamel'd and richly finish'd with gold £3 3s od.'

The group illustrates a scene from the legend of Jason and the Golden Fleece. Jason, son of Aeson, returns to his home land to find that Pelias has usurped the throne from his father and, wishing to be rid of the rightful king's son, sends him on the seemingly impossible mission to bring back from Colchis the Golden Fleece that is owned by King Aëtes. Jason builds the galley, *Argo*, and with a crew of fifty Heroes and after many adventures, lands at Colchis. Aëtes agrees to surrender the fleece if Jason can accomplish certain tasks. His daughter Medea falls in love with Jason and they make their solemn vows of marriage before the altar of Diana before she tells him how to carry out the requisite deeds. After capturing the fleece they return to Iolcus only to discover that during their absence Pelias had murdered Aeson. They wreak a bloody revenge and live happily together for many years before Jason deserts Medea for a younger woman. The new bride puts on the gown given to her by Medea as a wedding present and is consumed in flames.

Examples

A Twitchett, op. cit., pl. 103. Enamelled, $12\frac{3}{4}$ in (32.4 cm), no marks reported.
B Derby Museums and Art Gallery. Enamelled, 13 in (33 cm), incised 'No. 37'.
C Sotheby's, *Sale Catalogue*, 31 August 1979, lot 102. Enamelled, 13 in (33 cm), no marks reported. Wrongly identified as *Meleager Before Atalanta*.

References

1 A. J. Toppin, 'The Origin of Some Ceramic Designs', *Trans. ECC*, 2, 1948, no. 10, pp. 266–76.
2 Nightingale, op. cit., appendix, p. 41.

No. 38. *Not Identified*

HASLEM 'Prudence and Discretion: $5\frac{1}{2}$ ins., enamelled 7s od., biscuit 8s od.'
BEMROSE 'Pair Prudence and discression [sic].'

No models or groups incised 'No. 38' are known to the author. A pair of vases, after Sèvres originals, exist, incised 'No. 38', which have tapering necks and are decorated with festoons of drapery and lions' masks. They stand on octagonal bases with spreading feet adorned with satyrs' masks and are complete with covers.

Example
Bradley, op. cit., p. 28, no. 28. Enamelled, $12\frac{3}{4}$ in (32.4 cm), incised 'No. 38'. Private collection.

Nos. 39–45. *The Arts and Sciences* (seven groups)

HASLEM 'Seven Groups of Arts and Sciences: Various at 16s od. each with pedestals and 14s od. without pedestals.'
BEMROSE 'Group Arts and Scyances [sic].'

Each group is composed of two winged putti mounted on rectangular bases with detachable pierced and scrolled stands, overall 7 in (17.8 cm).

No. 39. *Architecture.* Two scantily clad putti, one seated the other standing amid architectural ruins.
No. 40. *Music.* A putto seated playing a lute while his companion holds a musical score.
No. 41. *Commerce.* A putto stands taking coins from a wallet as his associate writes upon a slate, with parcels scattered about them.
No. 42. *Painting and Sculpture.* A standing putto sculpts a bust while his seated companion makes a painting in a book.
No. 43. *Astronomy and Geometry.* A putto makes a measurement with a pair of dividers upon a celestial globe while his associate uses a spyglass.
No. 44. *Arithmetic.* A putto stands writing with a quill in a ledger as his companion supports the tome and holds an ink-well.
No. 45. *Literature.* A putto writes in a book held by his friend with scrolls and books scattered about them.

The Derby groups are copies of Meissen originals of about 1765 by Michel-Victor Acier.[1] The *Derby Sale Catalogues* of 9 and 10 February 1773[2] include: 'Two groups, music and painting and sculpture finely modelled in biscuit £1 10s od.' Also:[3] 'Two groups of the Arts and Sciences, viz: Painting and Sculpture and Astronomy, in biscuit £1 14s od.' A further entry for 29 March of the same year[4] reads: 'Pair of elegant groups Poetry and Music, on pedestals, in biscuit £1 14s od.' The term 'pedestals' here distinguishes No. 40 from No. 217, both of which represent *Music.*

Examples
A Barrett and Thorpe, op. cit., pl. 101. *Astronomy,* incised 'No. 43'; *Commerce,* incised 'No. 41'; and *Arithmetic,* incised 'No. 44'. All biscuit, 7 in (17.8 cm), as illustrated.

150 No. 40. Biscuit group of two putti representing *Music*. $5\frac{1}{2}$ in (14 cm). Incised 'No. 40'.
Fitzwilliam Museum

151 Three biscuit groups, each of two putti, with detachable stands. 7 in (17.8 cm). *Victoria and Albert Museum* No. 41. *Commerce* (centre). No. 42. *Astronomy and Geometry* (left). No. 44. *Arithmetic* (right).

B Sotheby's, *Sale Catalogue*, 15 July 1969, lot 12. *Painting and Sculpture*, 7 in (17.8 cm), incised 'No. 42'.

C Private Collection. *Literature*, biscuit, 7 in (17.8 cm), no marks.

D British Museum, ref. no. 1936, 7–15, 38. Biscuit, $7\frac{1}{4}$ in (18.4 cm), incised 'No. 45.T.'

E *Trans. ECC.*, 1967, vol. 6, pl. 223b. *Music*, biscuit, 7 in. (17.8 cm), incised 'No. 40'.

F Christie's, *Sale Catalogue*, 22 May 1989, lot 268, *Architecture*, 7 in (17.8 cm), incised 'No. 39'.

References

1 Berling (A)., op. cit. table 19, no. 9. *Astronomy and Geometry*, Meissen, by M. V. Acier.
2 Nightingale, op. cit., appendix, p. 40.
3 Ibid., p. 41.
4 Ibid., p. 44.

152 No. 45. Biscuit group of two putti representing *Literature*, without detachable stand. $5\frac{1}{2}$in (14 cm). *British Museum*

No. 46. *Boy and Girl Dancing a Reel* (group)

HASLEM 'Dancing Figures and Group: 5½ ins., enamelled 9s od.'
BEMROSE 'Small groups, two figs. dancing.'

A young man and a girl dancing a reel, their bodies facing in opposite directions and heads turned to regard one another; he holds the girl's left hand behind his back in his right whilst she holds his hand behind her in her right. Mounted on a mound base encrusted with leaves and flowers.

The Derby group is a copy of a biscuit Sèvres original entitled *La Danse Allemande,* created about 1765 by Étienne-Maurice Falconet.[1]

Examples

A Rackham, 1915, pl. 40, no. 415 (new no. 348). Enamelled, 6¼ in (15.8 cm), incised 'No. 46'.

B Twitchett, op. cit., pl. 119. Enamelled, 6¼ in (15.8 cm), incised 'No. 46'.

Reference

1 Émile Bourgeois and Georges Lechevallier-Chevignard, *Le Biscuit de Sèvres: Recueil des Modèles de la manufacture de Sèvres au xviii*[me] *siècle,* Paris, 1909, pl. 10, no. 169.

153 No. 46. *Boy and Girl Dancing a Reel.* 6¼ in (15.8 cm). Incised 'No. 46'.
Derby Museums and Art Gallery

No. 47. *The Four Grotesque Seasons* (set of four models)

HASLEM 'Grotesque Seasons: $5\frac{1}{4}$ ins., enamelled 16s od.'
BEMROSE 'Group, 4 Seasons.'

A set of four standing figures of strangely trunkated rustics.

Spring A bareheaded girl wearing a bodice, apron and skirt, who carries an oval basket filled with flowers in her dependent right hand and a posy in her left.

Summer A bareheaded boy attired in a shirt with sleeves rolled up and breeches, stooped over a corn sheaf.

Autumn A girl clad in a round hat, laced bodice, apron and skirt, holding grapes in a fold of her apron with her left hand and an apple in her right.

Winter A boy attired in a brimmed hat, jacket and breeches, holding a spoon-shaped container filled with burning charcoal in his right hand over which he warms his left.

Examples

A Gilhespy, 1961, pl. 89, fig. 161. Enamelled, $5\frac{1}{2}$ in (14 cm), incised 'No. 47'.

B Christie's, *Sale Catalogue*, 2 June 1968, lot 16. Enamelled, $5\frac{1}{2}$ in (14 cm), no marks reported.

C Sotheby's, *Sale Catalogue*, 21 December 1971, lot 21. Enamelled, $5\frac{1}{2}$ in (14 cm), example of *Summer* only, no marks reported.

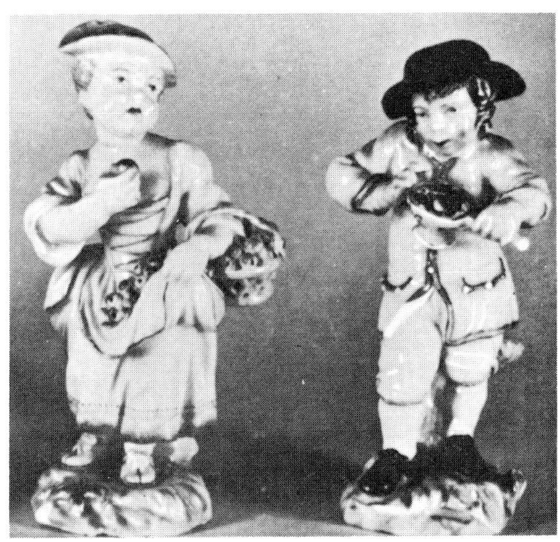

154 *The Four Grotesque Seasons*. $5\frac{1}{4}$ in (13.3 cm). All incised 'No. 47'. *Private Collection*
No. 47. *Spring* (left) and *Summer* (right).

155 No. 47. *Autumn* (left) and *Winter* (right).

No. 48. *The Four Elements* (four groups)

HASLEM 'The Elements in two Groups: $8\frac{3}{4}$ ins., enamelled £2 12s 6d., biscuit £3 4s 0d.'
BEMROSE 'Four Antique Seasons, group.'

Four groups, each of two winged putti about a leafing tree upon an irregular rocky mound.

Air A putto slides down a tree-trunk having robbed a robin's nest, while his companion stands beside a cage, basket in hand, ready to receive fledglings or eggs.
Earth A putto leans upon his spade while his friend sits holding a garland.
Fire A putto wearing a brimmed hat with a quiver slung from his belt, sharpens arrows on a grindstone while his partner holds a flaming torch.
Water A putto stands beside a tree against which his net is supported, holding a wicker pannier, while his companion sits removing a catch of fish from a creel.

156 *The Four Elements*, each represented by a biscuit group of two putti, by N. J. F. Gauron. $8\frac{1}{2}$in (21.6 cm). Incised 'No. 48'. No. 48. *Air. Derby Museums and Art Gallery*

157 No. 48. *Water* (left) and *Earth* (right). *David Thorn Collection*

158 No. 48. *Fire. David Thorn Collection*

The groups echo Tournai originals of about 1760, created by Nicolas-Joseph-François Gauron,[1] and have been ascribed to the same artist though they were cast from different moulds. The *Derby Sale Catalogues* of 9 and 10 February 1773[2] include: 'Two groups of elements, Earth and Air, finely modelled in biscuit £1 11s od.' Also: 'Two groups of the elements, Fire and Water, finely modelled in biscuit £1 9s od.'

Examples

A Derby Museums and Art Gallery, ref. nos. 633, 635 and 643. Biscuit examples of *Air, Earth* and *Fire*, $8\frac{1}{2}$ in (21.6 cm), incised 'No. 48', as illustrated.

B C. M. Scott and G. R. Scott, *Antique Porcelain Digest*, Newport, 1961, pl. 169, figs. 617–20. Complete set, biscuit, $8\frac{1}{2}$ in, incised 'No. 48'.

C Gilhespy, 1951, pl. 89, fig. 162. Biscuit examples of *Air and Fire*, $8\frac{1}{2}$ in (21.6 cm), incised 'No. 48'.

D Sotheby's, *Sale Catalogue*, 21 March 1972, lot 44. Enamelled examples of *Fire and Earth*, $8\frac{1}{2}$ in (21.6 cm), no marks reported.

References

1 H. Nicaise, 'Porcelaines de Tournay et de Chelsea-Derby', *Revue Belge d'Archéologie d'Histoire de l'Art*, 1935, vol. 5, pp. 5–15. See also: Clifford, 1969, pl. 121b, Tournai version of *Fire;* pl. 121c, Chelsea–Derby example of *Fire*.

2 Nightingale, op. cit., appendix, pp. 38–9.

No. 49. *Boy and Girl with Macaroni Dog and Cat* (pair)

HASLEM 'Cat and Dog Figures: $5\frac{3}{8}$ ins., enamelled 13s od.'
BEMROSE 'Pair grotesque cat and dog figures.'

A boy wearing a soft cap, ruffle, jacket and breeches beneath a short cape, kneels upon a mound with both arms encircling a spaniel that has a cocked hat upon its head. The companion girl, clad in a dress and apron beneath a cape, stands in a mirror pose with her arms about a cat. Mounted on mound bases encrusted with small leaves and flowers.

The pair is mentioned in the *Derby Sale Catalogue* of 29 March 1773:[1] 'A pair of laughing figures enamelled white and gold, dressing a macarony dog and cat.' Similar models portraying animals dressed in human garments were made at Longton Hall[2] and Champion's Bristol factory,[3] and appear to have been popular. Lady Charlotte Schreiber records in her journal:[4] 'Found at Mme. Faudin's a lovely pair of Derby-Chelsea figures, Boy with dog and Girl with cat. They were very dear but quite irresistable at £14 os od.' Modern taste may not be in harmony with this appraisal.

The term 'Macaroni' was employed during the eighteenth century to describe a male or female dandy or fop and was also applied to dogs or monkeys wearing decorative clothing (see also No. 91).

Examples

A Twitchett, op. cit., pl. 115. Enamelled, $6\frac{1}{2}$ in (16.5 cm), incised 'No. 49'. Victoria and Albert Museum, ref. nos. 414/416–1885 and 414/416a–1885.

159 No. 49. *Boy and Girl with Macaroni Dog and Cat.* 6½ in (16.5 cm). Incised 'No. 49'.
Victoria and Albert Museum

B Sotheby's, *Sale Catalogue*, 29 June 1971, lot 48. Enamelled female model only, 6½ in (16.5 cm), incised 'No. 49. G'.

C Barrett and Thorpe, op. cit., pl. 89. Enamelled male model only, 6½ in (16.5 cm), incised 'No. 49'. Derby Museums and Art Gallery, ref. no. 373.

References

1 Nightingale, op. cit., appendix, p. 45.

2 Bernard Watney, *Longton Hall Porcelain*, London, 1957, pls. 67b and 68b. *Gallant and Lady, each with a dog.*

3 Peter Bradshaw, *Eighteenth Century English Porcelain Figures* 1745–95, Woodbridge, 1981, pl. 142. Champion's Bristol models of *Gallant and Lady, each with a dog.*

4 Guest, op. cit., p. 184.

No. 50. *Huntsman and Lady* (pair)

HASLEM 'Sporting and Companion [sic]: 5⅝ ins., enamelled 12s 0d., biscuit 14s 0d.'
BEMROSE 'Pair small figures, Sportsman and companion.'

A huntsman clad in a brimmed hat, cravat, jacket, breeches and boots, a game-bag and powder-flask suspended by crossed belts, stands holding a flint-lock gun in his left hand. His female companion wears a round hat and jacket over her ankle-length dress, and has a game bird upon her left wrist and a gun in her right hand. Mounted upon flower-encrusted mound bases.

Blood sports were reserved for the aristocracy in Europe during the eighteenth century so that the possession of porcelain models of huntsmen and their ladies served to enhance the prestige of their owner. Both Chelsea[1] and Bow[2] issued very similar models based on Meissen prototypes though the precise source of the Derby examples is unknown. The *Derby Sale Catalogues* of 29 March–1 April 1773[3] include: 'A fine pair of figures enamelled, viz. a sportsman and companion with his dog and gun 16s od.' Later, the same two figures were refurbished to provide *Spring* and *Autumn* in a set known as the *Chelsea Seasons* (No. 125).

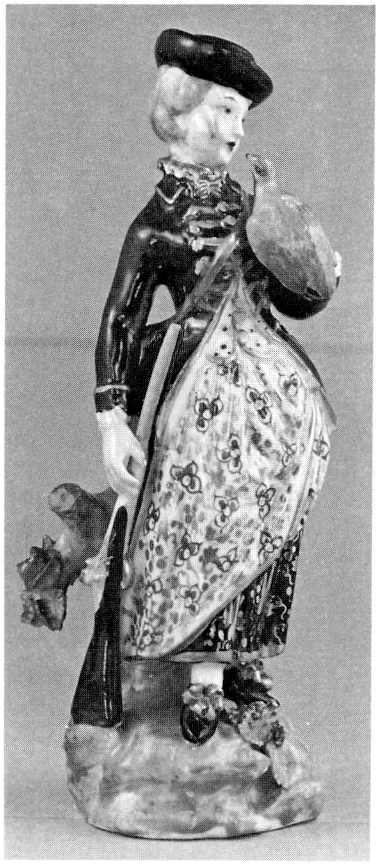

160 No. 50. *Huntsman* holding a gun with his dog. $5\frac{1}{2}$in (14cm). Incised 'No. 50'. *Hanbury Hall*

161 No. 50. *Lady* with a gun holding a falcon. $5\frac{1}{2}$in (14cm). Incised 'No. 50'. *Hanbury Hall*

Examples

A Hanbury Hall, the Watney Collection. Enamelled, $5\frac{1}{2}$ in (14 cm), incised 'No. 50', as illustrated.

B Sotheby's, *Sale Catalogue*, 16 March 1971, lot 388. Enamelled, $5\frac{1}{2}$ in, (14 cm), incised 'No. 50'.

References

1 F. Severne Mackenna, *Chelsea Porcelain, the Red Anchor Wares,* Leigh-on-Sea, 1951, pl. 71, fig. 141. A Chelsea pair of *Huntsman and Lady*.

2 Frank Stoner, *Chelsea, Bow and Derby Porcelain Figures,* Newport, 1955, col. pl. 5. Bow *Huntsman and Lady*.

3 Nightingale, op. cit., appendix, p. 46.

No. 51. *Gentleman and Lady with Dog and Cat* (pair)

HASLEM 'Cat and Dog Figures: 5 ins., enamelled 10s 6d., biscuit 14s 0d.'
BEMROSE 'Small cat and dog figures.'

A gentleman sits bareheaded upon a rocky ledge with a begging dog at his right side; his right hand is elevated to attract the animal's attention while with his left he supports the dog's front legs. The companion lady sits stroking a cat in her lap. Mounted on mound bases encrusted with leaves and flowers.

162 No. 51. *Gentleman and Lady with Dog and Cat.* 6 in (15.2 cm). Incised 'No. 51'.
Victoria and Albert Museum

The Derby pair follows a Meissen original by J. J. Kändler of about 1755.[1] The *Derby Sale Catalogues* of 9 and 10 February 1773[2] mention: 'A pair of sitting figures, with dog and cattle [sic], finely enamel'd and richly finish'd with lace £2 2s od.'

Examples

A Twitchett, op. cit., pl. 336. Enamelled, 6 in (15.2 cm), incised 'No. 51'. Victoria and Albert Museum, ref. nos. C. 1298–1919 and C. 1299–1919.

B Sotheby's, *Sale Catalogue*, 27 May 1970, lot 265. Enamelled, 6 in (15.2 cm), incised 'No. 51'.

References

1 Meissen prototypes were shown by Adams, Bond Street, London, at the International Ceramics Fair, held at the Dorchester Hotel, London, 15–18 June 1984.

2 Nightingale, op. cit., appendix, p. 38.

No. 52. *Griffin Candlestick*

HASLEM 'Dragon Candlesticks.'
BEMROSE No item mentioned.

A candlestick $9\frac{1}{4}$ in (23.5 cm), incised No. 52, composed of a seated griffin bearing a candle holder upon its head, mounted on a waisted circular base edged with beading on a shallow octagonal stand. It is likely Haslem transposed the titles of Nos. 52 and 53.
'One pair of dragon candlesticks green and gold 15s od.'

Example

Recent acquisition of the Derby Museums and Art Gallery, as described above.

Reference

1 Nightingale, op. cit., appendix, p. 63.

No. 53. *Pair of Grimacing Dwarfs*

HASLEM 'Griffin Candlesticks.'
BEMROSE No item mentioned.

A female dwarf, wearing a hat, laced bodice and skirt, is portrayed grinning, her head inclined to dexter and both hands before her. Her male companion is also clad in a hat as well as a shirt, waistcoat and breeches, and sits with legs crossed with both hands elevated before his face which is turned.

163 No. 53. Pair of *Grimacing Dwarfs*. $5\frac{1}{2}$ in (14 cm). Incised 'No. 53'. See also Plate XVI. *Bonham's*

The 'Griffin Candlesticks' mentioned by Haslem appear in the *Derby Sale Catalogues* of 18 and 19 February:[1] 'One pair griffin candlesticks blue and gold 15s 0d.' See No. 52.

Example
Bonhams, *Sale Catalogue*, 23 May 1986, lot 160. Enamelled, $5\frac{1}{2}$ in (14 cm), one example is marked in red enamel with a crown, crossed batons and script 'D', and is also incised 'No. 53'. Bloor period.

Reference
1 Nightingale, op. cit., appendix, p. 50.

No. 54 *Justice*

HASLEM 'Justice: $9\frac{1}{2}$ ins., enamelled 15s 0d.'
BEMROSE 'New Justice.'

Justice is portrayed as a woman standing with both eyes closed, wearing a mantle over a classical robe, holding in her right hand a short sword with upturned point and in her left the scales of Justice. Mounted upon a square base.

The model was first issued about 1760 (see E57 (Plate 95)) but was later reissued in a smaller size upon a square base. It must be distinguished from *Antique Justice* (No. 162), which may explain the use of the title 'New Justice' employed in the Bemrose version of the Factory List.

Examples

A Sotheby's, *Sale Catalogue*, 1 April 1980, lot 183. Enamelled, $9\frac{3}{4}$ in (24.8 cm), incised 'No. 54', mounted on a square base.

B Hughes, op. cit., pl. 9. Enamelled version of c. 1760, no incised marks reported.

C See E57 (Plate 95) for an earlier but similar model.

No. 55. *The Dresden Shepherds* (pair)

HASLEM 'The Dresden Shepherds, 2 sizes: 1st. $9\frac{1}{4}$ ins., enamelled £1 6s 0d. 2nd. $8\frac{3}{4}$ ins., enamelled £1 2s 0d.'

BEMROSE 'Dresden shepherd, 1st size, 2 figures, 3 sizes.'

164 No. 55. *Dresden Shepherd* with his dog. 8 in (20.3 cm).

165 No. 55. Female companion to the *Dresden Shepherd*. 8 in (20.3 cm). Incised 'No. 55'.
B. and T. Thorn Antiques

The shepherd wears a brimmed hat, jacket and breeches and a scrip hangs by a strap diagonally from his right shoulder. He holds a basket of fruit level with his left breast and proffers an apple with his right hand; a dog lies at his feet. The shepherdess, clad in a round hat, laced bodice and skirt, secures blossoms in her apron with her right hand and extends a posy in her left hand; at her feet there is a lamb. Mounted on mound bases edged with scrolls before waist-tall bocages.

The Dresden Shepherds follow Meissen prototypes of about 1745 by J. J. Kändler, first issued at Derby about 1758 (see D17 (Plates 55 and 56)). Pale Family examples are mounted on tall bases, but later during the 1760s mound bases decorated with scrolls were favoured both at Derby[1] and Chelsea.[2] Subsequently they receive mention in the *Derby Sale Catalogues* of 17–21 April 1771:[3] 'Lot 16. One pair Dresden Shepherds, richly enamel'd in flowers and elegantly finish'd in burnish'd gold £1 0s 0d.' Further examples were priced at between 18s and £1 16s, according to size.

Examples

A Twitchett, op. cit., pl. 334. Enamelled, 9 in (23 cm), mounted on scrolled bases, c. 1765, no marks reported.

B Sotheby's, *Sale Catalogue*, 9 January 1968, lot 150. Enamelled, $8\frac{1}{4}$ in (21 cm), incised 'No. 55' and '2nd Size', rectangular bases.

References

1 Hughes and Hughes, op. cit., pl. 5. Chelsea gold anchor version of *The Dresden Shepherds*.

2 Honey, W. B., *Old English Porcelain*, London, 1928, pls. 45A. and 45C. Derby *Dresden Shepherds* of c. 1765.

3 Nightingale, op. cit., appendix, pp. 16–36.

No. 56. *The Garland Shepherds* (pair)

HASLEM 'Garland Shepherds, 4 sizes: 1st. $9\frac{3}{4}$ ins., enamelled £1 6s 0d. 2nd. 9 ins., enamelled £1 2s 0d. 3rd. $7\frac{5}{8}$ ins., enamelled 18s 0d. 4th. $6\frac{3}{4}$ ins., enamelled 15s 0d.'

BEMROSE 'Pair of garland shepherds, 4 sizes.'

A shepherd wearing a brimmed hat, jacket and breeches, stands beside a seated dog, with his right hand on his hip and holding a letter in his outstretched left hand. Companion shepherdess stoops to place a garland about the neck of a ewe that has its front legs upon her knee. Mounted upon mound bases edged with scrolls, before small, waist-tall bocages.

The first Derby *Garland Shepherds* were issued about 1760, after which they were reissued in several sizes.[1] The subject portrayed suggests they may have

166 No. 56. *The Garland Shepherds.* $6\frac{1}{4}$ in (15.9 cm). Incised 'No. 56'. *Thornton's of Harrogate*

been adapted from French engravings after Boucher, though their source remains unknown. Early versions (E23).

Example
Thornton's of Harrogate. Enamelled, $6\frac{1}{4}$ in (15.9 cm), incised 'No. 56', as illustrated.

Reference
1 Twitchett, op. cit., pl. 60. enamelled, $10\frac{1}{2}$ in (26.7 cm), no incised marks.

No. 57. *The French Shepherds* (pair)

HASLEM 'French Shepherds, 6 sizes: 1st. [$7\frac{1}{2}$ ins.], enamelled £1 8s 0d., biscuit no price given. 2nd. [6 ins.], enamelled £1 2s 0d., biscuit no price given. 3rd. ——, enamelled 18s 0d., biscuit no price given. 4th. [$4\frac{1}{2}$ ins.], enamelled 14s 0d., biscuit no price given. 5th. ——, enamelled 10s 6d., biscuit 12s 6d. 6th. ——, enamelled 7s 0d., biscuit 8s 0d.'
BEMROSE 'French shepherds, 6 sizes.'

A boy shepherd stands bareheaded and barefoot supporting with his right hand a puppy that has jumped up with its front legs upon his chest, while holding aloft a ball in his left to attract the animal's attention. The companion girl holds a lamb in her arms. Mounted on shallow mound bases edged with scrolls.

The source of this pair of models is unknown although the title 'French' would suggest they were based either on a French engraving or porcelain models, perhaps from Tournai or Sèvres. Similar models made at Bow about 1765 are on four-footed bases,[1] while hard-paste versions from Champion's Bristol factory[2] show both figures wearing stockings and shoes.

Examples

A Bradshaw, op. cit., pl. 121. Enamelled, 6 in (15.2 cm), incised 'No. 57 Size 2'.
B Author's Collection. Biscuit, 4½ in (11.4 cm), incised 'No. 57 Size 4'.
C Twitchett, op. cit., pl. 113. Enamelled, 7½ in (19.1 cm), no marks reported but presumably Size 1. Victoria and Albert Museum, ref. nos. C.256–1935 and C.256a–1935.

References

1 John Cushion, *English Porcelain,* London, 1974, p. 32, pl. 24. Bow version of *French Shepherds.*
2 Private Collection.

167 No. 57. Biscuit examples of *The French Shepherds.* 4½ in (11.4 cm). Incised 'No. 57' and 'Size 4'. *Author's Collection*

No. 58. *Shepherd Playing a Reed-pipe*

HASLEM 'Piping shepherd: $6\frac{1}{2}$ ins., enamelled 15s od.'
BEMROSE 'Two pair piping Shepherd and companion.'

A shepherd clad in a brimmed hat, jacket and breeches, plays a reed-pipe, whilst a seated dog regards him with a woeful expression. Mounted on a scrolled base before a tree-stump support. For earlier version see E33 (Plate 87).

Example
Rackham (B), op. cit., pl. 26, no. 100. Enamelled, $6\frac{1}{2}$ in (16.5 cm), incised 'No. 58', as illustrated. Herbert Allen Collection.

168 No. 58. *Shepherd Playing a Reed-pipe* (missing) beside his dog. $6\frac{1}{2}$ in (16.5 cm). Incised 'No. 58'. *Victoria and Albert Museum*

169 *The Five Senses* represented by seated adolescents, each with a creature: No. 59. *Feeling*, represented by a lady accosted by Cupid. $7\frac{1}{2}$ in (19.1 cm). No incised marks. *Private Collection*

No. 59. *The Five Senses* (set of five models)

HASLEM 'Set of Five Senses: $7\frac{1}{2}$ ins., enamelled £2 12s 6d.'
BEMROSE 'Five sences [sic], small.'

A set of five seated figures of girls or boys, each with a creature appropriate to one of the Senses.

Feeling A bareheaded girl, with ornaments in her hair, wearing a laced bodice and full skirt, seated with both hands in her lap, regarding Cupid who stands with left arm upraised at her side, his quiver suspended from a tree-trunk.
Hearing A bareheaded girl, her hair decked with plumes, wearing a blouse and skirt, seated with a swan at her side, playing a lute.
Sight A youth clad in a plumed cap, jacket with lace collar, and breeches, seated with an eagle at his right side, holding a spy-glass.
Smell A bareheaded youth attired in jacket and breeches, with a cloak draped over his knees, seated beside a hound that he caresses with his left hand while holding a posy to his nose with his right.
Taste A bareheaded youth clad in a shirt, jacket and breeches, seated beside a leopard that he strokes with his right hand while elevating a bunch of grapes in his left.

These models were first issued from the Derby factory about 1765 (E72). Some have waist-tall bocages and they seem to have been made in two sizes. Although some have attributed them to Pierre Stephan, they were available some five years prior to his arrival in England.

Examples
A Reginald Blunt, *The Cheyne Book of Chelsea Pottery and China,* London, 1924, no. 252 and pl. 23. Enamelled set, $9\frac{1}{2}$ in (24.1 cm), no incised marks reported.
B King, 1925, fig. 48, *Hearing*; fig. 49, *Smell.* Both enamelled, $10\frac{1}{4}$–$10\frac{1}{2}$ in (26–26.7 cm), no marks reported.
C Twitchett, op. cit., pl. 133, *Sight* (identified wrongly as *Feeling*); pl. 134, *Smell*; pl. 135, *Feeling* (identified wrongly as *Sight*). Enamelled, about $7\frac{1}{2}$ in (19.1 cm), no marks reported.
D Hanbury Hall, the Watney Collection. *Sight, Hearing* and *Taste,* enamelled, as illustrated.
E British Museum, ref. no. 1936, 7–15, 133. Enamelled example of *Smell,* incised 'No. 59 G', as illustrated.

170 No. 59. *Hearing,* portrayed by a lady playing a mandoline seated beside a swan. $7\frac{1}{2}$ in (19.1 cm). Incised 'No. 59'. *Hanbury Hall*

171 No. 59. *Sight,* represented by a youth holding a spy-glass beside an eagle. $7\frac{1}{2}$ in (19.1 cm). Incised 'No. 59'. *Hanbury Hall*

173 No. 59. *Taste,* shown as a youth eating grapes beside a panther. $7\frac{1}{2}$ in (19.1 cm). Incised 'No. 59'. *Hanbury Hall*

172 No. 59. *Smell*, depicted by a youth smelling a posy beside a hound. $8\frac{1}{4}$ in (20.9 cm). Incised 'No. 59 G'. *British Museum*

No. 60. *The Singing Shepherds* (pair)

HASLEM 'Singers, 3 sizes: 1st. [$8\frac{1}{4}$ ins.], enamelled £1 0s 0d. 2nd. 7 ins., enamelled 16s 0d. 3rd. $5\frac{3}{8}$ ins., enamelled 9s 0d.'
BEMROSE 'Singers, 3 sizes.'

A shepherd and shepherdess stand bareheaded singing in mirror positions with one hand holding a song-sheet and the other on hip. The male wears a cloak over a tight-fitting jacket with a linen collar and breeches, while the female, also in a mantle, is clad in a blouse and skirt. Mounted on mound bases encrusted with leaves and flowers. For earlier version see E32.

174 No. 60. Male partner of *The Singing Shepherds*

175 No. 60. Female partner of *The Singing Shepherds*. Both $8\frac{1}{4}$ in (21 cm). Incised 'No. 60'. *Thornton's of Harrogate*

Examples

A Thornton's of Harrogate. Enamelled, $8\frac{1}{4}$ in (21 cm), incised 'No. 60', as illustrated.

B Twitchett, op. cit., pl. 118. Example probably c. 1765, enamelled, $8\frac{1}{2}$ in (21.6 cm), no marks reported.

C Stoner, op. cit., pl. 4. Enamelled, $8\frac{1}{2}$ in (21.6 cm), male figure only, no marks reported.

D Barrett and Thorpe, op. cit., pl. 68. Enamelled, $8\frac{1}{2}$ in (21.6 cm), no marks reported.

No. 61. *The Four Seasons* (set of four models)

HASLEM 'Four Sitting Seasons: 1st. size not given, enamelled £1 1s od.' No other information provided.

BEMROSE 'Pair Spring figures, 2 sizes.' Also: 'Group Arts and Scyances' [sic].

Four models of seated children with appropriate accessories, each mounted on scrolled and fenestrated bases before small bocages.

Spring A seated child clad in a blouse and skirt wearing a floral diadem and holding flowers.

Summer A similar girl crowned with corn-ears holding a cornsheaf.

176 No. 61. Three of *The Four Seasons*, each represented by a seated child. $4\frac{3}{4}$ in (12.1 cm). Incised 'No. 61'. *Thornton's of Harrogate*

Autumn A similar girl wearing a chaplet of vine leaves and grapes with grapes in her lap.

Winter A similar girl crowned with holly holding a charcoal burner.

Examples

A Thornton's of Harrogate. Enamelled, 4¾ in (12.1 cm), incised 'No. 71', as illustrated. Figure of *Winter* missing.

B Gilhespy 1951, fig. 148. Enamel example of *Spring* only.

C Sotheby's, *Sale Catalogue*, 16 March 1982, lot 122. Complete set, enamelled, 4½ in (11.4 cm), incised 'No. 61'.

No. 62. *The Welch Tailor and his Family* (pair)

HASLEM 'Welch Taylor [sic] and Family. 2 sizes: 1st. size not given, enamelled £2 12s 6d. 2nd. 5½ ins, enamelled £1 1s 0d.'

BEMROSE 'Welch tayler [sic], 2 sizes.'

A tailor astride a male goat, clad in a brimmed hat, jacket and breeches, holding a pair of scissors in his upraised right hand, and having upon his back pannier of kids. His wife, wearing a hat, blouse and skirt, rides a female goat that suckles a kid; she bears a child in her arms and a basket filled with babies is upon her back. Mounted on oval bases encrusted with leaves and flowers.

The story is told of how Count Heinrich von Brühl, Prime Minister of Saxony and director of the Meissen factory, rashly promised to grant any request made by his master tailor if he could deliver a special suit in time for a Court banquet. The garments were duly delivered and the tailor asked to be allowed to attend the feast. The Count accordingly placed him as a porcelain model upon the table since by reason of his humble birth he could not be invited to sit down with the nobility. Kändler's first model of the *Tailor*[1] of about 1737, depicted him resplendent in an order of knighthood astride a bespectacled goat that stood without attachment to any base. The following year a less grotesque version on an oval base was made and a companion model of the *Tailor's Wife*[2] was added by J. F. Eberlein. The first Derby copies were made in the 1760s (E79), and subsequently were advertised in the *Sale Catalogue* of 17 April 1771:[3] 'One small pair Welch taylor and family riding goats, elegantly finish'd in flowers and burnish'd gold £1 0s 0d.' Three similar entries followed. John Twitchett reminds us that the title 'Welch' was appended owing to a misunderstanding of the German: *Schneider, welcher auf einem Ziegenbock reitet* ('A tailor who rides on a goat').

177 No. 62. *The Welch Tailor and his Family.* $9\frac{1}{2}$ in (24.1 cm). Incised 'No. 62'. *Venner's Antiques*

Examples

A Twitchett, op. cit., pl. 303. Enamelled, no size given, unmarked, Bloor Derby versions.

B Barrett and Thorpe, op. cit., pls. 123 and 124. Enamelled, $10\frac{1}{2}$ in (26.7 cm), Derby Museums and Art Gallery, ref. nos. 364, 365 and 359.

C Gilhespy, 1951, fig. 151. Enamelled, 6 in (15.2 cm), incised 'No. 62'.

D Christie's, *Sale Catalogue*, 5 June 1968, lot 297. Enamelled, 7 in (17.8 cm), incised 'No. 62'.

References

1 Berling, 1910, fig. 47. Meissen model of *Welch Tailor* c. 1737, by J. J. Kändler.

2 Ibid., fig. 8. Meissen model of the *Welch Tailor* c. 1738, by J. J. Kändler.
Table 15, no. 12. Meissen model of the *Tailor's Wife*, c. 1738, by J. F. Eberlein.

3 Twitchett, op. cit., p. 236.

No. 63. *Boy and Girl in Turkish Costumes* (pair)

HASLEM 'Small Turks: $3\frac{1}{2}$ ins., enamelled 5s od., biscuit 6s od.'
BEMROSE 'Turks, 3 sizes.'

The boy, attired in a turban, long jacket, sleeveless gown and boots, stands left hand on hip with his head turned to dexter. The companion girl wears a stocking-cap and long dress that she holds out with her left hand while making a gesture with her right. Mounted on mound bases edged with scrolls.

178 No. 63. *Boy and Girl in Turkish Costumes.* $3\frac{3}{4}$ in (9.5 cm). Incised 'No. 63'. *Private Collection*

The first Derby versions (E40) of about 1760 appeared as Blackamoors and followed Meissen originals of about 1740 by Eberlein. Shortly afterwards they were reissued with white faces as a pair of Turks[1] and similar models were created at Bow.[2] The greatly diminished size of the Chelsea–Derby examples may have been due to their having been cast from secondary moulds.

Examples

A Gilhespy, 1951, pl. 99, fig. 181. Enamelled, $3\frac{3}{4}$ in (9.5 cm), incised 'No. 63'.

B Sotheby's, *Sale Catalogue*, 29 January 1980, lot 25. Enamelled, $3\frac{3}{4}$ in (9.5 cm), incised 'No. 63'.

References

1 Twitchett, op. cit., pl. 42. Pair of *Turks*, enamelled, 8 in (20.3 cm), Royal Crown Derby Museum, no marks reported.

2 Anton Gabszewicz and Geoffrey Freeman, *Bow Porcelain – The Collection Formed by Geoffrey Freeman*, London, 1982, pl. 242. Bow group of *Turks*.

No. 64. *Not Identified*

HASLEM 'Four Standing Seasons: $5\frac{1}{2}$ ins., enamelled 18s od.'

BEMROSE 'Set of small seasons, 3 sizes.'

No. 65. *Diana with a Hunting-dog*

HASLEM 'Diana, 2 sizes: 1st. [9¾ ins.], enamelled £1 1s 0d., biscuit £1 4s 0d. 2nd 8½ ins., enamelled 14s 0d., biscuit not given.'
BEMROSE 'Dyanna [sic], 2 sizes.'

Diana with a crescentic ornament in her hair, wearing flowing robes gathered at the waist by a sash, and sandals, stands before a ruined column; she grasps a long-bow in her right hand and holds a leashed hound with her left. Mounted on a square base with chamfered corners.

This model replaced an earlier copy of a Meissen original by J. F. Eberlein[1] and was mentioned in the *Derby Sale Catalogue* of 5 May 1778:[2] 'One figure of Diana'. This lacks the dramatic impact of the earlier version.

Diana was the daughter of Jupiter and Leto and the sister of Apollo. She was a Mother Goddess and as such wore a crescent, emblematic of the Moon. The protector of women in childbirth, she was also the virgin huntress of the forests. Her silver bow was a gift from the Cyclopes (one-eyed giants), and her three hounds were presents from Pan. The chariot in which she rode was gold and drawn by horned hinds, watered from gilded troughs and fed upon the sacred clover from Juno's pasture. She demanded absolute chastity from her devotees and, when an attendant nymph became pregnant by Jupiter, Diana transformed her into a bear which, had not Jupiter intervened, would have been torn to pieces by her hounds. The wretched Actaeon, who stumbled accidentally upon the goddess bathing, whilst he was hunting, was metamorphosed into a stag and slain by his own pack of hunting dogs.

Examples

A Sotheby's, *Sale Catalogue*, 8 July 1980, lot 236. Biscuit, 10 in (25.4 cm), incised 'No. 65'.
B Ibid., 2 October 1972, lot 195. Enamelled, 9¾ in (24.8 cm), incised 'No. 65 G.'

References

1 John Dixon, *English Porcelain of the Eighteenth Century*, London, 1952, pl. 38.
2 Nightingale, op. cit., appendix, p. 53.

No. 66. *Venus and Cupid* (group)

HASLEM 'Venus and Cupid: 6½ ins., enamelled 10s 6d., biscuit 12s 0d.'
BEMROSE 'Venus.'

Venus is portrayed as a young woman, her hair piled high on her head secured by a ribbon, wearing a loose robe gathered at her waist by a sash. She stands barefoot

179 No. 65. *Diana with a Hunting-dog*. $9\frac{3}{4}$ in (24.8 cm). Incised 'No. 65'. *Sotheby's*

180 No. 66. *Venus and Cupid* (group). $7\frac{1}{2}$ in (19.1 cm). No incised number. Courtesy of the *Birmingham Museum and Art Gallery*

holding an apple aloft in her right hand while with her left she restrains Cupid who reaches upwards to grasp the forbidden fruit. Mounted on an irregular mound base.

It has been mentioned above how the dry-edge Derby *Venus and Cupid* (B30) followed Eberlein's Meissen original and was reissued (E67a and b) during the 1760s in larger and more elaborate forms. The first Chelsea–Derby example reverts to a smaller size (No. 66), and appears on a mound base, but was later reissued as No. 115, on a square base.

Venus, Goddess of Love, was the daughter of Jupiter and the sea-nymph, Dione, although some believe she arose from the ocean foam fertilized when the severed genitals of Cronus had been hurled into the deep. She was married to Vulcan yet enjoyed many torrid affairs with both gods and men. She shared a mutual passion with Mars, the fruit of which was their son Cupid. Her other children included Rhodus and Herophilus by Neptune, Hermaphroditus by Mercury and Priapus by Bacchus. Once when she was in the company of the shepherd, Adonis, she was accidentally scratched by one of Cupid's arrows and as a result became besotted with the youth until he was slain by a wild boar; from the ground upon which his blood was spilled there grew anemones.

Example
Birmingham Museum. Enamelled, $7\frac{1}{2}$ in (19.1 cm), incised 'No. 66'.

No. 67. *Not Identified*

HASLEM 'Venus, Chelsea Model.'
BEMROSE 'Small ewer.' Also: 'Small Term Vase.'

No. 68. *The Four Seasons* (two groups)

HASLEM 'Group of Four Seasons: $9\frac{1}{4}$ ins., enamelled £1 10s 0d, biscuit £1 18s 0d.'
BEMROSE 'Group of 4 musical figures.'

Two groups composed of two standing figures, each taken from the earlier set of four single models (No. 35), arranged on either side of a leafing tree upon a rocky mound.

Spring and Winter A girl with a basket of flowers over her arm holding a posy, and a sportsman with a gun.
Summer and Autumn A girl holding a cornsheaf, and a youth with grapes in his inverted hat and in one hand.

These figures were later reissued once more as a single group arranged about an obelisk (No. 294).

Examples

A Rackham, 1915, pl. 40, no. 417 (new no. 356). Enamelled, *Summer and Autumn* only, $8\frac{3}{4}$ in (22.2 cm), incised 'No. 68'.

B Christie's, *Sale Catalogue*, 22 November 1971, lot 56. Enamelled, *Spring and Winter* only, $8\frac{3}{4}$ in (22.2 cm), incised 'No. 68'.

C Phillips. Biscuit, $8\frac{3}{4}$ in (22.2 cm), incised 'No. 68', as illustrated.

181 No. 68. Two biscuit groups representing *The Four Seasons*. $8\frac{3}{4}$ in (22.2 cm). Incised 'No. 68'. *Spring and Winter* (right) and *Autumn and Summer* (left). *Phillips*

No. 69. *Gentleman with a Flute and Lady with a Lute* (pair)

HASLEM 'Sitting Flute Figures: $6\frac{2}{3}$ ins., enamelled 6s od.'
BEMROSE 'Grotesque seasons, small.'

This pair is a reissue of No. 11, mounted upon octagonal bases.

Example
Twitchett, op. cit., col. pl. 18. Enamelled, male figure only, $6\frac{1}{2}$ in (16.5 cm), incised 'No. 69'.

No. 70. *Not Identified*

HASLEM 'Figure of Christie: $12\frac{1}{2}$ ins., enamelled £1 5s od.'
BEMROSE No item mentioned.

The *Derby Sale Catalogues* of 18 and 19 February 1778[1] mention: 'One figure of Christ, in biscuit 11s od.'

Reference
1 Nightingale, op. cit., appendix, p. 50.

182 No. 71. *Boy Seated with Cat.*
183 No. 71. Companion *Girl* likewise *with Dog*. Both $5\frac{1}{2}$ in (14 cm). Incised 'No. 71'.
B. and T. Thorn Antiques

No. 71. *Boy Seated with Cat and Girl with Dog* (pair)

HASLEM 'Pair Sitting Figures, with Cat and Dog: $5\frac{1}{2}$ ins., enamelled 16s od., biscuit £1 5s od.'
BEMROSE 'Boy and girl sitting in chair.' Also: 'A vase.'

A bareheaded youth, wearing a jacket and breeches, sits in a brown wood ladder-back chair, stroking a cat. His companion, clad in a simple dress, sits likewise caressing a dog on her lap. Mounted on square bases encrusted with leaves and flowers.

Examples

A B. and T. Thorn, Budleigh Salterton. Enamelled, $5\frac{1}{2}$ in (14 cm), incised 'No. 71', as illustrated.

B Sotheby's, *Sale Catalogue*, 29 June 1965, lot 116. Biscuit, $5\frac{3}{4}$ in (14.6 cm), incised 'No. 71'.

184 No. 72. *Pastoral Group with Dog*. $5\frac{3}{8}$ in (13.7 cm). Incised 'No. 72'.
D. M. and P. Manheim Ltd.

No. 72. *Pastoral Group with Dog* (group)

HASLEM 'Pastoral Group with a Goat: $5\frac{3}{8}$ ins., enamelled 12s od.'
BEMROSE No item mentioned.

A gallant sits cross-legged upon a grassy mound holding the hand of a shepherdess in his left hand and with his right arm about her waist as she stands beside him. A leafing tree is behind the couple and a spaniel lies at their feet. Mounted on an irregular-shaped mound base.

Examples

A Sotheby's, *Sale Catalogue*, 21 July 1970, lot 302. Enamelled, $5\frac{1}{2}$ in (14 cm), incised 'No. 72'.

B Ibid., 26 October 1971, lot 121. Similar to the above.

C D. M. and P. Manheim Ltd., London. Enamelled, $5\frac{3}{4}$ in (14.6 cm), no marks reported, as illustrated.

185 No. 73. *Pastoral Group with Dog and Lamb.* $5\frac{1}{2}$ in (14 cm). *Sotheby's*

No. 73. *Pastoral Group with Dog and Lamb* (group)

HASLEM 'Pastoral Group with a Dog: $5\frac{3}{8}$ ins., enamelled 12s od.'
BEMROSE 'Small group, boy and girl.'

A bareheaded lady attired in a fine gown sits upon a grassy mound stroking a lamb that lies in her lap while restraining with her left hand a gallant who stoops to caress her cheek; a dog sits looking away from the couple.

This group may have been inspired by an engraving after the painting by François Boucher entitled *Le Mouton Favorite* and was probably intended as a pair to 'No. 72'.

Examples

A Arthur Lane, *English Porcelain Figures of the Eighteenth Century*, London, 1961, pl. 70A. Enamelled, 6 in (15.2 cm), no marks reported, Victoria and Albert Museum.

B Sotheby's, *Sale Catalogue*, 26 October 1971, lot 121. Enamelled, $5\frac{1}{2}$ in (14 cm), incised 'No. 73' and 'G'.

No. 74. *Dancing Group* (group)

HASLEM 'Dancing Group: $6\frac{1}{2}$ ins., enamelled 12s od.'
BEMROSE 'Dancing group.'

A reissue of No. 16.

Example

Derby Museums and Art Gallery, ref. no. 1436. Enamelled, $6\frac{1}{2}$ in (16.5 cm), incised 'No. 74'.

No. 75. *Procris and Cephalus* (group)

HASLEM 'Group of Cephalus and Procris: $8\frac{1}{2}$ ins., enamelled £1 1s od.'
BEMROSE No item mentioned.

Cephalus, clad in a short tunic, breeches and sandals, stoops over his wife, Procris, who dying reclines against a tree-trunk, her left breast transfixed by an arrow. Mounted upon an oval base before a leafing tree.

The group was adapted from Noel Mire's engraving, after Charles Monnet's painting, illustrating the second volume of Le Mire and Basan's edition of Ovid's *Metâmorphoses*, published in 1768.[1] The *Derby Sale Catalogues* of 5–8 May 1778[2] mention: 'One pair of elegant flower pots enamelled in compartments with

Cephalus and Procris, Renaldo and Armida, in fine ultramarine blue and gold £4 0s 0d.'

When Venus caught the minor goddess, Eos, in bed with her beloved Mars, she cursed her with an insatiable sexual appetite for men. Eos first chose Ganymede but he was abducted by Jupiter. Next she seduced Tithonus and begged Jupiter to grant him eternal life, but she forgot to ask also for his eternal youth and in time he grew old and impotent. Eos then took Cephalus, son of Mercury and Herse, but he had recently married Procris and steadfastly repulsed her overtures. However, before she released him, Eos intimated that his wife's favours might readily be purchased for gold and he, anxious to test her, came to her in disguise proffering gold crowns when, to his dismay, she led him to her couch. Procris, then recognizing her husband, fled in shame to Diana, who gave her a javelin that never missed its mark and a hound which never lost the scent of a quarry. Procris returned to Cephalus incognito and offered him these gifts, provided he acceded to her charms. He accepted the bargain and there ensued mutual recriminations and

186 No. 75. *Group Portraying Procris and Cephalus* (right). No. 76. *Renaldo and Armida* (left). Both $8\frac{7}{8}$ in (21.6 cm). Incised respectively 'No. 75' and 'No. 76'. *Victoria and Albert Museum*

reconciliation. Many years afterwards Procris overheard Cephalus talking in endearing terms to the West Wind and, believing that Zephyr was the name of his mistress, decided to follow him when he next went out hunting. She concealed herself behind a bush but when Cephalus saw it move, thinking it was a wild boar, he hurled his javelin and slew his wife. The javelin of the myth is replaced in the porcelain model by an arrow.

Examples

A Twitchett, op. cit., pl. 149. Enamelled, $8\frac{7}{8}$ in (21.6 cm), incised 'No. 75'. Victoria and Albert Museum, ref. no. 180–1874, as illustrated.

B Gilhespy, 1951, op. cit., pl. 84, fig. 153. Enamelled, 7 in (17.8 cm), incised 'No. 75'. Birmingham Museum.

References

1 William King (B), 'Two Chelsea–Derby Groups and their Prototypes', *Connoisseur*, 69, 1924, pp. 211–13; no. I, Derby group; no. IV, Noel Mire's engraving.

2 Nightingale, op. cit., appendix, p. 52.

No. 76. *Renaldo and Armida* (group)

HASLEM 'Group of Renaldo and Armida: $8\frac{1}{2}$ ins., enamelled £1 1s od.'
BEMROSE 'Large group.' Also: 'French flower pots, 2 sizes.'

The comely youth Renaldo, wearing a cuirass, breeches and boots, lies asleep beneath a leafing tree, his shield and his sword at his side. The sorceress Armida stoops to cover him with leaves and flowers.

In Canto XIV of the narrative poem, *Gerusalemme Liberata*, published about 1575 by Torquato Tasso (1544–95), the sorceress Armida, bent upon the destruction of Renaldo, comes across him asleep and at her mercy in her enchanted garden. She is about to place a terrible curse upon him when she is overwhelmed by his beauty and, after covering him with flowers, passes on her way. The Derby model follows an engraving by Pierre de Bailliu after Van Dyck that illustrated a seventeenth-century edition of the work.

Examples

A Twitchett, op. cit., pl. 149. Enamelled, $8\frac{7}{8}$ in (21.6 cm), incised 'No. 76'. Victoria and Albert Museum, ref. no. 180–1874, as illustrated.

B Sotheby's, *Sale Catalogue*, 19 October 1970, lot 72. Similar example.

C Christie's, *Sale Catalogue*, 22 November 1971, lot 55. Similar example.

Reference

1 King, 1924, p. 212, no. II. Enamelled, $8\frac{1}{2}$ in (21.6 cm), incised 'No. 76'; no. III. Engraving by P. de Bailliu.

187 No. 77. *Stocking-mender Group*, c 1820. $7\frac{1}{2}$ in (19.1 cm). Incised 'No. 77'. *B and T. Thorn Antiques*

No. 77. *Stocking-mender Group*

HASLEM 'Stocking Mending: [$7\frac{1}{2}$ ins.], enamelled 12s 6d., biscuit 18s 0d.'
BEMROSE 'Stocking mender.'

A servant girl, wearing a crimped cap, blouse, apron and skirt, squats upon the ground to darn the left stocking upon the leg of a standing gallant.

This group, together with Nos. 78, 81 and 84, were based upon a set of biscuit Sèvres originals entitled *En Grande Toilette*, made by Etienne-Maurice Falconet about 1765. Early Derby copies of about 1779 are extremely rare and are mounted upon irregular mound bases. They are mentioned in the *Sale Catalogues* of 5–8 May 1779:[1] 'A pair of groups, shoemaker and stocking mender, in biscuit 12s 0d.' Most surviving examples date to the Bloor period and are mounted on oval bases with pierced scrollwork.

Examples

A Sotheby's, *Sale Catalogue*, 10 February 1981, lot 333. Biscuit, $6\frac{3}{4}$ in (17.1 cm), incised 'No. 77'.

B Ibid., 23 October 1979, lot 209. Enamelled, $6\frac{1}{2}$ in (16.5 cm), incised 'No. 77', c. 1820, Bloor period.

C Derby Museums and Art Gallery. Enamelled, $7\frac{1}{2}$ in (19.1 cm), incised 'No. 77', c. 1820.

Reference

1 Nightingale, op. cit., appendix, p. 56.

No. 78. *Shoe-maker Group*

HASLEM 'Shoemaker group of two Figures: $5\frac{7}{8}$ ins., enamelled 12s 0d., biscuit 18s 0d.'

BEMROSE 'Shoemaker.'

188 No. 78. *Shoe-maker Group*, c. 1820. $7\frac{1}{2}$ in (19.1 cm). Incised 'No. 78'. *B. and T. Thorn Antiques*

189 No. 78. *Shoe-maker Group*, c. 1775. $7\frac{3}{4}$ in (19.7 cm). Incised 'No. 78'. *Private Collection*

A bareheaded cobbler squats upon his right knee to fit a shoe to the left foot of an elegant lady who, standing on her right leg, holds on to a tree-trunk for support with one hand.

This group was issued en suite with Nos. 77, 81 and 84.

Examples

A Barrett and Thorpe, op. cit., pl. 131. Bloor enamelled, $6\frac{1}{2}$ in (16.5 cm), incised 'No. 78'. Derby Museum, ref. no. 346, as illustrated.

B Sotheby's, *Sale Catalogue*, 23 October 1979, lot 209. Bloor, enamelled, $7\frac{1}{2}$ in (19.1 cm), incised 'No. 78'.

Nos. 79 and 80. *Not Identified*

HASLEM No. 79. 'Complimenting Group of two: $6\frac{3}{4}$ ins., enamelled 13s od.'

No. 80. 'Spinning Group of two: size not given, enamelled 12s od.'

BEMROSE No. 79. No item mentioned. No. 80. 'Large oval vases, 2 sizes.'

No. 81. *Shoe-black Group*

HASLEM 'Shoeblack, Group of two: [$6\frac{1}{2}$ ins.], enamelled 12s od., biscuit 18s od.'

BEMROSE 'Shoeblack.'

A servant girl, wearing a linen cap, dress and apron, kneels to polish the right shoe of a standing gallant whose foot is resting upon a foot-stool.

Group issued en suite with Nos. 77, 78 and 84.

Examples

A Sotheby's, *Sale Catalogue*, 23 October 1979, lot 209. Enamelled, Bloor period, $6\frac{1}{2}$ in (16.5 cm), incised 'No. 81'.

B Gilhespy, 1951, fig. 63. Enamelled, Bloor period, $6\frac{1}{2}$ in (16.5 cm), incised 'No. 81'.

C Twitchett, op. cit., pl. 136. A rare early example, enamelled, $6\frac{3}{8}$ in (16.2 cm), no mark reported. Hermitage Museum, Leningrad, ref. no. 19871.

No. 82. *Not Identified*

HASLEM 'Fury Group, Broken Fiddle: $8\frac{1}{2}$ ins., enamelled, no price quoted.

BEMROSE 'Fury group, 2 figures.'

This group is presumably a pair to No. 83.

190 No. 81. *Shoe-black Group*, c. 1820. $7\frac{1}{2}$ in (19.1 cm). Incised 'No. 81'.
See also Plate XVIII. *B. and T. Thorn Antiques*

191 No. 83. *Fury Group with Broken Chair*. $5\frac{1}{2}$ in (14 cm). Incised 'No. 83'. *Sotheby's*

No. 83. *Fury Group with Broken Chair* (group)

HASLEM 'Fury Group, Broken Chair.'
BEMROSE No item mentioned.

A family quarrel in which the husband is shown reclining upon the wreckage of a broken chair, vainly attempting to ward off with his left arm a series of punches directed at him by his irate wife. Mounted upon an oval mound base.

The group is a mirror image adaptation of an original Frankenthal one made about 1762 by Karl Gottlieb Lück, entitled *Discord in Marriage.*[1] The prototype was paired with a second group, *Harmony in Marriage,*[2] which appears to have been ignored by the Derby modellers.

Example

Bradley, op. cit., no. 45. Enamelled, $5\frac{1}{2}$ in (14 cm), no marks reported. Victoria and Albert Museum, ref. no. 3016–1901.

References

1 Erica, Pauls-Eisenbeiss, *German Porcelain of the Eighteenth Century*, London, 1972, II, p. 172, *Discord in Marriage* by K. G. Lück.

2 Ibid., pp. 170–1, *Harmony in Marriage* by K. G. Lück.

No. 84. *Hairdresser Group*

HASLEM 'Hairdresser Group, two Figures: Size not given, enamelled 12s 0d., biscuit 18s 0d.'

BEMROSE 'Hairdresser.'

192 No. 84. *Hairdresser Group*. $7\frac{1}{4}$ in (18.4 cm). Incised 'No. 84'. See also Plate XVIII.
B. and T. Thorn Antiques

A group composed of a seated lady, wearing a fine gown, with a towel about her shoulders, having her hair dressed by a male servant who stands, clad in waistcoat, cravat, jacket and breeches. Mounted on a flower-encrusted mound base.

This group was issued en suite with Nos. 77, 78 and 81.

Examples

A Gilhespy, 1961, op. cit., fig. 63. Biscuit, 8 in (20.3 cm), no marks reported.

B Sotheby's, *Sale Catalogue*, 31 July 1979, lot 92. Enamel, 6¾ in (17.1 cm), incised 'No. 84'. Bloor Derby example.

C Twitchett, op. cit., pl. 395. Enamelled, 7 in (17.8 cm), incised 'No. 84'. Victoria and Albert Museum, ref. no. C.1302–1919.

Nos. 85 and 86. *Not Identified*

HASLEM No. 85. 'Macaroni: Size not given, enamelled 14s 0d.' No. 86. 'Set of Elements, in Groups of two figures each: Size not given, enamelled £2 2s 0d.'

BEMROSE No. 85. 'Macaroni.' No. 86. 'Pair boy and girl sitting on baskets.' Also: 'Four Elements groups.' Also: 'Large Term vase.'

No. 87. *Pair of Salutation Figures* (pair)

HASLEM 'Pair of Salutation Figures: 4¾ ins., enamelled 7s 0d.'

BEMROSE No item mentioned.

A bareheaded lady, wearing a fine gown, standing with a fan in her right hand and holding out the edge of her over-skirt with her left. No example of the male companion model is known to the author.

Example

Sotheby's, *Sale Catalogue*, 18 May 1982, lot 109. Enamelled, 7 in (17.8 cm), incised 'No. 87'.

No. 88. *Mrs Catherine Macaulay*

HASLEM 'Mrs. Catherine Macaulay.'

BEMROSE No item mentioned.

A portrait model of Mrs Catherine Macaulay, standing bareheaded attired in classical robes with a cloak draped over her right arm. She holds a quill in her hand and rests her right elbow upon a pile of books placed on a pedestal, while with her left she has a scroll inscribed 'Bill of Rights'. Early versions are on mound

193 No. 88. Biscuit figure of *Mrs Catherine Macaulay* with parcel gilt and blue enamel embellishments. 12 in (30.5 cm). Incised 'No. 88'. *Derby Museums and Art Gallery*

bases, later examples are on octagonal bases decorated in low relief with the Greek key-fret pattern.

The model was once thought to have been adapted from a marble by J. F. Moor, but John Mallet[1] pointed out that the description of this work in the *Dictionary of National Biography* does not accord with the appearance of the model so that, if this is correct, some other source must have been employed. The *Derby Sale*

Catalogues of 17–20 April 1780[2] mention: 'One figure of Mrs. Macaulay in biscuit and fine blue and gold 19s od.'

Catherine Macaulay (1731–91) was author of *The History of England from the Accession of the Stuarts*, the first volume of which appeared in 1763. This was a largely imaginative work in which she expressed her political opinions. Indeed, she was a notorious leveller whose name became linked with that of the rascally John Wilkes (No. 126). However, he evidently held her in no great esteem, for once when they met as she was returning from Paris, he described her as 'Painted up to the eyes and looking as rotten as an old Catharine pear'.[3] Dr Samuel Johnson wrote about her: 'One day when I was at her house I put on a very grave countenance and said, "Madam, I am now become a convert to your way of thinking. I am convinced that all mankind are upon equal footing; and I give you this unquestionable proof, Madam, that I am in earnest, here is a very sensible, civil, well behaved fellow citizen, your footman; I desire that he may be allowed to sit down to dine with us . . ." She never liked me since.'[4]

The lady retired to Bath in 1774[5] and took up residence in the home of the Rev. Dr Thomas Wilson, one-time Chaplain to George III and absentee Vicar of St Stephen's, Walbrook. He became besotted with her and commissioned J. F. Moor to sculpt her in the likeness of the Muse, Clio, which in due course was erected in the chancel of his church. Mrs Macaulay later became friendly with the Scottish quack, Dr Graham, who was the proud inventor of the 'Celestial Bed' which he set up in a 'Temple of Hymen', in London. When Catherine unexpectedly wed the good doctor's younger brother, James, then twenty-one years old, the marble statue was hurriedly removed.

Examples

A J. V. G. Mallet, *The Bearsted Collection: Porcelain*, Plaistow, 1964, no. 55. Enamelled, 13 in (33 cm), incised 'No. 88'. Octagonal base decorated with Greek key-fret.

B King, 1925, fig. 54. Biscuit, 13 in (33 cm), octagonal base.

C Derby Museum, ref. nos. 295 and 294. Biscuit with blue and gold embellishments, 12 in (30.5 cm), incised 'No. 88'.

References

1 Mallet, op. cit., pp. 18–19.
2 Nightingale, op. cit., appendix, p. 60.
3 Mallet, op. cit., pp. 18 19.
4 J. B. Hill (ed.), *Boswell's Life of Johnson*, London, 1891.
5 David Gadd, *Georgian Summer, Bath in the Eighteenth Century*, Bradford-on-Avon, 1971, pp. 162–3.

No. 89. *The Unfaithful Husband* (group)

HASLEM 'Fury Group Family.'
BEMROSE No item mentioned.

The wife, clad in a fine dress, stands confronting her husband, her left hand upon her hip and her right fist clenched. He stands with both hands clasped before him, his knees bent, looking guilty, whilst the cause for the dispute, a servant girl, weeps and holds a handkerchief to her eyes. Mounted on an octagonal base.

194 No. 89. Biscuit group of *The Unfaithful Husband*. $5\frac{1}{2}$ in (14 cm). Incised 'No. 89'.
Klaber and Klaber

Examples

A Klaber and Klaber, Kensington Church Street, London. Biscuit, $5\frac{1}{2}$ in (14 cm), incised 'No. 89', as illustrated.

B Sotheby's, *Sale Catalogue*, 9 July 1968, lot 114. Enamelled, $5\frac{3}{4}$ in (14.6 cm), incised 'No. 89' and 'Size 3'. Here the servant girl is identified as the daughter of the quarrelling couple!

No. 90. *A Cook*

HASLEM 'Cook and Companion.'
BEMROSE 'Cook and companion.'

A male cook wearing a cap, jacket, apron and breeches stands with a kitchen pot attached to the front of his belt, supporting an object (missing) with both hands upon a pole-like support. Mounted before a tree-stump on a mound base. The companion model has not yet been identified.

The model is possibly based on the Meissen *Street Cook with a Turkey*, of 1757, by Peter Reinicke, after a watercolour sketch by Christophe Huet.[1]

Example

Aldbury Antiques, Blockley. Enamelled, $8\frac{1}{4}$ in (21 cm), incised 'No. 90', as illustrated.

Reference

1 Len Adams and Yvonne Adams, *Meissen Portrait Figures*, London, Melbourne, Auckland and Johannesburg, 1987, p. 109, col. pl. xxxi.

No. 91. *Two Female Macaronis* (group)

HASLEM 'Female Macaroni: $7\frac{3}{4}$ ins., enamelled, 14s 0d.'
BEMROSE 'Macaroni.'

A pair of young ladies attired in flamboyant dress. One wears a huge bonnet, a fur-trimmed cloak, and a dress with a divided over-skirt revealing a floral petticoat beneath, and stands with her hands concealed in a fur muff. Her companion has an elaborate coiffure and is clad in a fine dress with a flounced petticoat edged with lace.

Example

Sotheby's, *Sale Catalogue*, 16 March 1983, lot 127. Enamelled, $7\frac{1}{2}$ in (19.1 cm), incised 'No. 91', as illustrated.

195 No. 90. *A Cook*. $8\frac{1}{4}$ in (21 cm). Incised 'No. 90'. *Aldbury Antiques*

196 No. 91. *Two Female Macaronis* (group). $7\frac{1}{2}$ in (19.1 cm). Incised 'No. 91'. *Sotheby's*

No. 92. *Three Figures Learning Music* (group)

HASLEM 'Three Figures learning Music.'
BEMROSE 'Fencer.' Also 'Small ewer, 2 sizes.'

A young lady clad in a brimmed hat and dress sits upon a grassy mound playing an end-flute. A male companion wearing a hat and contemporary attire sits at her right side, his left arm about her shoulders, while he points with his right forefinger to the musical score. Mounted upon a mound base encrusted with leaves and flowers which has a tongue-like projection in front supporting a third figure of a seated bagpiper.

François Boucher (1701–70) painted *L'Agréable Leçon* in 1748 portraying a bareheaded swain seated on the left of a peasant girl, holding an end-flute with his left hand to her lips, and with his right arm about her shoulders guiding with his right hand her fingers upon the stops of the instrument. This was engraved by René Gaillard and provided the basis for a biscuit Sèvres group by Étienne-

197 No. 92. *Three Figures Learning Music* (group). 8 in. (20.3 cm). Incised 'No. 92'. *Weston Park Museum*

198 *The Music Lesson*, Chelsea, c. 1765. 15 in (38.1 cm). *Sotheby's*
199 *La Leçon Agréable*, Sèvres, c. 1756. *Sotheby's*

Maurice Falconet.[1] An enamelled version was made by J. F. Lück at Frankenthal about 1759[2] as well as a gold anchor Chelsea version by Joseph Willems of about 1765[3] in which the figures were transposed. It seems likely that one of these groups prompted the Chelsea–Derby version though there are obvious dissimilarities. An accurate Derby copy of the Sèvres group (F28) has recently been identified.

Examples

A Weston Park Museum, Sheffield. Enamelled, 8 in (20.3 cm), incised 'No. 92', as illustrated.

B *Antique Dealer and Collector's Guide*, April 1974, p. 10. Enamelled, no size given and no marks cited.

References

1 Bradshaw, op. cit., pl. 50B. Sèvres biscuit group.

2 Peter Wilhelm Meister and Horst Reber, *European Porcelain of the Eighteenth Century*, Oxford, 1983, pl. 363. Frankenthal group.

3 Bradshaw, op. cit., pl. 50A. Gold anchor Chelsea group.

No. 93. *Children Playing Hazard* (group)

HASLEM 'Group of three figures playing hazard: 6 ins., enamelled £1 1s 0d.'
BEMROSE 'Children Group.'

A group of three children standing bareheaded about a fortune-telling wheel that resembles a sun-dial with a revolving pointer, supported upon a drum-like base. A boy operates the pointer, a girl stoops forward to observe the result, while a third child looks on. A crouching dog and a basket of fruit are at their feet. Mounted on an irregular pad base.

A painting by François Boucher of about 1736, entitled *Country Fair*, was engraved by Charles-Nicolas Cochin[1] which includes both the group of children playing hazard and another portraying a peep-show, together with some twenty-five other figures. Étienne-Maurice Falconet based his Sèvres biscuit group *Le Tourniquet présenté à la Foire par le Marchand de Plaisirs, ou La Loterie* on this engraving, but with modification of both major and minor details.[2] The plaster model may be seen in Cliché des Musées Nationaux.[3] This was issued about 1760. The *Derby Sale Catalogue* of 18 February 1778, includes:[4] 'One group of a galantee show, and one ditto playing hazard, in biscuit £1 12s 6d.'

200 No. 93. *Children Playing Hazard*, c. 1780. $5\frac{1}{2}$ in (14 cm). Incised 'No. 93'. *Klaber and Klaber*

Examples

A *Antique Dealer and Collector's Guide*, February 1983, p. 9. Enamelled, $5\frac{1}{2}$ in (14 cm), incised 'No. 93'. Advertisement for Klaber and Klaber, as illustrated.

B Shepherd Antiques, late of Buxton. Enamelled, $5\frac{1}{2}$ in (14 cm), incised 'No. 93'.

References

1 George Levitine, *The Sculpture of Falconet*, New York, 1972, pl. 47, *Country Fair*, engraved by C.-N. Cochin after Boucher.

2 E. Bourgeois and Georges Lechevallier-Chevignard, op. cit., no. 380, pl. 6, *La Loterie* by E. M. Falconet.

3 Levitine, op. cit., pl. 46. Plaster model of *La Loterie* in the Cliché des Musées Nationaux.

4 Nightingale, op. cit., appendix, p. 50.

No. 94. *Children at a Peep-show* (group)

HASLEM 'Group of three figures at a Raree Show: 6 ins., enamelled £1 1s 0d.'
BEMROSE No item mentioned.

A boy clad in a brimmed hat, scarf, jacket and breeches, stands turning the handle of a peep-show acting as showman. A girl stoops to peer at the viewing panel while a small child accompanied by a dog and with a basket of dairy products at her feet, attempts to attract her attention. Mounted upon an irregular pad base.

201 No. 94. *Children at a Peep-show*, c. 1775. $5\frac{1}{2}$ in (14 cm). Incised 'No. 94'. *Fitzwilliam Museum*

The group is complementary to No. 93 and also echoes a biscuit Sèvres group of Étienne-Maurice Falconet[1] adapted from an engraving by Charles-Nicolas Cochin entitled *La Lanterne Magique montrée à la Foire par le Savoyard, ou La Curiosité.*[2] The *Derby Sale Catalogue* of 18 February 1778[3] mentions this group. The two groups Nos. 93 and 94 continued to be reissued well into the nineteenth century and some later Bloor versions omit from the *Peep-show* group the figure of the standing child.[4]

Examples

A Bradley, op. cit., no. 44. Enamelled Bloor Derby example, $5\frac{1}{2}$ in (14 cm), incised 'No. 94', red crown and D mark.

B Barrett and Thorpe, op. cit., pl. 121. Bloor Derby example, $5\frac{1}{2}$ in (14 cm), incised 'No. 94'.

References

1 Bourgeoise and Lechevallier-Chevignard, op. cit., no. 308, pl. 6, *La Lanterne Magique* by Falconet.
2 Levitine, op. cit., pl. 47, *Country Fair*, engraved by C.-N. Cochin.
3 Nightingale, op. cit., appendix, p. 50.
4 Bradley, op. cit., no. 44.

202 No. 94. *Three Children at a Peep-show*, c. 1820 version. $5\frac{1}{2}$ in (14 cm).
Incised 'No. 94'.
Derby Museums and Art Gallery

Nos. 95–8 *Not Identified*

HASLEM No. 95. 'Sphinx Candlestick.' No. 96. 'Sphinx Vase.' No. 97. 'Griffin Vase.' No. 98. 'Group of Prudence and Discretion: 11½ ins., enamelled £2 2s 0d.'
BEMROSE No. 95. 'Sphinx and griffin candlesticks, 3 sizes.' No. 96. No item mentioned. No. 97. 'Vase supported by 3 griffins.' 'No. 98. 'Small ewer.' Also: 'Hydra.'

No. 99. *Aesculapius and Hygeia* (pair)

HASLEM 'Pair of Figures, Aesculapius and Hygeia: 7½ ins., enamelled 16s 0d., biscuit 18s 0d.'
BEMROSE 'Esculapius [sic] and companion.' Also: 'Small ewer.'

Aesculapius portrayed as a bearded youth clad in loose robes, stands bareheaded and barefoot, a scroll in his right hand, the forefinger of which rests upon his chin; a rustic club is at his side. Hygeia also stands bareheaded, a cloak draped from her right shoulder, carrying in her right hand a serpent and in her left a basin containing the bile of Medusa. Mounted on a rectangular pair of bases.

Timothy Clifford[1] suggested the figure of Aesculapius may have been a transposed adaptation of the Farnese Hercules, and noted how a club replaces the more customary caduceus. The models are mentioned in the *Derby Sale Catalogue* of 5 May 1779:[2] 'A pair of Aesculapius and Hygaea [sic].' This date is far too early for them to have been created by Rossi though it seems later versions may stem from his hand. In 1793 Lygo wrote in a letter to William Duesbury II:[3] 'Been with Mr. Vulliamy about a pair of figures modelled by Rossi. The drawing of the figure you have sent me is done for Aesculapius and is meant to hold a serpent. The other female figure is out of one of Mr. Vulliamy's books.' It may be noted that it is Hygeia and not Aesculapius who holds the serpent, while the source of the model of the goddess was probably *Thorp's Book of Ornament*.

Aesculapius was the son of Apollo and Coronis, daughter of the king of the Lapiths. While pregnant by Apollo, Coronis was unfaithful and was immediately slain with an arrow from Diana's long-bow. The child was born by Caesarian section after her death and reared by the centaur, Cheiron, who instructed him in the healing arts. Some time later Aesculapius wearied of curing the sick and instead began to raise the dead. Pluto complained to his brother Jupiter that he was being robbed of his subjects, and the Supreme Deity immediately struck the offender dead with a thunderbolt.

The title Hygeia was assumed by the goddess Minerva after she had miraculously

203 No. 99. *Aesculapius.* $6\frac{3}{8}$ in (16.2 cm). Incised 'No. 99'. *Victoria and Albert Museum*

204 No. 100. *Andromache Weeping over the Ashes of Hector.* $8\frac{1}{2}$ in (21.6 cm). Incised 'No. 100'.
Derby Museums and Art Gallery

saved the lives of Mnesicles and his friend who had fallen from a roof-top into the street in Propylae. The physic that she administered was the bile of the gorgon Medusa that had been given to her by Perseus.

Examples

A Clifford, 1969, pl. 126c. Biscuit model of *Aesculapius*, 10 in (25.4 cm), no marks reported, rectangular base. Victoria and Albert Museum, ref. no. C.305–1931.

B Rackham, 1915, pl. 40, no. 415 (new no. 351). Enamelled model of *Aesculapius*, $6\frac{3}{8}$ in (16.2 cm), incised 'No. 99', as illustrated.

C Sotheby's, *Sale Catalogue*, 12 May 1981, lots 143 and 144. White glazed models of *Aesculapius* and *Hygeia*, 10 in (25.4 cm), square bases. These were identified as 'Staffordshire' and the model of Aesculapius is transposed from the Derby biscuit version.

References

1 Clifford, 1969, p. 115.
2 Nightingale, op. cit., appendix, p. 56.
3 Gilhespy, 1961, op. cit., p. 67.

No. 100. *Andromache Weeping over the Ashes of Hector*

HASLEM 'Andromache weeping over the ashes of Hector: $9\frac{1}{4}$ ins., enamelled £1 10s 0d., biscuit £1 11s 6d.'

BEMROSE 'Large figure of Andromache weeping over the ashes of Hector, 2 sizes.' No further details mentioned.

Andromache, wearing a veil and classical robes, stands sorrowfully with a handkerchief in her left dependent hand, leaning with her right forearm upon a covered urn upon which she rests her head; she holds a laurel wreath in her right hand. Mounted upon a rectangular base.

The model was inspired by Thomas Burke's engraving *Andromache and Hecuba weeping over the ashes of Hector*, after Angelica Kauffmann[1], of about 1772. The *Derby Sale Catalogues* of 17–20 April 1780[2] mention: 'One figure Andromache weeping over the ashes of Hector'. A similar model was made about 1778 at Richard Champion's Bristol factory, and one such example is inscribed as a funerary memorial to the proprietor's daughter, Eliza Champion, who died on 13 October 1779, at the tender age of fourteen.

Andromache married Hector, the son of Priam, King of Troy, and Queen Hecuba. During the siege of that city by the Achaeans, Hector sought out their champion, Achilles, hoping to engage him in single combat. Knowing his adversary had earlier withdrawn from the hostilities and might be in poor physical training,

Hector induced him to chase him three times about the city walls, hoping thereby to tire him. The stratagem failed, for Achilles overtook him and slew him with his spear. Stripping the corpse of its armour, Achilles dragged it behind his chariot thrice around Troy for the horrified inhabitants to see, before hurling the remains to the dogs. King Priam went secretly by night to the Achaean lines and after ransoming Hector's body for its weight in gold, brought it back to the city where the appropriate funerary rites were observed. When Troy eventually fell, Andromache hurled her own son, Scamandrius, from the walls to his death and lived out her declining years with Helenus, one of Hector's brothers.

Examples

A Twitchett, op. cit., pl. 151. Enamelled, $8\frac{5}{8}$ in (22 cm), no marks reported. Victoria and Albert Museum, ref. no. C.234–1922.

B Sotheby's, *Sale Catalogue*, 29 January 1980, lot 39. Enamelled, $10\frac{1}{2}$ in (26.7 cm), incised 'No. 100'.

C Derby Museum. Enamelled, $8\frac{1}{2}$ in (21.6 cm), incised 'No. 100'. Illustrated in *Apollo*, June 1955, p. 78.

References

1 Bernard Watney, 'Some Parallels and Proto-types in Ceramics', *Trans. ECC*, 10, 1980, part 5, pl. 157c, engraving by Thomas Burke of *Andromache and Queen Hecuba weeping over the ashes of Hector*; pl. 157b, Richard Champion's Bristol model of *Andromache*.

2 Nightingale, op. cit., appendix, p. 58.

3 Llewellyn Jewitt, *The Ceramic Art of Great Britain* (revised edition), London and New York, 1983, p. 227, fig. 759. Champion's Bristol model of *Andromache* inscribed as a funerary memorial to Eliza Champion.

No. 101. *Boy Eating an Apple and Girl Curds-and-Whey* (pair)

HASLEM 'Pair, Grotesque Boy and Girl: $4\frac{1}{2}$ ins., enamelled 5s 0d.'
BEMROSE 'Pair small figures.'

Two children standing bareheaded. The boy has a basket of fruit over his left arm and eats an apple; the girl eats curds-and-whey from a wooden bowl with a spoon. Mounted on mound bases encrusted with leaves and flowers.

Examples

A Twitchett, op. cit., pl. 335. Female figure only, enamelled, $4\frac{1}{2}$ in (11.4 cm), no marks reported.

B Sotheby's, *Catalogue*, 21 March 1972, lot 13. Enamelled pair, $4\frac{1}{2}$ in (11.4 cm), incised 'No. 101'.

C Aldbury Antiques, Blockley. Enamelled, $4\frac{1}{2}$ in (11.4 cm), incised 'No. 101', as illustrated.

205 No. 101. *Boy Eating an Apple and Girl Curds-and-Whey*. $4\frac{1}{4}$ in (11.4 cm). Incised 'No. 101'.
B. and T. Thorn Antiques

Nos. 102–113. *Monks and Nuns* (pairs and groups)

HASLEM 'Twelve figures of Nuns and Monks.'

BEMROSE Nos. 102, 103, 105–8, 110 and 112–13, no items mentioned. No. 104. 'Six small vases.' No. 109. 'Dominican.' No. 111. 'A father confessor.'

Few surviving examples bear incised numbers, while sometimes two identical models will be numbered differently.

Nos. 102–5 are pairs of *Monk* and *Nun* seated upon studded coffers, reading from books, 4–$5\frac{1}{2}$ in (10.2–14 cm), enamelled, showing minor variations. For example, the book may be held in either or both hands whilst monks may have tonsured heads exposed or covered by a cowl.

Examples

A *Monk and Nun* with books held in both hands, enamelled, 4 in (10.2 cm), incised 'No. 102'. Sotheby's, *Sale Catalogue*, 1 April 1980, lot 177.

B *Monk* holding book in right and *Nun* in left hand, $4\frac{1}{2}$ in (11.4 cm), enamelled, incised 'No. 102'. Jupiter Antiques.

C *Monk* holding book in both hands, his tonsured head bare, enamelled, 4½ in (11.4 cm), incised 'No. 104', enamelled, 4½ in (11.4 cm). Ibid.

D *Monk* with head covered with his cowl, holding a book in his left hand, 4½ in (11.4 cm), enamelled, incised 'No. 105'. Gilhespy, 1951, pl. 85, fig. 155.

E *Monk* and *Nun*, with cowl and veil, with books held in both hands, enamelled, 7½ in (19.1 cm), no marks. Venner's Antiques, as illustrated.

Possibly Nos. 109 and 110. A Monk standing with a pointed cowl over his head, his habit gathered by a belt, standing among tomes and holding a rosary in one hand and a skull in the other. Companion *Abbess* standing displaying the text of an open book while making a gesture, seemingly to emphasize a quotation, with her right hand.

Examples

A John Cushion, *English Porcelain*, London, 1974, fig. 152. *Standing Monk and Abbess*, enamelled, neither measurements nor marks reported.

B *Monk*, enamelled, 7 in (17.8 cm), no marks reported. British Museum, ref. no. 6–11, 2.

C *Abbess*, enamelled, 7 in (17.8 cm), unmarked. Jupiter Antiques.

Confessional Group of Abbot and Nun. A veiled nun kneels before an abbot making her confession.

206 No. 105. Seated *Monk* and *Nun*, each reading a book. 7½ in (19.1 cm). No incised marks. *Venner's Antiques*

207 ? No. 109. *Monk* standing, holding a skull. 7 in (17.8 cm). No incised marks. *British Museum*

Examples

A Arthur Lane, *English Porcelain Figures of the Eighteenth Century*, London, 1961, pl. 70b. Enamelled, 5 in (12.7 cm), no incised marks reported, as illustrated.

B Kaye Chappell Antiques, Bakewell. Biscuit, 5 in (12.7 cm), no incised marks reported.

Confessional Group of Abbess and Nun. Companion group to the above with an abbess replacing the abbot.

Example

A Kaye Chappell Antiques, Bakewell. Biscuit, 5 in (12.7 cm), no marks reported.

Models of monks and nuns in quasi-humorous vein were created at Meissen during the 1740s and 1750s by J. F. Eberlein and J. J. Kändler.[1] Many were based on illustrations of the different habits worn by the several religious orders of the day, provided by numerous books published during the seventeenth and eighteenth centuries.[2] Several of the Meissen models were copied at Bow,[3] Chelsea[4] and Longton Hall.[5] Whether the Derby examples were based upon the Meissen or the English copies remains an open question.

References

1 C. H. Fischer, *Katalog der Sammlung Alt-Meissner Porzellan des Herren Reutners und C. H. Fischer in Dresden*, Cologne, 1906, pl. 4, *et seq.*

2 *Courte et solide Histoire de la Fondation des Ordres Religieux*, Amsterdam, 1688. Engravings by Adrien Schoonbeck. Later edition, Augsburg, 1692, engravings by Daniel Steudner. *Ordinum Religiosorum in Ecclesia Militante Catalogues*, Rome, 1658, engravings by Filippo Bonanni.

3 Sotheby's, *Sale Catalogue*, 10 February 1981, lot 60. Bow models seated *Monk* and *Nun*.

4 Ibid., 28 October 1980, lots 99 and 100. Chelsea seated *Monk* and *Nun*.

5 Bernard Watney, *Longton Hall Porcelain*, London, 1957, pl. 37a. Longton Hall seated *Nun*.

208 ? No. 111. *Confessional Group with Monk and Nun*. 5 in (12.7 cm). No incised marks. *Victoria and Albert Museum*

No. 114. *Mars*

HASLEM 'Pair of Figures, Mars and Venus: $6\frac{1}{4}$ ins., enamelled 16s 0d., biscuit 18s 0d.'
BEMROSE 'Mars' and also: 'Season vases' and 'A Group of 4 small musical figures.'

Mars represented as a Roman centurion wearing a crested helmet, cloak, chain armour, thonged kilt and sandals, stands with his right hand on hip and his left upon the hilt of a short sword; an oval shield and a flag are beside him. Mounted on a square base.

The Meissen prototype was made about 1746 at Meissen by J. J. Kändler[1] and may have been based, according to Timothy Clifford,[2] upon a statue of Louis XIV by Desjardins (1640–95) that has not survived. The first Derby copies (B24 (Plate 24)) were made about 1752, and during the 1760s larger more elaborate versions (D28) were issued, some before bocages[3] and others adapted as candlesticks.[4] Chelsea–Derby examples revert to smaller and simpler forms and are mounted on square bases. Similar gold anchor Chelsea models of Mars[5] may immediately be distinguished by their small heads, long torsos and squat legs.

Mars, the God of War, was the son of Jupiter and Juno. He was detested by the other Olympians with the exception of Pluto, who hoped that war would increase the number of his subjects, and Venus who shared with Mars a mutual passion, the fruit of which was their son Cupid. During the ascendancy of Rome, Mars became the symbol of the Militaristic State and often shared this role with Minerva.

Examples
A Bradley, op. cit., no. 36. Biscuit, $6\frac{3}{4}$ in (17.1 cm), incised 'No. 114'.
B Private Collection. Enamelled, $6\frac{3}{4}$ in (17.1 cm), incised 'No. 114', as illustrated.

References
1 K. Berling, *Königlich, Sächsische Porzellan Manufaktur Meissen 1710–1910*, Dresden, 1911, pl. 9, fig. 4. Meissen model of *Mars* by J. J. Kändler.
2 Bradley, op. cit., p. 14.
3 Bradshaw, op. cit., pl. 118. Derby *Mars* with bocage.
4 Bradley, op. cit., no. 18. Derby figure of *Mars* mounted before a candlestick.
5 Bradshaw, op. cit., pl. 45. Gold anchor Chelsea figure of *Mars*, as illustrated.

No. 115. *Venus and Cupid* (group)

HASLEM 'Pair of figures, Mars and Venus: $6\frac{1}{4}$ ins., enamelled 16s 0d.'
BEMROSE 'Venus.'

This group is a reissue of No. 66, mounted upon a rectangular base.

209 No. 114. *Mars* mounted on a square base. $6\frac{3}{8}$ in (17.8 cm). Incised 'No. 114'. *Private Collection*

210 *Mars*, Chelsea version, c. 1760, $7\frac{1}{2}$ in (19.1 cm). Showing the small head, long torso and squat legs. *Author's Collection*

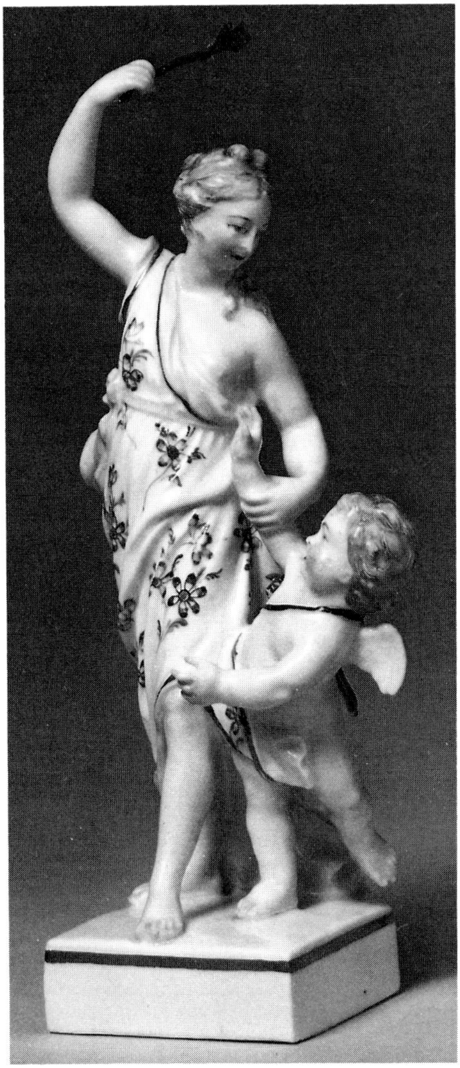

211 No. 115. *Venus and Cupid* (group). $6\frac{1}{2}$ in (16.5 cm). Incised 'No. 115 N.' *British Museum*

212 *Bronze Group of Aphrodite with a Child Centaur*, after the antique. 12 in (30.5 cm). *Author's Collection*

Examples

A Sotheby's, *Sale Catalogue*, 15 March 1966, lot 110. Enamelled, $6\frac{3}{4}$ in (17.1 cm), incised 'No. 115 N'.

B British Museum, ref. no. 1923, 3–14. Enamelled, $6\frac{1}{2}$ in (16.5 cm), incised 'No. 115 N', as illustrated.

No. 116. *Apollo*

HASLEM 'Apollo: $6\frac{3}{4}$ ins., enamelled 8s od., biscuit 9s od.'
BEMROSE 'Apollo.'

Apollo depicted as a long-haired youth wearing a laurel diadem and a long robe, who stands holding a lyre in his left hand. Mounted on a square base.

The Chelsea–Derby version of *Apollo* differs from the earlier dry-edge model that was based on a Meissen prototype,[1] but the source of its inspiration is undetermined.

Apollo, the son of Jupiter and Leto, was fed on ambrosia and was given his long-bow when only seven months old; he slew the Python, who was Mother Earth's Oracle at Delphi. Afterwards he exchanged his herd of cattle for Mercury's lyre, the seven strings of which symbolize the seven vowels of the ancient Greek tongue. He became the patron of the Arts, Archery and Mathematics and, as leader of the Nine Muses, assumed the title of Musagetes. He sired the Corybantes by Thalia and seduced the comely youth Hyacinth, who was later slain when the discus he had thrown was blown back by the West Wind and struck him on the head. Apollo's sister, Diana, shared his love of the chase.

Examples

A Sotheby's, *Sale Catalogue*, 20 May 1980, lot 103. Enamelled, $6\frac{1}{2}$ in (16.5 cm), incised 'No. 116'.
B See Plate 243 for a later example.

Reference

1 Bradshaw, op. cit., pl. 94. Dry-edge Derby *Apollo*.

No. 117. *Jupiter and an Eagle*

HASLEM 'Pair of figures, Jupiter & Juno: $6\frac{1}{2}$ ins., enamelled 16s od., biscuit 18s od.'
BEMROSE 'Jupiter.'

Jupiter stands, crowned and wearing royal robes, beside an eagle, his right hand elevated as if about to hurl a thunderbolt whilst he grasps a second dart in his dependent left. Mounted on a square base.

Derby models of both Jupiter and Juno issued during the 1760s (E56 and E53) were often very large and unattractive.[1] During the Chelsea–Derby period they both were reissued in smaller sizes in less elaborate forms on square bases. The *Derby Sale Catalogues* of 18 and 19 February 1778[2] mention: 'One pair of figures, Jupiter and Juno, and two pair fruit and flower figures, in biscuit 16s 6d.' A further

213 No. 117. *Jupiter and an Eagle* mounted on a square base. 7 in (17.8 cm). Incised 'No. 117'.
Sotheby's

entry of 11 December 1783[3] reads: 'A large figure of Jupiter'.

Jupiter was the sixth child of the Supreme Deity, Cronus, and his spouse, Rhea. Warned that any child born of Rhea would one day overthrow him, Cronus proceeded to swallow each baby soon after birth. In this manner he devoured Vesta, Pluto, Ceres, Juno and Neptune. Rhea determined to save her sixth child, Jupiter, and after his birth she presented Cronus with a boulder wrapped in swaddling bands which he swallowed. Jupiter was concealed and reared by the centaur Chiron. When he had grown to godhood, Jupiter returned and at his mother's prompting placed an emetic in his father's wine causing him to regurgitate intact the five progeny he had ingested. Jupiter obtained thunderbolts from the Cyclopes and waged war on Cronus, whom he defeated, to succeed him as Supreme Deity. He married his sister Juno and took the firmament for his realm, although he presided over the feasts of the gods on Mount Olympus. His brothers, Neptune and Pluto, became, respectively, Lord of the Lakes, Rivers and Oceans, and Lord of Tartarus.

Examples

A Barrett and Thorpe, op. cit., pl. 91. Enamelled, $6\frac{1}{4}$in (15.9 cm), incised 'No. 117'.
B Sotheby's, *Sale Catalogue*, 29 May 1980, lot 57. Enamelled, 7 in (17.8 cm), incised 'No. 117'.
C Christie's, *Sale Catalogue*, 22 May 1972, lot 169. Enamelled, $6\frac{1}{2}$in (16.5 cm), incised 'No. 117'.

References

1 King, 1925, fig. 46. Enamelled, 19 in (48.3 cm), scrolled base, c. 1765. Derby Museums and Art Gallery.
2 Nightingale, op. cit., appendix, p. 50.
3 Ibid., appendix, p. 82.

No. 118. *Neptune with a Dolphin*

HASLEM 'Neptune: $6\frac{3}{4}$ins., enamelled 8s 0d., biscuit 10s 6d.'
BEMROSE 'Neptune.'

Neptune is portrayed as a bearded and crowned man, his cloak blown out by the wind, holding a trident in his left hand and with a dolphin at his side. Mounted upon a square base.

The earliest dry-edge Derby model of Neptune (B26) of about 1752[1] was adapted from a small bronze by Michel Anguier (1612–86) in which the naked god stands beside a hippocampus.[2] An engraving by L. Desplaces[3] may have provided an intermediate source. The unacceptable nudity of the bronze was suitably draped and a dolphin substituted for the sea-horse. Basically the same model was reissued during the 1760s[4] and after 1770, although No. 118 is mounted on a square base, No. 229 upon a scrolled mound base, No. 299 on a tall base encrusted with marine life, and No. 300 upon a low mound. The *Derby Sale Catalogues* of 5–8 May 1778[5] include: 'One pair figures, Neptune and Amphitrite drawn by sea horses, in biscuit 19s 0d.' No item of this description is known to the author.

The strange happenings surrounding Neptune's birth have been mentioned (see No. 117). He received his trident from the Cyclopes for use in the war against Cronus and the Titans, and took for his kingdom the rivers, lakes and oceans. Initially he courted the water nymph (nereid) Thetis but, having heard the prophecy that any son she bore him would usurp his suzerainty, he deserted her and instead turned his attentions towards another nereid, Amphitrite, but she took fright and fled to the Atlas Mountains. Neptune dispatched Delphinius after her to plead his cause and this he did so well that Amphitrite returned to marry the god. In gratitude Neptune placed the image of Delphinius, a dolphin, in the firmament and the creature was ever afterwards sacred to his name.

Examples

A Gilhespy, 1961, fig. 2. Dry-edge Derby model of Neptune, $6\frac{3}{4}$ ins., no marks reported.

B Weston Park Museum, Sheffield. Enamelled, $6\frac{3}{4}$ ins., incised 'No. 229'.

C, D See Plates 97 and 299 for similar models.

No example upon a square base incised 'No. 118' is known to the author.

References

1 Gilhespy, 1961, fig. 2.

2 Bernard Watney, 'Some Parallels and Proto-types in Ceramics', *Trans. ECC*, 10, 1980, part 5, pp. 350–6: pls. 148a and 148b, dry-edge Derby porcelain Neptune; pls. 148c and 148c, bronze Neptune by Michel Anguier.

3 Jennifer Montagu, *Bronzes*, London, 1968, fig. 110, engraving by L. Desplaces of Neptune.

4 Derby Museums and Art Gallery.

5 Nightingale, op. cit., appendix, p. 52.

214 No. 119. *Juno with a Peacock* mounted on a square base. $6\frac{1}{2}$ in (16.5 cm). Marked with the 'Crown X and D', in red, and incised 'N. 119'. *Venner's Antiques*

215 No. 120. *Diana* holding a long-bow with a hunting-dog. $9\frac{1}{4}$ in (23.5 cm). No incised marks. *Late Raymond Shingler Collection*

No. 119. *Juno with a Peacock*

HASLEM No. 117 and No. 119. 'Pair of figures, Jupiter & Juno: $6\frac{1}{2}$ ins., enamelled 16s 0d., biscuit 18s 0d.'
BEMROSE 'Juno.'

Juno, wearing a crown over a veil, sumptuous robes and a cloak, stands holding an orb in her right hand and a sceptre in her left, a peacock at her side. Mounted on a square base.

During the 1760s some large models of Juno (E53) were issued on scrolled bases that were elaborately decorated. Simpler, smaller versions mounted on square bases were made during the Chelsea–Derby era, mentioned in the *Sales Catalogues* of 18 and 19 February 1778,[1] viz.: 'One pair of figures, Jupiter and Juno.'

Juno was both sister and spouse of Jupiter, who received as her wedding present from Mother Earth an orchard bearing golden apples on the slopes of Mount Atlas tended by the Hesperides. Thus the orb may be a golden fruit symbolizing Life. Since, however, Juno was a Triple-Moon Goddess and in her third person represented Death, the orb might alternatively have been a pomegranate, for only the dead were permitted to eat red-coloured food. Juno bore her husband three children: Mars, God of War, Vulcan, the patron of armourers and smiths, and Hebe, the cup-bearer to the gods. Once, when Jupiter was making love to the minor goddess, Io, fearing he had been observed, he transformed her into a white heifer. Juno became suspicious and sent the hundred-eyed Argus to guard the animal. Jupiter called Mercury to assist him, who sent Argus to sleep by relating to him a long and boring story, and then slew him. Juno placed the hundred eyes in the tail feathers of the peacock, which henceforth became sacred to her name.

Example
Barrett and Thorpe, op. cit., pl. 91. Enamelled, $6\frac{1}{2}$ in (16.5 cm), incised 'No. 119'. Derby Museums and Art Gallery, ref. no. 352.

Reference
1 Nightingale, op. cit., appendix p. 50.

No. 120. *Diana*

HASLEM 'Diana: $6\frac{1}{2}$ ins., enamelled 9s 6d, biscuit 10s 6d.'
BEMROSE 'Dianna [sic].'

This model is a reissue of No. 65, mounted on a square base.

Example
A. F. Hurlbutt (A), *Old Derby Porcelain*, London, 1925, pl. 13. Enamelled, $6\frac{1}{2}$ in (16.5 cm), incised 'No. 120'.

No. 121. *Minerva*

HASLEM 'Minerva: $6\frac{1}{2}$ ins., enamelled 8s od., biscuit 9s od.'
BEMROSE 'Minerva.'

Minerva stands, attired in a crested helmet, cuirass, thonged skirt and sandals, holding a spear in her right hand and with her left supporting an oval shield upon the centre of which is the head of Medusa. Mounted on a square base.

The Derby model was adapted from a garden statue by John Cheere[1] and is different from the Bow version[2] that echoes a Meissen original.[3]

When Jupiter became aware he had impregnated the Titaness, Metis, fearing the prophecy that any child she bore him would usurp his throne, he swallowed both her and the unborn child. Afterwards he complained of a headache and summoned Vulcan, who split open Jupiter's head with wedges and a hammer; Minerva stepped out from the wound. Initially she was peace-loving and only borrowed thunderbolts from her father when the need arose. In Roman times she evolved to become a martial goddess who became the symbol of the militaristic State. She helped Perseus in his quest to slay the Gorgon first by showing him how to distinguish Medusa, who was mortal, from her sisters, who were not, and also warning him to look only on the reflection of Medusa in his shield, for to look at her directly would result in his petrification. She provided him with the adamantine sickle, a script and winged sandals and, in addition, persuaded Pluto to loan him the Helmet of Darkness that rendered him invisible. Perseus presented Minerva with the head of Medusa, which she placed upon her aegis, together with bile from the monster which proved to be powerful healing medicine. Minerva was also patron of the Argonauts and intervened in the Trojan wars.

Example
Private Collection. Enamelled, $6\frac{1}{4}$ in (16.5 cm), incised 'No. 121'. A more elaborate example was later issued as No. 298.

References
1 M. Whinney, *Sculpture in Britain 1530–1830*, London, 1962, pl. 107b, lead statue of *Minerva* by J. Cheere.
2 Frank Hurlbutt, *Bow Porcelain*, London, 1926, p. 56.
3 Hugh Tait, *Porcelain*, London, 1962, pl. 34, Meissen figure of *Minerva*.

No. 122. *Winged Time*

HASLEM 'Hercules: $6\frac{1}{4}$ ins., enamelled 8s od., biscuit 9s od.'
BEMROSE 'Time.'

This model has been identified as Winged Time and was later reissued as No. 222.

Example
A See Plate 257 for later Bloor Derby example.

No. 123 *The French Seasons* (set of four models)

HASLEM 'Set of Seasons, from French, 4 sizes: 1st. ——, enamelled £4 4s od., biscuit ——. 2nd. [$8\frac{1}{2}$ ins.], enamelled £3 13s 6d., biscuit £4 4s od. 3rd. [$7\frac{1}{2}$ ins.], enamelled £3 3s od., biscuit £3 13s 6d. 4th. [6 ins.], enamelled £1 16s od., biscuit £2 2s 6d.'
BEMROSE 'Four French seasons, 4 sizes.' Also 'Vase by Spangler.'

A set of four models of standing adolescents:

Spring A youth wearing a brimmed hat, holding in both hands a posy before his face.
Summer A bareheaded girl, wearing a simple dress, stands barefoot, her left arm about a cornsheaf.
Autumn A girl clad in a bonnet, laced bodice, apron and skirt, holding a bunch of grapes in her left hand and with a basket of grapes over her arm.
Winter A bareheaded youth, dressed in a fur-trimmed cape, jacket, breeches and boots, bearing a bundle of faggots on his shoulder.

The models are copies of four out of eight, made at Tournai about 1760, by N. J. F. Gauron, based on designs by Boucher.[1] They are less competently modelled than their prototypes and stylistically resemble a set of *Rustic Seasons*[2] issued about 1773 by Champion's Bristol factory. The *Derby Sale Catalogue* of 7 May 1782[3] includes: 'One sett [sic] French seasons and one pair figures Bacchus and Ariadne in biscuit £1 15s od.' Early examples are on scrolled bases, later versions are mounted on shallow cylinders. John Twitchett[4] presents evidence to suggest that between 1791 and 1795 the original models were refurbished by William Coffee.

Examples
A Gilhespy, 1951, fig. 160. Enamelled, 6 in (15.2 cm), incised 'No. 123', cylindrical bases.

216 No. 123. Enamelled set of *The French Seasons*. $8\frac{1}{2}$ in (21.6 cm). *Grosvenor Antiques*

217 No. 123. Biscuit versions of *Spring* and *Summer*. $8\frac{1}{2}$ in (21.6 cm). Incised 'No. 123'.

218 No. 123. Biscuit versions of *Autumn* and *Winter*. $8\frac{1}{2}$ in (21.6 cm). Incised 'No. 123'.
Private Collection

B Twitchett, op. cit., pl. 148. Biscuit, $8\frac{1}{2}$ in (21.6), incised 'No. 123'.
C Bradshaw, op. cit., pl. 125. Enamelled, $8\frac{1}{2}$ in (21.6 cm), incised 'No. 123'. Grosvenor Antiques.

References

1 N. Nicaise, 'Porcelaines de Tournay et de Chelsea–Derby', *Revue Belge d'Archéologie et d'Histoire de l'Art*, 5, 1935, pp. 5–15, fig. 4. Eight Tournai models of *Boys and Girls after Boucher*, emblematic of *The Four Seasons* by N. J. F. Gauron.
2 Bradshaw, op. cit., pl. 151. Champion's Bristol *Rustic Seasons*.
3 Nightingale, op. cit. appendix, p. 71.
4 John Twitchett and Betty Bailey (1976) *Royal Crown Derby*, London, 1976, p. 33.

No. 124. *Time Clipping the Wings of Love* (group)

HASLEM 'Time and Cupid, 3 sizes: 1st. ——, enamelled £2 12s 6d., biscuit, no price given. 2nd. [$8\frac{1}{2}$ ins.] enamelled £1 11s 6d., biscuit, no price given. 3rd. [$7\frac{3}{4}$ ins], enamelled £1 1s 0d., biscuit, no price given.
BEMROSE 'Vase by Spangler.'

219 No. 124. *Time Clipping the Wings of Love*. $7\frac{3}{4}$ in (19.7 cm). Incised 'No. 124'. *Private Collection*

Time is represented by an elderly bearded man wearing loose robes who stoops over Cupid to clip his wings with shears. Mounted on a mound base ended with scrolls.

The group is adapted from Charles Phillips's engraving[1] after Van Dyck and is mentioned in the *Derby Sale Catalogues* of 17–20 April 1780:[2] 'A fine large figure of Time and Cupid 11s 6d.' An example in biscuit, mounted upon an ornamental clock by Benjamin Vulliamy, is in Buckingham Palace.[3]

Examples

A Barrett and Thorpe, op. cit., pl. 92. Biscuit, $7\frac{3}{4}$ in (19.7 cm), incised 'No. 124'.
B Rackham, 1915, pl. 40, no. 409. Enamelled, $8\frac{1}{2}$ in (21.6 cm), incised 'No. 124'.

References

1 Schreiber Collection, no. 1819, Victoria and Albert Museum. Engraving of *Time Clipping the Wings of Love* by C. Phillips, c. 1772. Painting of the same by Sir Anthony Van Dyck, once in the collection of the Duke of Marlborough, Blenheim House.
2 Nightingale, op. cit., appendix, p. 58.
3 L. G. G. Ramsey, 'A Masterpiece of Clockmaking', *The Connoisseur*, 38, 1956, p. 230, fig. 1.

No. 125. *The Four Chelsea Seasons* (four figures)

HASLEM 'Set of four Chelsea standing Seasons: 1st. $6\frac{5}{8}$ ins., enamelled £1 8s od. 2nd. $6\frac{1}{4}$ ins., enamelled £1 4s od. 3rd. $5\frac{1}{8}$ ins., enamelled 14s od., biscuit 16s od.'
BEMROSE 'Large Chelsea Seasons, 4 sizes.'

Spring A bareheaded woman wearing an apron and dress, standing with a basket of fruit over her left arm and a posy in her right hand, before a bocage of flowers and leaves.
Autumn A huntsman wearing a brimmed hat, jacket, breeches and supporting a gun with his left hand and holding grapes in his right, before a bocage of grapes and vine leaves.
Summer Unknown to author.
Winter Unknown to author.

No Chelsea prototypes have been recognized, although *Spring* and *Autumn* may have been adapted from No. 50, *Huntsman* and *Lady*.

Examples

A B. N. Clifford Collection (private). *Trans. ECC*, 7, 1969, part 2, pp. 108–17, pls. 124c and d. Biscuit, $5\frac{1}{2}$ in (14 cm), unmarked.
B Hanbury Hall. $6\frac{1}{4}$ in (15.8 cm).

220 No. 125. A sportsman standing before a bocage of vine leaves and grapes, emblematic of *Autumn*, from *The Chelsea Seasons*. $6\frac{1}{4}$ in (15.8 cm). *Hanbury Hall*

221 No. 126. Biscuit figure of *John Wilkes, MP*, with enamel and gilt embellishments. The mace of the Lord Mayor of London is upon the base. 12 in (30.5 cm). *Derby Museums and Art Gallery*

No. 126. *John Wilkes, MP*

HASLEM 'Wilkes: 12 ins., enamelled £1 5s od.'
BEMROSE 'John Wilkes Esqre.'

John Wilkes portrayed after the manner of Scheemakers' statue of Shakespeare in Westminster Abbey, standing left hand on hip and leaning with his right upon an architectural plinth from which two scrolls hang inscribed 'Magna Charta' and 'Bill of Rights'. A seated putto supports a tome entitled 'Lock on Govt.' and holds the Cap of Liberty; a mace lies at his feet.

The model was adapted from Nathaniel Dance's painting, now in the National Portrait Gallery, with the addition of a cloak probably to provide support in the kiln. A summary of the life of Wilkes has earlier been provided[1] in Chapter 4. Models of about 1764 appear on scrolled bases, No. 126 upon an octagonal base decorated with Greek key-fret.

Examples

A Derby Museums and Art Gallery, ref. no. 292. Biscuit, 12 in (30.5 cm), incised 'No. 126', as illustrated.

B Sotheby's, *Sale Catalogue*, 10 February 1981, lot 128. Enamelled, 12 in (30.5 cm), incised 'No. 126', as illustrated.

Reference

1 Horace Bleakley, *The Life of John Wilkes*, London, 1918.

Nos. 127–36. *Not Identified*

HASLEM No. 127. No item mentioned. Nos. 128–36. 'Nine figures.'

BEMROSE No. 127. No item mentioned. No. 128. 'Oval vase.' No. 129. 'Vase.' No. 130. 'Vases by Spangler, 3 sizes.' No. 131. 'Vases by Spangler, large.' Nos. 132–6. No items mentioned.

A biscuit group incised 'No. 129' was brought to the Derby Museums and Art Gallery for identification and is described in a memo: 'Venus standing, holding possibly a laurel wreath over the head of Cupid who looks up at her.'

No. 137. *The Prudent Mother* (group)

HASLEM 'Madonna, a Group.'

BEMROSE 'Pair figures, Madonna and prudent mother.'

A lady wearing a lace cap, long dress with pagoda sleeves, seated in a gilt-wood chair with an open book on her lap. Her left arm is about the shoulders of a small girl as she points with her right hand to the text. The dress is edged with lace and the group mounted on a square chamfered and fluted base.

The Haslem version of the Factory List transposed Nos. 137 and 138.

Examples

A Sotheby's, *Sale Catalogue*, 26 February 1980, lot 212. Enamelled, $8\frac{1}{4}$ in (21 cm), said to be incised 'No. 131' but probably misread from 'No. 137'.

222 No. 137. *The Prudent Mother*. $8\frac{1}{4}$ in (21.5 cm). Incised 'No. 137'. *Sotheby's*

B Ibid., 3 October 1972, lot 196. Enamelled, $8\frac{1}{4}$ in (21 cm), incised 'No. 137'.

C Derby Museums and Art Gallery, ref. no. 212. Enamelled, $8\frac{1}{4}$ in (21 cm), incised 'No. 137'.

No. 138. *Madonna and Child* (group)

HASLEM 'Prudent Mother, a Group: 8¼ ins., enamelled 18s od., biscuit £1 1s od.'
BEMROSE 'Pair figures, Madonna and prudent mother.'

The Blessed Virgin Mary is depicted as a young woman wearing a veil and loose robes, seated in a chair, with the Holy Child amidst flowers in her lap. Mounted on a shallow plinth with chamfered corners decorated with vertical fluting.

The similar presentation of Nos. 137 and 138 suggests they were intended to constitute a pair. The *Derby Sale Catalogues* of 18 and 19 February 1778[1] include: 'One pair of figures, Madonna and Prudent Mother, in biscuit 17s od.' Also on 5 May 1779[2] there appeared: 'A group of Madonna and Child and a pair of element groups, in biscuit 19s od.'

Examples

A Sotheby's, *Sale Catalogue*, 29 July 1980, lot 158. Enamelled, 8½ in (21.6 cm), incised 'No. 138'.
B British Museum. Enamelled, 8½ in (21.6 cm), incised 'No. 138'.

References

1 Nightingale, op. cit., appendix, p. 50.
2 ibid., appendix, p. 55.

No. 139. *Musical Group of Two Figures*

HASLEM 'Musical Group of two Figures: 6½ ins., enamelled 12s od.'
BEMROSE Nos. 139 and 140. 'Two groups boy and girl, two in each.'

A boy wearing a brimmed hat and contemporary dress is seated upon a grassy mound beneath a leafing tree, playing a reed-pipe and with a musical score in his lap. Placed at a slightly lower level, a girl also wearing a hat, is seated playing a French horn and with a tambourine at her side.

This group is intended to be paired with No. 140, but possibly both groups were made with and without the leafing tree for the two examples here presented are on this account not a true pair.

Examples

A Sotheby's, *Sale Catalogue*, 4 December 1962, lot 145. Enamelled, 8½ in (21.6 cm), incised 'No. 139'.
B Cecil Higgins Museum, Bedford, as illustrated.

223 No. 138. *The Madonna and Child.* $8\frac{1}{2}$ in (21.6 cm). Incised 'No. 138'. *Sotheby's*
224 No. 139. *Musical Group of Two Figures.* $8\frac{1}{2}$ in (21.6 cm). Incised 'No. 139'. *Cecil Higgins Museum*

No. 140. *Musical Group of Two Figures*

HASLEM 'Musical Group of two Figures: 6½ ins., enamelled 12s od.'
BEMROSE Nos. 139 and 140. 'Two groups boy and girl, two in each.'

A boy wearing a brimmed hat seated on a grassy mound playing a flute. At a slightly lower level a girl sits likewise surrounded by musical trophies, holding a score in her lap and with bagpipes. See No. 139 above.

Examples

A Sotheby's, *Sale Catalogue*, 28 October 1980, lot 104. Enamelled, 6½ in (16.5 cm), incised 'No. 140'.

B David Love Antiques, Harrogate. Enamelled, 6½ in (16.5 cm), incised 'No. 140', as illustrated.

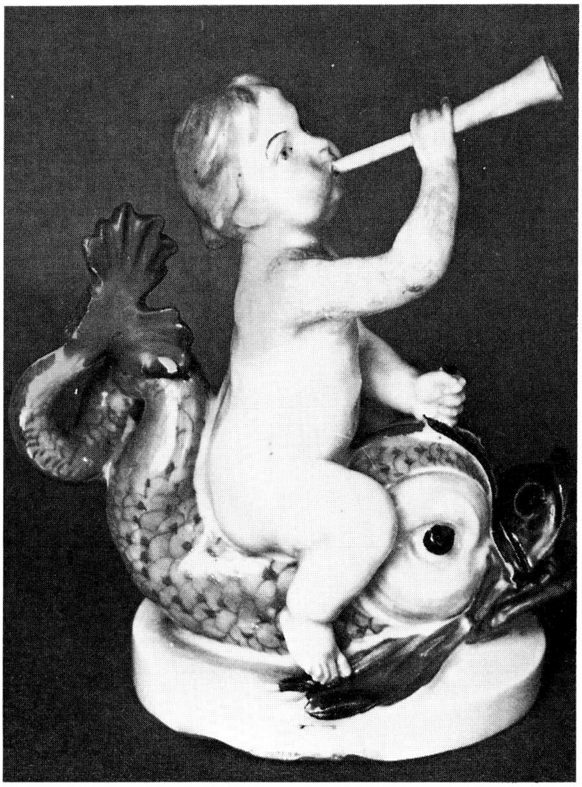

225 No. 140. *Musical Group of Two Figures*. 6½ in (16.5 cm). Incised 'No. 140'. *David Love Antiques*

226 ? No. 142. *Boy Riding a Dolphin*. 5½ in (14 cm). No incised marks.
Derby Museums and Art Gallery

No. 141. *Not Identified*

HASLEM 'Pair of Fighting Boys: $3\frac{1}{2}$ ins., enamelled 4s od., biscuit 5s od.'
BEMROSE 'Pair of small seasons, boy and girl.' Also: 'Fencing boy.'

Nos. 142 and 143. *Boy and Girl Riding a Dolphin and a Swan* (pair)

HASLEM 'Pair of small boys riding on Dolphin and Swan, 3 sizes: 1st. size not given, enamelled 12s od. 2nd. size not given, enamelled 10s od. 3rd. size not given, enamelled 7s od.'
BEMROSE 'Swan and Dolphin, 4 sizes.'

Two scantily draped putti, one astride a dolphin holding the reins with which it is harnessed and at the same time blowing a trumpet. Mounted on an oval base. Companion figure unknown to author.
The *Derby Sale Catalogues* of 18 and 19 February 1778[1] include: 'One pair of boys riding a dolphin and swan'. Also in Duesbury's *Account Book*[2] under the date 24 April 1787 appear:

'4 Boys riding Dolphins	14s od.
4 Boys riding Swans	14s od.'

Example
Barrett and Thorpe, op. cit., pl. 87. Enamelled *Boy Riding a Dolphin*, $5\frac{1}{2}$ in (14 cm), no incised marks reported.

References
1 Nightingale, op. cit., appendix p. 50.
2 Barrett and Thorpe, op. cit., p. 153.

Nos. 144 and 145. *Not Identified*

HASLEM No item mentioned.
BEMROSE No item mentioned.

Nos. 146 and 147. *Busts of Addison* and *Virgil*

HASLEM No items mentioned.
BEMROSE No items mentioned.

A pair of busts upon circular waisted plinths, $8\frac{3}{4}$ in (22.2 cm).

227 Pair of biscuit busts. $8\frac{3}{4}$ in (22.2 cm). Both by courtesy of *Connoisseur*: No. 146. *Addison* (left). No. 147. *Virgil* (right).

Addison (No. 146). Portrayed as a bareheaded young man wearing a shirt open at the neck, and a cloak about his shoulders.

Virgil (No. 147). Shown wearing a laurel diadem and a singlet draped about his shoulders.

Renewed interest in the ancient cultures of Greece and Rome was prompted by excavations conducted at Pompeii, Herculaneum and Spalatro and many ceramic establishments issued both busts and full-length models of antique and contemporary characters in biscuit. Josiah Wedgwood purchased moulds for busts of Addison, Virgil, Alexander Pope, Jean-Jacques Rousseau and others[1] from Hoskin and Oliver, John Cheere, and other craftsmen in this field. The *Derby Sale Catalogues* of 5–8 May 1779,[2] mentions: 'A pair of busts of Addison and Virgil, in biscuit 18s 0d.' Later from 9–14 May 1779:[3] 'A large bust of Addison.'

Joseph Addison (1672–1719), poet and author, is especially remembered for his 'Ancient Medals', 'The Campaign', 'Cato', amongst many other works. His association with literature relating to ancient Greece and Rome prompted the issue of his statue or bust as a companion to *Virgil* or similar classical heroes.

Virgil (70–19 BC) was author of *The Aeneid*, the *Georgics* and *Bucolics*, and is recognized as one of the greatest of all the epic poets of ancient Rome. He enjoyed the patronage of Augustus Caesar and died in old age at Brindisium. Joseph Wright painted a picture of the supposed tomb of Virgil beside the road from Puteoli to Naples, in 1779.

Example
Allam, op. cit., p. 30, no. II. Biscuit bust of Addison, 8¾ in (22.2 cm), incised 'No. 146'; also bust of Virgil, incised 'No. 147', in like manner.

References
1 G. Savage and Robin Reilly, *The Dictionary of Wedgwood,* Woodbridge, 1980, p. 192.
2 Nightingale, op. cit., appendix p. 56.
3 Ibid., appendix p. 76.

Nos. 148–55. *Not Identified*

HASLEM No items mentioned.
BEMROSE No items mentioned.

No. 156. *Bust of Zingara*

HASLEM No item mentioned.
BEMROSE No item mentioned.

A bust of a bareheaded young woman wearing a chin-cloth and with the upper portion of her shoulders draped.

An ancient Greek marble, lacking head, hands and feet, most probably representing Artemis (Diana), was among the antiquities of the Villa Borghese, where it was listed as *An Egyptian Woman.*[1] The missing head and appendages were replaced in bronze by an unknown artist who may have been Nicolas Cordier (1567–1612), who is known to have accomplished similar commissions. The statue was purchased by Napoleon Bonaparte in 1807; later it became the property of the Louvre, and is now at Versailles. During the eighteenth century the subject enjoyed great popularity; a half-size marble replica may be seen in the ante-room at Stourhead, Wiltshire, and both bronze and plaster statuettes were available in London and Rome. Peter Scheemakers offered plaster maquettes of Hercules, Flora, Venus, Faunus and the Zingara Egyptian Woman, in 1747 for five guineas. In 1774 Richard Parker fashioned a bust of Zingara, while Hoskins and Grant supplied moulds of Zingara to Josiah Wedgwood, who issued a black basaltes version. The name Zingara has been assumed to mean 'Gipsy Girl' and provided the name of a heroine in a burlesque held in Marylebone Gardens in 1773. The Derby bust was almost certainly based on one of many plaster and bronze replicas.

Example

R. L. Hobson, *Catalogue of the Collection of English Porcelain in the Department of British and Medieval Antiquities in the British Museum,* London, 1905, pl. 20, III. 8. Biscuit, 10½ in (26.7 cm), as illustrated.

Reference

1 Francis Haskell and Nicholas Penny, *Taste and the Antique,* New Haven and London, 1981, pp. 339–41.

228 No. 156. Biscuit *Bust of Zingara.* 10½ in (26.7 cm). Incised 'Stephan sculpt'. *British Museum*

229 Busts of two philosophers. $5\frac{3}{4}$ in (14.6 cm): No. 159. *Philospher Crying* (left). Incised 'No. 159'. No. 160. *Philosopher Laughing* (right). Incised 'No. 160'. *Sotheby's*

Nos. 157 and 158. *Not Identified*

HASLEM No items mentioned.
BEMROSE No items mentioned.

Nos. 159 and 160. *Busts of Two Philosophers*

HASLEM 'Pair of Laughing and Crying Philosophers: $5\frac{3}{4}$ ins., enamelled 10s 6d.'
BEMROSE No items mentioned.

A pair of small busts mounted upon circular, waisted plinths decorated in enamel and gilt with the anthemium, flowers and leaves. One philosopher wears a toque and is depicted frowning, the other is clad in a soft cap and is shown smiling.

Example
Sotheby's, *Sale Catalogue*, 20 November 1979, lot 121. Enamelled, 6 in (15.2 cm), incised 'No. 159' and 'No. 160', as illustrated.

No. 161. *Antique Figure of Wisdom*

HASLEM 'Antique Figure of Wisdom, 2 sizes: 1st. 8½ ins., enamelled 12s od., biscuit 18s od. 2nd. No details provided.'
BEMROSE 'Four figures, Wisdome, Justice, Peace and Pleanty [sic.].'

Wisdom is depicted as a tall, slender lady wearing a plumed helmet and a long robe gathered at the waist by a sash and sandals. She holds an orb or pomegranate in her right hand. Mounted upon a rectangular base encrusted with leaves and flowers.

Example
Plymouth Museum and Art Gallery, Reserve Collection. Enamelled, 8½ in (21.6 cm), incised 'No. 161', as illustrated.

No. 162. *Antique Figure of Justice*

HASLEM 'Antique Figure of Justice, 2 sizes: 1st. 8½ ins., enamelled 12s od., biscuit 18s od. 2nd. No details provided.'
BEMROSE 'Wisdome [sic.] and Justice, 2 sizes.'

Justice is portrayed as a tall, slender lady who stands bareheaded wearing a blindfold and loose garments gathered by a sash at her waist; she holds a sword in her right hand with its point directed towards the ground. Mounted on a rectangular base encrusted with leaves and flowers.

Example
Plymouth Museum and Art Gallery, Reserve Collection. Enamelled, 8½ in (21.6 cm), incised 'No. 162', as illustrated.

No. 163. *Antique Figure of Plenty*

HASLEM 'Antique Figure of Plenty, 2 sizes: 1st. 8½ ins., enamelled 12s od., biscuit 18s od.' 2nd. No details provided.
BEMROSE No item mentioned.

Plenty is represented by a slender lady wearing a coronet, loose robes and sandals, who stands proffering fruits and leaves in her right hand whilst supporting a cornucopia with her left. Mounted on a rectangular base.

The *Derby Sale Catalogues* of 23–28 May 1785[1] mention: 'Andromache and Plenty, a pair of enamelled figures £1 6s od.'

230 No. 161. *Antique Figure of Wisdom* (left). No. 162. *Antique Figure of Justice* (right). Both $8\frac{1}{2}$in (21.6 cm). Incised 'No. 161' and 'No. 162' respectively. *Plymouth City Museums and Art Gallery*

231 No. 163. *Antique Figure of Plenty*. 10 in (25.4 cm). Incised 'No. 163'. *Victoria and Albert Museum*
232 No. 164. *Antique Figure of Peace*. $6\frac{1}{2}$ in (16.5 cm). Incised '14'. *Hanbury Hall*

Example
Rackham, 1915, op. cit., pl. 41, no. 424. Biscuit, 10 in (25.4 cm), incised 'No. 163', as illustrated.

Reference
1 Nightingale, op. cit., appendix, p. 86.

No. 164. *Antique Figure of Peace*

HASLEM 'Antique Figure of Peace, 2 sizes: 1st. $8\frac{1}{2}$ ins., enamelled 12s od., biscuit 18s od.' 2nd. No details provided.
BEMROSE No item mentioned.

Peace is shown as a bareheaded girl wearing a long dress who kneels upon a ruined plinth, holding a dove in her right hand and an olive branch in her left; a basket of leaves and flowers lies at her feet. Mounted on an octagonal base.

Example
Hanbury Hall, Droitwich, Watney Collection. Enamelled, $6\frac{1}{2}$ in (16.5 cm), incised '14' without the prefix 'No.', as illustrated.

Nos. 165–75. *Not Identified*

HASLEM Nos. 165–74. No items mentioned. No. 175. 'Pair of Boy and Girl Figures: 4 ins., enamelled 4s od.'
BEMROSE Nos. 165–75. No items mentioned.

No. 176. *Grape-gatherers* (group)

HASLEM No item mentioned.
BEMROSE 'Hydra.'

A country girl sits upon a grassy mound, a basket of grapes over her right arm, proffering a grape with her left outstretched hand to a rustic swain seated at her left side. The youth holds a bouquet in his left hand which, as he looks at the girl, is being eaten by a sheep, whilst at his feet his inverted hat is filled with grapes.

223 No. 176. *Grape-gatherers.* $8\frac{1}{2}$ in (21.6 cm). No incised marks.
Victoria and Albert Museum

Mounted on an irregular mound encrusted with leaves and flowers.

The group echoes the biscuit Sèvres original by Étienne-Maurice Falconet of about 1752[1] that had been adapted from the engraving made by Jacques-Phillipe Le Bas in 1750 of the painting entitled *Pensent-ils au raisin?*, executed by Boucher in 1747, now in the National Museum, Stockholm.

Examples

A Twitchett, op. cit., col. pl. 17. Enamelled, $8\frac{3}{4}$ in (22.2 cm), no marks reported. Ronald W. Raven Collection.

B Rackham, 1915, pl. 43, no. 423 (new no. 355). Enamelled, $8\frac{1}{2}$ in (21.6 cm), no marks reported.

C Private Collection, biscuit, $8\frac{1}{2}$ in (21.6 cm), incised 'No. 176'.

Reference

1 Bourgeois and Lechevallier-Chevignard, op. cit., pl. 1, no. 398. Biscuit Sèvres group by E.-M. Falconet.

No. 177. *The Knot in the Cravat* (group)

HASLEM No item mentioned.
BEMROSE 'Hydra.'

A bareheaded lady, attired in a dress with puff-sleeves and panniered skirt, sits upon a four-legged stool adjusting the cravat of a gallant who squats upon his haunches before her. Mounted on an irregular rocky mound.

The group echoes a biscuit Sèvres original made by Étienne-Maurice Falconet about 1766, adapted from an engraving after the painting by Boucher entitled *L'Oracle, ou le Noeud de Cravate.*

Examples

A Clifford, 1969, pl. 125. Biscuit, 7 in (17.8 cm); incised 'No. 177'. Late B. N. Clifford Collection (private).

B Derby Museums and Art Gallery, ref. Nos. 454 and 452. Biscuit, 7 in (17.8 cm), incised 'No. 177'.

C See plate 270 for a later bocaged example.

Reference

1 Bourgeois and Lechevallier-Chevignard, op. cit., pl. 9, no. 481. Biscuit Sèvres group by E.-M. Falconet.

No. 178. *Alpine Shepherdess* (group)

HASLEM No item mentioned.
BEMROSE 'Macaroni.'

A bareheaded shepherdess sits upon a grassy mound with a recumbent lamb at her left side. Before her, and at a slightly lower level, a gallant reclines gazing into the eyes of the lady and holding her right hand in both of his own. Mounted on an irregular pad base encrusted with leaves and flowers.

The theme portrayed by the group is derived from a play adapted from Jean-François Marmontel's popular story, produced by Charles-Simon Favart (1710–92) and his talented actress wife, née Marie-Justine Duronceray, at the Opéra-Comique during the early 1750s. François Boucher painted *La Bergère des Alpes* and several other scenes from this and similar French operettas, and engravings brought this work to a wide public. Étienne-Maurice Falconet based his biscuit Sèvres group of about 1766[1] on one of these which was later copied at Derby.

234 No. 178. *Alpine Shepherdess* (group). 7 in (17.8 cm). Incised 'No. 178'. *Derby Museums and Art Gallery*

Examples

A Clifford, 1969, pl. 123. Biscuit group modified by the addition of a leafing tree behind and between the two figures, incised 'No. 256', 12 in.

B Derby Museums and Art Gallery, ref. nos. 452 and 461. Biscuit, 7 in (17.8 cm), incised 'No. 178'.

Reference

1 Bourgeoise and Lechevallier-Chevignard, op. cit., pl. 9. no. 10. Biscuit group by E. M. Falconet.

235 No. 179. *Four Children Playing Music* (group). 10 in (25.4 cm). *Sotheby's*

No. 179. *Four Children Playing Music* (group)

HASLEM 'Musical Group of four Figures: [13¼ ins.], enamelled £2 12s od.'
BEMROSE 'Four small musical figures.'

Four bareheaded children attired in contemporary dress stand around a leafing tree upon a rocky mount. Two boys respectively hold a French horn and an end-flute; two girls have either a lute or a tambourine, whilst musical trophies are scattered at their feet. Possibly adapted from Nos. 9 and 10.

Examples
A Sotheby's, *Sale Catalogue*, 31 July 1979, lot 77. Enamelled, 10 in (25.4 cm), incised 'No. 179'.
B Derby Museums and Art Gallery. Biscuit, 10 in (25.4 cm), incised 'No. 179'.
C Castle Museum, Norwich.

No. 180. *Autumn and Spring* (two models)

HASLEM 'Pair of Boys, Autumn and Spring: [6¼ ins.], enamelled 3s od.'
BEMROSE No item mentioned.

A pair of stiffly posed standing putti, each standing upon an irregular mound base before a small waist-high bocage.

Spring wears a diadem of flowers and holds a basket of blossoms as well as a posy.
Autumn stands likewise crowned with vine leaves and grapes and holds both a bunch and a basket full of the same fruit.

Example
Private Collection. Enamelled, 6¼ in (15.9 cm), incised 'No. 180'.

No. 181. *Not Identified*

HASLEM No item mentioned.
BEMROSE No item mentioned.

No. 182. *Cupids Riding Bucks* (pair)

HASLEM 'Pair of Cupids riding on Bucks: 5 ins., enamelled 10s 6d.'
BEMROSE 'Four boys riding on a goat and panther.'

236 No. 182. *Cupid Riding a Buck* (one of a pair). 5 in (12.7 cm). *Derby Museums and Art Gallery*

A pair of scantily draped winged Cupids, each with a quiver suspended diagonally from the left shoulder and holding a long-bow in one extended hand, in mirror poses, sitting astride either a stag or a doe. Mounted on irregular pad bases.

Example
Derby Museums and Art Gallery, ref. no. 378. Enamelled, 5 in (12.7 cm), incised 'No. 182' (*Cupid on a Buck* only).

No. 183. *Not Identified*

HASLEM 'Pair of Prudence and Discretion: Size not given, enamelled 4s od.'
BEMROSE 'Boy and girl, Cupid and discression [sic].'

The relatively low price cited suggests that this pair may be a small version of either No. 15 or No. 98.

No. 184. *Boy Reading a Book* and *Girl Tatting* (pair)

HASLEM 'Pair of Boy and Girl Figures: [5½ ins.], enamelled 4s od., biscuit 5s od.'
BEMROSE 'Small boy and girl.'

A boy attired in a wig, long coat, waistcoat and breeches, sits with legs crossed, holding his right ankle with his left hand, reading from a book held in his right hand at arm's length. Companion girl wears a linen cap, blouse and long skirt, sits likewise tatting and with her brimmed hat balanced upon her right knee.

The *Derby Sale Catalogue* of 17 April 1771[1] mentions: 'Lot 60. A pair of sitting figures, a gentleman reading, and a lady knotting most curiously ornamented with lace £5 2s 6d.' The unusually high serial number allotted to models issued in 1771 suggests that they were first issued with a lower number and that No. 184 represents a reissue some years later.

Examples

A Derby Museums and Art Gallery. Enamelled, $5\frac{1}{2}$ in (14 cm), incised 'No. 184'.

B G. A. Godden, *An Illustrated Encyclopaedia of British Pottery and Porcelain*, London, 1966, p. 140, pl. 227 (2nd and 4th models in photograph).

Reference

1 Nightingale, op. cit., appendix, p. 19.

237 No. 184. *Boy Reading a Book and Girl Tatting*. 238 No. 184. Both $5\frac{1}{2}$ in (14 cm). Incised 'No. 184'. *B. and T. Thorn Antiques*

Nos. 185–91. *Not Identified*

HASLEM No. 185. 'Cupids riding on Swan and Dolphin: No size given, enamelled 7s od.' Nos. 186–8. No item mentioned. No. 189. 'Boy riding on Sea-Horse: $4\frac{1}{2}$ ins., enamelled 4s od.' No. 190. 'Triton: 2 ins., enamelled 3s od.' No. 191. No item mentioned.

BEMROSE No. 185. 'Swan and dolphin.' Nos. 186–91. No items mentioned.

William Duesbury's Account Book contains entries for 19 April 1787[1] for:

'4 Small Tritons.	12s od.
2 Boys riding Sea-Horses.	9s od.'

Reference

1 Barrett and Thorpe, op. cit., p. 153.

239 No. 192. *Man and Woman Standing beside Hampers.* $8\frac{1}{2}$ in (21.6 cm). Incised 'No. 192'. *Springfield Antiques*

No. 192. *Man and Woman Standing beside Hampers* (pair)

HASLEM No item mentioned.
BEMROSE 'Neptune.'

A pair of rustics standing with rectangular open baskets before them. The man wears a brimmed hat, jacket and loose trousers, and his companion a headscarf, coat and skirt, both are barefoot and are mounted upon scrolled bases. Probably intended to serve as sweetmeat containers.

Examples
Springfield Antiques, Kensington Church Street, London. Shown at the Wakefield Ceramics Fair, Crown Hotel, Harrogate, 5–8 November 1987. Enamelled, incised beneath concave undersurface of base 'No. 192', about 8 in.

Nos. 193 and 194. *Bacchus and Ariadne* (pair)

HASLEM 'Pair large Bacchus and Ariadne, 3 sizes: 1st. 9 ins., enamelled £1 8s od., biscuit £1 11s od. 2nd. 8¼ ins., enamelled £1 1s od., biscuit £1 4s od. 3rd. 7½ ins., enamelled 16s od., biscuit 18s od.'
BEMROSE 'Bacchus and Areadny [sic], 2 sizes.'

Bacchus wears a chaplet composed of vine leaves and grapes and a loose robe; he stands holding aloft in his right hand a bunch of grapes, while in his left there is a goblet of wine. The companion figure of *Ariadne* stands bareheaded, and with her upraised left hand grasps the edge of a cloak draped diagonally from her right shoulder, while holding a scroll in her right.

The *Derby Sale Catalogues* of 18 and 19 February, 1778[1] mention: 'One pair of figures, Bacchus and Ariadne,' and these were subsequently offered again on 7 May 1782[2] and on 11 December 1783.[3] The Lygo correspondence of 1791, however, ascribes the models to John Charles Felix Rossi in that year. It seems likely that the first versions of *Bacchus* and *Ariadne* were created by some other unknown modeller in 1778 and that the pair to which Lygo refers represent different or refurbished examples. The model of *Bacchus* was transposed and adapted by the addition of drapery from the marble, now in the Bargello in Florence,[4] by Jacopo Sansovino (1486–1570). The prevailing prudery of the moral climate necessitated the masking of the nudity of the original. Some versions stand on circular and others on square bases. A black basaltes model was issued by Josiah Wedgwood's factory[5] derived from the same source. The origin of the model of *Ariadne* has not been identified but it is likely to have been adapted from a terracotta after the antique.

240 No. 193. Biscuit model of *Bacchus*, after Sansavino. $8\frac{1}{4}$ in (21 cm). *Liverpool Museum and Art Gallery*

241 No. 194. Biscuit model of *Ariadne*. $6\frac{1}{2}$ in (21.6 cm). Incised 'No. 194'. *Derby Museums and Art Gallery*

242 No. 194. Enamelled version of *Ariadne*. $8\frac{1}{2}$ in (16.5 cm). *Venner's Antiques*

The strange events relating to the birth and earlier life of Bacchus are later presented (see No. 376). Ariadne was the daughter of Minos, king of Crete, and his spouse queen Pasiphae. The monarch's half-brother was the Minotaur, a monster part-bull and part-man, who dwelt in a labyrinth upon the island. Seven youths and seven maidens were sent every nine years as a tribute from Athens to be sacrificed to the odious creature. Theseus and a band of Athenian warriors determined to rid their city of this scourge and arrived in Crete disguised as sacrificial maidens. Ariadne, who had fallen in love with Theseus, after extracting from him a promise of marriage, showed him how to secure the escape from the maze by tying a golden thread to the portals and unwinding it as he proceeded into it. Having strangled the Minotaur with his bare hands Theseus embarked with Ariadne on his ship. They landed at Naxos where Theseus deserted her and where she was subsequently discovered by Bacchus, Silenus and their band of satyrs. Bacchus married Ariadne who bore him and Minos many children including: Catreus, who succeeded Minos as king of Crete, Phaedra, who wed Theseus, and Acacallia who was seduced by Apollo.

Examples

A Sotheby's, *Sale Catalogue*, 21 March 1972. Enamelled Bacchus, 5½ in (14 cm), incised 'No. 293', mounted on a square base.

B Canterbury Museum. Ariadne, biscuit, 6½ in (16.5 cm), no incised number reported.

C Clifford, 1969, pl. 127A. Biscuit Bacchus, 8½ in (21.6 cm), incised 'No. 193'. B. N. Clifford collection (private).

D Derby Museums and Art Gallery, ref. no. 402. Biscuit Bacchus, 8½ in (21.6 cm), incised 'No. 193'.

E Idem. Biscuit Ariadne, 9½ in (24.1 cm), incised 'No. 194'.

References

1 Nightingale, op. cit., appendix p. 50.
2 Ibid., p. 67.
3 Ibid., p. 83.
4 Clifford, 1969, pl. 127A, marble Bacchus by Jacopo Sansovino; pl. 127B, Derby biscuit Bacchus.
5 Wedgwood and Bentley, *Sale Catalogue*, 1779. Class XII, section II, no. 9, 'Bacchus from Sansovino, 2 ins'.

No. 195. *Two Virgins Awakening Cupid* (group)

HASLEM 'Group of two Virgins awakening Cupid: 12½ ins., enamelled £2 2s 0d., biscuit £3 3s 6d.'

BEMROSE 'A group Virgins awakening Cupid.'

Two maidens stand bareheaded and barefoot regarding Cupid who sleeps upon a grassy mound, his long-bow beside him, while one tickles his ear with a blade of grass. Mounted on an irregular mound encrusted with leaves and flowers.

The two groups Nos. 195 and 196, and possibly also No. 235, form a *garniture de cheminé* and all three were based on stipple engravings made about 1776 by Francesco Bartolozzi after paintings by the talented Swiss artist Angelica

243 No. 195. *Two Virgins Awakening Cupid* (group). $12\frac{1}{2}$ in (31.8 cm). *Derby Museums and Art Gallery*

Kauffmann. Stipple engraving had been introduced into England by William Wynne Ryland (1732–83) who also enjoyed the doubtful distinction of having been hanged for fraud. Angelica Kauffmann (1741–1803) came to England in 1766 via Italy to paint in the Neo-Classical style both for private clients and for Robert Adam. The porcelain group is mentioned in the *Derby Sale Catalogues* of 5–8 May 1778:[1] 'A fine group of two Virgins awakening Cupid, in biscuit £1 19s 6d.' It has been ascribed to Pierre Stephan for stylistic reasons. The same group was also made at Zurich, entitled *Schlafender Amor*.[2]

Examples

A Lane, op. cit., pl. 71. enamelled, 11½ in (29.2 cm), incised 'No. 165'. British Museum.

B Twitchett, op. cit., pl. 144. Biscuit, 12¼ in (31.1 cm), incised 'No. 195'. Victoria and Albert Museum.

C Derby Museums and Art Gallery, no. 1535. Biscuit, 12½ in (31.8 cm), incised 'No. 195'.

References

1 Nightingale, op. cit., appendix p. 52.

2 S. Ducret, *Zürcher Porzellan*, Zurich, 1953, p. 25.

No. 196. *Two Bacchantes Adorning a Bust of Pan* (group)

HASLEM 'Group of two Bacchantes adorning Pan: 12½ ins., enamelled & gilt £2 2s od, biscuit £3 3s od.'

BEMROSE 'Two Virgins adorning Pan'.

Two bareheaded and barefoot female revellers bedeck a bust of Pan with garlands of flowers.

The group was adapted from an engraving by Francesco Bartolozzi after Angelica Kauffmann, and is complementary to Nos 195 and 235. It was mentioned in the *Derby Sale Catalogues* of May 1778:[1] 'One large group of two Bacchantes dressing Pan with a garland of flowers, in biscuit £1 15s od.'

Examples

A Twitchett, op. cit., pl. 125. Enamelled and gilt, 10⅛ in (25.7 cm), incised 'No. 196'. Victoria and Albert Museum reg. no. C.307–1940.

B Clifford, 1969, pl. 121d, biscuit, 12½ in (31.8 cm), incised 'No. 196'.

C Barrett and Thorpe, op. cit., pl. 98. Enamelled and gilt, 11 in (28 cm), incised

244 No. 196. *Two Bacchantes Adorning a Bust of Pan* (group). 12 in (30.5 cm). Incised 'No. 196'. *Sotheby's*

'No. 196'. Derby Museums and Art Gallery, ref. no. 1525.

D Sotheby's, *Sale Catalogue*, 10 February 1981, lot 124. Enamelled and gilt, 12 in (30.5 cm), incised 'No. 196'.

Reference

1 Nightingale, op. cit., appendix p. 53.

No. 197. *Not Identified*

HASLEM 'Cupid riding on a Sea-lion: $2\frac{3}{4}$ ins., enamelled & gilt 4s od.'

BEMROSE No item mentioned.

No. 198. *Pair of Haymakers* (pair)

HASLEM 'Pair of Haymakers: $6\frac{1}{2}$ ins., enamelled 15s od., biscuit 16s od.'
BEMROSE 'Haymaker and companion.'

A male rustic wearing a brimmed hat, jacket and breeches, holds a wine keg attached to a pole over his shoulder. His companion attired in linen cap, apron and dress, holds a wine flask in her dependent right hand. Mounted on scrolled bases.

245 No. 198. *Haymaker* carrying a keg attached to a pole.

246 No. 198. *Haymaker's Companion* with a wine-flask. 7 in (17.8 cm). Both incised 'No. 198'.
Thornton's of Harrogate

The *Derby Sale Catalogues* of 7–11 May 1782[1] include: 'One pair of haymakers, and 1 pair of sporting figures, ditto 18s od. Lord Monson.'

Examples

A Sotheby's, *Sale Catalogue*, 6 June 1972, lot 82. Female figure only, enamelled, $6\frac{1}{2}$ in (16.5 cm), incised 'No. 198G'.

B Victoria and Albert Museum. Female figure only, enamelled, $6\frac{1}{2}$ in (16.5 cm), incised 'No. 198'.

C *Connoisseur*, 88, 1930, no. 328, p. x. Male figure only, enamelled, no marks reported.

D Burnley Antiques. Displayed at the Antique Dealers' Fair, Buxton, April 1981. Pair, enamelled, 7 in (17.8 cm), incised 'No. 198'.

Reference

1 Nightingale, op. cit., appendix p. 68.

No. 199. *Harlequin and Columbine* (pair)

HASLEM 'Pair of Harlequin and Columbine: $5\frac{1}{2}$ ins., enamelled 10s 6d., biscuit 12s od.'

BEMROSE 'Harlequin and Columbine.'

Harlequin stands with left foot advanced and his right hand upon his breast. He wears a brimmed hat decorated with a rabbit's scut, face-mask and the motley and carries slap-sticks beneath his left arm. Columbine, who wears a falling ruffle, jacket and skirt, stands bareheaded, a posy in her left hand and her right arm outstretched. Mounted on irregular mound bases before tree-stump supports.

Harlequin and Columbine were amongst the first models to be made at Meissen initially adapted from engravings by Jacques Callot but subsequently based on illustrations by François Joullain in Luigi Riccoboni's *Histoire du théâtre italien,* published between 1727–32. Between 1736–40, J. J. Kändler created a series of Harlequin models[1] and in 1743–4 collaborated with Peter Reinicke to make a set of Italian Comedy models to commemorate the nuptuals of the Duke of Weissenfels[2] from which most of the English Comedy figures were copied. The *Derby Sale Catalogues* of 5–8 May 1778[3] mention: 'One pair of harlequins, 1 pair of gardeners, and a set of small grotesque seasons, in biscuit 16s od.' Also: 'One figure of Time, 1 pair of sitting figures, 1 Harlequin and Columbine £1 5s od.'[4]

The history of the *Commedia dell' Arte* (Italian Comedy) has been reviewed by Duchartre.[5] Harlequin (Arlecchino) was supposedly born in Bergamo, was employed as the servant of one of the main characters, namely Pantaloon

(Pantalone), or the Lover (Cynthio del Sole), and was the husband or lover of Columbine (Columbina), a maid in the same household. During and after the sixteenth century, troupes played throughout Europe where they were widely acclaimed. Harlequin spent most of his time on stage in romantic dalliance, plotting mischief, or engaged in bawdy repartee and acrobatics. By the mid-eighteenth century audiences became more sophisticated and the Comedy degenerated into light musical entertainments known as Harlequinades, some of which were performed in London. The Chelsea–Derby models here presented must have been amongst the last to have been issued by an English porcelain factory.

Examples

A Twitchett, op. cit., p. 58. Harlequin, enamelled, $5\frac{1}{2}$ in (14 cm), no marks incised. Ashworth Collection (private).

247 No. 199. *Harlequin and Columbine* in biscuit. $5\frac{1}{2}$ in (14 cm). Incised 'No. 199'. *Venner's Antiques*

248 No. 199. Enamelled version of *Harlequin*. $5\frac{1}{2}$ in (14 cm). *Private Collection*

B Brian Bowden Antiques, Doncaster. Harlequin, enamelled, $5\frac{1}{2}$in (14 cm), incised 'No. 199'.

C Christie's *Sale Catalogue*, 17 January 1972, lot 107. Columbine, enamelled, $5\frac{1}{2}$in (14 cm), incised 'No. 199'.

D Venner's Antiques, London. Biscuit Harlequin and Columbine, as illustrated.

References

1 Erica Pauls-Eisenbeiss, *German Porcelain of the Eighteenth Century*, London, 1972, I, Meissen: p. 263, Harlequin with bagpipes; p. 265, Harlequin drinking; p. 297, Harlequin alarmed; Harlequin with a Pug; p. 315, Harlequin dancing.

2 Ibid., pp. 319–41. Set of Italian Comedy figures made for the Duke of Weissenfels c. 1743–4.

3 Nightingale, op. cit., appendix p. 52.

4 Ibid., appendix p. 59.

5 Pierre-Louis Duchartre, *The Italian Comedy* New York, 1929, reprinted 1966 by Dover Publications.

No. 200. *The Four Quarters of the Globe* (set of four models)

HASLEM 'Set of Four Quarters of the Globe, 2 sizes: 1st. 6 ins., enamelled £1 12s od., biscuit £1 12s od. 2nd. $5\frac{1}{4}$ins., enamelled £1 4s od., biscuit £1 4s od.'

BEMROSE 'Four quarters, 2 sizes.'

Four models of standing children with appropriate accessories:

Africa A blackamoor wearing an elephant headdress, drapery and a cloak, holding a crab and a cornucopia, stepping over a lion.

America A Red Indian girl clad in a tunic and feathered headdress, holding a long-bow in her left hand and selecting with her right an arrow from a quiver on her back, an alligator at her feet.

Asia A Levantine girl clad in a toque, dress and cloak, holding a perfume-burner in her right hand and feeding a camel with berries with her left.

Europe A girl stands crowned wearing royal robes, holding an orb and sceptre in either hand, a recumbent horse at her feet.

F. E. Meyer created a more elaborate set of adult models at Meissen[1] c. 1750, that were followed by juvenile versions within that year.[2] These were copied about 1759 at Chelsea[3] and by the following year (E71) Derby versions appeared.[4] In both of them *America* differs from later Chelsea–Derby examples by reason of a feathered skirt and by holding the long-bow in her right hand and an arrow in her left. It would seem that the Chelsea–Derby *America* was based upon J. F. Eberlein's model of *Diana* after a seventeenth-century French bronze, copied at Derby about 1758,[5] subsequently adapted to provide *America* at Longton Hall about 1759[6] and reissued at Plymouth about 1770;[7] this in turn was reproduced in juvenile form at

Derby. The *Derby Sales Catalogues* of 9–14 May 1783[8] mention: 'A very elegant biscuit group representing the four quarters £1 7s od.' This relates to No. 295 in which the same four figures were combined as a group.

Examples

A Bradshaw, op. cit., col. pl. R. Enamelled, $5\frac{1}{4}$ in (13.3 cm), incised 'No. 200'. John and Diana Mould Collection (private).

B Sotheby's, *Sale Catalogue*, 18 May 1982, lot 130. Enamelled, $5\frac{1}{2}$ in (14 cm), no incised marks reported.

C Christie's, *Sale Catalogue*, 12 May 1969, lot 170. Enamelled, $5\frac{1}{4}$ in, impressed Derby factory device but no serial number.

References

1 Pauls-Eisenbeiss, op. cit., pp. 142 and 143. *Large Continents* by J. J. Kändler.
2 Sotheby's, *Sale Catalogue*, 9 June 1963, lot 165. Paired seated children as two groups, emblematic of the *Four Quarters of the Globe*, by F. E. Meyer, from which he later made standing versions.
3 Lane, op. cit., pls. 22b and 23b. Chelsea *Four Quarters of the Globe*.
4 Twitchett, op. cit., pl. 104. Derby *Four Quarters* c. 1760.
5 John Dixon, *English Porcelain of the Eighteenth Century*, London, 1952, pl. 38.
6 Bernard Watney, *Longton Hall Porcelain*, London, 1957, pl. 80d.
7 F. Severne Mackenna. *Cookworthy's Plymouth and Bristol Porcelain*, Leigh-on-Sea, 1946, figs. 91–4.
8 Nightingale, op. cit., appendix p. 75.

249 No. 200. *The Four Quarters of the Globe*. $5\frac{1}{2}$ in (14 cm). No incised marks reported. *Sotheby's*

250 No. 202. Biscuit *Cupid* with gun and leashed hound. No. 205. Biscuit *Cupid* with hunting-horn. Both $4\frac{5}{8}$ in (11.8 cm). Unmarked. *Warner Antiques*

Nos. 201 and 202. *Pair of Cupids*

HASLEM 'Pair of Cupids: [4 ins.], enamelled 5s od., biscuit 7s od.'
BEMROSE 'Two pair small Cupids.'

Cupid scantily draped and wearing a brimmed hat, holds a leashed hound with his left hand and has a fowling-piece under his right arm. His female companion stands holding an end-flute leaning upon a birdcage.

These models together with others of Cupid are taken from two groups, each of four figures, Nos. 251 and 257 depicting *Cupids Out Hunting*. These were available singly or in pairs and many surviving examples are unmarked.

Examples

A Sotheby's, *Sale Catalogue*, 3 October 1972, lot 224. Biscuit, $4\frac{1}{2}$ in (11.4 cm), incised 'No. 201'. Male figure only.

B Ibid., 16 March 1971, lot 388a. Biscuit, $4\frac{1}{4}$ in (10.8 cm), incised 'No. 202'. Female figure only.

No. 203. *Pair of Cupids*

HASLEM 'Pair of Cupids with Dog and Falcon: $5\frac{1}{4}$ ins., enamelled, [no price given], biscuit 10s 6d.'
BEMROSE No item mentioned.

Cupid standing as a shepherd, wearing a brimmed hat and scantily draped, plays an end-flute and with a dog at his feet. Female model unknown to author but presumably holds a falcon.

Example
Sotheby's, *Sale Catalogue*, 6 May 1969, lot 136. Enamelled, $5\frac{1}{4}$ in (13.3 cm), incised 'No. 203'.

No. 204. *Gardener and Companion* (pair)

HASLEM 'Pair of Gardeners: 5 ins., enamelled 8s od., biscuit 12s od.'
BEMROSE 'Pair of small gardeners.'

A gardener walking and holding a pannier of flowers beneath his right arm, wearing a brimmed hat, jacket, apron and breeches. The companion woman holds a watering-can and is clad in a laced bodice, apron and skirt. Mounted on an irregular mound encrusted with leaves and flowers.

251 No. 204. *Gardener* carrying a pannier of flowers. $5\frac{1}{2}$ in (14 cm). Incised 'No. 204'. *Venner's Antiques*

252 No. 204. *Gardener's Companion* with a watering-can. $5\frac{1}{2}$ in (14 cm). Incised 'No. 204 and N.W.' *Fitzwilliam Museum*

Examples

A Venner's Antiques. Enamelled, 5½ in (14 cm), incised 'No. 204'. Female figure only.

B Fitzwilliam Museum, ref. no. C.21–1938. Enamelled, 5½ in (14 cm), incised 'No. 204'. Male figure only.

Nos. 205 and 206. *Pair of Cupids*

HASLEM 'Pair of Cupids: 4½ ins., enamelled 5s od., biscuit 7s od.'
BEMROSE 'Pair small Cupids.'

Cupid scantily draped but wearing a brimmed hat, stands with a scrip slung by a strap diagonally from his left shoulder, playing an end-flute. His female companion blows a hunting-horn.

Examples

A Christie's, *Sale Catalogue*, 17 January 1972, lot 113. Biscuit Cupid with hunting-horn, 4½ ins., incised 'No. 206'.

B David Siers Collection (private). Enamelled, 4½ in (11.4 cm), incised 'No. 206'.

C Warner Antiques. See No. 262.

Nos. 207–12. *Not Identified*

HASLEM No. 207. 'Sea Nymph riding on a Dolphin: 4½ ins., enamelled 4s. 6d.' No. 208. 'Sea Nymph playing the Tabor: 3 ins., enamelled 2s 6d.' No. 209. 'Syren with a Shell: 2½ ins., enamelled 2s 6d.' No. 210. 'Triton: 3 ins., enamelled 2s 6d.' Nos. 211 and 212. No items mentioned.
BEMROSE Nos. 207–10. Ditto. Nos. 211 and 212. 'Fame and Mercury.'

The *Account Book* of William Duesbury[1] includes the following entries:

24 April 1787.	'4 Small Tritons	12s od.
	4 Sea Nymphs	12s od.
	4 Syrons with Shells	12s od.
	4 Boys riding on Dolphins	14s od.'

Reference

1 Barrett and Thorpe, op. cit., p. 153.

Nos. 213 and 214. *Cupids Seated with Dog and Falcon* (pair)

HASLEM 'Pair of Cupids, with Dog and Falcon: $4\frac{3}{8}$ ins., enamelled 10s 0d., biscuit 10s 6d.'

BEMROSE 'Pair small figures, Dog and Falcon.'

A pair of scantily clad Cupids, each seated on a rocky mound beneath a leafing tree; one holds a front paw proffered by a dog that licks his face, the other supports a falcon upon his wrist.

253 No. 213. *Cupid Seated with Dog* on rocks beneath a tree. $5\frac{1}{2}$ in (14 cm). Incised 'No. 213'.

254 No. 214. Companion *Cupid with a Falcon*. $5\frac{1}{2}$ in (14 cm). Incised 'No. 214'.

Derby Museums and Art Gallery

Examples

A Twitchett, op. cit., pl. 147. Biscuit, 5 in (12.7 cm). Stated to be incised 'No. 123', but this must be a typographical error.

B Derby Museum, ref. nos. 671 and 437. Biscuit, 5 in (12.7 cm), incised 'No. 213' and 'No. 214'.

C Sotheby's, *Sale Catalogue*, 16 March 1971, lot 390. Biscuit, 5½ in (14 cm), no marks reported.

No. 215. *Not Identified*

HASLEM No item mentioned.
BEMROSE 'Four small seasons.'

Nos. 216 and 217. *Poetry and Music* (two groups)

HASLEM 'Pair, group Music and Poetry, 3 sizes: 1st. 9¾ ins., enamelled £3 3s 0d., biscuit £3 15s 0d. 2nd. ——, enamelled £2 16s 0d., biscuit £3 3s 0d. 3rd. ——, enamelled £2 10s 0d., biscuit £2 16s 0d.'
BEMROSE 'Music and Poetry.'

Poetry, No. 216, is represented by a lady attired in a long robe, standing bareheaded and barefoot, holding a book or a scroll, attended by two putti. One sits holding a quill and parchment, the other stands holding aloft a scroll. The group also includes a ruined fluted column with trophies scattered both over it and upon the base.

Music, No. 217, is portrayed by a similar female figure playing a flute, with two companion putti, one seated holding a violin and musical score, the other standing holding aloft a song-sheet.

The *Derby Sale Catalogues* of 5–8 May 1778[1] mention: 'One large music group in biscuit £1 10s 0d.', though this might refer to No. 40. However, the identities of groups mentioned in the *Sale Catalogues* of 23–28 May 1985[2] seems assured: 'A beautiful pair of groups representing Poetry and Music, in biscuit £2 15s 0d.' Both groups have been tentatively ascribed to Pierre Stephan for stylistic reasons.

Examples

A Rackham, 1915, pl. 40, no. 424 (new no. 356). Biscuit *Music Group*, 9½ in (24.1 cm), incised 'No. 217'. Schreiber Collection.

B Derby Museums and Art Gallery, ref. no. 460. Biscuit *Poetry Group*, 10½ in (26.6 cm), incised 'No. 216'.

255 No. 216. Biscuit group emblematic of *Poetry*. 9½ in (24.1 cm). Incised 'No. 216'.
Birmingham Museum and Art Gallery

256 No. 217. Biscuit group emblematic of *Music*. 9½ in (24.1 cm). Incised 'No. 217'.
Derby Museums and Art Gallery

C Birmingham Museum, ref. no. 101–31. Biscuit *Poetry Group*, 9½ in (24.1 cm), incised 'No. 216'.

D Christie's, *Sale Catalogue*, 13 May 1968, lot 58. Biscuit groups of *Music and Poetry*, 10½ in (26.6 cm), incised respectively 'No. 217' and 'No. 216'.

References

1 Nightingale, op. cit., appendix p. 52.

2 Ibid., appendix p. 91.

Nos. 218–21. *Not Identified*

HASLEM No. 218 and No. 219. No items mentioned. No. 220 and No. 221. 'Pair Basket Figures, 2 sizes: 1st. $6\frac{1}{2}$ ins., enamelled 15s 0d. 2nd. $5\frac{1}{4}$ ins., enamelled 10s 6d.'

BEMROSE No. 218. No item mentioned. No. 219. 'Pair of basket figures.' No. 220 and No. 221. 'Pair of basket figures.'

Stiffly posed standing putti, adorned with floral diadems and diagonal garlands slung from one shoulder, holding baskets of flowers, are generally known as *Basket Figures*, about $4\frac{1}{2}$ in (11.4 cm), but without any incised serial numbers.

257 No. 222. *Winged Time* with an hour-glass and scythe, c. 1820 version. 7 in (15.2 cm). Incised 'No. 222'. *B. and T. Thorn Antiques*

No. 222. *Winged Time* (group)

HASLEM 'Figure of Time: 6½ ins., enamelled 9s 0d., biscuit 10s 6d.'
BEMROSE 'Hercules.'

Time is portrayed as a bearded and winged man wearing a robe draped over his left shoulder, holding in both hands an hour-glass, standing with one foot upon a terrestrial globe. Astrological instruments are scattered about him.

Although the precise source of this group is unknown, Timothy Clifford has suggested it may have been adapted from the marble Venus[1] in the Boboli Grotto by Giovanni da Bologna (1529–1608). It is mentioned in the *Derby Sale Catalogue* of 17 April 1771:[2] 'Lot 52. A figure of Time, richly finish'd £1 10s 0d.' Also between 10–14 May 1781:[3] 'A figure of Time and a set of seasons, enamelled £1 15s 0d.' The group should be distinguished from *Time clipping the wings of Love* (No. 124).

Examples

A Clifford, 1969, pl. 127. Biscuit, 6½ in (16.5 cm), square base, incised 'No. 222'. B. N. Clifford Collection (private).

B B. and T. Thorn Antiques. Enamelled, 6 in (15.2 cm), Bloor Derby version mounted upon a circular base.

References

1 Clifford, 1969, p. 115.
2 Nightingale, op. cit., appendix p. 19.
3 Ibid., appendix p. 63.

Nos. 223–5. *Not Identified*

HASLEM No items mentioned.
BEMROSE Ditto.

No. 226. *Cupid in Disguise as a Shepherd*

HASLEM No item mentioned.
BEMROSE Ditto.

Cupid attired as a shepherd, wearing a brimmed hat and playing an end-flute, stands beside his dog.

Example

Fitzwilliam Museum. Enamelled, 3½ in (8.9 cm), incised 'No. 226'.

258 No. 227. *Pair of Dwarfs,* after J. Callot. 7 in (17.8 cm). Incised 'No. 227'. *Sotheby's*

No. 227. *Pair of Dwarfs* (two models)

HASLEM 'Pair of Grotesque Punches: 7 ins., enamelled 18s od.'
BEMROSE 'Pair of grotesque punches.'

An *Adult Dwarf* with a moustache, stands, left hand on hip, grasping a staff in his right; his hat resembles an inverted wine-funnel and he wears a decorative waistcoat, flounce and cloak.

An *Adolescent Dwarf* is usually clean-shaven, though in some models he has a sparse downward-turned moustache. He stands with both thumbs in his belt, and wears a conical hat, waistcoat, sash and trousers. Both mounted on pad bases encrusted with leaves and flowers.

The models ultimately stem from etchings made by Jacques Callot of a troupe of performing dwarfs that visited the Medici Court in Florence, illustrating his *Varie figure Gobbi*, published in 1616 in Antwerp.[1] These depict a 'Dwarf with a tall hat and drooping belly', and a 'Dwarf with a big belly'. The first of these prompted models at Meissen,[2] Mennecy[3] and Chelsea.[4] However, these were all issued with different companions, that made at Chelsea being paired with a female dwarf.[5] Chelsea–Derby versions are gaily painted with patterns composed of lozenges upon their garments, and in some early examples scarves are draped over

259 Etching by J. Callot of a dwarf with a big belly.
260 Etching by J. Callot of a dwarf with a tall hat.

their hats, though in later ones these are replaced by labels carrying advertisements. Legend holds that in Tudor times two dwarfs, a father and son, stood outside the Mansion House bearing advertisements for small fees, and a woodcut, supposedly illustrating their activities, is preserved in the Guildhall. This accounts for the name 'Mansion House Dwarfs' sometimes employed. Joseph Lygo[6] in a letter to William Duesbury II written in 1790 mentions: '... cannot get a print of Callot's ...'. They proved to be extremely popular figures and continued to be reproduced well into the nineteenth century.

Examples

A Barrett and Thorpe, op. cit., pl. 133. Enamelled, 7 in (17.8 cm), incised 'No. 227'. Derby Museums and Art Gallery.

B Gilhespy, 1951, pl. 78, figs. 142 and 142a. The same examples as the above.

C Sotheby's, *Sale Catalogue*, 26 November 1974, lot 70. Enamelled, 7 in (17.8 cm), incised 'No. 227'.

References

1 Howard Daniel, *Callot's Etchings*, London and New York, 1974, nos. 137 and 139.

2 W. B. Honey, *German Porcelain*, London, 1947, pls. 3b and 3c. Meissen *Dwarfs* after Callot.

3 George Savage, *Seventeenth and Eighteenth Century French Porcelain*, London, 1960, pl. 30b. Rue de la Charonne *Dwarfs* after Callot.

4 F. Severne Mackenna, *Chelsea Porcelain, the Triangle and Raised Anchor Wares*, Leigh-on-Sea, 1948, pl. 39, fig. 80. Chelsea *Male Dwarf* after Callot.

5 F. Severne Mackenna, *Chelsea Porcelain, the Red Anchor Wares*, Leigh-on-Sea, 1951, pl. 58, fig. 116. Chelsea Female Dwarf.

6 Gilhespy, 1961, p. 72.

No. 228. *Not Identified*

HASLEM No item mentioned.
BEMROSE Ditto.

No. 229. *Neptune with a Dolphin*

HASLEM No item mentioned.
BEMROSE Ditto.

This model is a reissue of No. 118, mounted upon a base decorated with symmetrically arranged scrolls.

Examples

A Barrett and Thorpe, op. cit., pl. 96. Enamelled, 8 in (20.3 cm), incised 'No. 229'. Derby Museums and Art Gallery.
B Weston Park Museum, Sheffield. Same specifications as above.

No. 230. *Not Identified*

HASLEM No item mentioned.
BEMROSE Ditto

No. 231. *James Quinn as Sir John Falstaff*

HASLEM 'Large Falstaff.'
BEMROSE 'Figure of a nun, large.'

The actor James Quinn portrayed as Sir John Falstaff, a corpulent, bearded and moustachioed knight with long hair, standing with his legs apart holding a sword and an oval shield; he is clad in a plumed hat, shirt with ruffles at neck and cuffs, a doublet gathered by a leather belt, baggy breeches and boots.

The first Derby model (E4) was adapted from an engraving of about 1760 by James McArdell after a portrait by Francis Hayman. This differs from a Bow model which is based on Grignion's engraving of the actor David Garrick in the role.[1] Haslem ascribes the Derby model to John Bacon[2] without supporting evidence. The *Derby Sale Catalogues* of 5–8 May 1779[3] include: 'A large figure of Falstaff 16s od.' It was obviously popular, for subsequently it was reissued as No. 291, in five different sizes. Some show a bill of fare tucked into the knight's belt:

A Capon	2s 0d.
Sauce	4s 0d.
Sack	5s 0d.
	11s 0d.

James Quinn (1693–1766) was the illegitimate son of an Irish barrister and one-time Lord Mayor of Dublin, of the same name. Born in London, educated in Ireland, he made his debut on the Dublin stage and, following his father's death, came to London in 1714. He played minor roles at Drury Lane until 7 November 1716 when at short notice he took over the part of Bajazet in *Tamerlane,* from Mills, who had been ill. He was an unqualified success and thereafter starred in both Shakespearian plays and contemporary dramas. He was, perhaps, one of the last proponents of the declamatory style characterized by loud and bombastic

261 No. 231. *James Quinn as Sir John Falstaff.* 13 in (33 cm). Incised 'No. 231'. *Sotheby's*

flowery speeches frequently interrupted by loud applause, in sharp contrast to the more natural manner favoured by Garrick. Quinn was a flamboyant and quarrelsome character who killed two opponents in duels yet was a brilliant conversationalist. He referred to Garrick as 'A new religion' which prompted the retort, 'Pope Quinn damns all churches but his own.' Quinn played Falstaff for the first time in 1742 at Drury Lane where John Rich was manager. When the 1747–8 London season was over, Quinn wrote to Rich: 'I am in Bath, yours James Quinn.' He received the reply, 'Stay there and be damned, yours John Rich.' He retired to Bath in 1751 where increasingly he came to resemble Falstaff by his corpulence, insatiable thirst for wine and a gargantuan appetite. Tobias Smollett relates how one Friday night when Quinn had dined well at the Three Tuns Inn, he gave instructions that six bottles of claret should be sent up to his room and nobody should disturb him until noon on Sunday. Although during his stage career he remained aloof from other actors and actresses, in his twilight years he became very friendly with David Garrick.

Examples

A Barrett and Thorpe, op. cit., pl. 62. Enamelled, 5¼ in (13.3 cm), c. 1765, Derby Museums and Art Gallery.

B Sotheby's, *Sale Catalogue*, 10 February 1981, lot 126. Enamelled, 13 in (33 cm), incised 'No. 231'.

C Ibid., 16 March 1982, lot 116. Enamelled, 8½ in (21.6 cm), no marks.

D Twitchett, op. cit., pl. 66. Enamelled, 13 in (33 cm), no marks reported.

E Rackham, 1915, pl. 21, no. 204. Enamelled, 13 in (33 cm), Victoria and Albert Museum, Schreiber Collection.

References

1 A. J. Toppin, 'The Origin of Some Ceramic Designs', *Trans. ECC*, 2, 1948, no. 10, pp. 266–76, pl. CId, Bow model of *Falstaff*; pl. CIc, engraving by Grignion.

2 Haslem, op. cit., appendix p. 152.

3 Nightingale, op. cit., appendix p. 55.

No. 232. *Not Identified*

HASLEM No item mentioned.
BEMROSE No item mentioned.

No. 233. *Pair of Cupids* (two models)

HASLEM No item mentioned.
BEMROSE No item mentioned.

These models are reissues of No. 201, Cupid with a leashed hound, and No. 211, Cupid leaning upon a bird-cage holding an end-flute.

Examples

A Rackham, 1915, pl. 41, no. 429 (new no. 355). Biscuit, Cupid with a leashed Hound, $3\frac{1}{2}$ in (8.9 cm), incised 'No. 233'.
B A. E. Dodson Collection (private). Cupid leaning on a bird-cage holding an end-flute, biscuit, $3\frac{1}{2}$ in (8.9 cm), incised 'No. 233'.

No. 234. *Four Cupids Bird's-nesting*

HASLEM 'Group of Four Cupids: 10 ins., enamelled £1 1s 0d., biscuit £1 11s 6d.'
BEMROSE 'Group of 4 Cupids.'

262 No. 234. *Four Cupids Bird's-nesting* (group). 9 in (22.9 cm). Incised 'No. 234'.
Derby Museums and Art Gallery

Four winged and scantily clad Cupids upon a rocky mound about a leafing tree: one slides down the tree-trunk, one stands holding a nest of fledglings, a third removes a chick from the nest, while the fourth sits amid nets and cages.

Example

Barrett and Thorpe, op. cit., pl. 94. Biscuit, 9 in (22.9 cm), incised 'No. 234 N' and with a small triangle. Derby Museums and Art Gallery.

No. 235. *Three Graces Distressing Cupid* (group)

HASLEM 'Group of Three Graces distressing Cupid, 2 sizes: 1st. 14½ ins., enamelled £3 13s 6d., biscuit £4 4s od. 2nd. 13 ins., enamelled £2 12s 6d., biscuit £3 3s od.'
BEMROSE 'Three virgins distressing Cupid, 3 sizes.'

Three bareheaded and barefoot maidens stand about Cupid bound to a tree; one kneels to examine his quiver, another stoops to examine his long-bow, while the third pelts him with flowers.

This group, like Nos. 195 and 196, was adapted from Francesco Bartolozzi's engraving after Angelica Kauffmann. It is mentioned in the *Derby Sale Catalogues* of 7–11 May 1782[1] as: 'A beautiful group of three Graces distressing Cupid, in biscuit £2 3s od.'

Examples

A Barrett and Thorpe, op. cit., pl. 99. Biscuit, 13 in (33 cm), incised 'No. 235'. Derby Museums and Art Gallery, ref. no. 451.

B Twitchett, op. cit., pl. 131. Biscuit, 13¼ in (33.7 cm), incised 'No. 235'. This shows a variation with one of the maidens looking round the tree-trunk at Cupid.

C Ibid., pl. 232. Enamelled, 15¼ in (38.7 cm), incised 'No. 235'. Victoria and Albert Museum, ref. no. C.194–1926.

Reference

1 Nightingale, op. cit., appendix p. 70.

Nos. 236–42. *Not Identified*

HASLEM Nos. 236 and 237. 'Pair of Cupids: 4 ins., enamelled 5s od., biscuit 7s od.' No. 238. No item mentioned. No. 239. 'The Virgin Mary: 10½ ins., enamelled £1 1s od.' No. 240. 'Pastoral Group of two figures: 7½ ins., enamelled 8s od.' Nos. 241 and 242. No items mentioned.

263 No. 235. *Three Graces Distressing Cupid* (biscuit group). 13 in (33 cm). Incised 'No. 235'.
Derby Museums and Art Gallery

264 No. 235. Enamelled example of *Three Graces Distressing Cupid*. 13 in (33 cm). Incised 'No. 235'.
Private Collection

BEMROSE Nos. 236–239. No items mentioned. No. 240. 'Group of two figures.' No. 241. 'Large fountain group.' Also 'Four Quarters, 3 sizes.' No. 242. No item mentioned.

No. 243. *Apollo*

HASLEM 'Apollo: $9\frac{1}{2}$ ins., enamelled £1 1s 0d.'
BEMROSE No item mentioned.

Apollo is depicted as a long-haired youth wearing a laurel diadem and loose robe, playing a lyre. This is a reissue of No. 116.

Example
Sotheby's, *Sale Catalogue*, 20 May 1980, lot 103. Enamelled, $10\frac{1}{4}$ in (26 cm), incised 'No. 243'. Offered with companion figure of *Diana* (No. 65).

No. 244. *Plenty*

HASLEM 'Plenty: $9\frac{3}{8}$ ins., enamelled £1 4s 0d.'
BEMROSE 'Figure of Plenty.'

Plenty, portrayed as a lady wearing a laurel crown and long robe, stands with her left arm resting upon an urn on which lies a bunch of fruit, and holding leaves and flowers in her right hand. Mounted on an octagonal base decorated with the Greek key-fret pattern in low relief.

Examples
A Sotheby's, *Sale Catalogue*, 5 June 1968, lot 323. Biscuit, $9\frac{1}{2}$ in (24 cm), incised 'No. 244'.
B Ibid., 31 July 1968, lot 256. Enamelled, $9\frac{1}{2}$ in (24 cm), incised 'No. 244'.

No. 245. *Charlotte Weeping for Werther*

HASLEM 'Peace: $9\frac{1}{4}$ ins., enamelled £1 4s 0d., biscuit £1 11s 6d.'
BEMROSE No items mentioned.

The young Charlotte stands wearing a feathered head-dress, tunic, skirt and sandals, a scarf draped over her right arm, leaning her left hand upon an urn upon a plinth, and holding a fan in her right.

The model illustrates a scene from Goethe's *The Sorrows of Young Werther*, published in 1774. Werther, a young student, falls in love with Charlotte only to discover she is already married. He writes her a farewell letter and, taking her

265 No. 243. *Apollo.* 10¼ in (26 cm). Incised 'No. 243'. *Sotheby's*

266 No. 245. *Charlotte Weeping for Werther.* 9½ in (24.1 cm). Incised 'No. 245'. *Late Raymond Shingler Collection*

husband's pistol, he kills himself. The tale was translated into English in 1779 by Richard Graves and, in 1785, was adapted by Frederick Reynolds for the stage when it opened at Covent Garden. The subject prompted Meissen models during the 1780s, while a relief plaque designed by Lady Elizabeth Templeton was executed by Hackwood and issued by Wedgwood in 1790.

Examples

A Raymond Shingler Collection (private). Enamelled, $9\frac{1}{2}$ in (24.1 cm), incised 'No. 245', as illustrated.

B Sotheby's, *Sale Catalogue*, 31 July 1968, lot no. unknown. Enamel, $9\frac{1}{2}$ in (24 cm), incised 'No. 245'.

No. 246. *Not Identified*

HASLEM No item mentioned.
BEMROSE 'Pair small figures.'

No. 247. *The Grape-gatherers* (group)

HASLEM 'Pastoral Group of two Figures: $12\frac{1}{4}$ ins., enamelled £2 5s od.'
BEMROSE No item mentioned.

This group is adapted from No. 176 with the addition of a leafing tree placed behind and between the two figures.

Example

J. V. G. Mallet, *The Bearsted Collection: Porcelain*, Plaistow, 1964, no. 70. Biscuit, 11 in (28 cm), incised 'No. 247 B'. Upton House.

No. 248. *The Antique Seasons* (group)

HASLEM 'Group of Four Seasons, Antique: 11 ins., enamelled £1 11s 6d., biscuit £2 2s od.'
BEMROSE 'A group of antique seasons.'

A group of four ancient divinities standing upon a rocky mound about an obelisk upon an architectural plinth. *Flora* holds flowers in a fold of her dress, *Ceres* holds a cornsheaf, *Bacchus* crowned with vine leaves and grapes holds a goblet and grapes in either hand, *Vulcan* gathers his robe about him and stands beside a brazier.

This group incorporates the same models as those initially issued in a set of four, No. 5.

267 No. 248. *The Antique Seasons* (biscuit group). 10 in (25.4 cm). Incised 'No. 248'.
Victoria and Albert Museum

Examples

A Victoria and Albert Museum. Biscuit, 10 in (25.4 cm), incised 'No. 248'.

B Derby Museums and Art Gallery, ref. no. 412. Biscuit, 11 in (28 cm), incised 'No. 248'.

C Christie's, *Sale Catalogue*, 18 December 1972, lot 298. Biscuit, 11 in (28 cm), incised 'No. 248'.

Nos. 249 and 250. *The Four Elements* (two groups)

HASLEM No items mentioned.
BEMROSE No. 249. No item mentioned. No. 250. 'Two small Elements.'

Fire and Water are represented by a youth igniting faggots with a burning-glass and a girl with a fishing-net holding a catch in a fold of her dress (No. 249).

Earth and Air comprise a gardener leaning upon his spade and a girl who holds aloft a bird and carries a hunting-horn (No. 250).

Each pair stand upon a rocky mound on either side of a leafing tree. The models are the same as those by Pierre Stephan (No. 3).

Example
Allam, op. cit., p. 33, nos. III and IV. Biscuit, 10½ in (26.7 cm), incised as above.

No. 251. *Four Cupids Hunting* (group)

HASLEM 'Group of 4 Cupids: 9 ins., enamelled 18s 0d., biscuit £1 5s 0d.'
BEMROSE 'Group of 4 Cupids.'

A group of four winged and scantily clad Cupids wearing brimmed hats upon a rocky mound about a leafing tree. One holds a leashed hound, one plays a hunting-horn, another leans against a bird-cage and holds an end-flute, while the fourth holds a gun and has a scrip suspended by a diagonal strap from his shoulder.

Example
Derby Museums and Art Gallery. Biscuit, 9 in (22.9 cm), incised 'No. 251', as illustrated.

No. 252. *Group of Three Cupids*

HASLEM 'Group of 3 Cupids: 13½ ins., enamelled £1 1s 0d., biscuit £1 11s 6d.'
BEMROSE 'Group of 3 Cupids.'

x Pair of *Minuet Dancers* (E18), c. 1760. $10\frac{3}{4}$ and 11 in (27.4 and 28.1 cm). The floral sprays are in the manner of *indianische Blumen* (see p. 60). See also Plate 76. *Victoria and Albert Museum*

XI Group of *Tyrolean Dancers* (E19), c. 1760. $7\frac{1}{2}$ in (19.1 cm). Here the more usual floral sprays have been replaced by patterns composed of circles, lines, dots and stars (see p. 83) which echo the decoration upon the Meissen prototype in the collection of Lord Fisher. *Fitzwilliam Museum*

XII *David Garrick as Tancred*, from the play *Tancred and Sigismunda* (E7), c. 1760. $8\frac{7}{8}$ in (22.6 cm). *Victoria and Albert Museum*

XIII The *Garland Shepherds* (E23), c. 1765. $7\frac{1}{2}$ in (19.1 cm). The earlier plain washes of colour used upon garments are here broken by reserves containing stylized stems, leaves and florets simulating brocades (see p. 83). *Albury Antiques*

XIV *George III in Van Dyck dress* (F10), c. 1773. 14 in (35.6 cm). The biscuit figure is adapted from Richard Earlom's engraving after Johann Zoffany's portrait of the Royal Family and was issued en suite with two other groups. *British Museum*

XV The *Alpine Shepherdess* group (No. 256), c. 1785. 12 in (30.5 cm). The use of transparent light-green enamel and more natural colouring of garments reflects the Louis Seize taste.
See also Plate 270.
Victoria and Albert Museum

XVI Pair of *Grimacing Dwarfs* (No. 53), c. 1775. $5\frac{1}{2}$ in (14 cm). See also Plate 163. *Bonhams*

XVII *Lady Feeding a Sheep with Hay* (No. 395), c. 1795. 14 in (35.6 cm). The warm tone of the biscuit and satin-like sheen are characteristic of Derby in the eighteenth century and the figure was one of the last to have been made by Jean-Jacques Spengler. See also Plate 333.
Victoria and Albert Museum

XVIII *The Shoe-black* and *Hairdresser* groups (Nos. 81 and 84), c. 1820. $7\frac{1}{2}$ in (19.1 cm). These were first issued c. 1780 but the late versions are in the dark opaque colouring of the Bloor period. See also Plates 190 and 192. *Victoria and Albert Museum*

XIX *Sleeping Nymph* (G50), c. 1845. $5\frac{1}{2}$ in (14 cm). The figure is adapted from the Cupid in the earlier group *Two Virgins awakening Cupid* (No. 195), and is ascribed to John Whitaker. See also Plate 364. *Timothy Kendrew Antiques*

268 No. 251. *Four Cupids Hunting* (biscuit group). 9 in (22.9 cm). Incised 'No. 251'. *Derby Museums and Art Gallery*

269 No. 252. *Group of Three Cupids*, one with a dog, one playing a mandoline, and one holding a crib (biscuit). $13\frac{1}{2}$ in (34.3 cm). No incised mark. *Sotheby's*

A group of three winged and scantily clad Cupids about a leafing tree upon a rocky mound. One stands playing a lute, another holds a basket of flowers, the third sits with right arm upraised beside a recumbent dog. The base is encrusted with shells and leaves.

Example
Sotheby's, *Sale Catalogue*, 16 June 1981, lot 163. Biscuit, 13½ in (34.3cm), no marks reported, as illustrated.

No. 253. *Pair of Cupids*

HASLEM 'Pair of Cupids with Dog and Birdcage: 3¾ ins., enamelled 4s od., biscuit 7s od.'
BEMROSE 'Pair small Cupids, dog and birdcage.'

Cupid wearing a brimmed hat and scantily draped, holding a leashed hound. Companion likewise carrying a wicker bird-cage. These models are reissues of Nos. 233 and 251.

Example
Private Collection.

No. 254. *Pastoral Group*

HASLEM 'Pastoral Group of two Figures: 13½ ins., enamelled £2 10s od.'
BEMROSE 'Large group.'

A memorandum in the Derby Museums and Art Gallery indicates that a group incised 'No. 254' was brought by an anonymous collector to the museum for identification and was described as follows: 'A shepherdess sits upon a grassy mound beneath a leafing tree with a basket of flowers close to her right foot. A young shepherd boy stoops over her. Mounted on an irregular mound base.'

No. 255. *The Knot in the Cravat*

HASLEM 'Pastoral Group of two Figures: 12 ins., enamelled £2 os od.'
BEMROSE 'Pastoral group.'

This group was adapted from No. 177 by the addition of a leafing tree behind and between the two figures.

270 No. 255. *The Knot in the Cravat* (left). Incised 'No. 255'.
No. 256. *Alpine Shepherdess* (right). Incised 'Nȯ. 256'. See also Plate xv. Both 12 in (30.5 cm).
Victoria and Albert Museum

Example

A Rackham, 1915, pl. 42, no. 420 (new no. 352). Enamelled, 11½ in (29.2 cm), incised 'No. 255'.

No. 256. *Alpine Shepherdess* (group)

HASLEM 'Pastoral Group of two Figures: 12¼ ins., enamelled £2'os od.'
BEMROSE 'Pastoral group.'

A reissue of No. 178 with the addition of a leafing tree.

Examples

A Rackham, 1915, pl. 42, no. 420 (new no. 352). Enamelled, 12¼ in (31.1 cm), incised 'No. 256'.

B Twitchett, op. cit., col. pl. 16. Biscuit, 14 in (35.6 cm), incised 'No. 256'. Royal Crown Derby Museum.

No. 257. *Four Cupids Hunting* (group)

HASLEM 'Group of four Cupids: 9¾ ins., enamelled £1 1s 0d., biscuit £1 11s 6d.'
BEMROSE 'Group of four Cupids.'

Four winged and scantily clad Cupids wearing brimmed hats grouped about a leafing tree upon a rocky mound, similar to No. 251 but with different models including one holding a pair of leashed hounds, one bearing a flaming torch, another carrying a quiver full of arrows, while the last stoops to sharpen an arrow-head.

Models of Cupids included in the two groups Nos. 251 and 257 were issued singly or in pairs, as previously indicated.

Examples

A Rackham, 1917, pl. 32, no. 118. Biscuit, 8¼ in (21 cm), incised 'No. 257'.
B Sotheby's, *Sale Catalogue*, 16 March 1971, lot 391. Biscuit, 8 in (20.3 cm), no marks.

No. 258. *Not Identified*

HASLEM 'Pair of Sitting Boy Candlesticks: 6½ ins., enamelled 16s 0d.'
BEMROSE No item mentioned.

Although no examples bearing appropriate incised numbers are known, there are several unmarked ones that might fill the void.

No. 259. *Britannia*

HASLEM 'Britannia, 3 sizes: 1st. [no size given], enamelled £2 2s 0d. 2nd. no size given, enamelled £1 11s 6d. 3rd. [no size given], enamelled £1 1s 0d.'
BEMROSE 'A large Britannia, 2 sizes.' Also: 'Five small elements.'

Britannia stands supporting a shield upon which is emblazoned the device formed by the intersecting crosses of St George and St Andrew, beside a lion couchant. She wears a plumed helmet and dress with sleeves rolled up and the hem of her skirt looped to her waist, and holds a trident in her right hand.

Models of *Britannia* were included in a large consignment of Derby porcelain dispatched for sale to London in 1763,[1] some of which may have been adapted upon lead garden statuary by John Cheere[2] representing *Minerva*. The *Derby Sale Catalogues* of 5–8 May 1779[3] include: 'A large figure of Britannia £1 3s 0d'. There is an interesting and rare variant now in the Bowes Museum in which Britannia stands before a small bocage of acorns and oak leaves with a shield bearing the device of a wild boar and a lion. This might be a rebus 'Boarslion' or the emblem of some secret society. The *Sale Catalogues* of 11 –14 December 1783,[4] marking the closure of the Chelsea works, included: 'The moulds of a Large figure of Britannia, 5 feet high, £2 2s od.', which is likely to have been made for casting terracotta rather than porcelain.

Examples

A Clifford, 1969, pl. 126a. Biscuit. 12½ in (31.8 cm), no incised marks reported. B. N. Clifford Collection.

B Bowes Museum. Enamelled, 13 in (33 cm), as illustrated.

References

1 Jewitt, Llewellynn, *The Ceramic Art of Great Britain*, London, 1878, II, pp. 68–9.
2 Clifford, 1969, pp. 113–14.
3 Nightingale, op. cit., appendix p. 56.
4 Ibid., p. 82.

271 No. 259. *Britannia*. 13 in (33 cm). No incised mark. *Bowes Museum*

No. 260. *Boy Crying* and *Girl Laughing* (pair)

HASLEM 'Crying Boy and Laughing Girl, 2 sizes: 1st. [$8\frac{1}{2}$ ins.], enamelled ——. 2nd. $7\frac{5}{8}$ ins., enamelled 14s od.'
BEMROSE 'Crying boy and laughing girl, 2 sizes.'

A bareheaded girl laughs as she holds a small boy's ball out of his reach while he reaches out vainly with his right hand and dries his tears with a handkerchief in his left.

Examples

A B. and T. Thorn. Enamelled pair, $8\frac{1}{2}$ in (21.6 cm), incised 'No. 260', as illustrated.
B Sotheby's, *Sale Catalogue*, 22 October 1968, lot 106. Enamelled, 8 in (20.3 cm), no incised marks reported.

272 No. 260. *Girl Laughing*, holding her brother's ball.

273 No. 260. Companion *Boy Crying* with hand outstretched. Both $8\frac{1}{2}$ in. (21.6 cm). Incised 'No. 260'. *B. and T. Thorn Antiques*

No. 261. *Not Identified*

HASLEM No item mentioned.
BEMROSE 'Peace & Plenty, 2 sizes.' Also: 'Pair large Cupids, Dove and Key.'

Nos. 262–78. *Cupids in Disguise*

HASLEM 'Seventeen Figures of Cupid in Disguise: [$4\frac{1}{2}$–$4\frac{3}{4}$ ins.], enamelled 2s 6d. [each].'
BEMROSE No items mentioned.

The majority of the Derby Cupids do not bear any incised number and in a few instances different numbers may appear on identical examples. All appear to have been cast from gold anchor Chelsea moulds and are slightly smaller with restyled bases. Some original wax models survive and are at Copeland's factory, Stoke-on-Trent.[1] Red anchor Chelsea Cupids are mostly slightly smaller than both the gold anchor and Derby versions.

Cupid, as a Bewigged Lawyer, playing an end-flute. Fitzwilliam Museum, ref. no. C.98–1950, as illustrated.
Cupid with a Magic Lantern. Ibid., ref. no. C.97–1950.
Cupid as a Lady's Maid, with powder box and puff. Author's Collection.

274 Nos. 262–78. Five *Cupids in Disguise.* $4\frac{1}{4}$–$4\frac{3}{4}$ in (10.8–12.1 cm). No incised marks. *Fitzwilliam Museum*

Cupid as a Nursemaid, carrying a baby in a crib. Fitzwilliam Museum, ref. no. C.3674–1928.
Cupid as a Girl with a Hurdy-gurdy. Ibid., ref. no. C.97–1950; Author's Collection, as illustrated.
Cupid as a Money-Lender, holding a purse. David Thorn Collection, as illustrated.
Cupid as a Shepherd, piping with a dog. Fitzwilliam Museum, ref. no. C.99–1950.
Cupid as a Shepherdess, with a lamb. Peter and Heather Jackson.
Cupid as a Chimney Sweep, wearing a round hat with a sack over his left shoulder. Burnley Antiques.

These are mounted on either cylindrical or scrolled bases, the latter embellished with light blue enamel and gilt. It is likely that the eight remaining Cupids follow some of the following Chelsea models:

Cupid as a Cook, holding a saucepan over a brick oven. Mackenna, 1951, pl. 76, fig. 152.
Cupid as a Scullion, wearing a toque and holding before him a dish in both hands. Ibid., pl. 76, fig. 152.
Cupid with a Flail, wearing a tricorn-hat. Mackenna, 1951, pl. 60, fig. 47.
Cupid with Bagpipes. Cheyne Book, pl. 19, no. 239.
Cupid as Bacchus, crowned with vine leaves and grapes, holding a tambourine. Ibid., pl. 16, no. 114.
Cupid as a Drummer Boy, wearing a hat. Mackenna, 1951, pl. 60, fig. 118.
Cupid as Pantaloon, bearded, wearing a cloak and holding a money-bag. Cheyne Book, pl. 16, no. 113.
Cupid as a Wounded Soldier, with bullet-torn hat, a wooden leg and arm in a sling. Lane, pl. 23a.

Cupid (Eros), the son of Mars and Venus, was usually depicted as a naked child, with or without wings, carrying a long-bow and a quiver full of golden arrows. Cupids wearing helmets and either bearing arms or playing musical instruments appear in murals in the House of the Vetii, excavated at Pompeii, together with others engaged in a variety of trades. Putti were incorporated into a bronze font by Donatello at Siena about 1429, while they became almost the speciality of the sculptor Nicolo Roccatagliata during the late sixteenth and early seventeenth centuries. They were employed in some of the paintings of Antoine Watteau (1684–1721), such as his *L'Ile de Cythère,* and in the work of contemporary artists. The apogee of the Cupid was, however, manifest in the paintings and engravings of François Boucher (1701–70) whose scantily clad goddesses were often depicted with putti in attendance. In 1749, J. J. Kändler was sent to Paris by Augustus III to ensure the safe delivery of a belated wedding present of Meissen porcelain to his daughter, Maria-Josepha, the Dauphine. Kändler took this opportunity to purchase prints and engravings from the art dealer, Jean-Charles Huet, which he hoped might provide a much-needed fresh source of inspiration to the Meissen manufactory.

During the early 1750s, Meissen models began to appear reflecting the French influence and, amongst these, were *Cupids in Disguise*. Some, like *Cupid as a Wounded Soldier*, were entirely novel, whilst others echoed in humorous vein

275 Nos. 262–78. *Cupid Disguised as a Money-lender*. $4\frac{1}{2}$ in (11.4 cm). No incised mark.
B. and T. Thorn Antiques

276 Nos. 262–78. *Cupid Disguised as a Hurdy-gurdy Girl*. $4\frac{3}{4}$ in (12 cm). No incised mark.
Author's Collection

277 *Cupid Disguised as a Hurdy-gurdy Girl*, Chelsea, c. 1756, red anchor mark. $4\frac{1}{2}$ in (11.4 cm).
Author's Collection

earlier more serious work. Thus Cupids were dressed in the costumes of Italian Comedy players, shepherds and shepherdesses, street criers, musicians and artisans.[2] K. Berling[3] wrote of them: 'Kändler is quite in his element when creating together with his fellow craftsmen, those robust little Cupids in all imaginable impersonations, poses and costumes. They breathe such original freshness and life, and they are so boldly and humerously conceived, that they conquered the world in a trice.'

Copies of the Meissen Cupids were first issued at Chelsea between 1755 and 1756 when the *Chelsea Sale Catalogues*[4] mention 'Six beautiful small figures of different sorts representing Love in Disguise, for Desert', and again, 'Six beautiful Cupids, representing Love in Disguise, playing on different sorts of music.' Later, during the gold anchor period, about 1759–69, the red anchor Cupids were reissued and further fresh ones were added which are slightly larger, brighter in colouring, and mounted on restyled bases. Their moulds were evidently among those purchased by Duesbury in 1770.

References

1 Frank Stoner, *Chelsea Moulds and Models*. The Cheyne Book of Chelsea China and Pottery, ed. Reginald Blunt, London, 1924, pp. 104–8.
2 Cecil Vavasseur, the Lord Fisher, 'Love in Disguise', *Apollo*, LXI, 1966, no. 364, pp. 183–8.
3 Berling, *Festive Publication to Commemorate the 200th Jubilee of the Oldest European China Factory, Meissen*, 1910, Meissen, p. 37.
4 William King, *Chelsea Porcelain*, London, 1922. Reproductions of the *Chelsea Sale Catalogues* of 1755 and 1756.

No. 279. *Not Identified*

HASLEM No item mentioned.
BEMROSE No item mentioned.

No. 280. *Seated Musicians with Bagpipes and Guitar* (pair)

HASLEM 'Pipe and Guitar Candlesticks: $8\frac{1}{2}$ ins., with ornamental branches £1 10s 0d. Ditto, with chandelier branches £1 16s 0d.'
BEMROSE 'Two chandelier figures.'

Seated figures of a shepherd wearing a soft cap and contemporary dress playing bagpipes, and a lady playing a lute. Each mounted on a steep mound base before a bocage flanked by candle sconces.

278 No. 280. *Seated Musicians with Bagpipes and Guitar.* $8\frac{1}{2}$ in (21.6 cm). Incised 'No. 280'. *Sotheby's*

Examples

A Sotheby's, *Sale Catalogue*, 2 April 1968, lot 62. Enamelled, $8\frac{1}{2}$ in (21.6 cm), incised 'No. 280'.

B Derby Museums and Art Gallery, ref. no. 362. Enamelled, $8\frac{1}{2}$ in (21.6 cm), no marks reported.

No. 281. *Spring Candlesticks* (pair)

HASLEM 'Pair Spring Candlesticks: $6\frac{1}{2}$ ins., enamelled 16s od.'
BEMROSE 'Two spring candlesticks, boy and girl.'

No examples bearing appropriate incised serial numbers are known to the author. Two possible contenders are:

A pair of scantily draped putti with floral diadems, seated in mirror positions, each proffering a posy with the other hand about a candle nozzle (missing in illustration, pl. 280), before small bocages.

A pair of standing figures of a boy and girl, each with flowers gathered in their aprons, before bocages upon scrolled based candlesticks.

279 ? No. 281. Girl standing with flowers, possibly a *Spring Candlestick*. $7\frac{3}{4}$ in (19.7 cm). No incised mark. *Private Collection*

280 ? No. 281. Pair of putti with flowers adapted as *Spring Candlesticks* (candle-holders missing). $6\frac{1}{2}$ in (16.5 cm). No incised marks. *Author's Collection*

281 ? No. 283. Pair of *Gardener Candlesticks*. $6\frac{1}{2}$ in (16.6 cm). No incised mark. *Sotheby's*

No. 282. *Not Identified*

HASLEM 'Pair of small Fame and Mercury Candlesticks: $8\frac{1}{2}$ ins., enamelled 18s od.'
BEMROSE No item mentioned.

These are probably smaller examples of No. 302 with added candlesticks.

No. 283. *Gardener Candlesticks* (pair)

HASLEM 'Pair of Gardener Candlesticks: $6\frac{7}{8}$ ins., enamelled 16s od.'
BEMROSE 'Gardener candlesticks.'

A bareheaded boy wearing contemporary dress stands holding a posy in either hand and his companion likewise, before a bocage that rises to support a candle-holder, mounted upon circular pierced scroll bases.

Example
Sotheby's, *Sale Catalogue*, 15 April 1969, lot 168. Enamelled, 6½ in (16.5 cm), incised 'No. 283'.

Nos. 284 and 285. *Not Identified*

HASLEM 'Pair Pipe and Guitar Candlesticks: 9½ ins., enamelled £1 10s od.'
BEMROSE 'Pair Bagpipe candlesticks.'

These are probably a reissue of No. 280.

Nos. 286 and 287. *Not Identified*

HASLEM No. 286. No item mentioned. No. 287. 'Pair Garland Shepherd Candlesticks, 2 sizes: 1st. 9½ ins., enamelled £1 10s od. 2nd. 8 ins., enamelled £1 6s od.'
BEMROSE No. 286. No item mentioned. No. 287. No item mentioned.

No. 288. *Mars and Venus Candlesticks* (pair).

HASLEM 'Pair of Mars and Venus Candlesticks: 8 ins., enamelled £1 6s od.'
BEMROSE 'Pair Mars and Venus.'

These models are reissues of Nos. 114 and 66 and are mentioned in the *Derby Sale Catalogues* of 9–14 May 1783: 'A pair of Mars and Venus candlesticks £3 os od.'

Example
Arthur Hayden, *Catalogue of the Lady Ludlow Collection*, London, 1932, pl. 190, no. 200. An earlier version of c. 1765.

No. 289. *Not Identified*

HASLEM No item mentioned.
BEMROSE 'Large old Diana.'

No. 290. *Minerva*

HASLEM No item mentioned.
BEMROSE No item mentioned.

A reissue of *Minerva*, No. 144, which later reappeared as No. 298.

282 No. 288. Pair of *Mars and Venus Candlesticks*. 8 in (20.3 cm). Incised 'No. 288'. *Burnley Antiques*

Example

Christie's, *Sale Catalogue*, 13 May 1968, lot 140. Enamelled, 10 in (25.4 cm), incised 'No. 290'.

No. 291. *Quinn as Sir John Falstaff*

HASLEM 'Falstaff, 5 sizes: 1st. [15$\frac{1}{2}$ ins.], enamelled £2 12d 6d. 2nd. ——, enamelled £1 11s 6d. 3rd. ——, enamelled £1 5s 0d. 4th. [8$\frac{3}{4}$ ins.], enamelled 15s 0d. 5th. [6$\frac{1}{2}$ ins.], enamelled 12s 6d.'

BEMROSE 'Falstaff, 5 sizes.'

A reissue of No. 231, mounted on a scrolled base.

Examples

A Sotheby's, *Sale Catalogue*, 23 July 1985, lot 218. Enamelled, 15$\frac{1}{4}$ in (38.7 cm), incised 'No. 291 Size 1'.

B Ibid., 4 February 1969, lot 100. Enamelled, 8$\frac{1}{2}$ in (21.6 cm), Bloor Derby version, no marks reported.

C Ibid., 8 July 1967, lot 118. Enamelled, 8$\frac{3}{4}$ in (22.2 cm), incised 'No. 291 Size 4'.

D Derby Museums and Art Gallery. Enamelled, 15$\frac{1}{2}$ in (39.4 cm), incised 'No. 291'.

No. 292. *Pair of Dessert Gardeners*

HASLEM 'Pair of Dessert Gardeners, 2 sizes: 1st. $5\frac{1}{4}$ ins., enamelled 7s 0d. 2nd. $4\frac{3}{8}$ ins., enamelled 6s 0d.'
BEMROSE No item mentioned.

A gardener wearing a stocking-cap, smock and apron, holds a basket in both hands before him. Companion woman clad in a linen cap, dress and apron, likewise. Mounted upon scroll bases before small, waist-tall bocages.

These models echo earlier larger figures holding flowers in either hand in place of baskets, mounted before bocages surmounted by candle tulips.[1] There are so many different Derby models of gardeners and their companions mentioned in contemporary sale catalogues that it is not possible to determine which one of them is relevant to the present pair. Early nineteenth-century Berlin versions[2] are also known. The baskets are clearly too small to contain sweetmeats and it is probable they were meant to hold comfits, or breath sweeteners, aromatic for men and scented for women. These must have been welcome in the days of poor dental hygiene when guests spent hours at the dining-table in heavily curtained rooms.

283 No. 292. Pair of *Dessert Gardeners*. $4\frac{3}{8}$ in (11.2 cm). Incised 'No. 292' and 'Second Size'.
Author's Collection

Examples

A Twitchett, op. cit., pl. 75. Enamelled male figure only, $5\frac{1}{4}$ in (13.3 cm), no marks reported. John Neat Collection (private).

B Bradshaw, op. cit., pl. 119. Enamelled pair, $4\frac{3}{8}$ in (11.1 cm), incised 'No. 292 2nd Size'.

C Gilhespy, 1951, pl. 99, fig. 180. Enamelled, 5 in (12.7 cm), incised 'No. 292'.

References

1 Egan Mew, *Chelsea and Chelsea-Derby China*, London, 1909, col. pl. II. Herbert Allen Collection, no. 43.
2 Collection of A. E. Dodson (private).

No. 293. *Tithe Pig Group*

HASLEM 'Tythe Pig Group, three figures: 7 ins., enamelled 15s od.'
BEMROSE Tyth [sic] pig group.'

A group showing a farmer's wife proffering her tenth child to the horrified parson while her husband keeps a tight hold on the tithe pig; behind them there is a flowering tree and at their feet is scattered farm produce.

284 No. 293. *Tithe Pig Group*. $6\frac{1}{4}$ in (15.9 cm). Incised 'No. 293'. *Private Collection*

The Derby group was adapted from an engraving by Boitard after J. S. Muller of about 1751.[1] This snide reference to the established Church proved to be popular and this prompted a Derby group of about 1765 as well as three separate models en suite,[2] together with numerous pottery versions.[3] Boitard's engraving was also transfer-printed on to both porcelain and earthenware,[4] often including the following verse:

> The Parson comes, the Pig he claims,
> And the good Wife with Taunts inflames,
> But she quite Arch bow'd low and smil'd
> Kept back the Pig and held the Child.
> The Priest look'd gruff, the Wife look'd big,
> Zounds, Sir quoth she, no Child, no Pig.

Examples

A Barrett and Thorpe, op. cit., pl. 66. Enamelled, 8½ in (21.6 cm), incised 'No. 293'. Derby Museums and Art Gallery.

B Bradshaw, op. cit., pl. 120. Enamelled, 6¼ in (15.9 cm), George Savage.

C Author's Collection. Enamelled, 7¾ in (19.7 cm), unmarked.

References

1 H. B. Lancaster, 'The Origins of the Tithe Pig Pottery Group', *Connoisseur*, 105, 1940, pp. 253–5.

2 Gilhespy, 1961, fig. 154. Set of three models, enamelled.

3 Sotheby's, *Sale Catalogue*, 20 November 1979, lot 65. Staffordshire version *Tithe Pig*.

4 E. N. Stretton, 'Early Sadler Prints on Wedgwood Creamware', *Proc. Wedgwood Society*, 8, 1970, pl. 16.

No. 294. *The Four Seasons* (group)

HASLEM 'Group of Four Seasons, with an Obelisk: 8 ins., enamelled £1 11s od., biscuit £2 2s od.'

BEMROSE 'Two seasons group.'

The group is composed of the same four figures that earlier had been issued both as a set of four (No. 35), and as two groups (No. 68), but grouped about an obelisk on a mound base.

Examples

A Hugo Morley-Fletcher. *Investing in Pottery and Porcelain*, London, 1968, p. 138. Enamelled, 8¼ in (21 cm), no marks reported, as illustrated.

B Sotheby's, *Sale Catalogue*, 21 March 1972, lot 12. Enamelled, 8¼ in (21 cm), incised 'No. 294'. A Bloor Derby example.

285 No. 294. *The Four Seasons,* represented by four children about an obelisk. $8\frac{1}{4}$ in (21 cm). Incised 'No. 294'. *Hugo Morley-Fletcher*

286 No. 295. *The Four Quarters of the Globe,* portrayed by four children about an obelisk. 10 in (25.4 cm). Incised 'No. 295'. *Royal Crown Derby Museum*

No. 295. *The Four Quarters of the Globe* (group)

HASLEM 'Group of the Four Quarters of the Globe: $10\frac{3}{8}$ ins., enamelled £2 2s 0d., biscuit £2 12s 0d.'

BEMROSE 'Group, 4 quarters, large.'

A group of four standing children, previously issued as a set of four figures (No. 200), standing about an obelisk.

Examples

A Sotheby's, *Sale Catalogue*, 22 October 1968, lot 107. Enamelled, 10½ in (26.7 cm), incised 'No. 295'.

B Twitchett, op. cit., pl. 164. Enamelled, 10 in (25.4 cm), incised 'No. 295'. Royal Crown Derby Museum.

No. 296. *Pair of Haymakers* (pair)

HASLEM 'Pair of Haymakers: 9¼ ins., enamelled £1 11s 6d.'
BEMROSE 'Pair of haymakers.'

These models are larger versions of those earlier issued No. 198.

Examples

A Christie's, *Sale Catalogue*, 2 June 1969, lot 118. Enamelled male figure only, 10 in (25.4 cm), incised 'No. 296.'

B Thornton's of Harrogate. Enamelled, 9 in (22.9 cm), incised 'No. 296', both figures.

287 No. 296. *The Haymaker's Companion* (biscuit version). 9 in (22.9 cm). Incised 'No. 296'. *Thornton's of Harrogate*

288 No. 297. *John Milton* (right). Incised 'No. 297'. No. 305. *William Shakespeare* (left). Both mounted on chamfered and fluted bases. 9½ in (24.1 cm). *Sotheby's*

No. 297. *John Milton*

HASLEM 'Milton: 10⅝ ins., enamelled £1 5s 0d., biscuit £1 11s 6d.'
BEMROSE 'Shakespeare and Milton.'

John Milton stands bareheaded, wearing traditional Puritan dress, leaning upon a circular plinth decorated in relief with scenes depicting the expulsion of Adam from the Garden of Eden, with a scroll in his hand. Mounted upon a square base with chamfered corners decorated with vertical fluting.

The first Derby models of Milton and Shakespeare (D12 and D13) were issued about 1758. That of Milton was adapted from a plaster maquette by Peter Scheemakers[1] or, alternatively, from a copy made by John Cheere[2] at his atelier at Hyde Park Corner, for an example, painted to simulate bronze, survives that is signed *J. Cheere fecit 1749*.[3] Early examples appear on Rococo scrolled bases; later Chelsea–Derby versions on square bases with chamfered corners decorated with vertical fluting in sympathy with the Neo-Classical taste. A Chelsea model is also known which differs in some details and which may have been taken from a different source.[4] The *Derby Sale Catalogues* of 29 March–1 April 1773[5] mention: 'A pair of figures, Shakespeare and Milton, enamelled and ornamented with gold £3 2s od.'

John Milton (1608–74), author, poet and playwright and a leading Puritan of his day, is best remembered for *L'Allegro, Il Penseroso, Comus, Lycidas*, and for the three-volume work *Paradise Lost* and its sequel *Paradise Regained*. Milton was an advocate of the Commonwealth and justified the execution of Charles I by the regicides in his *The Tenure of Kings and Magistrates*. He married three times though his last wife survived him, and became blind in 1652. Following the restoration of the monarchy he went temporarily into hiding but, after the *Act of Oblivion*, lived out his twilight years in peace.

Examples

A Clifford, 1969, pl. 126b. Biscuit, 10 in (25.4 cm), incised 'No. 297'. B. N. Clifford Collection (private).

B Lane, op. cit., pl. 64. Enamelled version of c.1758.

C Sotheby's, *Sale Catalogue*, 29 January 1980, lot 71. Enamelled, 9½ in (24.1 cm), incised 'No. 297'.

D Derby Museums and Art Gallery, ref. nos. 287 and 290. Biscuit, Milton incised 'No. 297', Shakespeare 'No. 305', both 11 in (28 cm).

References

1 William King, 'Chelsea Chronology', *Trans. ECC*, 1, 1933, p. 10.

2 T. Friedman and T. Clifford. *The Man at Hyde Park Corner, Sculpture by John Cheere, 1709–87*, Twickenham, 1974, nos. 54 and 55, pls. 11 and 12.

3 The City Art Gallery, New York, USA.

4 *Apollo*, 37, 1943. Chelsea model of *Milton*.

5 Nightingale, op. cit., appendix p. 45.

No. 298. *Minerva*

HASLEM 'Minerva, 3 sizes: 1st. [10 ins.], enamelled £2 2s od., biscuit £2 12s 6d. 2nd. ——, enamelled £1 11s 6d., biscuit £2 2s od. 3rd. ——, enamelled £1 1s od., biscuit £1 10s od.'

289 No. 298. *Minerva.* 10 in (25.4 cm). Incised with a star and 'No. 298'. *Upton House*

BEMROSE 'Large figure of Minerva.'

The model is a larger and more elaborate version of No. 121, with an owl seated upon a pile of books at the feet of the goddess. Symbols of a crow and an owl were originally associated with the third person of a Moon Goddess representing the crone or death, but here the association with books was probably intended to portray wisdom.

Example
Mallet, op. cit., no. 66. Enamelled, 10 in (25.4 cm), incised 'No. 298' and also with a star. Upton House, Lord Bearsted's Collection.

No. 299. *Neptune with a Dolphin*

HASLEM 'Neptune on a Rock Pedestal, 2 sizes: 1st. [$9\frac{1}{4}$ ins.], enamelled £1 1s od., biscuit £1 4s od. 2nd. [$8\frac{3}{4}$ ins.], enamelled 16s od., biscuit 18s od.'
BEMROSE 'Small Neptune without rock.' Also: 'Large neptune, 2 sizes.'

All Derby Models of Neptune are basically the same, including B26, D30, E61, Nos. 118, 299 and 300. No. 299, unlike the others, is mounted upon a tall rock-like mound encrusted with shells.

No. 300. *Neptune with a Dolphin*

HASLEM 'Neptune without a pedestal: $5\frac{3}{8}$ ins., enamelled 9s od., biscuit 10s 6d.'
BEMROSE No item mentioned.

The same as the above but mounted on a shallow mound base.

Example
Sotheby's, *Sale Catalogue*, 31 July 1979, lot 89. Enamelled, 6 in (15.2 cm), incised 'No. 300'.

No. 301. *Shepherd Bagpiper and Lady with Guitar* (pair)

HASLEM 'Pair sitting Pipe and Guitar, 3 sizes: 1st. ——, enamelled £1 os od., biscuit ——. 2nd. $6\frac{1}{4}$ ins., enamelled, 16s od., biscuit ——. 3rd. $5\frac{3}{8}$ ins., enamelled, 12s 6d., biscuit 18s od.'
BEMROSE 'Pair single Bagpipers, 3 sizes.'

These models are a reissue of No. 280, without their candle-holders.

Examples
A Sotheby's, *Sale Catalogue*, 8 July 1980, lot 242. Enamelled, 6 in., (15.2 cm), incised 'No. 301', male figure only.
B,C,D See Nos. E13, 278 and 292 for other examples.

No. 302. *Fame and Mercury* (pair)

HASLEM 'Pair of Fame and Mercury: [11 ins.], enamelled £1 1s od., biscuit £1 11s 6d.'
BEMROSE 'Fame and Mercury, 2 sizes.'

The god Mercury is depicted as a clean-shaven youth, wearing a round helmet, tunic, cloak and winged sandals, standing with a money-bag in his upraised right hand and holding the caduceus in his left. Fame is portrayed as a winged angel,

290 No. 299. *Neptune with a Dolphin*, mounted on a tall base. $9\frac{1}{4}$ in (23.5 cm). Incised 'No. 299'.
Sotheby's

291 No. 302. Pair of candlesticks, *Fame* (left) and *Mercury* (right). 11 in (27.9 cm). Incised 'No. 302'. *Fitzwilliam Museum*

bareheaded and scantily draped, blowing a trumpet. Both bases take the forms of billowing clouds.

Mercury (Hermes) was the son of Jupiter and Maia, daughter of the Titan, Atlas. He was a precocious godling who greatly amused his father when he stole cattle belonging to Apollo. When his crime was exposed, he gave Apollo his lyre in exchange for the herd and persuaded Jupiter to appoint him his divine messenger. Jupiter gave him a round helmet to protect him from the rain, winged sandals to speed him on his journeys, and a staff of office which traditionally had white ribbons attached to it. This subsequently was altered to the caduceus, a staff entwined by two serpents.

Examples

A Twitchett, op. cit., pl. 195. Biscuit model of *Fame*, $8\frac{3}{4}$ in (22.2 cm), incised 'No. 302'. Dr John Freeman Collection (private).

B Rackham, 1915, pl. 40, no. 179 (new no. 340). Enamelled model of *Mercury*, c. 1765.

C Sotheby's, *Sale Catalogue*, 24 April 1968, lot 157. Enamelled pair, 11 in (28 cm), incised 'No. 302'.

D Fitzwilliam Museum, ref. no. C.20–1928 and C.20B–1928, as illustrated.

Nos. 303 and 304. *Not Identified*

HASLEM No. 303. 'Pair of Pipe and Tabor, 2 sizes: 1st. ——., enamelled 17s 0d. 2nd. $6\frac{3}{8}$ ins., enamelled 14s 0d.' No. 304. No item mentioned.
BEMROSE No. 303. 'Old pipe and tabor, 3 sizes.' No. 304. 'Pair peasant figures.'

No. 305. *William Shakespeare*

HASLEM 'Shakespeare: $10\frac{1}{2}$ ins., enamelled £1 5s 0d., biscuit £1 11s 6d.'
BEMROSE 'Milton.'

William Shakespeare is portrayed wearing the traditional tight-fitting jacket, breeches and cloak, standing cross-legged, leaning his right elbow on a pile of books resting upon an oval plinth. This is decorated with relief masks in the supposed likeness of Richard II, Queen Elizabeth I, and Henry V, to commemorate some of the bard's historical dramas. A scroll hanging from the plinth is inscribed with lines from *The Tempest*:

The cloud capt towers,
The gorgeous palaces,
The solemn temples,
The great globe itself,
Yea all which it inherit
Shall dissolve and, like
This insubstantial pageant
Fade leave not a rack behind.

The porcelain model was adapted from the marble by Peter Scheemakers (1681–1761) in Westminster Abbey about 1751, though it is likely an intermediate source was employed. The model was often sold as a pair with another of Milton (No. 297).

Examples

A Twitchett, op. cit., pl. 67. Enamelled, $9\frac{1}{2}$ in (24.1 cm), on a scrolled base, c. 1760.
B Lane, op. cit., pl. 65. Enamelled, $9\frac{1}{2}$ in (24.1 cm) on a scrolled base, c. 1760.
C Sotheby's, *Sale Catalogue*, 29 January 1980, lot 71. Enamelled, $11\frac{1}{2}$ in (29.2 cm), incised 'No. 305', square base with vertical fluting and chamfered corners.

No. 306. *Not Identified*

HASLEM No item mentioned.
BEMROSE 'Large sitting Cupid.'

292 No. 307. *Seated Bagpiper and Lady with a Lute*. $6\frac{2}{3}$ in (17 cm). Incised 'No. 307'. *Sotheby's*

No. 307. *Seated Bagpiper and Lady with a Lute* (pair)

HASLEM 'Set of Four Seasons, sitting: $4\frac{5}{8}$ ins., enamelled £1 0s 0d.'
BEMROSE No item mentioned.

A seated gallant extravagantly attired in a plumed cap, cravat, waistcoat, short-sleeved jacket revealing lace cuffs secured with ribbons and knickerbockers gathered below the knees, playing bag-pipes with a dog at his feet. Companion lady wearing a head-dress incorporating both plumes and a veil, bodice, apron and skirt, playing a lute (or guitar) with a sheep at her feet. Mounted upon scrolled bases before bocages.

Similar models were issued during the 1760s at both Derby[1] and Chelsea,[2] presumably from a common source that has not yet been identified (see Nos. E12 and 13).

Examples

A Sotheby's, *Sale Catalogue*, 20 May 1980, lot 99. Enamelled, $6\frac{2}{3}$ in (17 cm), incised 'No. 307'.

B D. G. Rice, *Derby Porcelain, the Golden Years 1750–70*, London and New York, 1983, col. pl. J. Enamelled, $7\frac{1}{2}$ and 8 in (19.1 and 20.3 cm), no marks reported, c. 1765.

References

1 Sotheby's, *Sale Catalogue*, 23 October 1979, lot 183.

2 Ibid., 20 November 1979, lot 110.

No. 308. *Not Identified*

HASLEM No item mentioned.
BEMROSE No item mentioned.

No. 309. *Musical Group*

HASLEM 'Musical Group of four Figures, with Obelisk: 10 ins., enamelled £1 11s 0d.'
BEMROSE No item mentioned.

A group of four youths, each wearing a brimmed hat, jacket and breeches, playing different musical instruments that include a flute, fiddle, tambourine and reed-pipe. They stand upon a mound base about an obelisk.

Example

Private Collection, $9\frac{3}{4}$ in (24.8 cm), incised 'No. 309'.

No. 310. *Not Identified*

HASLEM No item mentioned.
BEMROSE 'Old justices, 4 sizes.'

No. 311. *The Idyllic Musicians* (pair)

HASLEM 'Pair of Pipe and Tabor Figures: $8\frac{1}{4}$ ins., enamelled £1 0s 0d.'
BEMROSE 'Pair pipe and triangle figures, 2 sizes.'

The gallant stands wearing a soft triple plumed cap, short-sleeved tunic and breeches, playing a flageolet and tabor. His companion, her hair decked with plumes and wearing a bodice, apron and skirt, plays a triangle. Mounted before waist-tall bocages on scrolled and fenestrated bases.

The models are refurbished from earlier versions (E9) of about 1760,[1] and known also in Bow versions[2] which were later married on a single base.[3] The original Bow and Derby examples wore brimmed hats and long-sleeved jackets and were called by Egan Mew *The Idyllic Musicians*.

Examples

A Derby Museums and Art Gallery, ref. nos. 1518 and 381. Enamelled, $7\frac{1}{2}$ in (19.1 cm), no marks reported.

B Sotheby's, *Sale Catalogue*, 14 October 1969, lot 213. Enamelled, $7\frac{1}{2}$ in (19.1 cm), no marks reported.

C Raymond Shingler Collection (private). Enamelled, $8\frac{1}{2}$ in (21.6 cm), incised 'No. 311', as illustrated.

References

1 Fitzwilliam Museum, ref. nos. C.64 and C.65. Enamelled.

2 Frank Hurlbutt, *Bow Porcelain*, London, 1926, pl. 62.

3 Yvonne Hackenbroch, *Chelsea and Other English Porcelain, Pottery and Enamel in the Irwin Untermyer Collection*, Cambridge, Mass., 1957, pl. 83, fig. 246.

No. 312. *Not Identified*

HASLEM No item mentioned.

BEMROSE No item mentioned.

Nos. 313 and 314. *Boy Reading a Book and Girl Tatting* (pair)

HASLEM 'Pair of sitting Figures: $5\frac{3}{4}$ ins., enamelled £2 2s od., biscuit £3 3s od.'

BEMROSE No. 313. No item mentioned. No. 314. 'Two pair Dresden figures.'

These models are reissues of No. 184.

Examples

A Rackham, 1915, pl. 33 no. 127. Enamelled, $5\frac{1}{2}$ in (14 cm), incised 'No. 314'.

B Derby Museums and Art Gallery, ref. nos. 653 and 655. Enamelled, $5\frac{1}{2}$ in (14 cm), incised, 'Nos. 313 and 314'.

293 No. 311. *Male Musician*, standing with flageolet and tabor.

294 No. 311. *Companion Female* with a triangle. Both $8\frac{1}{2}$ in (21.6 cm). Incised 'No. 311'.

Late Raymond Shingler Collection

No. 315. *Not Identified*

HASLEM 'Set of Four Seasons, sitting: 7 ins., enamelled . . .' no other details given.
BEMROSE No item mentioned.

No. 316. *Sailor and his Lass* (pair)

HASLEM 'Sailor and Lass, 3 sizes: [$9\frac{3}{4}$ ins.], enamelled £1 16s od. [$8\frac{3}{4}$ ins.], enamelled ——. [$7\frac{1}{2}$ins .], enamelled ——.'
BEMROSE 'Saylor [sic] and lass.'

A sailor clad in a tricorn hat, waistcoat, jacket and knickerbockers, stands holding a telescope in his right hand while he displays three gold coins in the palm of his left. The lass sports a saucy hat, blouse, apron and skirt, and stands beckoning him with her right forefinger. Mounted on scrolled and fenestrated bases before waist-tall bocages.

The models are believed to represent Henry Woodward and Nancy Dawson in character roles, possibly connected with Gray's ballad 'The Farewell of Sweet William to Black-eyed Susan', first published in 1720. D. G. Rice[1] illustrates examples of the models that he dates to about 1765 which would seem possibly too early.

295 No. 316. *Sailor and his Lass.* $9\frac{1}{2}$ in (24.1 cm). Incised 'No. 316'. *Venner's Antiques*

Examples

A Bradshaw, op. cit., pl. 130. Enamelled, $7\frac{1}{2}$ in (19.1 cm), incised 'No. 316'. Grosvenor Antiques, as illustrated.

B Twitchett, op. cit., pl. 61. Enamelled, $8\frac{3}{4}$ in (22.2 cm), incised 'No. 316'.

C Sotheby's, *Sale Catalogue*, 13 January 1970, lot 212. Enamelled, $9\frac{1}{2}$ in (24.1 cm), no marks reported. Bloor period examples.

Reference

1 Rice, 1983, pl. 54. Enamelled, $9\frac{1}{2}$ in, no marks reported.

Nos. 317 and 318. *Pair of Dancing Figures*

HASLEM 'Pair of Dancing Figures, 2 sizes: 1st. ——., enamelled 18s 0d. 2nd. [$7\frac{1}{2}$ ins.], enamelled, 14s 0d.'

BEMROSE No items mentioned.

296 Nos. 317 and 318. *Pair of Dancing Figures*. 7 and $7\frac{1}{2}$ in (17.8 and 19.1 cm). Male incised 'No. 317', female unmarked. *Sotheby's*

A bareheaded gallant, wearing a jacket, waistcoat and breeches, is shown dancing. The companion lady holds open her divided skirt with both hands to display her petticoat as if about to dance. Mounted on scrolled bases before waist-tall bocages.

Example
Sotheby's, *Sale Catalogue*, 2 April 1968, lot 64. Enamelled, 7 and $7\frac{1}{2}$ in (17.8 and 19.1 cm), one model only, incised 'No. 317'.

Nos. 319–22. *Not Identified*

HASLEM Nos. 319–21. 'Three Figures.' No. 322. 'Pair of Hen and Chicken Candlesticks: $6\frac{1}{4}$ ins., enamelled £1 1s 0d.'
BEMROSE No. 319. No item mentioned. No. 320. 'Four coronation figures.' Nos. 321–2. No items mentioned.

No. 323. *Cupid and Flora Candlesticks* (pair)

HASLEM 'Pair Cupid and Flora Candlesticks: $8\frac{3}{4}$ ins., enamelled £2 2s 0d.'
BEMROSE No items mentioned.

A scantily draped seated Cupid with his right arm about a tree-stump upon which there was once a candle-holder. Mounted on a rock-like base. Companion figure unknown.

Example
Weston Park Museum, Sheffield. Biscuit, $8\frac{3}{4}$ in (22.2 cm), incised 'No. 323', as illustrated.

Nos. 324 and 325. *Not Identified*

HASLEM No. 324. No item mentioned. No. 325. 'Set of Four Elements.'
BEMROSE No. 324. No item mentioned. No. 325. No item mentioned.

No. 326. *The Singing Shepherds* (pair)

HASLEM 'Pair of Singers, 4 sizes: 1st–3rd. [No details provided.] 4th. $5\frac{3}{4}$ ins., enamelled ——.'
BEMROSE No items mentioned.

These models are reissues of No. 69. The author has seen a badly damaged example of the male figure incised 'No. 326'.

297 No. 323. *Cupid Candlestick* (sconce missing). $8\frac{3}{4}$ in (22.2 cm). Incised 'No. 323'. *Weston Park Museum*

Nos. 327–31. *Not Identified*

HASLEM Nos. 327–30. No item mentioned. No. 331. 'Pair of Candlesticks with Bird and Dog: $11\frac{1}{4}$ ins., enamelled £3 3s od.'
BEMROSE Nos. 327–31. No items mentioned.

No. 332. *The Four Quarters of the Globe* (set of four models)

HASLEM 'Set of Four Quarters of the Globe, 3 sizes: 1st & 2nd [no information provided]. 3rd. size not given, enamelled £1 16s od.'
BEMROSE No items mentioned.

Models emblematic of *Africa* and *Asia* are reissues of No. 200. *America* is a different model of a Red Indian girl wearing a feathered dress, holding a long-bow in her right hand and with a quiver at her left side. *Europe* is similar to that included in No. 200 but with the recumbent horse omitted.

Examples

A L. G. G. Ramsey, *The Complete Encyclopaedia of Antiques*, London, 1962, p. 995, pl. 355. Enamelled, 9 in (22.9 cm), no marks.
B Bradshaw, op. cit., pl. 113. Early versions of *Africa* and *Asia* only, c. 1760.
C Grosvenor Antiques. Enamelled, $9\frac{1}{2}$ in (24.1 cm), incised 'No. 332', as illustrated.

298 No. 332. *The Four Quarters of the Globe.* $9\frac{1}{2}$ in (24.1 cm). Incised 'No. 332'. *Grosvenor Antiques*

299 No. 333. *Four Boys Playing Music* (biscuit group). $10\frac{1}{4}$ in (26 cm). Incised 'No. 333'. *Private Collection*

No. 333. *Four Boys Playing Music* (group)

HASLEM 'Group of four Boys: 9 ins., enamelled £1 11s 6d., biscuit £2 2s 0d.'
BEMROSE 'Group. Four musical boys.'

A group of four boys each clad in a brimmed hat, jacket and breeches, playing different musical instruments, grouped about a leafing tree upon a rock-like base. The two standing play a clarinet and French horn, the two seated hold a flute and cymbals.

Examples

A Derby Museums and Art Gallery, ref. no. 450. Biscuit, 9 in (22.9 cm), incised 'No. 333', as illustrated.

B Christie's, *Sale Catalogue*, 17 November 1969, lot 36. Biscuit, $10\frac{1}{4}$ in (26 cm), incised 'No. 333'.

No. 334. *Group of Four Boys with Pets* (group)

HASLEM 'Group of four Boys: 10½ ins., enamelled, £1 11s 6d., biscuit £2 2s 0d.'
BEMROSE 'Pastoral group, 4 boys.'

A group of four boys, each wearing a brimmed hat, jacket and breeches, arranged about a leafing tree upon a rocky mound. Two stand, one holding a nest of fledglings, the other a puppy; two are seated, one feeds a lamb the other plays with a kid.

This group was assembled by a repairer from old models. The *Boy with a Puppy* is adapted from the male member of the *French Shepherds* (No. 57) with the addition of a hat. The other three appear to have been based on figures included in the group *Four Boys Playing Music* (No. 333).

Examples

A A. E. Dodson Collection (private). Biscuit, 10½ in (26.7 cm), incised 'No. 334', as illustrated.

B E. Percival Allam, op. cit., p. 34, no. VI. Biscuit, 11 in (28 cm), incised 'No. 334'.

Nos. 335–57. *Not Identified*

HASLEM Nos. 335–59. 'Twenty-five Spangler's and Coffee's Figures and Groups.'
BEMROSE No. 335. 'Group, 4 boys.' Nos. 336–50. No items mentioned. Nos. 351–3. 'Four quarters of the Day.' No. 354. 'Pair figures.' Nos. 355–7. No items mentioned.

No. 358. *Cupid Disarmed by Euphrosyne* (group)

HASLEM *Vide supra.*
BEMROSE 'Large Venus and Cupid.'

Euphrosyne wearing a diaphanous robe gathered by a sash, stoops forward upon her left knee, grasping a bundle of arrows in her left hand and holding Cupid's long-bow aloft in her right. Cupid reaches upwards in a vain attempt to regain possession of his weapon. Mounted on an oval base.

The porcelain group is adapted from an engraving made in 1784 by Thomas Burke after Angelica Kauffmann[1] and the same source prompted an enamel painting by James Bamford upon a Derby bough-pot.[2]

Euphrosyne, together with Pasithea and Cale, constituted the Three Graces (or Charities). Often they would protect those mortals that they favoured by deflecting Cupid's arrows or removing his long-bow, so that they might be spared the pangs of love.

300 No. 334. *Four Boys with Pets* (group) (biscuit). $10\frac{1}{2}$ in (26.7 cm). Incised 'No. 334'.
Private Collection

301 No. 334. Reverse view of *Four Boys with Pets*.

302 No. 358. *Cupid Disarmed by Euphrosyne* (biscuit group). $10\frac{3}{4}$ in (27.3 cm). Incised 'No. 358'. Courtesy of the *Connoisseur*

Examples

A Clifford, 1978, pp. 146–53, fig. 8b. Biscuit, $10\frac{3}{4}$ in (27.3 cm), incised 'No. 358'. B. N. Clifford Collection (private).

B Allam, op. cit., no. VIII. Biscuit, $10\frac{3}{4}$ in (27.3 cm), incised 'No. 358'.

References

1 Clifford, 1978, fig. 8a. Thomas Burke's engraving after Angelica Kauffmann.

2 Twitchett, op. cit., pl. 209.

No. 359. *Gardener and Companion*

HASLEM See Nos. 335–59.
BEMROSE 'Gardener and companion.'

Two distinct items, including a pair of figures and a single figure, are all incised 'No. 359', viz:

(i) A bareheaded gardener stands supporting his chin in his cupped right hand while leaning upon his spade with his left. His companion, also bareheaded, stands with her left hand upon her breast while she arranges a flowering plant resting

303 No. 359. *Gardener* leaning upon a spade (missing) (biscuit).

304 No. 359. *Companion* lady with flowers. Ascribed to J. W. Coffee. Both $5\frac{5}{8}$ in (14.3 cm). Incised 'No. 359'. *Derby Museums and Art Gallery*

305 No. 359. *Gardener* (biscuit), ascribed to J. J. Spengler. $9\frac{5}{8}$ in (24.5 cm). Incised 'No. 359'. *Victoria and Albert Museum*

upon a plinth with her right. Mounted on rectangular bases.

Joseph Lygo[1] credits William John Coffee with this pair of models and describes one of the figures, presumably the gardener, as 'One of the stupidest things I ever saw . . .'

Examples

A Derby Museums and Art Gallery, ref. nos. 456 and 439. Biscuit, $5\frac{5}{8}$ in (14.3 cm), incised 'No. 359', as illustrated.

B Clifford, 1969, fig. 7. Biscuit, $9\frac{5}{8}$ in (24.5 cm) incised 'No. 359'.

(ii) Another model of a gardener stands bareheaded, his right knee raised as he leans on a tree-stump with his outstretched right hand. Mounted upon a square base.

The admirable sense of movement of this model is in sharp contrast to the wooden pose of Coffee's figure and suggests the hand of Spengler.[2]

Example

Clifford, 1978, fig. 6. Victoria and Albert Museum, ref. no. C.262–1976. Late B. N. Clifford Collection.

References

1 Llewellynn Jewitt, *The Ceramic Art of Great Britain*, London, 1878, II, p. 96.

2 Clifford, 1973, fig. 6.

No. 360. *Johnny Wapstraw and Companion* (group)

HASLEM 'Johnny Wapstraw and Companion: [size not given] enamelled £1 16s 0d.'

BEMROSE 'Shepherd and shepherdess.'

A memorandum in the Derby Museums and Art Gallery indicates that a Derby group incised 'No. 360' was brought for identification when it was described: 'The figure of a girl watching two doves billing and cooing at her feet. Mounted on a square pedestal, 9 in (22.9 cm). A similar model is recorded in Sotheby's Catalogue of 25th October, 1966.'

No. 361. *Gardener and Companion* (pair)

HASLEM 'Pair, Gardener and Companion: $10\frac{1}{2}$ ins., enamelled £1 16s 0d., biscuit £2 2s 0d.'

BEMROSE 'Pair figures Fruit and flowers.'

A gardener stands proffering a flower in his right outstretched hand while supporting with his left a basket of blossoms behind his back that rests upon a

306 No. 361. *Gardener*. $10\frac{1}{2}$ in (26.7 cm). Mark of crown X and D in red, incised 'No. 361'.
Fitzwilliam Museum

tree-stump. His companion stands leaning slightly forward and to her left, holding a posy in her left hand and with her right securing flowers in a fold of her apron.

Examples

A Sotheby's, *Sale Catalogue*, 29 January 1980, lot 50. Enamelled, 10 in (25.4 cm), incised 'No. 361', male figure only.

B Fitzwilliam Museum, ref. no. C. 101–1932. Enamelled, $10\frac{1}{2}$ in (26.7 cm), incised 'No. 361'.

307 No. 362. Seated biscuit figures of *Boy with Macaroni Dog and Girl with Cat*. 8 in (20.3 cm). Incised 'No. 362'. *Derby Museums and Art Gallery*

No. 362. *Boy with Macaroni Dog and Girl with Cat* (pair)

HASLEM 'Pair Sitting Cat and Dog, William and Mary: 8 ins., enamelled £1 10s 0d.'
BEMROSE 'Boy and companion with bird's nest.'

A boy wearing a tricorn hat, jacket and breeches sits upon a stool holding a brimmed hat over the head of a dog that wears a jacket. The girl, attired in bodice and skirt, sits likewise, feeding a cat with a spoon.

The models are copied from Meissen originals of about 1750 by J. J. Kändler.[1] The *Derby Sale Catalogues* of 10 and 11 February 1773[2] contain the entry: 'A pair of sitting figures with dog and cattle [sic]. This may, however, refer to either No. 49, No. 51 or No. 71, since the serial number No. 362 is too high to have been issued in 1773.

Examples

A Derby Museums and Art Gallery, ref. no. 537. Enamelled, 8 in (20.3 cm), incised 'No. 362', as illustrated. Note that in this example the hat held over the dog's head is missing.

B Sotheby's, *Sale Catalogue*, 31 July 1979, lot 95. Enamelled, $8\frac{1}{4}$ in (21 cm), incised 'No. 362'. Bloor period.

References

1 Meissen originals were displayed by Adams, of Old Bond Street, London, at the International Ceramics Fair held 15–18 June 1987, at the Dorchester Hotel.

2 Nightingale, op. cit., appendix p. 38.

No. 363. *Two Figures Burying a Dead Bird* (pair)

HASLEM 'Pair, figures, with dead bird: 8 ins., enamelled £1 5s od.'
BEMROSE 'Two pair female figures with dead bird, Spangler.'

A young lady clad in a bonnet and décolleté dress stands sorrowfully leaning her left elbow upon an empty bird-cage and regarding a dead bird in her dependent right hand. Her youthful companion is shown digging a diminutive grave, his right

308 No. 363. *Two Figures Burying a Dead Bird* (biscuit). $7\frac{1}{2}$ in (19 cm). Incised with crown and 'D', and 'N. 363'. *British Museum*

foot upon the upper edge of a spade. Mounted on rectangular bases.

This rather sentimental theme was portrayed in different versions at most of the eighteenth-century porcelain manufactories including Meissen, Lunéville and Sèvres. Joseph Lygo, in a letter to his employer, William Duesbury, in 1793[1] wrote: 'Spengler has modelled two female figures with a dead bird.'

Examples

A Lane, op. cit., pl. 74b. Biscuit, 7½ in (19.1 cm), incised 'No. 363'.
B Twitchett, op. cit., pl. 143. Enamelled, 8½ in (21.6 cm), incised 'No. 363'. Collection of Andrew Dando (private).
C Clifford, 1978, fig. 9. Biscuit, 8 in (20.3 cm), incised 'No. 363'.

Reference

1 Gilhespy, 1961, p. 67.

No. 364. *Gallant and Lady Waltzing* (group)

HASLEM 'Group of Figures Waltzing: 6½ ins., enamelled £1 1s 0d.'
BEMROSE 'Small group, two figures.'

This rare group seemingly survives only in a badly damaged example. A gallant clad in a tie-wig, cravat, coat and breeches, dances with a lady who wears a tall brimmed hat and a décolleté dress and holds what appears to be a vanity-bag in her dependent left hand. Mounted on a wide cylindrical base.

Example

Derby Museums and Art Gallery, as illustrated. Biscuit, 6¼ in (15.9 cm), incised 'No. 364'. The modelling style is reminiscent of that employed in Spengler's group, *Palemon and Lavinia* (No. 366).

No. 365. *Boy Piping and Girl Dancing with Cymbals* (pair)

HASLEM 'Pair of Dancing Figures: Size not given [7½–8 ins.], enamelled 18s 0d.'
BEMROSE 'Pair small figs. Symbols [sic] and pipe.'

A bareheaded youth plays a reed-pipe that he holds in both hands. The companion girl dances with cymbals held aloft in her upraised hands. Mounted on cylindrical bases encrusted with leaves and flowers.

The models were adapted from an engraving by Charles White which also prompted paintings upon Derby coffee-cans executed by Richard Askew.[1] Mentioned in the *Derby Sale Catalogues* of 23–28 May 1783[2] are also: 'Two Ewer form'd vases to complete a set, the front one represents an enamel Tambourine

Boy, the front of the other the Cymbal Girl, delicately finish'd from C. White's beautiful plates £15 15s od., Simson.' Surviving models indicate that they were issued in at least two sizes in biscuit and enamel.

Examples

A British Museum, ref. no. 1935, 7–15, 32. Biscuit, 8 in (20.3 cm), incised 'No. 365'.

B Sotheby's, *Sale Catalogue*, 16 March 1971, lot 396. Biscuit, 7⅜ in (18.7 cm), mark of an incised star.

C An exhibition held at Manchester University, 3–31 March 1976, *People and Pots*, no. 69. Biscuit, 6⅜ in (16.2 cm), incised 'No. 365'.

References

1 Barrett and Thorpe, op. cit., pl. 136. Coffee-can painted by R. Askew, depicting the *Girl with cymbals*.

2 Nightingale, op. cit., appendix p. 89.

309 No. 364. Damaged biscuit group of *Gallant and Lady Waltzing*. 6¼ in (15.9 cm). Incised 'No. 364'. *Derby Museums and Art Gallery*

310 No. 365. Enamelled figure of *Boy Piping as He Dances*. 8 in (20.3 cm). *British Museum*

311 No. 365. Biscuit version of *Boy Piping*. 8 in (20.3 cm).
312 No. 365. *Companion Girl Dancing with Cymbals*. 8 in (20.3 cm). Both incised 'No. 365'.
British Museum

No. 366. *Palemon and Lavinia* (group)

HASLEM 'Spanish Group: [12 ins.], enamelled £1 16s 0d.'
BEMROSE 'Large Venus and Cupid.' Also: 'Paliman [sic] and Lavinia.'

The young Palemon, elegantly clad in a plumed hat, jacket, breeches, and boots, a cloak thrown over one shoulder, stands facing Lavinia, holding her right hand in both of his. She wears a simple dress and averts her gaze demurely. Mounted on a wide flat base with an irregular contour.

313 No. 366. Biscuit group of *Palemon and Lavinia*. 12 in (30.5 cm). Incised 'No. 366' and a star.
Private Collection

The group was adapted from Charles Knight's engraving after Angelica Kauffmann that illustrates the 1788 edition of *The Seasons*, by James Thomson. In 1791 in a letter to William Duesbury II, Joseph Lygo wrote to inform him: 'The Spanish figures belonging to M. Daguesant are to be copied.' These may possibly have been terracottas based on Knight's engraving. The group has been ascribed to Spengler for stylistic reasons.

The poem for *Autumn* in Thomson's *The Seasons*, relates the tale. Lavinia, the beautiful daughter of Acasto, was constrained by poverty when her father died, to work in the fields to support her aged mother and herself. Palemon, the son of the new landowner, discovers that Lavinia is the daughter of his one-time friend and benefactor and, struck by her loveliness, falls in love, proposes marriage, and is accepted. 'They flourished long in tender bliss and reared numerous offspring, lovely like themselves and good, the grace of all the country round.'[1]

Examples

A Clifford, 1969, fig. 3. Biscuit, 12 in (30.5 cm), incised 'No. 366'.

B Miss Phyllis Winterton Collection (private). Biscuit, 12 in (30.5 cm), incised 'No. 366'. Exhibited in the Derby Museums and Art Gallery in 1981 to commemorate the death of William Bemrose.

Reference

1 James Thomson, *The Seasons*, London, 1788. Reprinted 1977, ed. J. Sambrock, Oxford, p. 94, lines 176–210.

No. 367. *Not Identified*

HASLEM No item mentioned.

BEMROSE 'Bugbear and companion.'

No. 368. *Not Identified*

HASLEM 'Pair of Dancing Figures: [no size given] enamelled 18s od., biscuit £1 1s od.'

BEMROSE 'Pair Tryangle and tamborene figures [sic].'

No. 369. *Shepherd and Shepherdess Playing Flutes* (pair)

HASLEM 'Shepherd and Shepherdess: [10 ins.], enamelled £1 16s od., biscuit £2 2s od.'

BEMROSE 'Pair Shepherd and shepherdess playing on fluit [sic].'

314 No. 369. *Shepherd Playing Flute.* 10 in (25.4 cm). Incised 'No. 369'. *British Museum*
315 No. 369. *Companion Shepherdess Playing Flute* (missing). 10 in (25.4 cm). *British Museum*

A shepherd stands legs crossed, his left elbow resting upon a tree-stump, playing a flute beside a sheep at his feet. His shepherdess in rustic dress with a scarf draped over her right shoulder, also plays a similar instrument. Mounted upon cylindrical bases encrusted with leaves and flowers.

The male model was adapted from a sixteenth-century Florentine bronze of a nude youth with a pelt slung from his right shoulder, playing an end-flute.[1] This in turn, was based on a marble of the Imperial Roman Age which had been prompted by a fourth-century Hellenistic bronze.[2] Reproductions may be seen in the Louvre and Vatican museum as well as in the Capitol in Rome.[3] This last mentioned gave rise to the title of *The Capitoline Faun*. In the Derby version the pagan nudity of the original was clothed to comply with the climate of moral opinion, and the end-flute was replaced by a flute. The female model was adapted from the same source. Joseph Lygo, in a letter to William Duesbury II dated 10 January 1791, attributes the models to Spengler.

Examples

A Bradley, op. cit., no. 38. Biscuit Shepherd only, 10½ in (26.7 cm), incised 'No. 369' and with a star.

B British Museum, ref. no. 1936, 7–15 and 17–18. Biscuit pair, 10 in (25.4 cm), incised 'No. 369' and with a star.

C R. J. Charleston and Donald Towner, *English Ceramics 1580–1830*, London, 1977, no. 151. Biscuit Shepherd only, 10¼ in (26 cm), incised 'No. 369'.

References

1 Watney, 1980, part 4, p. 353.

2 S. Reinach, *Répertoire de la Sculpture grecque et romaine*, Paris, 1903, Tome II, vol. 1, p. 135, fig. 5.

3 John Warrack, *Greek Sculpture, One Hundred Illustrations*, London, 1903, fig. 50.

No. 370. *Belisarius and his Daughter* (group)

HASLEM 'Belisarius and Daughter, Spangler: 9½ ins., enamelled £1 16s 0d.'
BEMROSE '2 figs. Group, blind beggar and daughter.'

The blind Belisarius is portrayed as an elderly bearded man, clad in a tunic, breeches and cloak, holding a staff in his right hand and with his left resting upon the shoulder of his young daughter who guides him. Mounted on a wide cylindrical base.

The group was based upon Charles Vasseur's engraving after an original by Hubert Gravelot of 1767, but it is possible the intermediate source was employed of a Lunéville group made by Louis Paul Cyfflé.[1] The *Catalogue of Sale* held on 11 December 1783[2] of 'All finished and Unfinished Stock of the Chelsea Porcelain Factory', included: 'A beautiful large group of Belisarius, in artificial stone £1 5s 0d and moulds of ditto £1 2s 0d', which were sold to Mr Lygo. The Derby porcelain version was created by J. J. Spengler.

Belisarius (AD 505–65) was a general who served the Byzantine emperor, Justinian. He defeated the Persian army in 530, and in 532 suppressed an insurrection in Constantinople. His campaigns against the Vandals, Ostrogoths, Persians, Goths and Huns were all successful but, in 562, he was falsely accused

316 No. 370. Biscuit group of *Belisarius and his Daughter*. $9\frac{1}{4}$ in (23.5 cm). Presence of marks unknown to author. *Liverpool Museum and Art Gallery*

of conspiracy against the emperor and imprisoned. He was exonerated and restored to his former office. There appears to be no truth in the rumour that he was blinded and died a beggar.

Examples

A Clifford, 1969, fig. 5. Biscuit, $9\frac{1}{4}$ in (23.5 cm), incised 'No. 370'. Liverpool Museum.

B Stuart C. Davis, 'Some English Pottery and Porcelain Figures connected with Alsace Lorraine, *Burlington Magazine*, LI, 1927, pp. 221–8, pl. IIb, Derby group; pl. IIa, Lunéville group by Cyfflé.

References

1 Davis, op. cit., pl. IIa.

2 Nightingale, op. cit., appendix p. 82.

No. 371. *Not Identified*

HASLEM No item mentioned.
BEMROSE 'Pair of small figures, Spangler.'

No. 372. *The Proposal* (two figures)

HASLEM 'Sailor and Lass.'
BEMROSE 'Sailor and Lass.'

A bareheaded gallant wearing a wig, cravat, frock-coat and breeches, stands with his left hand upon his heart, while making a gesture of his undying love with his right. The lady he addresses is also bareheaded with her hair in curls and is attired in an elegant dress; she raises her left hand as if to reject a proposal. Mounted on a shallow cylindrical base encrusted with leaves and flowers.

Examples

A Bradley, op. cit., no. 40. Biscuit, $7\frac{5}{8}$ in (19.4 cm), incised 'No. 372'. Private Collection, as illustrated.

B Clifford, 1978, figs. 10a and 10b. Biscuit, $7\frac{5}{8}$ in (19.4 cm), no numbers incised.

317 No. 372. Pair of biscuit figures known as *The Proposal*. $7\frac{5}{8}$ in (19.4 cm). Incised 'No. 372'. *Aldbury Antiques*

318 No. 373. Biscuit group of *Four Figures, Subject Unidentified.* $6\frac{1}{4}$ in (15.9 cm). Incised 'No. 373'. *Royal Crown Derby Museum*

No. 373. *Four Figures, Subject Unidentified* (group)

HASLEM No item mentioned.
BEMROSE 'Figure of Spangler.'

A lady, draped but with both breasts exposed, reclines with her legs supported upon a foot-stool. In attendance there are two nude putti: one standing upon a second foot-stool holds up a mantle above the lady's head, the other stands facing away from her. A fourth figure, a youth wearing a tunic, stoops on one knee before the lady as if to console her.

Example
Twitchett, op. cit., pl. 218. Biscuit, $6\frac{1}{4}$ in (15.9 cm), incised 'No. 373'. Royal Crown Derby Museum, as illustrated.

Nos. 374 and 375. *Not Identified*

HASLEM No item mentioned.
BEMROSE No. 374. 'Large Britannia.' No. 375. 'Pompey's poems.' Also: 'Group of 3 Virgins distressing Cupid.'

No. 376. *The Infant Bacchus with Nymphs on Mount Nysa* (group)

HASLEM No item mentioned.
BEMROSE No item mentioned.

The infant Bacchus lies in the lap of a seated Muse holding a cloak with her left hand over her head. Two other Muses stand in attendance while a youth, probably Mercury, stands regarding the child. Mounted on an irregular mound base encrusted with leaves and flowers.

The source of this fine group, executed in the style of J. J. Spengler, is not known.

Jupiter came in disguise to Semele, the daughter of Cadmus the king of Thebes, and seduced her. Juno determined to avenge herself on the adulteress, advised Semele to withhold her favours if her lover failed to reveal his identity. This she did, but Jupiter, infuriated at this action, struck her dead with a thunderbolt, not knowing she was carrying his child. Mercury performed a post mortem Caesarian section and saved the unborn infant Bacchus who was sewn into a fresh wound made in his father's thigh where he remained until capable of an independent existence. Juno again took her revenge by inciting the Titans to tear the infant into pieces. These were boiled in a cauldron but Rhea, Bacchus's grandmother, magically reconstituted him. Next he was raised in the women's quarters of the palace belonging to King Athamas and Queen Ino, but Juno sent the Spirit of Madness upon the royal couple, causing them to hunt and kill their son, Laerches, believing him to be a stag. Finally Jupiter ordered Mercury to take Bacchus to be reared on Mount Nysa by Macris, Erato, Bromie, Nysa and Bacche, though some hold that there were only three Nymphs. Here the child was reared in safety and learnt how to ferment the grape to make wine. When he had grown to manhood, he was maddened by Juno, and set off on peregrinations with his tutor Silenus and a band of satyrs, introducing debauchery and the cult of wine to all nations.

Example
Allam, op. cit., p. 36, no. IX. Biscuit, $9\frac{1}{2}$ in (24.1 cm), incised 'No. 376'.

319 No. 376. Biscuit group of *The Infant Bacchus with Nymphs on Mount Nysa*. $9\frac{1}{2}$ in (24.1 cm). Presence of marks unknown to author. Courtesy of *The Connoisseur*

No. 377. *Not Identified*

HASLEM No item mentioned.
BEMROSE No item mentioned.

No. 378. *Scotsman and his Lass* (pair)

HASLEM 'Pair, Scotsman and Lass, Coffee, $7\frac{1}{4}$ ins., enamelled £1 16s 0d.'
BEMROSE No item mentioned.

A Scotsman, wearing a glengarry, jacket, plaid, kilt and stockings, stands with his left hand raised away from his side and his right upon his breast. The lass stands clad in bonnet, shawl, blouse and skirt, carrying a basket of flowers and with her right hand upon her heart. Mounted upon shallow cylindrical bases.

The models, which Haslem ascribes to William Coffee, probably represent characters from the ancient Scottish ballad 'Donald of the Isles'[1] subsequently republished as 'Leezie Lindsay'.[2]

320 No. 378. *Scotsman and his Lass.* $11\frac{1}{4}$ in (28.6 cm). Incised 'No. 378'. *Burnley Antiques*

'Will ye gang to the Hielands, Leezie Lindsay?
Will ye gang to the Hielands wi' me?
Will ye gang to the Hielands, Leezie Lindsay,
My bride and my darling to be?'

'To gang to the Hielands wi' you, sir
I dinna ken how that may be;
For I ken na the land that ye live in,
Nor ken I the lad I'm gaun wi'.'

'O, Leezie lass, ye maun ken little
If sae ye dinna ken me;
For my name is Lord Ronald MacDonald,
A chieftan O' high degree.'

She has kilted her coats o' green satin,
She has kilted them up to her knee,
And she's off wi' Lord Ronald MacDonald,
His bride and his darling to be!

Examples

A Gilhespy, 1951, p. 73, no. 76.
B Sotheby's, *Sale Catalogue*, 6 November 1979, lot 146. Enamelled, 11¼ in (28.6 cm), incised 'No. 378'.
C Burnley Antiques, as illustrated.

References

1 Ballad from Kinloch MSS, by Aytoun.
2 Alfred Moffat, *The Minstrelsy of Scotland*, 1896, (2nd ed.).

No. 379. *Music* (group)

HASLEM No item mentioned.
BEMROSE No item mentioned.

A lady, possibly Calliope, stands wearing classical robes, holding a harp, beside a plinth-like altar, attended by two putti holding flowers.

Example

Aldbury Antiques. Biscuit, 10¼ in (26 cm), incised 'No. 379' and Derby factory mark.

321 No. 379. Biscuit group emblematic of *Music*. 10¼ in (26 cm). Incised 'No. 379'. *Aldbury Antiques*

No. 380. *Art, Literature* and *Astrology* (group)

HASLEM No item mentioned.
BEMROSE No item mentioned.

A group of three maidens, probably representing *Art, Literature* and *Astrology*, stand about an architectural plinth on which lies a covered urn. One holds a scroll inscribed 'The Poet's eye in a fine frenzy Rolling doeth glance from Heaven to Earth, from Earth to Heaven'.[1] Other objects held by the figures are missing. Mounted upon a cylindrical base on which an orb, a sheet of parchment bearing upon it an inscribed triangle and circle, and a book are scattered.

Timothy Clifford[2] has established the source of this rare group to be an engraving by Marcantonio Raimondi, after Raphael, intended as a design for a pounce-pot or funerary monument to Francis I, c 1518–19, once in the Church of Celestines but now in the Louvre. The Derby version is in the style of Spengler, and is described in the *Sale Catalogue* of William Bemrose's Collection[3] as: 'A Group –

322 No. 380. Biscuit group emblematic of *Art, Literature and Astrology*. 12½ in (31.8 cm). Incised 'No. 380'. *Derby Museums and Art Gallery*

323 No. 380. Reverse view of *Art, Literature and Astrology*.

three female figures grouped round a pedestal, on which is a vase, with festoons of delicate raised flowers; the figures represent Art, Literature and Astrology. Modelled by Spengler . . .'

Example

Clifford, 1969, pl. 128. Biscuit, 12½ in (31.8 cm), incised 'No. 380'. Derby Museums and Art Gallery, as illustrated.

References

1 William Shakespeare, *A Midsummer Night's Dream*, Act V, Scene I, line 7.

2 Clifford, 1969, pl. 128, engraving by Marcantonio Raimondi; pl. 128, monument of the *Heart of Henri II*.

3 *Catalogue of the William Bemrose Collection*, 1909, p. 24, lot 336. Messrs T. Neal and Son, Nottingham.

No. 381. *Not Identified*

HASLEM No item mentioned.
BEMROSE 'Pair figures, Spangler.'

No. 382. *Dancing Girl*

HASLEM No item mentioned.
BEMROSE 'Pair of figures.'

A dancing girl stands with her right hand on her hip, leaning slightly towards her left, holding out her skirt with her left hand. She wears a wide ribbon to secure her hair and a three-quarter length dress gathered at the waist by a sash. Mounted on a rectangular base.

Example
Clifford, 1969, fig. 13. Biscuit, $6\frac{1}{2}$ in (16.5 cm), incised 'No. 382'. Late Peerage Antiques.

No. 383. *Not Identified*

HASLEM No item mentioned.
BEMROSE 'Farming figures.'

No. 384. *Admiral Lord Howe*

HASLEM No item mentioned.
BEMROSE 'Lord Howe.'

A portrait model of Admiral Lord Howe, standing with his left hand on his hip, and with his right resting upon the muzzle of a cannon. He wears a cocked hat, cravat, belted waistcoat, jacket, breeches and buckled shoes. Upon his breast is the ribbon of the *Order of the Bath*, and a sword hangs at his right side.

The model was adapted from Mather Brown's portrait of the admiral standing upon the quarter-deck of HMS *Queen Charlotte* after his defeat of the French fleet on the 'Glorious first of June, 1794', now in the National Maritime Museum, Greenwich. Joseph Lygo mentioned in a letter to William Duesbury II, dated 2 July 1794,[1] that Lady Howe had been shown a print brought by a Mr Latiefieri which she declared was no true likeness of her husband. The model must have been issued about 1794–5 and a clay maquette survives that is incised 'P. Stephan'.[2]

Admiral Richard Earl Howe (1726–99) was the second son of the second viscount, Emanuel Scrope Howe. Educated at Eton College, he later joined the senior service in the family tradition. He proved himself to be a competent naval commander who was abreast, though scarcely ahead, of his time. He led the task force that relieved Gibraltar in 1782, and was First Lord of the Admiralty between 1783 and 1788. His finest hour was the defeat of the French fleet on 1 June 1794,

324 No. 384. Biscuit model of *Admiral Lord Howe*. $10\frac{1}{4}$ in (26 cm). Incised 'P. Stephan'.
Victoria and Albert Museum

though this was effected more by the superiority of the British men and equipment than as the result of tactical brilliance. He was awarded the *Order of the Garter*, but for personal reasons for a while declined the honour that he ultimately accepted. His portraits by Gainsborough and Singleton hang respectively in the National Portrait Gallery and Trinity House.

Examples

A Bradley, op. cit., no. 41. Clay maquette of *Admiral Howe*, 10¼ in (26 cm), signed 'P. Stephan'. Victoria and Albert Museum, ref. no. C.134–1937.

B Mallet, op. cit., no. 58. Enamelled, 11¼ in (28.6 cm), incised 'No. 384'. Bearsted Collection, Upton House.

C R. T. H. Hasley, 'Ceramic Americana of the Eighteenth Century', Part IV, *Art in America*, V, 1916, pp. 55–6, fig. 12b.

References

1 Gilhespy, 1961, op. cit., p. 70.

2 Victoria and Albert Museum, ref. no. C.134–1937.

No. 385. *Aesculapius and Hygeia* (pair)

HASLEM No item mentioned.

BEMROSE 'Farmer figure.'

The above designation has been confirmed by Barrett and Thorpe, although examples are unknown to the present author. When Joseph Lygo wrote to William Duesbury II in 1793 that Rossi had completed a model of Aesculapius, this could not have been No. 99, for such a low serial number relates to about 1780, long before that artist came to model for Derby. Recently fine models of Aesculapius and Hygeia, which closely follow descriptions given by Lygo, came to auction. These were attributed to Staffordshire and not to Derby though an illustration is here provided.

Example

A See Plate 262 for white glazed Staffordshire porcelain examples.

Nos. 386 and 387. *Not Identified*

HASLEM No items mentioned.

BEMROSE No. 386. No item mentioned. No. 387. 'Large group, 4 figures, Russian Shepherd.'

325 No. 385. Pair of Staffordshire white glazed figures of *Aesculapius and Hygeia*. These correspond to descriptions by Lygo of Derby models. $9\frac{1}{2}$ in (24.1 cm). *Sotheby's*

326 No. 388. Biscuit group of four putti representing *The Four Seasons*. $10\frac{1}{2}$ in (26.7 cm). Incised 'No. 388'. *Derby Museums and Art Gallery*

327 No. 388. Reverse view of *The Four Seasons*.

No. 388. *The Four Seasons* (group)

HASLEM No item mentioned.
BEMROSE No item mentioned.

Four winged and scantily draped putti are arranged upon a rocky mound about a leafing tree.

Spring A putto standing with a garland about his waist and a posy in either hand.
Summer A putto stooped over a sheaf of corn which he binds.
Autumn A putto crowned with vine leaves and grapes holding a bunch of grapes aloft in his right hand.
Winter A seated putto attaching an ice-skate to his left foot.

Examples

A Derby Museums and Art Gallery, $10\frac{1}{2}$ in (26.7 cm), incised 'No. 388', as illustrated.

B Ibid. Enamelled, $10\frac{1}{2}$ in (26.7 cm), incised 'No. 388'. Bloor example.

No. 389. *The Alpine Shepherds* (pair)

HASLEM No item mentioned.
BEMROSE 'Pair of figures.'

A shepherd wearing a brimmed hat, sleeveless jacket and breeches, stands slightly stooped, playing an end-flute. The shepherdess, who is clad in a soft cap, blouse, skirt and apron, holds a crook and dances. Mounted on a mound base encrusted with leaves and flowers.

328 No. 389. *The Alpine Shepherds.* $10\frac{3}{4}$ in (27.3 cm). Incised 'No. 389'. *British Museum*

The models were adapted from engravings by Francesco Bartolozzi made about 1785, after Angelica Kauffmann's painting entitled *The Alpine Shepherds*. This portrays the male figure seated upon a boulder which was changed in the model to provide a pair.[1]

Example
Clifford, 1978, fig. 12b. Biscuit, $10\frac{3}{4}$ in (27.3 cm), incised 'No. 389'. British Museum, ref. no. 1936, 7–15, 15 and 7–15, 15A, as illustrated.

Reference
1 Clifford, 1978, fig. 12a. Engraving by F. Bartolozzi after Angelica Kauffmann.

No. 390(i). *Gualtieri and Griselda* (group)

HASLEM 'Group of Gaultherus and Griselda: [size not given] enamelled £1 11s 6d.'
BEMROSE 'Pair of single figures.'

No example has been seen by the author but a memorandum in the Derby Museums and Art Gallery describes a group brought in by a member of the public for identification that was 12 in (30.5 cm), biscuit, and incised 'No. 390'.

The beautiful young Griselda clad in a simple dress kneels before Gualtieri, and regards him as if pleading with him. He is portrayed wearing a plumed cap, tunic, breeches and riding-boots with a mantle thrown over his left shoulder. Mounted before a tree-trunk support upon a wide cylindrical base.

The group appears to have been based on an illustration in one of many possible editions of Boccaccio's *Decameron*, and relates to the 'Tenth Day, Novel X'. Gualtieri, Marquis of Saluzzo, is urged by his subjects to abandon his pleasure-loving ways and marry. He agrees to wed provided he may select his bride, and chooses Griselda, the daughter of a shepherd named Giannucolo, believing that her lack of sophistication and gentle sweetness will allow him to continue to indulge himself. Later, he comes to love her but cannot rest until he has tested her devotion to himself. Accordingly, when she bears him first a daughter and then a son, he tells Griselda that they pose a serious threat to his position and asks her to hand them over to him to be slain. Trusting in his natural goodness, she kisses them and surrenders them to his mercy. In due course Gualtieri pretends to love another woman and tells his wife he has obtained an annulment of their marriage. Meekly she returns his ring and, abandoning all her possessions, returns to live in her father's humble home. Finally she is commanded to attend the nuptial ceremony of her ex-husband but, when she arrives, she learns that her children have been reared secretly in Bologna, and that a great feast has been prepared in her honour.

She is reunited with Gualtieri and her children, and resumes her role as mother and wife.

No. 390(ii). *Flora*

An entirely different model also bears the incised 'No. 390'. This is a slender dancing maiden holding in either hand the two ends of a floral garland. She wears a cap secured beneath her chin with ribbons and is clad in a laced bodice and ankle-length skirt. Mounted on a cylindrical base before a truncated column.

This model, executed in the style of Spengler, was adapted from an engraving

329 No. 390 (ii). *Flora* holding a garland. 10 in (25.4 cm). Incised 'No. 390'. *Private Collection*

made in 1771 by Grignion after Brandoin, entitled *An Opera Girl of Paris in the Character of Flora.*[1]

Example

Bradshaw, op. cit., pl. 129. Biscuit, 10 in (25.4 cm), incised 'No. 390'. Collection of Dr H. G. M. Edwards (private).

Reference

1 Anthony Ray, 'Liverpool Printed Tiles', *Trans ECC*, 9, 1973, part 2, p. 61, appendices D5–26. Design for a tile of *Flora*.

No. 391. *Prince Frederick Augustus, Duke of York*

HASLEM No item mentioned.
BEMROSE 'Duke of York.'

A portrait model of Frederick Augustus, Duke of York, standing in military uniform consisting of a cocked hat, red jacket with epaulettes and blue facings, a cream waistcoat, breeches and boots. A flag and a cannon are at his feet.

Joseph Lygo mentions in a letter written to William Duesbury in 1794 that:[1] 'He had obtained a full length engraving of the Duke of York by Dickinson.' Also, 'Mr. Catherine had got a scratch from a picture of the Duke of York, which is going to be engraved.'

Frederick Augustus, Duke of York (1763–1827), was the younger brother of George IV and the son of George III and Queen Charlotte. He followed a military career and commanded the English army in Flanders against the French. After minor victories he was defeated at Hondschoote and Tournai and, in 1799, compelled to sign the Convention of Alkmaar. He resigned his position as Commander-in-Chief in 1809 when it was revealed his mistress, Mary Anne Clarke, was trafficking in appointments, but he was reinstated in 1811. The Derby model includes a replica of a flag bearing the device of the two crosses of St Andrew and St George prior to the incorporation of the cross of St Patrick, not implemented until 1801.

Examples

A Mallet, op. cit., no. 57. Enamelled, 11¼ in (28.6 cm), incised 'No. 391'. Bearsted Collection, Upton House.

B Christie's, *Sale Catalogue*, 8 December 1924, lot 133. Possibly the same model as the above.

Reference

1 Gilhespy, 1961, p. 70.

330 No. 391. *Prince Frederick Augustus, Duke of York.* $11\frac{1}{4}$ in (28.6 cm). Incised 'No. 391'. *Upton House*

No. 392. *Not Identified*

BEMROSE 'Pair of large figures.'

No. 393. *The Russian Shepherds* (group)

BEMROSE 'Russian shepherd and shepherdess.'

The group is composed of four interlocking sections, viz: A bareheaded bearded Russian peasant sits on a rocky mound, wearing a shirt, jacket, breeches and fur-lined boots, playing a balalaika. A lady stands at his right side, attired in flowing

331 No. 393. Biscuit group of *The Russian Shepherds*, with a detachable stand. 13 in (33 cm). Incised with crown X and 'D', and also a star but no number. *British Museum*

garments, singing. The two are mounted on a semi-mound with its vertical flat side facing posteriorly. A second semi-mound abuts against it on which there is a seated bareheaded youth playing bagpipes. The two sections are contained by an oval collar and the whole slots into an elaborate oval stand decorated with festoons of leaves and flowers between fluted pilasters.

Benjamin Vulliamy ascribed this group to Spengler and it was based on J. B. Tallard's engraving, after Le Prince, *Les Bergers Russes*. The *Sale Catalogue* of the Bemrose Collection of 1909 includes an example of the group said to be incised 'No. 395'. This, however, is known to be the *Lady Feeding a Sheep*. The incised numerals '5' and '3' are not dissimilar and it may be recalled that Severne Mackenna[1] interpreted an incised date upon a Chelsea *Goat and Bee* creamer as '1743' when most would read it as '1745'.

Examples

A Lane, op. cit., pl. 75. Biscuit, 13 in (33 cm), incised with a crown, crossed batons and script letter 'D', also with a star but with no numerals.

B Allam, op. cit., p. 30, no. I. Biscuit, 12 in (30.5 cm), incised numbers said to be either 'No. 387' or 'No. 367'.

C Clifford, 1978, fig. 4. Biscuit, 12 in (30.5 cm), no marks reported.

Reference

1 F. Severne Mackenna, *Chelsea Porcelain, the Triangle and Raised Anchor Wares*, Leigh-on-Sea, 1948, pl. 1.

No. 394. *Seated Piper*

BEMROSE No item mentioned.

A youth seated cross-legged playing a reed-pipe, being the rear section from *The Russian Shepherds*, No. 393.

Example

Sotheby's, *Sale Catalogue*, 18 May 1982, lot 136. Biscuit, $9\frac{1}{4}$ in (23.5 cm), incised 'No. 394', as illustrated.

332 No. 394. *Seated Piper*. $9\frac{1}{4}$ in (23.5 cm). Incised 'No. 394'. *Burnley Antiques*

333 No. 395. Biscuit group of *Lady Feeding a Sheep with Hay*. 14 in (35.6 cm). Incised 'No. 395'. See also Plate XVII. *Victoria and Albert Museum*

No. 395. *Lady Feeding a Sheep with Hay*

BEMROSE 'Shepherd and shepherdess.'

A young lady, wearing a bonnet, scarf and ankle-length dress, holds on to a rustic gate and feeds a sheep with hay; behind her a recumbent dog sleeps. Mounted on an oval base encrusted with leaves and flowers.

In 1793 Lygo wrote to William Duesbury II:[1] 'I could not get that beautiful figure of Rosina without buying it at a price of six shillings. Spengler is going to model it – have not found a male figure to match it and S. wants to do one of his own idea.' Rosina is the heroine in a novel, *Rosina – Or Love in a Cottage*, by Francis Brooke, published in 1785 and illustrated by an engraving by Charles Knight after Thomas Stothard. This, it was once believed, may have prompted the Derby model, but Timothy Clifford[2] has identified the source as an engraving of *Adelaide*, by J. Hogg after Francis Wheatley, published in July 1787. The model was the penultimate example of Spengler's work.

Examples

A Twitchett, op. cit., pl. 193. Biscuit, 11 in (28 cm), incised 'No. 395'. British Museum, ref. no. C.9–1975.

B Barrett and Thorpe, op. cit., pl. 122. The same model as the above said to be incised 'No. 369' (typographical error).

C Lane, op. cit., pl. 77. Biscuit, 14 in (35.6 cm), incised 'No. 395'. Lady Lever Gallery, Port Sunlight.

References

1 Gilhespy, 1961, p. 67.

2 Clifford, 1978, pp. 146–53.

No. 396. *Shepherd with his Dog*

BEMROSE 'Shepherd and shepherdess.'

A bareheaded shepherd stands hat in hand, leaning his left elbow upon a tree-trunk; at his right side sits a dog with one paw raised, regarding his master, while on his left there lies a sheep. Mounted on a cylindrical base encrusted with leaves and flowers.

The model was adapted from a terracotta that once belonged to the artist Joseph Wright, of Derby. The identity of the figure was, until recently, believed to be Antinous, favourite of the Roman emperor, Hadrian, drowned while attempting to cross the river Nile in AD 121. A classical original, which lacks a right arm, from the Praxiteles School, dates from the fourth century BC and clearly cannot be Antinous; it may be seen in the Vatican Museum, Belvedere. Almost certainly it portrays Hermes (Mercury). Pierre Legros (1629–1714) reproduced the statue complete in marble, and a terracotta is in Wentworth Castle, Yorkshire.[1] Bronze copies were also made in Florence[2] during the sixteenth century and have been copied during the eighteenth and nineteenth centuries.

Although Arthur Lane,[3] together with both Barrett and Thorpe,[4] have ascribed the Derby model to William John Coffee, the style is indubitably that of Spengler.

Examples

A Twitchett, op. cit., pl. 94. Biscuit, 14 in (35.6 cm), incised 'No. 396'. Victoria and Albert Museum, ref. no. 384–1896.

B Lane, op. cit., pl. 76. Biscuit, $13\frac{3}{4}$ in (35 cm), incised 'No. 396'.

C Barrett and Thorpe, op. cit., pl. 122. Biscuit, $13\frac{3}{4}$ in (35 cm), incised 'No. 396'.

References

1 G. B. Foggim, *Connoisseur*, 141, 1958, p. 223, pl. 7.

2 *Apollo*, December 1966, p. xxxiii.

3 Lane, op. cit., p. 111.

4 Barrett and Thorpe, op. cit., p. 86.

334 No. 396. *Shepherd with his Dog* (biscuit). Based on a transposed adaptation of *Hermes*. 14 in (35.6 cm). Incised 'No. 396'. *Victoria and Albert Museum*

335 *Bronze, after the antique, of Hermes*. 11 in (27.9 cm). *Author's Collection*

No. 397. *Cupid Entreating a Virgin* (group)

BEMROSE 'Venus and boy, large.'

A virgin stands, barehead and barefoot, attired in classical robes which she holds with her left hand while her right rests upon her forehead as if posed in thought. A winged Cupid faces the maiden with his left hand elevated in supplication whilst in his right he grasps his long-bow. Mounted upon an oval base which has a vertical circumference.

Example
Derby Museums and Art Gallery, ref. no. 1250. Biscuit, $12\frac{1}{2}$ in (31.8 cm), incised 'No. 397', as illustrated.

336 No. 397. Damaged biscuit group of *Cupid Entreating a Virgin*. $12\frac{1}{2}$ in (31.8 cm). Incised 'No. 397'. *Derby Museums and Art Gallery*

Part IV

8 · The Last Derby Soft-paste Models, 1796–1810

Following the departure of Jean-Jacques Spengler and William John Coffee, only a handful of new soft-paste models were created at Derby, the most notable of which are portrait figures of admirals whose naval victories had earned them nationwide renown. Admiral Hood (1727–1814) served under Admiral Lord Howe in both the English Channel and the Straits of Gibraltar, sharing with him the honours of the 'Glorious First of June', 1796. The porcelain model of *Lord Hood* (F4) shows him wearing a cocked hat and naval uniform, standing with a sword in his right hand and a telescope in his left. Admiral Sir Adam Duncan (1731–1804) is famed for his victory off Cape St Vincent in 1780 and the successful blockade of the Texel, but above all for his defeat of the Dutch fleet on 11 October 1797 at Camperdown. The model of *Admiral Duncan* (F3) portrays him standing bareheaded in uniform, left hand on hip, holding a baton in his right and with trophies scattered at his feet. George Bridges Rodney (1719–92) was Officer Commanding the Leeward Islands and also on two separate occasions Jamaica, where he served with distinction. In 1782 he captured De Grasse with seven of his ships off Dominica, a feat which established British naval hegemony in the area, although the full significance of the achievement was not appreciated until after the admiral's death. The model of *Lord Rodney* (F8), which was probably issued about 1795, depicts him clad in a cocked hat standing with his right hand which grasps a sword resting upon the barrel of a cannon, pointing with his left supposedly towards the enemy line of battle.

John Drinkwater (1762–1844) was the son of a naval surgeon who assumed the name 'Bethune'. When, at the age of only fifteen, he learned of the British defeat at Saratoga, he enlisted in the Royal Manchester Volunteers but was posted not, as he had hoped, to the American Colonies but to Gibraltar, where, between June 1779 and February 1783, he was besieged by the Spanish fleet. He reverted to civilian life and in 1785 wrote *The History of the Siege of Gibraltar*. Later he re-enlisted, serving a second tour of duty on the Rock before accompanying his regiment to Toulon and Corsica. He wrote the *Battle of Cape St Vincent* that linked his name thereafter with that event. Afforded the courtesy title 'General' he was in fact commissary general to the Helder Force in 1799. The model of *John Drinkwater* (F2) shows him standing bareheaded, right hand on hip with his left resting upon the muzzle of a cannon. All four of these portrait figures are stylistically akin to that of *Admiral Lord Howe* (No. 384), mentioned earlier, of which one example is incised 'P. Stephan'.[1] Black basaltes versions of Admirals Rodney and Hood survive which closely resemble their Derby counterparts and may have been made at Etruria. Stephan is known to have worked freelance to supply Josiah Wedgwood.[2] The evidence suggests that the five portrait Derby figures were all created by Stephan between about 1794 and 1798.

The sculptor François Hardenburg was engaged to replace Spengler and Coffee and probably arrived at Derby about 1796. However, he left after only a few months to establish his own atelier in the metropolis, and no soft-paste examples of his sojourn at Derby are extant. A model of *George III* (G27) of about 1820, now in the National Portrait Gallery, is ascribed to Hardenburg and, if this attribution is correct, it would seem he continued to supply master models to the manufactory from his London studio. His services are likely to have been engaged for portraits of royalty such as *George IV* (G28), *Queen Victoria* (G30), and other notables. John Twitchett[3] credits him with 'A rare unidentified figure of a stocky man', which he illustrates. This truncated figure is scarcely likely to represent the work of a sculptor and it is, in fact, the model of a *Warden*, from the set described as *Vicars, Curates and Wardens* (G41), by Edward Keys.

Between 1810 and 1815 – the precise date is uncertain – the soft paste was replaced by bone china. Haslem[4] relates how for a while the new formula was reserved for useful wares while models continued to be cast in soft paste. Both were fired in the same kiln, when models which required a lower temperature were placed on the bottom shelves and articles of bone china above them. This practice led to an unacceptable number of wasters amongst figures and accordingly the soft paste was abandoned altogether.

1 H. G. Bradley (ed.), *Ceramics of Derbyshire 1750–1976*, Tiverton, 1978, pl. 41. Victoria and Albert Museum, ref. no. C.134–1937.
2 R. T. H. Hasley 'Ceramic Americana of the Eighteenth Century', Part IV, *Art in America*, V, 1916, pp. 55–6: fig. 10, black basalted model of *Admiral Lord Hood*; fig. 11, Derby biscuit model of *Admiral Lord Rodney*; fig. 12, black basaltes model of *Admiral Lord Howe*; fig. 12a, black basaltes model of *Admiral Lord Rodney*; fig. 12b, Derby enamelled and gilt model of *Admiral Lord Howe*.
3 John Twitchett, *Derby Porcelain*, London, 1980, pl. 363.
4 John Haslem, *The Old Derby China Factory*, London, 1876, p. 147.

9 · Bone China Derby Models, 1810–48

PASTE AND GLAZE

Thomas Cookworthy rediscovered the means of making hard-paste porcelain, after the manner of the Chinese, during the mid-1760s at Plymouth. This entailed the formation of a paste with china clay (kaolin), china stone (petuntse), alkaline flux and water. Items were either thrown upon a wheel or shaped in plaster of Paris moulds and baked in a kiln at about 1,350°C. In practice, however, figures were given a preliminary firing at a lower temperature, dipped into a vat of liquid glaze, and then subjected to the full kiln heat. Richard Champion of Bristol bought Cookworthy's patent rights, but resold them in 1781 to a consortium of potters from Shelton who established the New Hall porcelain manufactory. During the early years of the nineteenth century several other factories made hard paste, but Josiah Spode then added to the mix bone ash, obtained from calcined cattle bones, to create bone china. Within a decade this had become the standard porcelain body adopted by almost every English manufacturer, including Derby. Barrett and Thorpe[1] have presented several formulae that differ in small details, found in a notebook that supposedly was once the property of Robert Bloor.

The new bone china was clad in a glaze composed of 140 parts of frit mixed with 28 of Cornwall stone, 28 of Cornish clay, 30 of white lead and 5 of pearl ash. It appears that this or a similar formula was in use as late as 1837, despite the invention of a lead-free glaze by John Rose of Coalport, which earned him a gold medal from the Royal Society of Arts in May 1820. Lead poisoning, which had constituted a serious health hazard in the ceramic industry, was virtually eliminated by this advance, although many potters failed to avail themselves of it, doubtless because they believed it to be inferior to the lead-containing feldspathic formula.

The bone china body was immensely strong and translucent, and provided greater stability in the kiln. It facilitated the creation of larger models in more ambitious poses, while its greater plasticity allowed the reproduction of sharper moulded

1 F. A. Barrett and A. L. Thorpe, *Derby Porcelain*, London, 1971, pp. 119–23.

detail and reduced fire-cracks, surface-tearing of paste and other earlier blemishes. The exposed paste presents a chalky-white appearance and feels dry to the touch. The glaze usually displays slight crazing which may help to distinguish Bloor figures from those reissued by Stevenson and Hancock.

BASES

Several new shapes were introduced, of which the most common are either circular or oval with the vertical circumference composed of pierced white scrolls accented with gilt, or alternatively shallow cylinders decorated with a gilt band or octagonal bases, on which the facets were often adorned by the Greek key-fret pattern in low relief. Most of these different forms were painted an opaque yellow-green over their upper surface. Small models appear on shallow mounds edged with gilt scrolls and accented with either green or turquoise enamel, or more rarely upon squares, some of which have chamfered corners, while figures of animals were mounted upon irregular green pads encrusted with small leaves and flowers. The under-surfaces are mostly concave, glazed and perforated by a small ventilation hole, although occasionally the underneath may be flat, when faint spur-marks may be evident, though larger patch-marks are not encountered.

MARKS

The factory device of a jewelled crown over crossed batons flanked on either side by three dots, surmounting a script letter 'D', continued to be used on some items. Between 1784–1810 this was neatly pencilled in blue or puce enamel over glaze but afterwards was often carelessly drawn in red. After 1825 the words 'Bloor Derby' may be written horizontally beneath a crown, or may be contained within two concentric circles when the central area may include a crown. These too are executed in red enamel. Pseudo-Meissen marks of crossed swords, or imitations of the entwined letters 'L' of Sèvres, are pencilled in blue on some models derived from these sources. A script letter 'N', enamelled or incised, may rarely be seen as well as Arabic numerals lacking the prefix 'No.' and lower case letters which probably refer to painters and gilders.

ENAMEL COLOURS

The enamel palette introduced about 1800 is noticeably much darker in tone than that previously used, while the opacity of some of the colours, especially of the blues, mauves and greens, tends to mask the translucency of the bone china, imparting to it the superficial appearance of earthenware. A yellow-green, derived from chrome oxide, first introduced about 1795, was now liberally used upon many of the bases.

A purplish, glossy and opaque dark blue provided a rather heavy nuance together with a greenish-blue that has a matt surface. Deep maroon, egg-yellow, brick-red, ultramarine, dark brown, purple and black complete the spectrum. Often washes of these colours, especially of green and black, flaked off the surface in patches to create a rather drab effect, clearly seen in Plates 359 and 360, Plate 373 (pair of *Topers* (G39), and an *Elephant* (G79). This may have been due to a failure to achieve a sufficiently high temperature in the muffle kiln to fix the enamel to the feldspathic glaze.

The pink flesh tints of the Chelsea–Derby era now darken to become almost a tan, while human hair that had invariably been blond or light brown was now portrayed brunette or raven-black. Although eyelids, lashes and eyebrows continued to be suggested in the former manner, china-blue eyes make their debut. A certain carelessness in the pencilling used to denote nostrils became evident, while the touch of colour required to enliven the inner canthus of the eyes was sometimes omitted altogether. Garments were decorated in the current Regency fashion with a preference for vertical stripes painted in three or more colours or patterns composed of geometrical shapes, lines and dots. When floral sprays were occasionally used they are small in scale and stylized after the manner of *indianische Blumen*.

GILDING

Around 1800 honey-gilding was replaced by the mercury process. This necessitated the formation of an amalgam with mercury and gold, known as gold water, which was added to a mixture of fat dissolved in alcohol to facilitate application with a brush. The mercury vaporized in the muffle kiln leaving a brilliant, though rather pale, gold precipitate. Bloor purchased gold from Read and Lucas of Sheffield for 85 shillings per fine ounce, well below the current London price. The material probably contained metallic impurities which may account for the coppery appearance of late Derby gold. It may be recalled here that in 1832 there were no fewer than forty-one male gilders and thirty-nine female burnishers working at Derby in a total work-force of 129 souls.

The lavish use of gold upon figures served to enliven the dark enamel colouring, and one delightful feature was the pencilling of gilt flowers that are small in scale upon a dark blue, or occasionally a dark green ground. This recalls the exquisite work executed at Vincennes when gilt sprays were laid upon *gros bleu*, or later at Sèvres upon *bleu-de-roi*.

MODELLING

Unfortunately the improvements afforded to modellers in paste, glaze and enamels were more than offset by the reduced skills of the craftsmen. Most of the new models are less than 6 in (15.2 cm) tall, are stiffly posed and appear to stare vacantly into space. Their faces are heart-shaped, with pointed chin and receding hair-line, mouths are stylized to resemble a rose-bud, while noses of adults are long and thin and those of children short and upturned. The naive representation of drapery further reduces any semblance of animation. Accessories like musical instruments and garden tools are usually carelessly finished and flowers, formerly cast from pitcher-moulds or made by hand, are often reduced to a mound of slip roughly indented. Moreover inadequate fettling often left junctions between separately cast parts visible. Apart from these deficiencies, in many instances models either have the characteristics of lampoons or exhibit semi-grotesque qualities, with the deliberate distortion of anatomical proportions.

Many copies were made of soft-paste models and groups. Often the original moulds had worn out and new ones were formed from clay squeezes. These bone china copies lack the crispness of detail found in their prototypes and, owing to shrinkage of paste in the kiln, are usually slightly smaller. Despite their deficiencies they number among the most attractive to have been issued during this period.

MODELS

Most of the bone china copies of earlier Derby items show only minor adaptations from the original theme, but in a few instances the subject was altered almost beyond recognition. The fine group *Belisarius and his Daughter* (No. 370) was refurbished by the replacement of the child with a lady, attired in a high-waisted Regency dress and a picture-hat, and by transforming the Byzantine general to become her elegant bearded escort (G25). A similar biscuit version was issued by George Cocker at a small manufactory at Friar's Gate, Derby.[2] The figure of Cupid in the group *Two Virgins Awakening Cupid* (No. 195) was adapted by John Whitaker to provide a *Nymph Asleep amidst Flowers* (G50), while according to Haslem, the seated dog at the feet of the male member of *The Dresden Shepherds* (No. 55) was also issued separately. The ever-popular *Putti* decked with flowers (E77) continued to be sold as *Basket Boys* (G52), and the group of two putti, emblematic of *Fire*, from the set of *The Four Elements* (No. 48) became two *Cupids Grinding* (G47).

Haslem provided a number of supplementary lists including one of models and

2 F. Brayshaw Gilhespy, *Derby Porcelain*, London, 1961, fig. 67.

groups supposedly cast either from Chelsea or Bow moulds. None of these can today be accepted although there is a fine pair consisting of a standing *Peasant Fiddler and Woman playing a Mandoline* (G37) that are known in Bow[3] and Chelsea[4] examples based on Meissen prototypes. The Derby *Stag and Doe at Lodge* (G67), as well as *Cats with Prey* (G61), seated *Pug Dogs on Cushions* (G75), together with sundry *Sheep* (G88–91) and *Cattle* (G64–6) are all known in Meissen prototypes, although Bow copies may have provided intermediate sources. Again, there are two Derby *Monkey Musicians* (F27) based upon the Meissen *Affenkapelle*[5] and, although at least ten red anchor Chelsea versions exist,[6] it is interesting to find that the specific monkey instrumentalists are not among the Chelsea models, so here Derby may have copied Meissen originals. A pair of delightful seated *Squirrels* eating nuts (G92), are noticeably slimmer than earlier Derby examples (E98), although both may have been inspired by a first-period Chelsea model.[7]

A second supplementary list includes items that are not, strictly speaking, figures, and these are presented in an amended form on p. 143. Some articles are mentioned in the *Derby Sale Catalogues* of 17–20 April, 1781: 'A pair of Satyr's Head drinking cups, blue and gold, 7s 6d.', 'Pair Neptune's Head drinking cups 7s od.' and 'Pair of large Fox Heads 8s 6d.' On 10–14 May, 1782[8] were offered: 'Neptune Heads', 'Hare's Heads', etc. These, it appears, continued to be manufactured during the first quarter of the nineteenth century.

The most interesting of the new models are those relating to the contemporary stage which have been ascribed to Samuel Keys (*fils*) by John Haslem, issued between 1825 and 1830. John Liston (1776–1848) abandoned his career as a schoolmaster for the acting profession and became the favourite comedy actor of George III. Between 1805 and 1837 he trod the boards of the Haymarket, Drury Lane and Olympic theatres. A porcelain model depicts him in the title role of *Paul Pry* (G5) of John Poole's play that opened on 13 September 1825. It was adapted from an engraving made in 1826 by J.W. Gear,[9] which also prompted the Rockingham

3 Robert Schmidt, *Porcelain as an Art and as a Mirror of Fashion*, London, 1932, fig. 43. Bow models of a *Fiddler and Lady Playing a Mandoline*.

4 F. Severne Mackenna, *Chelsea Porcelain, the Red Anchor Wares*, Leigh-on-Sea, 1951, pl. 74, fig. 147, Chelsea model of the *Lady Playing a Mandoline*.

5 John Cushion, *Animals in Pottery and Porcelain*, London, 1966, p. 21. See also *Apollo*, 79, 1964, p. 365, fig. 2, Meissen *Affenkapelle* by J. J. Kändler.

6 John C. Austin, *Chelsea Porcelain at Williamsburg*, Virginia, 1977, pls. 121–9, *Ten Chelsea Monkey Musicians*, after Meissen originals.

7 Ibid., pl. 104, Chelsea model of a red *Squirrel*, first period.

8 J. E. Nightingale, *Contributions towards the History of Early English Porcelain*, Salisbury, 1881, appendix pp. 58, 60 and 61.

9 Ibid., pp. 64 and 65.

version. Haslem records how Liston spotted the model of himself in the window of Bloor's showrooms in Bond Street and immediately purchased it. The same author mentions other models of Liston as *Maw Worm* (G6) and *Domine Sampson* (G7), although these do not seem to have survived. The Rockingham factory also produced a series of Liston models[10] in the roles of Simon Pengander, from *Twixt Cup and Lip*; Tristan Sappy, from *Deaf as a Post*; Billy Lackaday, from *Sweethearts and Wives*; and in the female parts of Madam Vestris and Moll Flagon, from *Lord of the Manor*.

Lucia Elizabeth Bartolozzi (1797–1856) was the grand-daughter of the engraver Francesco Bartolozzi. In 1813 she married an Italian dancer named Auguste Armand Vestris, but he deserted her four years later. She possessed a melodious, if largely untrained, contralto voice and, after performing minor roles in the Italian Opera then in Paris, came to London where she starred in light musical entertainments. She popularized the song 'Cherry Ripe' and in 1826 appeared in *The Hundred Pound Note*, attired as a Bavarian peasant woman, to sing the aria 'Buy a Broom'. The model of *Madam Vestris* (G9), based on a lithograph by J. Dickinson, shows her in this role. Alwyn and Angela Cox[11] remind us of how, on 6 November 1826, Madam Vestris and John Liston, both dressed as Bavarian women, appeared together at the Haymarket to sing 'Buy a Broom' as a duet. This event was immortalized by J. H. Lynch's engraving, which formed the basis for a Rockingham model of Liston in drag.

Maria Foote (1797–1867) made her stage début upon the boards of her father's theatre in Plymouth. In 1814 she played in London in *The Child of Nature*. The breeches role of Arinette, in William Diamond's *Little Jockey*, which had a revival at the Olympic theatre, prompted a Derby model (G2) but also proved to be her swan-song for, later that year, she married Charles Stanhope, the fourth Earl of Hartington.

Other models accredited to Samuel Keys include a set of three *Tyrolese Singers* (G8) depicting two men and a woman wearing green jackets and plumed hats, the males in breeches and boots, representing three of five members of the Rainer family, who toured Britain in 1827; based on a lithograph made by E. Wilson in 1828. They typify the puppet-like models of the period, together with *Billy Waters* (G10) the one-legged negro fiddler, and *Dusty Bob* and *African Sal* (G1), adapted from George Cruikshank's illustrations in Pierce Egan's *Life in London or the Day and Night Scenes of Jerry Hawthorn, Esq: and his elegant friend Corinthian Tom in their rambles and sprees through the Metropolis*, published in 1821. This subsequently

10 Ibid., pp. 67, 68 and 70.

11 Dennis G. Rice, *Rockingham Ornamental Porcelain*, London, 1965, p. 55.

prompted the musical extravaganza *Tom and Jerry*. The rare model of the clown *Grimaldi* (G3) was attributed by Haslem to Thomas Griffin. Joseph Grimaldi (1779–1837) made his stage début in 1781 at the age of only two years and continued to tread the boards at Sadler's Wells and Drury Lane until his retirement in 1828.

Thirteen models of *Dr Syntax* (G11–23) and one of his *Landlady* (G24) are ascribed to Edward Keys. These are mostly 4–6 in (10.2–15.2 cm) tall, mounted upon either shallow cylinders or pads or squares, some with chamfered corners. The character was created by William Gilpin (1724–1804) but was popularized by narrative verse, appearing as instalments in *Ackerman's Poetical Magazine* during 1809, composed by William Combe (1741–1823). These were expanded to provide three volumes: *The Tour of Dr Syntax in Search of the Picturesque* (1812), *The Tour of Dr Syntax in Search of Consolation* (1820), and *The Tour of Dr Syntax in search of a Wife* (1821). They relate the adventures of a curate–schoolmaster who sets off upon his dapple-grey horse, Grizzle, to tour Britain, hoping that later he may publish his exploits illustrated by his own watercolour sketches. The trilogy is illustrated with coloured engravings by Thomas Rowlandson: nine in Volume I and two in Volume II provide the prototypes for the models. A few others appear to have been somewhat loosely adapted. Several authors anxious to reap a ready profit from what proved to be a popular subject, wrote similar works and published these anonymously. An engraving in one of these, entitled *Dr Syntax in Paris: or a Tour of the Grotesque*, prompted the group of *Dr Syntax landing at Calais* (G23) upon the back of his landlady who wades ashore. The subject of both the engravings and the models has been reviewed by Gough.[12] After 1848 several Dr Syntax models were reissued by Stevenson and Hancock and some show minor variations. For example, *Dr Syntax Seated Sketching* (G12) reappears between geese.[13]

Mention has earlier been made of the fine model of *George III* (G27). *George IV* (G28) stands in regal robes beside a plinth upon which rests the crown. This, together with a figure of the *Duke of Wellington* (G31), and of the young *Queen Victoria* (G30), most probably issued to commemorate her accession to the throne in 1837, survives in biscuit, and the competence of their execution suggests the hand of a sculptor. An enamelled replica of *Napoleon Bonaparte* (G26) must have been issued after his death in 1821. It has been suggested that the *Mazeppa Group* (G29) was prompted by the appearance of Ada Isaacs Meukin in the opera of that name in London. However, this event did not take place until 1861, many years after the

12 B. G. Gough, 'Doctor Syntax, Rowlandson's Popular Schoolmaster in Print and in Porcelain', *Antique Collector*, February 1967, pp. 24–8.

13 Bradley, op. cit., no. 329, Stevenson and Hancock model of *Dr Syntax Sketching*, flanked by two geese.

Derby factory had failed. Ivan Stephanovitch Mazeppa (1644–1709) was the scion of a noble house in the Ukraine who was sent to the Polish Court as a page. There he seduced the wife of a courtier who, having caught the miscreant *in flagrante delicto*, bound him naked to the back of a wild horse and whipped up the animal in the snow-clad forests of winter. Miraculously he was carried back to the Ukraine unharmed to be elected *hetman* of the Cossacks and, later, was created Prince of the Ukraine by Peter the Great. When the Czar attempted to curb the power of the Cossacks, Mazeppa threw in his lot with Charles XII of Sweden but his hopes were shattered when the Swedish army was routed at Pultowa in 1709. He fled with Charles to Bender but died there the following year.

There are two different Derby versions of the *Man and Woman with Milk Churns*. In the first (G35), they stand in mirror poses holding milk churns in either hand at different heights off the ground. In the second (G36), the containers (pails) are suspended from a yoke. Only two models, a *Vicar* and a *Warden*, are known to the author from the set of *Vicars, Curates and Wardens* (G41). These are oddly truncated figures upon square bases. Also in semi-grotesque vein are the *Topers* (G39). Tradition holds that the pair entitled *Steady, Lads, Steady*, together with a model of a *Dying Drunk*, were designed by Dr Douglas Fox, a resolute campaigner against the demon drink. The sight of the third figure in this trio was evidently deemed to be too terrible to warrant commercial production, although an example may be seen in the Brighton Museum.

The sentimental mood of the age is reflected by several models of children and adolescents. There is a *Boy and Girl Gathering Flowers* (G55), a pair of *Boy and Girl, each with a Dog* (G53), or with a greyhound and a falcon (G54). Models of a child kneeling to clean her shoes, and another saying her prayers, sometimes labelled *Good Morning* and *Good Night* (G57) were doubtless intended to stress moral virtues, and this may also apply to the pair known as the *Industrious Boy and Girl* (G34). The two sit upon chairs, their frivolous toys scattered at their feet ignored, the boy cross-legged reading a book held at arm's length, the girl sewing. Another couple, the *Romantic Boy and Girl* (G40) are purely decorative and shown standing in mirror poses beside a ewer on a plinth and a vase upon a fountain; the girl holds a lamb in a fold of her apron and is transposed in an otherwise similar Rockingham version.[14] Perhaps the strangest of all is the model of a *Girl Seated in a Chair* (G56). Her left leg is amputated below the knee and she wears a party frock trimmed with lace: her picture-hat lies at her feet. This was adapted from a painting by Chalon,[15] and the

14 Rice, op. cit., pl. 106, *Industrious Boy and Girl*, Rockingham; pl. 107, *Industrious Boy and Girl*, Derby.
15 Twitchett, op. cit., pl. 384, and legend.

same subject was enamelled by John Haslem in 1839 upon a Derby plate.[16] One must suppose the subject represents a broken doll rather than a juvenile amputee!

There are two large models of *Hebe* and *Innocence* (G49), that stand 28 in (71.1 cm) tall. According to Haslem[17] they were modelled by Samuel Keys the Younger, enamelled and gilded by his father, and their bases decorated by Leonard Lead. Uncommon models include that of a *Turk Seated,* cross-legged upon a cushion (G45), and a pair of *Cantonese Girls* (G43). Others cited by Haslem including an *Angel* (G46), the *Virgin Mary* (G51), a pair of *Archers* (G48), an *Eastern Lady* (G42) and six *Paris Cries* (G38) have not been identified.

An extremely ugly set of a seated *Monkey Orchestra* (G59), wearing jackets with falling ruffles, mounted upon square bases, were issued in two different sizes and are attributed to Edward Keys. These should not be confused with standing *Monkey Musicians* mentioned earlier which echo Meissen prototypes, although they do bear more than a passing resemblance to a *Dog Orchestra*[18] made during the period of the gold anchor mark at Chelsea. Turning to the more conventional replicas of animals, some of those listed by Haslem must either be very rare or have failed to survive. Amongst them are *Cats* (G60–3), *Worcester Mice* (G84), and *Rabbits* described as without (G86) and with (G87) plinths. More familiar are models of the *Stag and Doe at Lodge* (G67) which are known in two slightly different versions, both of them based on Meissen originals.[19] An extensive kennel is composed of *Pug Dogs* (G74 and G75), some seated upon cushions and most with cropped ears that proclaim their Continental origin, *Poodle Dogs* (G72 and G73), and both a prowling (G76) and a recumbent *Setter* (G77) of which at least one example is incised 'W. Coffee'. There is a large flock of rather banal *Sheep* (G88–91), a herd of *Cattle* (G64–6), from which only a few examples are here listed, and some splendid wild animals. A pair of prowling *Leopards* (G85) are refurbished from earlier models (E89) and appear to have been painted to resemble either *Panthers* or *Tigers*, while there are also *Elephants* (G78–80) issued in two sizes, with and without 'driver' (mahout).

Only a few birds of this period survive, of which the *Peacock amongst Flowers* (G94) by John Whitaker is by far the most attractive and, indeed, is to this day being reproduced by Coalports.

16 Ibid., col. pl. 77. Derby plate painted by John Haslem.

17 Haslem, op. cit., p. 161.

18 George Savage, Harold Newman and John Cushion, *Dictionary of Ceramic Terms*, London, 1974, p. 98. Gold anchor Chelsea models of a *Dog Orchestra*.

19 Siegfried Ducret, *Meissner Porzellan 1710–1810*, Munich, 1966, Nos. 1150 and 1151. *Stag and Doe at Lodge*, Meissen, by J. J. Kändler.

Before concluding this brief survey of Derby figures it should be noted that many were also issued between 1826–42 by the Rockingham manufactory. Dennis Rice[20] suggested that possibly Samuel Keys the Younger may have created both versions together with additional theatrical models peculiar to Rockingham. This would seem unlikely for it would have been beyond the capacity of any one modeller to have achieved this in a few months. In any event the same sources of inspiration must have been available to the various factories, while a modeller was able to sell moulds or clay squeezes to more than one client. The following figures are common to Derby and Rockingham:

No.	*Derby Model*	*Alteration Made at Rockingham*	*Rockingham Mould No.*
101	*Boy Eating an Apple and Girl Curds-and-whey*	Painted to depict beggar children	36
G5	*Liston as Paul Prye*	Nil	9
G9	*Madam Vestris as a Bavarian Peasant Woman*	Liston portrayed in the same role	6
G26	*Napoleon Bonaparte*	Nil	42
G34	*Industrious Boy and Girl*	Nil	28
G39	*Pair of Topers*	One Toper's arm repositioned	2 and 29
G40	*Romantic Boy and Girl*	Girl model transposed	26
G63	*Cat with Gold Collar*	Nil	57
G67	*Stag and Doe at Lodge*	Nil	100
G74	*Pug Dogs* (pair)	Nil	80
G89	*Sheep* (pair)	Nil	104
G90	*Sheep* (pair)	Nil	108
G92	*Squirrels* (pair)	More slender models	76

George Cocker's small manufactory at Friar's Gate, Derby, which operated about 1826–40 before being transferred to Bedford Square, London, copied the Derby group adapted from *Belisarius and his Daughter* (G25) and two *Topers* (G39) to which a third representing a *Dying Drunk*[21] was added. The factory of Thomas Minton at Stoke-on-Trent reproduced some old Derby models in a chalky-white biscuit from about 1798 as well as in enamelled bone china after about 1810, and subsequently after 1850 in Parian, which was known as the *Majolica Body*. Some

20 Rice, op. cit., pp. 48–54.
21 The Brighton Museum.

examples include *Queen Victoria* (G30), the *Romantic Boy and Girl* (G40), and *Good Morning* and *Good Night* (G57), all of which are illustrated by Geoffrey Godden.[22]

Finally, the establishment of the King Street factory in 1848 by a group of ex-employees from the Nottingham Road manufactory, led to the reissue of several of the old models and groups and this topic has been fully presented and discussed by Twitchett and Bailey.[23]

22 Geoffrey Godden, *An Illustrated Encyclopaedia of British Pottery and Porcelain*, London, 1966, pp. 232 and 233.

23 John Twitchett and Betty Bailey, *Royal Crown Derby*, London, 1976.

LIST G. DERBY MODELS 1810–48

THEATRICAL

G1 *Dusty Bob and African Sal* (pair). 4½ in (11.4 cm). Twitchett and Bailey, p. 33.

G2 *Maria Foote as Arinette*. 6 in (15.2 cm). Venner's Antiques.

G3 *Grimaldi the Clown*. 7 in (17.8 cm). Derby Museums and Art Gallery.

337 G2. *Maria Foote as Arinette*. 6 in (15.2 cm). *Venner's Antiques*

338 G3. *Grimaldi the Clown*. 7 in (17.8 cm). *Derby Museums and Art Gallery*

G4 *Edmund Kean as Richard III.* 9½ in (24.1 cm). A reissue of No. 21 with a new head. Twitchett, pl. 296. See Plate 144.

G5 *John Liston as Paul Pry.* 6¾ in (17.1 cm). David Thorn Collection.

G6 *John Liston as Maw Worm.* Example unknown to author.

G7 *John Liston as Domine Sampson.* Example unknown to author.

G8 *Tyrolese Singers* (three figures). 4¾ in (12.1 cm). Derby Museums and Art Gallery.

G9 *Madam Vestris as a Bavarian Peasant Woman.* 6¾ in (17.1 cm). Based on an engraving by J. Dixon. B. and T. Thorn Antiques. Based on a lithograph by J. H. Lynch; Venner's Antiques.

G10 *Billy Waters.* 4½ in (11.4 cm). A one-legged negro fiddler. Derby Museums and Art Gallery.

339 G5. *John Liston as Paul Pry.* 6¾ in (17.1 cm). *David Thorn Collection*

340 G8. *Three Tyrolese Singers.* 4¾ in–5 in (12.1–12.7 cm). *Derby Museums and Art Gallery*

341 G9. *Madam Vestris as a Bavarian Peasant Woman*, after an engraving by J. Dixon. 6¾ in (17.1 cm). *David Thorn Collection*

342 G9. *Madam Vestris*, after a lithograph by J. H. Lynch. 6¾ in (17.1 cm). *Venner's Antiques*

343 G10. *Billy Waters*, the one-legged negro fiddler. 4½ in (11.4 cm). *Derby Museums and Art Gallery*

THE DR SYNTAX SERIES

G11 *Dr Syntax Retiring to Bed.* 4½ in (11.4 cm). David Thorn Collection.

G12 *Dr Syntax Seated Sketching.* 4 in (10.2 cm). David Thorn Collection.

G13 *Dr Syntax Crossing a Lake.* Example unknown to author.

G14 *Dr Syntax at the Bookseller's.* He reads from one tome and stands among books. 4¼ in (11.4 cm). Gough, col. pl. 1.

G15 *Dr Syntax Playing a Violin.* 3¼ in (8.3 cm). David Thorn Collection.

G16 *Dr Syntax Reciting in the Greenroom.* 5½ in (14 cm). David Thorn Collection.

G17 *Dr Syntax at York Races.* 6 in (15.2 cm). He dances in fury at having lost money. David Thorn Collection.

G18 *Dr Syntax Chased by a Bull.* 6 in (15.2 cm). Gough, p. 24; David Thorn Collection.

344 G11. *Dr Syntax Retiring to Bed.* $4\frac{1}{2}$ in (11.4 cm). *David Thorn Collection*

345 G12. *Dr Syntax Sketching.* 4 in (10.2 cm). *David Thorn Collection*

346 G15. *Dr Syntax Playing a Violin.* $3\frac{1}{4}$ in (8.3 cm). *David Thorn Collection*

347 G16. *Dr Syntax Reciting in the Green Room.* $5\frac{1}{2}$ in (14 cm). *David Thorn Collection*

348 G17. *Dr Syntax at York Races,* dancing in a fury at having lost his money. 6 in (15.2 cm). *David Thorn Collection*

349 G18. *Dr Syntax Chased by a Bull.* 6 in (15.2 cm). *David Thorn Collection*

350 G22. *Dr Syntax Astride his Horse Grizzle.* 6 in (15.2 cm). *Derby Museums and Art Gallery*

351 G23. *Dr Syntax Landing at Calais.* 5 in (12.7 cm). *David Thorn Collection*

G19 *Dr Syntax Bound by Robbers to a Tree*. Example unknown to author.

G20 *Dr Syntax Walking*. 4 in (10.2 cm). *Antique Dealer and Collector's Guide*, December 1971, p. 63.

G21 *Dr Syntax Scolding his Landlady*. Example unknown to author.

G22 *Dr Syntax Astride his Horse Grizzle*. 6 in (15.2 cm). Derby Museums and Art Gallery.

G23 *Dr Syntax Landing at Calais*. 5 in (12.7 cm). He is carried upon the back of his landlady as she wades ashore. Gough, p. 25; David Thorn Collection.

G24 *Dr Syntax's Landlady*. Example unknown to author.

NOTABLES

G25 *Gallant and Lady* (group). 8½ in (21.6 cm). A bearded gallant escorts a lady wearing a fine Regency gown. Adapted from the group of *Belisarius and his Daughter* (No. 370). Twitchett, pl. 365.

G26 *Napoleon Bonaparte*. 5 in (12.7 cm) and 8¼ in (21 cm). Large version: Christie's, *Sale Catalogue*, 23 February 1987, lot 226.

G27 *George III*. Height uncertain. He is shown bareheaded, wearing a frock-coat, breeches and boots, the garter star and walking with a gold-headed cane. National Portrait Gallery; Twitchett, pl. 386.

G28 *George IV*. 10 in (25.4 cm). He stands beside a plinth upon which are placed the crown jewels (biscuit). Castle Museum, Nottingham.

G29 *Mazeppa Group*. 5½ in (14 cm). The naked count is bound to the back of a wild stallion that is chased by wolves. Derby Museums and Art Gallery.

G30 *Queen Victoria*. 10½ in (26.7 cm). The young Queen c. 1837, is portrayed in biscuit wearing a bonnet and a long gown. Castle Museum, Nottingham.

G31 *Duke of Wellington*. 10½ in (26.7 cm). Portrayed in biscuit, standing. Castle Museum, Nottingham.

G32 *Small Busts of Admiral Lord Nelson and George IV*. Both about 4 in (10.2 cm). Gilhespy, 1961, col. pl. III.

G33 *Bust of Queen Victoria*. Cited by J. Haslem but unknown to the author.

PASTORAL AND PEASANT

G34 *Industrious Boy and Girl* (pair). 5¼ in (13.3 cm). The two are seated bareheaded in chairs, their toys scattered at their feet ignored; the boy reads and his companion sews. Rice, 1965, pl. 107; Twitchett, pl. 73.

G35 *Man and Woman with Milk Churns*. 6½ in (16.5 cm). Sotheby's, *Sale Catalogue*, 23 July 1985, lot 216.

352 G26. *Napoleon Bonaparte.* $8\frac{1}{4}$ in (21 cm). Inscribed 'Born Aug 15th 1760 Died May 5th 1821'. *Christie's*

353 G28. Biscuit model of *George IV*. 10 in (25.4 cm). *Derby Museums and Art Gallery*

354 G29. Biscuit group of *Mazeppa* bound naked to a horse chased by wolves. $5\frac{1}{2}$ in (14 cm). *Derby Museums and Art Gallery*

355 G30. Biscuit figure of the young *Queen Victoria*. $10\frac{1}{2}$ in (26.7 cm).
Castle Museum, Nottingham

356 G31. Biscuit figure of *The Duke of Wellington.* $10\frac{1}{2}$ in (26.7 cm). *Castle Museum, Nottingham*

357 G34. The female member of the *Industrious Boy and Girl.* $5\frac{1}{4}$ in (13.3 cm). *Derby Museums and Art Gallery*

358 G35. *Man and Woman with Milk Churns.* 6½ in (16.5 cm). *Sotheby's*

359 G39. A semi-grotesque *Toper*. Note how enamel has flaked off the breeches. $3\frac{3}{4}$ in (9.7 cm). *Derby Museums and Art Gallery*

360 G39. Companion *Toper*. $3\frac{3}{4}$ in (9.5 cm).

G36 *Man and Woman with Milk Pails*. 6 in (15.2 cm). Each has two pails suspended from a yoke. Victoria and Albert Museum; Twitchett, pl. 392.

G37 *Peasant Fiddler and Woman Playing a Mandoline* (pair). $6\frac{3}{4}$ in (17.1 cm). The male musician wears a brimmed hat, jacket and breeches, while his companion is clad in a headscarf, blouse, apron and skirt. Meissen originals and red anchor Chelsea as well as Bow versions are known. David Goldblatt Collection; Gilhespy, 1961, fig. 148; Royal Crown Derby Museum; Twitchett, pl. 366.

G38 *Paris Cries* (six figures). *A Woman Asparagus Seller*, in the Victoria and Albert Museum, may come from this series which is otherwise unknown to the author.

G39 *Topers* (pair). $4\frac{1}{4}$ in (10.8 cm). These semi-grotesque models are entitled *Steady, Lads, Steady*. Derby Museums and Art Gallery.

361 G40. Pair of biscuit figures known as the *Romantic Boy and Girl*. $5\frac{1}{4}$ in (13.3 cm).
Derby Museums and Art Gallery

G40 *Romantic Boy and Girl* (pair). $5\frac{1}{4}$ in (13.3 cm). The boy, wearing a brimmed hat, stands cross-legged leaning upon an ewer placed upon a plinth; his companion holds a lamb in a fold of her apron and stands in mirror pose beside a fountain. Derby Museums and Art Gallery. Rice, 1979, pl. 105 shows an example of the boy from Rockingham and the girl from Derby.

G41 *Vicars, Curates and Wardens*. $4\frac{1}{4}$–5 in (11.4–12.7 cm). These are truncated models of which only two, the *Vicar* and a *Warden*, are known to the author. Sotheby's (see Plate 360).

FOREIGN PERSONAGES

G42 *Eastern Lady*. Cited by J. Haslem but unknown to author.

G43 *Cantonese Girls* (pair). 5 in (12.7 cm). They wear conical hats, long robes and stand holding fans. Victoria and Albert Museum; Hughes, pl. 42.

G44 *Children in Turkish Costume* (pair). $3\frac{3}{4}$ in (8.3 cm). A reissue of No. 63.

G45 *Turk Seated*. $5\frac{1}{2}$ in (14 cm). He wears a turban and eastern dress and sits cross-legged upon a cushion upon a detachable stand. Victoria and Albert Museum; Twitchett, pl. 337.

ALLEGORICAL AND RELIGIOUS

G46 *Angel.* Cited by J. Haslem but unknown to author.

G47 *Cupid Grinding.* $8\frac{1}{2}$ in (21.6 cm). A reissue of the group from *The Four Elements* (No. 48), emblematic of *Fire*.

G48 *Archers* (pair). Cited by J. Haslem but unknown to author.

G49 *Hebe and Innocence* (pair). 28 in (71.1 cm). Hebe, wearing a classical robe and laurel chaplet, stands pouring wine from an ewer into a basin. Innocence in similar attire holds a sacrificial lamb upon a plinth-like altar. Gilhespy, 1951, fig. 167.

G50 *Nymph Asleep amidst Flowers.* $5\frac{1}{2}$ in (14 cm). T. Kendrew Antiques. See Plate XIX. A similar model of Cupid, without floral arbour, also exists in biscuit, $4\frac{1}{2}$ in (11.4 cm). Derby Museums and Art Gallery.

G51 *Virgin Mary.* Cited by J. Haslem but unknown to author.

CHILDREN AND PUTTI

G52 *Basket Boys.* $4\frac{1}{2}$–$5\frac{1}{4}$ in (11.4–13.3 cm). Adapted from F16. B. and T. Thorn Antiques.

G53 *Boy and Girl, each with a Dog.* Cited by J. Haslem but unknown to author.

362 G41. *A Warden* (left) and *A Vicar* (right), from the set of *Vicars, Curates and Wardens.* $4\frac{1}{2}$ in (11.4 cm). *Sotheby's*

363 G50. *Sleeping Nymph* taken from the group *Two Virgins Awakening Cupid* (No. 195). $4\frac{1}{4}$ in (10.8 cm). *Derby Museums and Art Gallery*

364 G50. *Nymph Asleep Amidst Flowers*. $5\frac{1}{2}$ in (14 cm), by J. Whitaker. See also Colour Plate xix. *Timothy Kendrew Antiques*

G54 *Boy with Greyhound* and *Girl with Falcon* (pair). Cited by J. Haslem but unknown to author.

G55 *Boy and Girl Gathering Flowers*. 5 in (12.7 cm). The boy kneels to pick flowers which he places in his inverted hat; his companion also kneels, and holds a posy in either hand. Lita Kay Antiques; Twitchett, col. pl. 42d.

G56 *Girl Seated in a Chair*. 6 in (15.2 cm). The girl, or doll, sits with one leg amputated below the knee, wearing a lace-trimmed dress and with her picture-hat under her gilded chair. G. Godden Antiques; Twitchett, pl. 384.

G57 *Good Morning* and *Good Night* (pair). A pair of kneeling children respectively cleaning shoes and saying prayers. Both $3\frac{1}{4}$ in (8.3 cm). Godden, pl. 227; Herbert Allen Collection.

MISCELLANEOUS

G58 *Sweetmeat Containers*. (pair). 9 in (22.9 cm). A gallant stands bareheaded in sumptuous apparel, holding open with both hands the lid of a rectangular hamper, a dog at his feet. Companion wears a laced bodice with pagoda sleeves and a panniered skirt, and stands in mirror pose. Gilhespy, 1951, fig. 144.

G59 *Monkey Orchestra*. (in two sizes). $4\frac{1}{2}$ in (11.4 cm) and 6 in (15.2 cm). Seated monkeys wear jackets with falling ruffles and are mounted upon square bases:

365 G59. *Monkey Orchestra*. $4\frac{1}{2}$ in (11.4 cm), second size. *Derby Museums and Art Gallery*

366 G60. Pair of *Cats* on cushions. $1\frac{1}{2}$ in (3.8 cm). *Private Collection*

instrumentalists include a cymbalist, harpist, trumpeter, bass-drummer, players on both the recorder and penny-whistle, and two cellists; there are also two vocalists holding song-sheets, and a conductor. Victoria and Albert Museum; Twitchett, pl. 391; Derby Museums and Art Gallery.

ANIMALS

G60 *Cats* seated on cushions (pair). $1\frac{1}{2}$ in (3.8 cm). Private Collection.

G61 *Cats with Prey*. Cited by J. Haslem but unknown to author.

G62 *Cats Recumbent* (pair). $2\frac{1}{2}$ in (6.4 cm). Rice, 1983, pl. 112.

G63 *Cat with Gold Collar*. Cited by J. Haslem but unknown to author.

G64 *Cows, Lean*. Cited by J. Haslem but unknown to author.

G65 *Cow, Lowing*. $3\frac{1}{2}$ in (8.9 cm). Recumbent before a flowering shrub. Gilhespy, 1961, fig. 125.

G66 *Cow and Calf* (group). They stand beneath a leafing tree. Hermitage Museum. Twitchett, pl. 323; Private Collection.

G67 *Stag and Doe at Lodge* (pair). 6 in (15.2 cm). Private Collection; Bradley, no. 20.

G68 *Stag and Doe* (pair). $3\frac{1}{2}$ in (8.9 cm). Gilhespy, 1961, fig. 151; Twitchett, pl. 71; Rice, 1965 (B), pl. 118.

G69 *Stags* (group). $8\frac{1}{2}$ in (21.6 cm). Two stags, one wearing a collar and trailing chain attached, stand beneath a tree, in biscuit. Phillips, *Sale Catalogue*, 9 December 1987, lot 200.

367 G66. *Cow and Calf* beneath a leafing tree. $5\frac{1}{2}$ in (14 cm). *Private Collection*

G70 *Hounds* (group). $5\frac{1}{2}$ in (14 cm). Mounted in biscuit upon an oval base. Weston Park Museum.

G71 *King Charles Spaniel, Scratching*. 6 in (15.2 cm). Harris, p. 60.

G72 *Poodle Dog*. $4\frac{1}{2}$ in (11.4 cm). Seated with back bent forwards. Derby Museums and Art Gallery.

G73 *Poodle Dog*. $4\frac{1}{2}$ in (11.4 cm). Seated with straight back. Derby Museums and Art Gallery.

G74 *Pug Dogs* (pair). $2\frac{1}{4}$ in (5.7 cm). Seated on mound bases. Twitchett, pl. 69; Gilhespy, 1951, fig. 165; Rice, 1983, pl. 77.

G75 *Pug Dogs on Cushions* (pair). Cited by J. Haslem but unknown to author.

G76 *Setter, Prowling*. $4\frac{1}{2}$ in (11.4 cm) long. D. John's Collection; Twitchett, pl. 121; Derby Museums and Art Gallery.

G77 *Setter, Recumbent*. $3\frac{1}{4}$ in (8.3 cm). Bradley, no. 42.

368 G70. Biscuit group of two *Hounds*. $5\frac{1}{2}$ in (14 cm). *Weston Park Museum*

369 G72. Seated *Poodle Dog* with its back arched. $4\frac{1}{2}$ in (11.4 cm). *Derby Museums and Art Gallery*

370 G73. Seated *Poodle Dog* with its back straight. $4\frac{1}{2}$ in (11.4 cm). *Derby Museums and Art Gallery*

371 G74. Pair of seated *Pug Dogs*. $2\frac{1}{4}$ in (5.7 cm). *Private Collection*

372 G76. *Pointer* or *Setter, Prowling*. $4\frac{1}{2}$ in (11.4 cm) long. *Derby Museums and Art Gallery*

373 G79. *Elephant without Mahout*. 6 in (15.2 cm). *Derby Museums and Art Gallery*

G78 *Elephant with Mahout*. $5\frac{1}{2}$ in (14 cm). Sotheby's, *Sale Catalogue*, 29 September 1987, lot 238.

G79 *Elephant without Mahout*. 6 in (15.2 cm). Derby Museums and Art Gallery.

G80 *Elephant, Small*. $4\frac{1}{2}$ in (11.4 cm). Private Collection.

G81 *Fox, Seated*. 4 in (10.2 cm). An example of c. 1878 is illustrated by Bradley, no. 327.

G82 *Horse, Standing*. 4 in (10.2 cm). Victoria and Albert Museum; Twitchett, pl. 346.

G83 *Lion and Lioness* (pair). $3\frac{1}{4}$ in (8.3 cm). Gilhespy, 1951, fig. 166.

G84 *Worcester Mice*. Cited by J. Haslem but unknown to author.

374 G85. *Leopard, Prowling* (one of a pair), adapted from E89. $4\frac{3}{4}$ in (12 cm). *Derby Museums and Art Gallery*

G85 *Leopards, Prowling* (pair). $4\frac{3}{4}$ in (12 cm) long. Examples may be enamelled to portray either species. Adapted from E89. Derby Museums and Art Gallery.

G86 *Rabbits.* Cited by Haslem but unknown to author.

G87 *Rabbits* on plinths. Cited by Haslem but unknown to author.

G88 *Sheep, Standing* (pair). $3\frac{1}{4}$ in (8.3 cm). *Ewe and Ram.* Gilhespy 1951, fig. 165.

G89 *Sheep, Recumbent* (pair). $2\frac{1}{4}$ in (5.7 cm). Barrett and Thorpe, pl. 126.

G90 *Sheep, Recumbent* (pair). $4\frac{3}{4}$ in (12 cm). A horned *Ewe and Ram.* Derby Museums and Art Gallery.

G91 *Sheep* (group). 5 in (12.7 cm). *Ewe Suckling a Lamb* on a scrolled mound base. Private Collection.

G92 *Squirrels* (pair). $3\frac{1}{4}$ in (8.3 cm). Reissue of E98. Derby Museums and Art Gallery.

BIRDS

G93 *Parrots* (pair). 9 in (22.9 cm). Examples of c. 1770, from which Bloor models were probably copied. Victoria and Albert Museum; Rice, 1983, pl. 71.

G94 *Peacock amongst Flowers.* $6\frac{1}{2}$ in (16.5 cm). Derby Museums and Art Gallery.

G95 *Swan,* standing on rock-like base. $3\frac{1}{2}$ in (8.9 cm). Sotheby's, *Sale Catalogue,* 14 October 1985, lot 230.

375 G90. *Ewe, Recumbent.* $4\frac{3}{4}$ in (12.1 cm) long.

376 G90. *Companion Ram, Recumbent.* Both *Derby Museums and Art Gallery*

377 G91. *Sheep* (group). $4\frac{1}{2}$ in (11.4 cm) long. *Derby Museums and Art Gallery*

378 G92. *Squirrel* seated with a nut, a reissue of E98. 3 in (7.6 cm). *Derby Museums and Art Gallery*

379 G94. *Peacock amongst Flowers*. $6\frac{1}{2}$ in (16.5 cm). *Derby Museums and Art Gallery*

Appendices

Appendix A · Sculptors, Modellers and Craftsmen, 1770–96

BACON, John

John Bacon (1740–99) was born at Southwark, the son of a clothmaker. In 1755 he was apprenticed to Nicholas Crisp who, with his partner Thomas Sanders, owned a pottery adjacent to Bow Churchyard in Cheapside. There he must have become familiar with terracottas brought in by sculptors to be fired and may himself have been employed for a time modelling and painting ceramic figures.[1] Haslem,[2] citing a passage from Allan Cunningham's *The Lives of the Most Eminent British Sculptors and Architects*, published in 1883, wrote:

> Bacon, in 1754, when he was fourteen years of age, apprenticed himself to one Crispe, of Bow Churchyard, an eminent maker of porcelain, who taught him the art of modelling various groups, such as the Deer and the Holly-tree, the Bird and the Bush, the Shepherd and Shepherdess, and birds of all shapes and beasts of every kind yet made for show or use in our manufactories.

Normally Bacon would have been bound to Crisp until 1762, but he did not free himself until 1764 when both his employers were declared bankrupt. He attended the schools of sculpture at the Royal Academy until 1768 when he was appointed sculptor–manager at Eleanor Coade's Artificial Stone Works in Lambeth. This enterprise specialized in the manufacture of statues, busts and other architectural embellishments cast in an exceptionally hard and durable stoneware. Bacon made copies of both antique and contemporary sculpture as well as creating his own original work. Examples include figures representing *Vigilance* and *Patience*, mounted beside an ornamental clock now in Buckingham Palace, and a marble bust of *George III*, at Christ Church, Oxford, while his bronzes include *Hercules*, *Atlas* and a group portraying *George III as Father Time*.

Bacon undertook commissions for Josiah Wedgwood, William Duesbury and others. Duesbury made two payments to Bacon, one in 1769 for £75 7s 4d., the

1 *Gentleman's Magazine*, 1799, p. 808.

2 Haslem, op. cit., pp. 151 and 156.

other in 1772 for an unspecified sum.[3] These may have been for terracottas used for instruction of modellers and enamellers rather than master models to be translated into porcelain. Haslem[4] credits Bacon with 'Statuettes of Quin [sic] in Falstaff, and Garrick in Richard III', but provides no supporting evidence. Timothy Clifford[5] has pointed out that the arrangement of clothing about the neck of the Derby model of *King George III* differs from that seen in Richard Earlom's engraving after Zoffany, from which the figure was adapted, but closely resembles that seen on Bacon's marble bust in Christ Church. Certainly, if a famous sculptor like Bacon ever made master models for Derby his services would most likely have been reserved for the three groups depicting the *Royal Family*. William Bemrose,[6] in a supplement to his version of the Derby Factory list, includes *Large Seasons, Bacon*.

BANKS, Thomas

Thomas Banks (1735–1805) was the son of William Banks, steward to the Duke of Beaufort. He was apprenticed sculptor to William Barlow and later studied under Peter Scheemakers. In 1763 he was awarded a prize by the Society of Arts for a group in Portland stone entitled *The Death of Epaminondas* and, in 1770, won a gold medal for his bas-relief portraying *The Rape of Persephone*. Between 1772 and 1779 he furthered his studies in Rome, before establishing a studio in London, and, in 1786, was elected Royal Academician. Several busts from his hand are in Westminster Abbey, St Paul's Cathedral and lesser City churches. He also made both plaster models and terracottas that may have provided the basis for Derby porcelain models although none have been traced back to this source. In 1787 Joseph Lygo wrote to William Duesbury II:[7] 'Mr. Banks is the modeller in the same way as Mr. Bacon.'

CATHERINE, Mr

The name 'Catherine' occurs in two of the Lygo Letters. In 1787: 'He made moulds of two little boys', and in 1790 it is recorded: 'Large Sale of Save [Sèvres] – all the nobility there. Mr. Catherine will copy some of the designs.'

3 Ibid., p. 152.
4 Ibid.
5 Timothy Clifford, 'Derby Figures and Decorative Vases', a lecture given at Morley College on 26 November 1977, in a seminar devoted to Ceramics of Derbyshire, 1750–1975.
6 William Bemrose, *Bow, Chelsea and Derby Porcelain*, London, 1898, pp. 67–85.
7 F. Brayshaw Gilhespy, *Derby Porcelain*, London, 1961, p. 67.

CHEERE, John

John Cheere (1709–87) was the younger brother of the sculptor, Sir Henry Cheere, who in 1739 took over the atelier of John Nost at Hyde Park Corner. The enterprise specialized in the provision of inexpensive garden statuary in lead and stone. In 1742, for example, John Cheere supplied statues of the *Farnese Hercules*, *Flora*, *Ceres* and *Father Time*, in lead, and in 1749 created *Diana*, the *Four Seasons*, and sundry other figures in stone. Both the Derby porcelain models of *Minerva* (Nos. 121 and 298) and *Britannia* (No. 259) were adapted from Cheere's lead statues.[8] Josiah Wedgwood[9] purchased moulds from Cheere for busts of *Addison* and *Virgil*, and it is likely that the Derby versions of these, Nos. 146 and 147, were adapted from the same source. The Hyde Park Corner works also produced small plaster models after contemporary sculpture and the antique, some of which were painted to simulate bronze. These included *Shakespeare* after Peter Scheemakers, *Milton* and the *Zingara* woman. These may possibly have been used by the modellers at Derby.

COFFEE, William

William Coffee (c. 1746–1840) and his wife Catherine were residents of the Parish of St Clement Danes and the baptism of their first-born son, William John, appears in the register dated 12 September 1773. The elder Coffee was employed as a modeller at Eleanor Coade's Artificial Stone Works in Lambeth. He himself claimed to have 'worked the apostles and prophets around the pulpit and reading desk', in the Chapel of the Royal Naval College at Greenwich, as well as 'the angels under the communion table'. These were designed by Benjamin West and were modelled in artificial stone in 1789. It is possible that prior to being appointed at Coade's, Coffee (*père*) may have worked at a pottery in Chelsea and at the Derby porcelain manufactory and, if this is true, it would explain why Derby models such as *The Grotesque Seasons* (No. 47) and *Aesculapius and Hygeia* (No. 99) have traditionally been ascribed to Coffee. They cannot have been executed by Coffee (*fils*) who would then have been only a small child. I am indebted to Brian R. Bricknell, who is himself a descendant of William Coffee, for this information and also for other details pertaining to William John Coffee.

8 T. Friedman and T. Clifford, *Men at Hyde Park Corner, Sculpture by John Cheere, 1709–1787*, Twickenham, 1974, nos. 54 and 55, pls. 11 and 13. et seq.

9 G. Savage and Robin Reilly, *The Dictionary of Wedgwood*, Woodbridge, 1980, p. 192.

COFFEE, William John

William John Coffee (1773–c. 1846), the son of William Coffee, was also employed at Eleanor Coade's factory in Lambeth and was still working there on 25 July 1792, for on that day Eleanor Coade wrote him a letter[10] answering complaints he had made about a man named Prichard who had told lies about him to the manager, Mr Sealey. She advised him to make up his quarrel and concentrate upon his work. On 21 May 1792, Coffee had married Martha Dudley. Mr Bricknell has pointed out that a letter dated 23 March 1790 is reproduced by Jewitt,[11] written by Lygo to Duesbury, in which he mentions a fireman at Coade's who was probably dismissed, being 'a drunken bad chap, but clever at his business'. This appears in the text adjacent to Eleanor Coade's letter to Coffee and prompted several authors, including myself and Timothy Clifford, to suppose Coffee was the fireman which, clearly, he was not. Coffee (*fils*) probably had a disagreement with his employer and most likely during the first quarter of 1793 he left Lambeth in high dudgeon at short notice and was engaged as a modeller at Derby. During his absence, his wife was admitted to the British Lying-in Hospital, Covent Garden and, on 23 May, 1793, was delivered of her first-born son, Henry. The occupation of the father is recorded as 'artist', a title normally applied to modellers at Coade's. In July 1793, Lygo paid Mrs Coffee $3\frac{1}{2}$ guineas to enable her to join her husband in Derby. Prior to this, Coffee had signed an agreement with Duesbury: 'To receive 3s 6d. for each ten hour day, or a rate of 7s 0d for any single figure six inches in height, whether standing or in any other action, which if standing would be six inches high; all figures should be roughed out naked in correct proportions ...' The inclusion of the last clause implies that Duesbury had no great faith in the artist's modelling talent, a view evidently shared by Lygo,[12] who wrote: 'I do not much admire Mr. Coffee's modelling from what I have yet seen. The figure 359 [Gardener & Companion] is one of the most stupid looking things I ever saw, and the figure of Apollo in group 379 is very vulgar about the bosom, for sure never such bubbys was seen and so much exposed – the design is pretty enough.' (In fact, No. 379 has recently been identified as a Musical Group that does not include Apollo.) Charles King, the Derby works manager, underlined the artist's shortcomings:[13] 'Mason has had some conversation with me about Coffee's work, he thinks it so very imperfect as not to answer your purpose however low it may come.' According to

10 Llewellynn Jewitt, *The Ceramic Art of Great Britain*, London, 1878, II, p. 141.

11 Ibid., II, p. 139.

12 John Twitchett, *Derby Porcelain*, London, 1980, p. 221.

13 Letter from Charles King to William Duesbury, 8 December, 1794. Duesbury Papers in the Derby Local Studies Library.

Haslem: 'The figures in the modelling of which Coffee chiefly excelled were either animals, or subjects of a rustic or grotesque character.'

Haslem designated Nos. 335–59 as 'Twenty-five Spangler's and Coffee's Figures and Groups'. Only a few of them have been identified, including the gardener and companion, which incurred Lygo's strictures and are vastly inferior to Spengler's gardener, although Coffee was then only nineteen while Spengler was an experienced modeller of thirty-two. A *Scotsman and his Lass* (No. 378) also ascribed to Coffee are, however, scarcely more acceptable. A recumbent *Setter* (G77) is incised 'W. Coffee', and a Spanish *Pointer* (F28) is in a similar style. The evidence suggests that at this time Coffee possessed only modest skills and was employed chiefly making models of small animals that were mounted to complement the sophisticated figures of human subjects, issued in biscuit, created by Spengler. Haslem refers to the collection of plaster and terracotta models once owned by Joseph Wright:[14]

> To the modellers the collection was of still greater advantage, for it furnished them with many useful and valuable hints. Coffee, for example, having made a shepherd as a companion to a shepherdess, which Stephan had modelled before leaving the factory, did not hesitate to take a cast of Adonis, which was in the collection, for his model.'

Here, Haslem confuses Stephan for Spengler, who created the *Lady Feeding a Sheep with Hay* (No. 395), while the terracotta represented Hermes and not Adonis. Further, whatever capabilities Coffee may or may not have possessed, the *Shepherd with his Dog* (No. 396) reflects the inimitable style of Spengler.

An undated letter most probably written by Coffee in 1794 to Duesbury expresses dissatisfaction with his wages, and it would appear he left Derby in the last quarter of that year. He was then unemployed for a short time in London before joining Sir Nigel Gresley in a pottery at Burton-on-Trent in 1795. The chronology of his subsequent peregrinations is difficult to establish, but he worked for Michael Kean, later with Billy Duesbury at Friar's Gate, and between 1810 and 1814 on his own account in Derby. He is credited with a large statue of *Aesculapius* that once stood upon the roof of the Derbyshire Royal Infirmary; also with a bust of *Charles Darwin*, and with a copy of the *Florentine Boar* for the Derby Arboretum. A catalogue from the old King Street, Derby factory refers to 'Coffee Seasons' which during his second spell in Derby he may have refurbished from the originals (No. 123). In 1816 Coffee emigrated to America where he established a fine reputation both as painter and sculptor prior to his death in 1846. The following Derby models have been ascribed to him:

14 John Haslem, *The Old Derby China Factory*, London, 1876, pp. 155 and 156.

No.	*Derby Models*	*Authority*
F28	A Spanish *Pointer*	John Haslem
G74	*Pug Dogs* (pair) in three sizes	John Haslem
G77	A recumbent *Setter*	Incised 'W. Coffee'
359(i)	A Gardener and Companion	Joseph Lygo
378	A Scotsman and his Lass	John Haslem
379	Group said by Lygo to incorporate Apollo but is here said to be a Musical Group.	Joseph Lygo

DEARE, John

John Deare (1759–98) was born in Liverpool, the son of a jeweller, and was apprenticed sculptor to Thomas Carter; he also studied in the schools of sculpture at the Royal Academy, where he was awarded a gold medal for his group *Paradise Lost*. He modelled a *Cupid* for John Cheere, and carried out commissions for John Bacon. In 1783 he established his independent studio in London but in 1785 travelled to Rome where he spent three years in postgraduate study. According to Llewellynn Jewitt,[15] Mr Duesbury employed Deare, who was then a young sculptor living in London, to create models for him in 1784. Joseph Lygo also mentions him as a modeller of repute and, in a letter to Duesbury dated 19 September 1784 informs him: 'I will wait on Mr. Deare in the morning.' No Derby porcelain models attributed to him have so far been identified.

FARNSWORTH, Isaac

Isaac Farnsworth (c. 1735–1821) was employed as a repairer at the Derby manufactory in the early 1750s. Between about 1775–1800 he used a personal mark of a star formed with three short intersecting lines incised beneath the base of figures. He was described by Haslem as 'Spengler's old overlooker' and became head of the figure department about 1795. He was one of the men chosen to help draw up a Factory List of moulds in 1810 used in a law suit, Duesbury *versus* Kean.

GAURON, Nicolas-Joseph-François

Nicolas-Joseph-François Gauron (1735–c. 1780) was born in Paris and in 1748 may possibly have been apprenticed silversmith to his uncle, Jacob Gauron, in the City of London. If this is so, he did not stay long in England, for in 1753 he was working as a modeller at the Mennecy porcelain factory in the Rue de la Charonne. The

15 Jewitt, op. cit., II, p. 109.

history of the Gaurons, father and son, has been traced by W. H. Tapp.[16]

An ornamental clock framed by white glazed porcelain models of *Diana* and a *River Deity* is signed *Gauron 1754*. This is in the Louvre and has been ascribed to Mennecy.[17] A somewhat similar clock, mounted with almost identical figures, to which a reclining Cupid is added, in the Victoria and Albert Museum, is thought to have been made at Vincennes. If this is correct, then it would seem that Gauron modelled at Vincennes before going to Mennecy. In 1758 he was modeller at Tournai, where the cathedral registers[18] record his marriage to Caroline Guery, and the following year, the baptism of his son, Nicolas. Gauron himself claimed to have been a sculptor at the Académie Royale, Paris, before he became a modeller of porcelain and, if this is true, he would then have been only seventeen years of age. He also boasted that he was responsible for making the first biscuit models at Tournai and refuted the suggestion that the credit properly belonged to Jacques Lefèbre. Here he confused Jacques, an oil painter, with his brother François who was a modeller at Tournai. During his time there Gauron made the following models:

The Four Seasons[19] represented by four pairs of standing children after Boucher.
The Four Elements[20] portrayed by four groups, each of two putti.
Minerva crowning Constancy and Hercules killing the Hydra,[21] a composition of two groups separated by an obelisk.
A Bust of Charles D'Outremont, Prince Bishop of Liège.[22]
A group showing the *Apotheosis of Charles D'Outremont*,[23] made to commemorate his coronation in 1764.

In 1764 Gauron left Tournai and made application for permission to establish a small modelling factory to the City Councillors of Brussels, which was refused. In July 1765 Gauron and François Lefèbre jointly petitioned the City Councillors of Liège for a licence to set up a porcelain factory at Caronmeuse, which was granted. The venture was beset with technical and financial problems and, in 1770, Gauron

16 W. H. Tapp, 'The Gaurons, Father and Son, Sculptors of Tournai and Chelsea', *Apollo*, 35, 1942, pp. 62–4 and 89–92.

17 Ibid., fig. I.

18 Ibid., fig. II.

19 H. Nicaise, 'Porcelaines de Tournay et de Chelsea-Derby', *Revue Belge d'archéologie d'histoire de l'art*, 5, 1935, pp. 1–15, fig. 4, eight models of boys and girls, emblematic of the *Four Seasons*, after Boucher.

20 Tapp, op. cit., fig. III, Tournai groups emblematic of *Earth* and *Air*, by Gauron.

21 Timothy Clifford, 'Derby Biscuit', *Trans. ECC*, 7, 1969, pt. 2, pp. 108–17, fig. 121a, Tournai group of *Minerva Crowning Constancy and Hercules Killing the Hydra*.

22 Tapp, op. cit., fix. X, *Bust of Charles D'Outrement*, by Gauron.

23 Ibid., fig. IX, group of *The Apotheosis of Charles D'Outrement*, by Gauron.

abandoned the enterprise. In the same year, Thomas Morgan, who for some months had been looking after William Duesbury's interests at Chelsea, wrote to him: 'I am informed by Mr. Viveur [Duvivier] that a modeller named Garon [sic] is willing to come to England.' Gauron probably came to this country in the autumn of 1770 and appears to have remained until about 1783.[24] *Barton's Account Book* contains the entry: '19th June, 1773. Gauron – 5 days at 8s 9d.–£2 10s 3d.' This level of remuneration is much the same as that given to Pierre Stephan (see below). Gauron may possibly have given Duesbury advice relating to the design of models and groups to be issued in biscuit, but it is unlikely that the nature of the soft paste was modified as the result of his suggestions. The following Derby models and groups have been ascribed to Gauron:

No.	*Derby Models and Groups*	*Reason for Attribution*
F14	*Minerva Crowning Constancy and Hercules Killing the Hydra*	Tournai group by Gauron
48	*The Four Elements* (four groups)	Tournai group by Gauron
176	*The Grape-gatherers*	Traditional belief and style
177	*The Knot in the Cravat*	Traditional belief and style
178	*The Alpine Shepherdess*	Traditional belief and style
179	Musical Group of 4 Children	Stylistic reasons
247	*The Grape-gatherers*	Reissue of No. 176
251	*Four Cupids Hunting*	Stylistic reasons
252	*Group of Three Cupids*	Stylistic reasons
255	*The Knot in the Cravat*	Reissue of No. 177
256	*The Alpine Shepherdess*	Reissue of No. 178
257	*Four Cupids Hunting*	Stylistic reasons
333	*Boys Playing Music*	Stylistic reasons
334	*Boys with Pets*	Stylistic reasons
388	*Four Putti as Seasons*	Stylistic reasons

HILL, Joseph

Said to have been among the first apprentices bound to William Duesbury I, and to have worked as a repairer between about 1756 and 1795. He used a personal mark of a small impressed triangle.

24 Ibid., p. 92.

HOLMES, George

This name appears in the Clerkenwell Rate Books for 1746–7 as an enameller[25] and it seems likely he learned his trade from Thomas Hughes. A model of a *Shepherd*, now in the Lady Leverholme Collection, is incised George 'Holmes did this figer 1765'.[26]

LAURENCE, John

This name is incised beneath the base of a Derby model of about 1770,[27] though nothing more is known about this man.

MASON family

Chaffers[28] mentions a Mason who claimed he had been an enameller at Chelsea from about 1751–7, then migrated to Bow, returning to Chelsea in 1759 and from there going on to Derby. None of his work while at Derby has been identified. His son, M. Mason, was also a painter at Derby who in October 1792 left to join Mr Barr at Worcester.[29] A man named Thomas Mason was apprenticed repairer at Derby between September 1772 and 1776.[30]

MORTLIDGE, John

A man of this name was apprenticed repairer at Derby in September 1772 for a term of seven years.

PEART, Charles

Charles Peart (1759–98) was accepted by the Royal Academy Schools of Sculpture in 1781 and the following year won a gold medal for his group *Hercules and Omphale*. He assisted another sculptor, John Charles Lochee, and later accepted commissions from Josiah Wedgwood. In 1787 Benjamin Vulliamy presented Lygo with 'A bill for 30 guineas to Mr. Peart who had modelled and moulded two new figures'. When, some time afterwards, Duesbury II wrote to Lygo asking him if Thomas Banks would make figures and moulds for him, he received the reply: 'Mr. Vulliamy says Banks is the modeller just in the same way as Mr. Bacon, and he does not think

25 W. H. Tapp, 'Thomas Hughes, First Enameller of English China of Clerkenwell, *Trans ECC*, 2, 1939, no. 6, pp. 53–65.
26 John Twitchett, *Derby Porcelain*, London, 1980, p. 252.
27 Sotheby's, *Sale Catalogue*, 20 May 1969, lot 243.
28 William Chaffers, *Marks and Monograms on European and Oriental Pottery and Porcelain*, London, 1965, (15th revised ed.), II, p. 292.
29 Ibid.
30 Twitchett, op. cit., p. 253.

he will do it for you – nor does he know of any one so capable of doing your work in the modelling way as Mr. Peart and if you have any figures you would have done he will give them to him to do.'[31] Presumably this means that neither Banks nor Bacon, as famous sculptors, would be prepared to make moulds though Peart would do so.

ROSSI, John Charles Felix

John Charles Felix Rossi (1762–1839) was born in Nottingham, the son of an Italian physician who came to England from Siena. He studied under Locatelli and attended the Royal Academy Schools of Sculpture in London. In 1784 he won a gold medal for his group *Venus Conducting Helen to Paris* and a scholarship that enabled him to continue his studies for the next three years in Rome. Returning to England in 1787 he joined J. Bingley in a venture specializing in the production of terracottas. Evidently his work caught the eye of Joseph Lygo who wrote in 1788 to William Duesbury: 'The figure Mr. Rossi is modelling is a female sacrifice figure from a drawing out of one of Mr. Vulliamy's books [Thorpe's Book of Ornament] and has not [sic] particular name than a sacrifice figure ...'[32] These cannot have been the *Pair of Sacrifice Figures* (No. 14) mentioned in the *Derby Sale Catalogue* of 29 March 1773[33] when Rossi was only eleven years old.

Between about 1788–90 Benjamin Vulliamy ordered 'Cherubs and other small Figures from Rossi', doubtless to be mounted beside his clocks and barometers. Lygo also ascribed to Rossi the *Burning of Cato*, and *Anatomy*, which have not been identified, and *Aesculapius and Hygeia*. Models of this designation numbered No. 99 were mentioned in the *Derby Sale Catalogue* of 1778, long before Rossi was working for the factory, although recently later versions, incised 'No. 385' have been described which may represent Rossi's work. He has also been credited with bas-reliefs of *Salamis* and the *Philistines*.

Rossi was employed also by Eleanor Coade in her Artificial Stone Works in Lambeth and was honoured by royal appointments to the Prince of Wales, George IV and William IV. His magnum opus was a bronze equestrian group of the *Duke of Wellington Flanked by Fame and Victory*.

SARTINE, Mr

Benjamin Vulliamy recommended a modeller of the name Sartine to William Duesbury as a suitable craftsman to be employed at Derby in 1790.

31 Lygo Letters in the Local Studies Library, Derby. Cited by F. Brayshaw Gilhespy, *Derby Porcelain*, London, 1961, p. 67.

32 Gilhespy, 1961, p. 67. Excerpts from the Lygo letters in the Derby Local Studies Library.

33 J. E. Nightingale, *Contributions towards the History of Early English Porcelain*, Salisbury, 1881, appendix p. 47.

SMITH, Constantine

The Clerkenwell Rate Books of 1747 include the name Constantine Smith as a 'painter on China'[34] and he, like George Holmes, may have been apprenticed to Thomas Hughes. It seems probable that he was employed for a time at the pottery works on Cockpit Hill in Derby before joining the staff at the porcelain manufactory. The register of All Saints Church, Derby, records his marriage on 11 July 1757 to Hannah Storer and gives his occupation as 'china painter'. According to Llewellyn Jewitt,[35] Smith was among the best of the old hands, who served both as an enameller preparing his own colours and gilder. He was the inventor of a blue enamel that bears his name introduced about 1770 as a substitute for underglaze blue which had proved difficult to control in the decoration of useful wares. Haslem preferred to credit the invention to William Smith, his son, but it appears upon items issued too early for this thesis to be tenable. Smith witnessed the signing of the agreement between Duesbury and Stephan in 1770 but was probably working on his own account by 1773 since his son, William, was apprenticed to himself rather than to Duesbury. In 1778 Duesbury assumed responsibility both for Smith's son and wife which suggests the enameller may that year have died or become incapable. Some have sought to identify Constantine Smith with the 'Cotton-stem' or 'Secondary Bird' painter though without providing supporting evidence.

SMITH, William

The son of Constantine Smith, apprenticed enameller in 1773 to his father but later, between 1778 and 1780, to Duesbury. He left Derby shortly afterwards and established his own decorating studio that was initially in St Alkmund's Churchyard, later in Spring Gardens, and finally at Iron Gate, all venues being in Derby. A teapot decorated in underglaze blue in a style suggesting a date about 1785, which is now in the Royal Crown Derby Museum, is signed beneath the lid 'Smith enameller Derby'. Smith's efforts to run an independent business were evidently not successful for in 1790 he was re-employed by Duesbury at the main Derby factory at a weekly wage of £1 0s 0d., later raised to £1 5s 0d.

SPENGLER, Jean-Jacques

Jean-Jacques Spengler, or Spangler (1755–?), was a French-speaking Swiss of German extraction, born at Schaffhausen, the son of Johann Jakob Wilhelm Spengler. His father had been modeller at the Höchst porcelain factory and was later

34 Tapp, op. cit., p. 60.

35 Jewitt, op. cit., II., p. 109.

appointed manager at Zurich. The life and works of Spengler (*fils*) have been presented by Timothy Clifford.[36]

Most probably Spengler was apprenticed modeller at Zurich between 1772 and 1779 where he may have been bound to the talented sculptor, Valentin Sonnenschein (1749–1828), whose elegant style so closely resembles his own. Ducret[37] credits Spengler with the Zurich version of *Virgins Awakening Cupid*, and John Twitchett[38] suggested that Spengler may also have created the Derby group about 1775 on a visit to England. The work was based on an engraving after Angelica Kauffmann which was readily available to most of the porcelain manufactories of the day and it seems unnecessary to postulate that Spengler made both groups. Certainly his behaviour in 1790 when he arrived in London did not point to any previous familiarity with Duesbury or the Derby establishment. Timothy Clifford believes Spengler may have accompanied Sonnenschein to Berne when in 1779 he was appointed professor of design at the *Kunstschule*, though Spengler's movements until 1790 remain a mystery.

Spengler was in London by the spring of 1790 when Vulliamy wrote of him to Duesbury as 'A foreigner who wants employment as a modeller'. While still in the metropolis, Spengler successfully completed a trial model of *Astronomy* from drawings supplied by Lygo and received payment of £13 2s 6d. for the work. In August he created a pair of models emblematic of *Morning* and *Noon*, each portrayed by a lady standing beside a vase, and also a group of *The Three Graces*.[38] Earlier, after repeated delays due both to the language barrier and Spengler's artistic temperament, an agreement was signed that has been reproduced by John Twitchett:[39]

> London, July 13th, 1790. A Memorandum. That the Bearer Mr. J. Spangler, has agreed to come down to the Manufactory at Derby, to work as Modeller, etc. and to receive for the first month at the rate of three guineas per week, and his expenses paid by coach. His hours of work to be from Seven o'clock in the morning till the rest of the People in the Manufactory give Over in the evening. It is further agreed on, that after the expenditure of the first Month, if the parties like each other and they agree time to come, the Bearer, Mr.

36 Timothy Clifford, 'J. J. Spangler, a Virtuoso Swiss Modeller at Derby', *Connoisseur*, 198, 1978, pp. 146–53.

37 S. Ducret, *Die Zürcher Porzellanmanufaktur*, Zurich, 1944, p. 25.

38 Twitchett, op. cit., p. 269.

39 Jewitt, op. cit., II., p. 94.

Spangler, is then only to receive after the rate of two pounds ten shillings per week from the first day he began to work in the Manufactory

Witness	B. Vulliamy.
Signed	J. Spangler.
For Mr. Duesbury	J. Lygo.

The reason why Spengler left Zurich for London is not known, although Timothy Clifford noted that following the death of his mother in 1787 his father remarried a woman only twenty-six years of age. Spengler was one of the most talented modellers ever to work in England although he chose a rather large scale of seldom less than 10–12 in (25.4–30.5 cm) and most of his work survives in biscuit. The heads of his male figures have tight natural curls, full rounded cheeks and prominent chin, while noses, seen in profile, form a straight line with the forehead. His female models are lithe and graceful with elaborately tressed or coiffed hair. Drapery is represented with meticulous care which may, to the modern eye, appear to be too detailed to be artistically successful. Overall the style of presentation, though influenced by Neo-Classicism, is essentially romantic and more attuned to the nineteenth than to the eighteenth century.

Spengler was quarrelsome, dishonest and completely unamenable to discipline. In 1792, before his contract had expired, he borrowed £30 from his employer, on the security of his household effects, and while attempting to embark at Ramsgate for the Continent, was arrested. He was committed to the King's Bench Prison but was bailed by his friend, the miniature painter Henry Hurter (1734–99). He made arrangements to pay off his debt in instalments from his wages and, on promise of good behaviour, was re-employed at Derby but almost at once was once again in trouble. The story is told by Hurter,[40] in a letter to Duesbury:

Sir,

I received your favour of 24th Inst. only this day, in Answer I shall tell you that on 7th Inst. I wrote to Spengler to know whether I was discharged from my bail, he answered me by the 9th that he was working indefatigably to bring under the pretended debt (as he called it) and that he was allowed out of his weekly wages barely enough to maintain himself, upon this I thought he would continue to work 'till he had completely discharged your debt. But how great was my astonishment when last Saturday sen'night I saw him arrive, in a most pity full condition. I asked him immediately what brought him hither, and whether he had settled with you and cleared me of my responsibility. I rec'd

40 Twitchett, op. cit., p. 272.

no answer, but that nobody would ever ask me anything and that you owed him money; without saying anything more he sate down to dinner with me and after dinner he went up to my room to shave and dress his hair; a little while after my servant going up to make my bed found him in it and told him he could not remain in the house, all the rooms being engaged, he begged to be left to take a little rest (being very ill) and would rise again. I good naturedly never intended to disturb him, and thought he really slept in my room! 'till 11 o'clock when I went up to take a few things I wanted I found him gone and on looking round I missed several things which he had made free with to the amount of £4 4s. Notwithstanding this I think he is still in London or in its vicinity and that he will have the impudence enough to call on me or write: however I give up every thought of making any good of him. Therefore must beg you to dispose to the best advantage of those things left in your possession, and to let me know what further sum is coming to you, without any more law proceedings. When I know your demand I shall endeavour to settle it with Mr. Lygo to whom you may give your orders for the purpose.

I remain Sir Yr. most Obedt. Hble. serv.
H. Hurter. London 28 Nov. 1792.

On 22 January 1793, Spengler was again in prison when he was visited by Hurter who wrote to Duesbury of the matter:

I this morning went to the Bench and found him one of the most miserable reches that can possibly be, he is nothing but rags and has not had a Change of lining since he was in prison, no money, no vituals to eat. He is quite agreeable to everything you propose....

Surviving letters written by Lygo to Duesbury have helped to identify some of Spengler's work although it is not always possible to match models to descriptive titles in the Factory List. In 1791 Spengler completed a 'sitting figure' for Mr. Vulliamy. In 1793 Lygo wrote:

I could not get that beautiful figure of Rosina without buying it at the price of six shillings. Spengler is going to model it – have not found a male figure to match it and S wants to do one of his own idea. He is making two female girls with a little poultry before them – for two guineas ... two female figures with dead birds ... Done Rosina, now a male figure.

Rosina was the heroine in the novel illustrated by Thomas Stothard, entitled

Rosina – Or Love in a Cottage, published in 1785. No model of this description has been identified.

After the turbulent events of 1792–3, Spengler returned to Derby to work out the remainder of his contract. In August 1793 he took to the road, as Haslem records:[41]

> Shortly after leaving Derby he passed through the town on tramp, dressed in the cast off clothes of a soldier, and was in such low water that a little refreshment and money which Isaac Farnsworth, his old overlooker, gave him was very acceptable. Not long after he again passed through the town and at this time was altogether in better guise.

In 1794 Duesbury re-engaged Spengler but placed him in London under the watchful eye of Lygo who took him to view monuments in Westminster Abbey. Later Lygo wrote: 'Spengler has modelled two sitting boys which are not worthy of your attention.' Again, on 3 February he wrote: 'Spengler will set out for Derby tomorrow, he intends walking it as it will not be so expensive and he might as well be walking to Derby as staying here doing nothing ...' His last comment on this wayward artist was: 'Spengler is the greatest rascal I ever had anything to do with – it would a been well if you had not employed him here.' Timothy Clifford cites a memorandum written on the back of an envelope supposedly in the hand of William Duesbury: '11th July 1795. Have given Spengler notice.' Spengler departed from the Derby ceramic scene in the autumn of that year and his subsequent fate remains undetermined. The following Derby models have been attributed to him:

No.	*Derby Model or Group*	*Authority for Attribution*
F12	*Astronomy* (trial model)	J. Lygo
——	*Morning* and *Noon*	L. Jewitt
——	Group of *Three Graces*	L. Jewitt
358	*Cupid Disarmed by Euphrosyne*	J. Haslem
359(ii)	*Gardener*	J. Haslem
363	*Two Figures Burying a Dead Bird*	J. Lygo
366	*Palemon and Lavinia*	J. Lygo
369	*Shepherd and Shepherdess Playing Flutes*	J. Lygo
370	*Belisarius and his Daughter*	Style
372	*The Proposal*	Style
373	Unidentified Group	Style

41 Haslem, op. cit., p. 153.

376	*Bacchus with Nymphs on Mount Nysa*	Style
382	*Dancing Girl*	Style
389	*Alpine Shepherds*	J. Lygo
390(ii)	*Flora*	Style
393	*Russian Shepherds*	J. Lygo
394	*Seated Piper* (part of No. 393)	J. Lygo
395	*Lady Feeding a Sheep with Hay*	J. Lygo
396	*Shepherd with his Dog* (previously ascribed to Coffee)	Style

STEPHAN, Pierre

Little is known about the early life of Pierre Stephan except that he was a French-speaking Swiss who had been employed about 1760 at Tournai as a porcelain modeller. Arthur Lane[42] pointed out that the name 'Stephan' did not appear in the records of the manufactory which subsequently, during the Second World War, were destroyed. This is strange because Mlle M. Jottrand[43] discovered in the Archives of the City of Brussels:

> Archives de la Villes de Bruxelles, portefeuille 174. Tournay le 14 Octobre 1769. Monsieur Antoine parent de bruxelles doit aux Sieur peterinck et Campaignie de Tournay:
>
> | | |
> |---|---|
> | 1 groupe de 3 figures pastorales a fl. | |
> | 2 dito, de fig. idem a fl. | 1800 |
> | 4 figures les elemens | 800 |
> | 4 dito, elemens de Stephan | 700 . . . |

Mlle Jottrand illustrates two of the 'Elemens de Stephan' which though a trifle chubbier than their Derby versions are otherwise similar. On 17 September 1770, Stephan signed an agreement with Duesbury to work at Derby as a modeller for three years.[44] He received a weekly wage of £2 12s 6d. On 3 August 1773, Stephan married Catharine Yates in St Alkmund's Church, Derby, and on 24 October 1774, their daughter, Frances, was baptised in the same church.[45] Meanwhile in September 1773 Stephan left Derby for employment at Wirksworth pottery where

42 Arthur Lane, *English Porcelain Figures of the Eighteenth Century*, London, 1961, p. 105, n.6.

43 M. Jottrand, 'Tournai Porcelain and English Ceramics', *Trans. ECC*, 10, 1977, pt. 2, pp. 130–5, pls. 61a and 61b.

44 W. H. Tapp, 'Wirksworth China', *Antique Collector*, November 1932, pp. 389–94.

45 Ibid.

he remained until May the following year. On 9 May 1774, he wrote to Josiah Wedgwood:[46]

Sir,

I was informed some time agoe by several persons (particularly Mr. Gardiner of Derby the Architect) that you gave encouragement to Artists in the Modelling Branch, at which time I was engag'd with Mr. Duesbury, and since then with the China Factory at Wirksworth both which now I am disengag'd from and have for some time thoughts of goeing to London, but first take the Liberty of informing you that if I could meet with agreeable Employment and that Encouragement my work deserves I should be glad to have the opportunity of being Employ'd by persons of Taste and Merrit which I hear is the Character of your Manufactory but at the same time chould chuse to have some part of my Employment in London on account of haveing a greater opportunity of improving my ideas in the Art of Modelling; but hope you will be so kind as to favour me with a line as soon as possible as I shall leave this place in a fortnight or three weeks at the farthest which will muche oblige

Your Obedt. servt.
P. Stephan.

Wirksworth 9th May, 1774.
P.S. please to direct for me at the Post Office in Wirksworth.
P.P.S. I work in Figures, Vasses, or any sort of Useful as Business may require.

Wedgwood provided Stephan with drawings of *Hope and the Conquered Province* that he had obtained in London, as the basis for a pair of trial models. These were duly completed and earned Stephan £2 10s 0d. In August 1774 Wedgwood wrote of the matter to his partner, Thomas Bentley:[47]

... I have received and examined Mr. Steven's moulds of Hope and the Conquered Province, and I am glad to find the drawing and the proportions so well preserved, but in everything else they are infinitely short of the exquisite originals. The drapery is hard and unfinish'd & the characters of the Faces are those of common mortals of the Lower Class. The armour of the Conquered Province comes out too much a great deal. The face of the figure is crooked, greatly so and there is a total want of finishing in both pieces. They are in my opinion far from being equal to our figures of the same class ... Mr. Steven's

46 Ibid.
47 Eliza Meteyard, *The Life of Josiah Wedgwood*, London, 1866, I, pp. 326–7.

can do better than us, if he would bestowe a little more attention and labour on them.

Despite these criticisms Wedgwood gave Stephan several commissions. It would seem that Stephan worked freelance until about 1798 when he made several portrait models of admirals. A letter written by Richard Champion, proprietor of the Bristol porcelain factory, dated 17 February 1772[48] is thought to have been directed to Stephan though the Derby modeller is not named:

> ... I have seen the Four Elements which were made at Derby, they are very beautiful, their dresses easy, the forms fine, two in particular Air and Water are charming figures. I apprehend you made ye moulds and therefore hope for your execution the following Fancies will not look amiss ...

Detailed specifications follow for two sets of models, representing the *Four Elements*[49] and the *Four [Classical] Seasons*.[50] Both were duly completed about 1773 and are stylistically similar to the Derby set of *Four Elements* (No. 3). The same style is evident in the three Derby groups, Nos. 195, 196 and 235, after Angelica Kauffmann. A large but rather crudely modelled bust of an unidentified woman in the British Museum, incised 'Stephan sculpt', is likely to have been made by Pierre Stephan's son, Charles. The set of the *Five Senses* (No. 59), and several models relating to the scandal of *John Wilkes,* have also been attributed to Stephan, despite the fact that they first appeared about 1764, many years before he arrived in England. Possibly because Stephan is known to have worked for both Derby and Champion's Bristol factories he has, without other evidence, been identified as the modeller responsible for the Derby *French Seasons* (No. 123), and the *Bristol Rustic Seasons*. Both of these, together with several other models issued by both factories, depict children with over-large heads, button-noses, smirking visages and short arms. They are totally dissimilar from any work that can with reasonable certainty be attributed to Stephan and it is hard to accept his authorship of them.

The following Derby models have been attributed to Stephan:

No.	*Derby Model or Group*	*Reason for Attribution*
3	*The Four Elements*	Tournai models by Stephan
12	*Pastoral Group by a Fountain*	Factory List after Bemrose
124	*Time Clipping the Wings of Cupid*	Stylistic reasons

48 Hugh Owen, *Two Centuries of Ceramic Art in Bristol*, London, 1873, Facsimile No. 4.

49 F. Severne MacKenna, *Champion's Bristol Porcelain*, Leigh-on-Sea, 1946, figs. 100–3.

50 Bernard Rackham, *Catalogue of the Schreiber Collection*, 1915, I, pl. 79, no. 730 (new no. 742).

195	*Two Virgins Awakening Cupid*	Stylistic reasons
196	*Two Bacchantes Adorning a Bust of Pan*	Stylistic reasons
235	*Three Graces Distressing Cupid*	Stylistic reasons
249	Group of *Fire and Water*	Adapted from No. 3
250	Group of *Earth and Air*	Adapted from No. 3
384	*Admiral Lord Howe*	Incised 'P. Stephan'
F2	*General John Drinkwater*	Stylistic reasons
F3	*Admiral Sir Adam Duncan*	Stylistic reasons
F4	*Admiral Lord Hood*	Wedgwood model by Stephan
F5	*William Pitt, the Lord Chatham*	Stylistic reasons
F8	*Admiral Lord Rodney*	Wedgwood model by Stephan

Appendix B · Modellers and Other Craftsmen 1796–1848

BRADLEY, Louis

Haslem wrote: 'Thomas Griffin, John Perkins, James Goadsby, Louis Bradley, John Mountford &c. were amongst the cleverest modellers and ornamental potters who learned the art at Derby.' Two *Dancing Figures* are ascribed to Bradley but have not been identified.

GRIFFIN, Thomas

Little is known of the early life of Thomas Griffin who, after Samuel Keys (*fils*) left in 1826, was appointed head of the modelling department. He is credited with the figure of *Grimaldi the Clown* (G3) during the few months he remained at the factory. Dr Alwyn and Angela Cox[1] have found that a potter named Thomas Griffin was at Swinton in 1827 and that the same name is incised upon one of the Rockingham *Continental Peasant* models, viz. 'T. Griffin/July 15th 1830'. Also, in 1832 Griffin was engaged on a dessert-service ordered from Rockingham by William IV.

HARDENBURG, B. François

Hardenberg was a sculptor of German extraction who may have been a modeller at Tournai before coming to England in the mid-1780s to provide statues and architectural embellishments for Caughley Place which Thomas Turner refurbished in the style of a French château. He arrived at Derby about 1796, via London, as a replacement for Coffee but within a year left to establish his own atelier in Mount Street, Grosvenor Square, London. There he specialized in marble and plaster busts of both classical and contemporary personalities and also made a fine bronze of the Duke of Wellington. He was one of four men entrusted with drawing up a list of moulds in 1810 that later was to form the Bemrose version of the Derby Factory List. Twitchett credits him with a model of *George III* (G27),

1 Alwyn Cox, Angela Cox, 'Rockingham Porcelain Figures', *Trans. ECC*, 12, 1986, pt. 3, pp. 240–9.

made in 1820, an example of which is now in the National Portrait Gallery. He may also have supplied models of notables freelance from his London studio, including *George IV* (G28), the young *Queen Victoria* (G30) and the *Duke of Wellington* (G31) which are well conceived and finely executed in a manner that suggests the hand of a sculptor.

HOLMES, Charles

Haslem attributes the following small models of animals to Holmes:[2]

Sheep, Lying down	4s od.	(G90)
Sheep in 2 smaller sizes.		
Sheep & Lambs, large pair.	7s od.	(G91)
Lambs with sprigs.	2s od.	(G89)

KEYS, Edward

Edward Keys was apprenticed modeller at Derby about 1812 and, following the death of Isaac Farnsworth in 1821, succeeded him as foreman in the modelling department. He left Derby in 1826 to join Henry Neal at Shelton and was later employed at Minton's at Stoke-on-Trent. Haslem attributes the following Derby models to him:

Archers, a pair.	£1 16s od.	(G48)
Bust of Admiral Nelson.	5s od.	(G32)
Dusty Bob & African Sal.	——	(G1)
'Key's Fancy Figures'.	9s od. each.	——
Napoleon, large.	3s 6d.	(G26)
Napoleon, small.	3s od.	
Paris Cries, 6 figures.	£1 4s 6d.	(G38)
Doctor Syntax, 13 models.	4s od–12s 6d. each.	(G11–23)
Doctor Syntax's Landlady.	3s 6d.	(G24)
Vicars, Curates & Wardens.	6s od.	(G41)
Billy Waters.	——	(G10)
Cats on cushions, large.	2s od.	(G60)
Cats on cushions, small.	1s 6d.	
Cats new, with prey.	1s 6d.	(G61)
Elephant with driver.	10s 6d.	(G78)

2 John Haslem, *The Old Derby China Factory*, London, 1876: references to this work recur throughout the text of this section.

Elephant without driver.	9s od.	(G79)
Elephant, small.	1s 6d.	(G80)
Foxes sitting, small.	1s 6d.	(G81)
Lion and Lioness.	2s od.	(G83)
Mice, Worcester.	2s od.	(G84)
Poodle Dogs, new.	2s od.	(G73)
Pugs seated on cushions.	1s 6d.	(G75)
Monkey Musicians, large.	7s 6d. each.	(G59)
Monkey Musicians, small.	5s od. each.	

KEYS, Samuel (père)

Samuel Keys was apprenticed enameller and gilder at Derby about 1785 and, according to Haslem, was: 'one of the best Derby hands who excelled in the elaborate decoration of china figures in the Dresden style, at which kind of work he could not be surpassed.' Tradition holds he enamelled the large figures of *Hebe* and *Innocence* that his son, Samuel, had modelled. He had three sons: Edward (see above) and Samuel (see below), both of whom were modellers, and John who was an enameller. Haslem writes of John: 'His manner was between that of Billingsley and the more florid style which painters afterwards practiced.' Samuel Keys senior left Derby for Minton's about 1830.

KEYS, Samuel (fils)

Samuel Keys (*fils*) was apprenticed modeller at Derby about 1814 and, when his brother Edward left in 1826, Samuel was passed over as head of the modelling department in favour of Thomas Griffin. However, Griffin also departed after a few months when Samuel Keys succeeded him. Later, in 1831, he too left Derby to work first at Minton's and, in 1840, he joined John Mountford in a small venture that specialized in Parian figures and won a commendation for work submitted to the Great Exhibition of 1851. Lady Charlotte Schreiber mentions in her Journals that she met Samuel Keys when he was an old man of seventy-three at Peterinck's porcelain manufactory at Tournai. The following Derby models are accredited to him:

Cantonese Girls, pair.	7s 6d.	(G43)
The 'Industrious Boy & Girl'.	15s od.	(G34)
Hebe & Innocence.	——	(G49)
Liston as 'Paul Pry'.	8s 6d.	(G5)
Liston as 'Domine Sampson'.	7s 6d.	(G7)

Liston as 'Maw Worm'.	——	(G6)
Maria Foote as 'Arinette'.	——	(G2)
Madam Vestris as a 'Broom-Seller'.	6s od.	(G9)
The 'Romantic Boy & Girl'.	——	(G40)
Bucks & Does, biscuit.	——	(G67)
Horse, large standing.	——	(G82)
Rabbits, without plinths.	1s od.	(G86)
Rabbits, on plinths.	2s od.	(G87)
Sheep, small standing.	7s od.	(G88)

WHITAKER, John

According to Haslem, John Whitaker was the son of Richard Whitaker who had been one of the first persons apprenticed to the first William Duesbury. John was apprenticed modeller about 1818 and, following the departure of Samuel Keys (*fils*), succeeded him to become head of the figure department until 1848 when the manufactory failed. He was subsequently employed at Minton's and died at the age of sixty-seven years at Stoke-on-Trent. Haslem ascribes the following Derby models to him:

An Angel.	(G46)
Boy & Girl, each with a Dog.	(G53)
Boy & Girl with greyhound & Falcon.	(G54)
An Eastern Lady.	(G42)
Girl amputee seated in a Chair.	(G56)
Girl playing a Guitar.	?(G37)
Mazeppa Group.	(G29)
Nymph asleep amidst Flowers.	(G50)
Bust of Queen Victoria.	(G33)
The Virgin Mary.	(G51)
Group of Hounds.	(G70)
Group of Stags.	(G69)
A Parrot.	(G93)
Peacock amongst Flowers.	(G94)

Bibliography

Adams, L. and Adams, Yvonne, *Meissen Portrait Figures,* London, 1987.

Allam, E. Percival, 'The Artist Modellers of the Old Derby Porcelain Factory', *Connoisseur,* lxxxii, 1928, pp. 29–37.

Barrett, F. A. and Thorpe, A. L., *Derby Porcelain,* London, 1971.

Bemrose, William, *Bow, Chelsea and Derby Porcelain,* London, 1898.

Berling, K., *Festive Publication to Commemorate the 200th Jubilee of the Oldest European China Factory, Meissen,* Meissen, 1910.

Berling, K., *Königlich-Sächsische Porzellan Manufaktur Meissen 1710–1910,* Dresden, 1911.

Bleakley, Horace, *The Life of John Wilkes,* London, 1918.

Blunt, Reginald (ed.), *The Cheyne Book of Chelsea China and Pottery,* London, 1924.

Bourgeois, Emile and Lechevallier-Chevignard, Georges, *Le Biscuit de Sèvres: I Recueil des modèles de la Manufacture de Sèvres au XVIII*[me.] *Siècle,* Paris, 1913.

Bradley, H. G. (ed.), *Ceramics of Derbyshire, 1750–1975,* Tiverton, 1978.

Bradshaw, Peter, *Eighteenth Century English Porcelain Figures, 1745–95,* Woodbridge, 1981.

Catalogues:

- Bonhams, Montpellier Galleries, Knightsbridge, London.
- Christie, Manson and Woods, 8 King Street, London.
- Neal and Son, Nottingham. *The Catalogue of the Bemrose Collection,* 1909.
- Phillips, Blenstock House, New Bond Street, London.
- Sotheby's, New Bond Street, London.
- Sotheby's, York Avenue, New York, USA.

Charleston, R. J. and Towner, Donald, *English Ceramics 1580–1830,* London, 1977.

Clifford, Timothy, 'Derby Biscuit', *Trans. ECC,* 7, 1969, part 2, pp. 108–17.

Clifford, Timothy, 'J. J. Spangler, a Virtuoso Swiss Modeller at Derby', *Connoisseur* 198, 1978, no. 196, pp. 146–53.

Clifford, Timothy, *Chelsea–Derby Royal Family Groups*, London, 1985. Catalogue of an exhibition mounted by the Derby Porcelain International Society, September 1985, at Burlington House, London.

Craven, Babette, 'Derby Figures of Richard III', *Trans. ECC*, 10, 1977, part 2.

Cushion, John, *English Porcelain*, London, 1974.

Daniel, Howard, *Callot's Etchings*, London and New York, 1977.

Davis, Stuart, 'Some English Pottery and Porcelain Figures Connected with Alsace Lorraine', *Burlington Magazine*, 51, 1927, pp. 221–8.

Dixon, John, *English Porcelain of the Eighteenth Century*, London, 1952.

Ducret, Siegfried, *Zürcher Porzellan*, Zurich, 1955.

Fischer, C. H., *Katalog der Sammlung Alt Meissner Porzellan des Herren Reutners und C. H. Fischer in Dresden*, Cologne, 1906.

Foggim, G. B., 'Art Treasures in Wentworth House, Yorkshire', *Connoisseur*, 141, 1958, p. 223.

Friedman, T. and Clifford, T., *The Man at Hyde Park Corner – Sculpture by John Cheere, 1709–87*, Twickenham, 1974.

Gabszewicz, Anton and Freeman, Geoffrey, *Bow Porcelain – The Collection Formed by Geoffrey Freeman*, London, 1982.

Gadd, David, *The Georgian Summer – Bath in the Eighteenth Century*, Bradford-on-Avon, 1971.

Gilhespy, F. Brayshaw, *Crown Derby Porcelain*, Leigh-on-Sea, 1951.

Gilhespy, F. Brayshaw, *Derby Porcelain*, London, 1961.

Godden, Geoffrey, *An Illustrated Encyclopaedia of British Pottery and Porcelain*, London, 1966.

Guest, Montague J. (ed.), *The Lady Charlotte's Journals, Confidences of a Collector of Ceramics and Antiques etc.* London and New York, 1966.

Hackenbroch, Yvonne, *Chelsea and Other English Porcelain, Pottery and Enamels in the Irwin Untermyer Collection*, Cambridge, Mass., 1957.

Harris, Nathaniel, *Porcelain Figurines*, Maidenhead, 1975.

Haskell, Francis and Penny, Nicholas, *Taste and the Antique*, Newhaven and London, 1981.

Haslem, John, *The Old Derby Porcelain Factory*, London, 1876.

Hasley, R. T. H., 'Ceramic Americana of the Eighteenth Century', Part IV, *Art in America*, V, 1916, pp. 55–8.

Hayden, Arthur, *Catalogue of the Lady Ludlow Collection*, London, 1932.

Hill, J. B., *Boswell's Life of Johnson*, London, 1891.

Hobson, R. L., *A Guide to English Pottery and Porcelain in the Department of British and Mediaeval Antiquities, British Museum*, London, 1910.

Honey, W. B., *German Porcelain,* London, 1947.
Hoyte, Anthony and Swain, Marilyn, 'A New Look at Ceramics from Private Collections', *Antique Dealer and Collector's Guide,* September 1985, pp. 58–60.
Hughes, G. Bernard, *English Pottery and Porcelain Figures,* London, 1964.
Hughes, G. Bernard and Hughes, Therle, *English Porcelain and Bone China,* London, 1955.
Hurlbutt, Frank, *Old Derby Porcelain, its Artists and Workmen,* London, 1925.
Hurlbutt, Frank, *Bow Porcelain,* London, 1926.
Jewitt, Llewellynn, *The Ceramic Art of Great Britain,* London, I and II, 1878.
Jewitt, Llewellynn, *The Ceramic Art of Great Britain,* (revised ed.), London and New York, 1883.
Jottrand, Mlle M., 'Tournai Porcelain and English Ceramics', *Trans. ECC,* 10, 1977, part 2, pp. 130–5.
King, William, *Chelsea Porcelain,* London, 1922.
King, William, 'Two Chelsea-Derby Groups and their Prototypes', *Connoisseur,* 69, 1924, pp. 211–13.
King, William, *English Porcelain Figures of the Eighteenth Century,* London, 1925.
King, William, 'Chelsea Chronology', *Trans. ECC,* I, 1933, p. 10.
Lancaster, H. B., 'The Origin of the Tithe Pig Pottery Group', *Connoisseur,* 105, 1940, pp. 253–5.
Lane, Arthur, *English Porcelain Figures of the Eighteenth Century,* London, 1961.
Mackenna, F. Severne, *Champion's Bristol Porcelain,* Leigh-on-Sea, 1946.
Mackenna, F. Severne, *Chelsea Porcelain, the Triangle and Raised Anchor Wares,* Leigh-on-Sea, 1948.
Mackenna, F. Severne, *Chelsea Porcelain, the Red Anchor Wares,* Leigh-on-Sea, 1951.
Mackenna, F. Severne, *Chelsea Porcelain, the Gold Anchor Wares,* Leigh-on-Sea, 1952.
Mallet, J. V. G., *The Bearsted Collection: Porcelain at Upton House,* Plaistow, 1964.
Meister, Peter, Wilhelm and Reber, Horst, *European Porcelain of the Eighteenth Century,* Oxford, 1983.
Mew, Egan, *Chelsea and Chelsea Derby China,* London, 1909.
Moffat, Alfred, *The Minstrelsy of Scotland,* London, second ed., 1896.
Morley-Fletcher, Hugo, *Investing in Pottery and Porcelain,* London, 1968.
Nicaise, N., 'Porcelaines de Tournay et de Chelsea-Derby', *Revue Belge d'Archéologie et d'Histoire de l'Art,* V, 1935, pp. 5–15.
Nightingale, J. E., *Contributions towards the History of Early English Porcelain,* Salisbury, 1881.
Owen, Hugh, *Two Centuries of Ceramic Art in Bristol,* London, 1873.

Pauls-Eisenbeiss, Erica, *German Porcelain of the Eighteenth Century,* London, I and II, 1972.
Rackham, Bernard, *Catalogue of the English Porcelain, Earthenware, Enamels and Glass, collected by Charles Schreiber Esq., M.P., and The Lady Charlotte Elizabeth Schreiber and presented to the Museum* [Victoria and Albert] *in 1884,* London, 1915.
Rackham, Bernard, *Catalogue of the Herbert Allen Collection of English Porcelain,* London, 1917.
Ramsey, L. G. G., 'A Masterpiece of Clockmaking', *Connoisseur,* 38, 1956, p. 130.
Ramsey, L. G. G., *A Complete Encyclopaedia of Antiques,* London, 1962.
Ray, Anthony, 'Liverpool Printed Tiles', *Trans. ECC,* 9, 1973, pp. 36–66.
Reinach, S., *Répertoire de la Sculpture grecque et romaine,* Paris, 1903.
Rice, Dennis G., *Rockingham Ornamental Porcelain,* London, 1965.
Rice, Dennis G., *Derby Porcelain, the Golden Years 1750–1770,* London, 1983.
Savage, George, *Eighteenth Century German Porcelain,* London, 1958.
Savage, George, *Seventeenth and Eighteenth Century French Porcelain,* London, 1960.
Savage, George and Reilly, Robin, *A Dictionary of Wedgwood,* Woodbridge, 1980.
Scott, C. M. and Scott, G. R., *Antique Porcelain Digest,* Newport, 1961.
Stoner, Frank, 'Chelsea Moulds and Models'. See Blunt, Reginald, pp. 104–8.
Stoner, Frank, *Chelsea, Bow and Derby Porcelain Figures,* Newport, 1955.
Stretton, E. N., 'Early Sadler Prints on Wedgwood Creamware', *Proceedings of the Wedgwood Society,* 8, 1970, pl. 16.
Tait, Hugh, *Porcelain,* London, 1962.
Thompson, James (ed. J. Sambrock), *The Seasons,* London, 1740. Reprinted Oxford, 1977.
Toppin, A. J., 'The Origin of Some Ceramic Designs', *Trans. ECC,* 2, 1948, no. 10, pp. 266–76.
Twitchett, John, *Derby Porcelain,* London, 1980.
Twitchett, John and Bailey, Betty, *Royal Crown Derby,* London, 1976.
Vavasseur, Cecil, the Lord Fisher, 'Love in Disguise', *Apollo,* 61, 1966, no. 364, pp. 183–8.
Warrack, John, *Greek Sculpture, One Hundred Illustrations,* London, n.d. (c. 1910).
Watney, Bernard, *Longton Hall Porcelain,* London, 1957.
Watney, Bernard, 'Some Parallels and Proto-types in Ceramics', *Trans. ECC,* 10, 1980, part 5, pp. 350–6.
Whinney, M., *Sculpture in Britain, 1530–1830,* London, 1962.

Index

Numbers in italics refer to plate numbers.

Absinthe-seller, 28, 38, *20*
Abyssinian Archer and Negress, 89, 108, *90*
Académie Royale, 449
Acier, Michel-Victor, 154, 157, 173, 197
Ackerman's Poetical Magazine, 413
Actor, 16, 18, 27, 35, *15*
Actress, 95
Adam, Robert, 297
Addison, Bust of, 160, 277–9, 445, *227*
Addison, Joseph, 160, 277–9, *227*
Adelaide, Queen, 394
Admiral Lord Hood, 136, 461
Admiral Lord Howe, 161, 386–8, 406, 461, *324*
Admiral Lord Nelson and George IV, Small Busts of, 422
Admiral Lord Rodney, 138, 461
Admiral Nelson, Bust of, 463
Admiral Sir Adam Duncan, 136, 405, 461
Aesculapius and Hygeia, 250–2, 388, 445, 452, *203*, *325*
Aesop's Fables, 133, 135
Africa, 117, 302–3, 360, *72*, *102*, *249*
Air, 23, 30, 50, 140, 168, 203, *121*, *126*, *156*
Albert, Prince Consort, 144
Albrechtsburg Castle, 151
Alexander Pope, 135, 138
All Saints Church, Derby, 453
allegorical models:
  1770–1810, 140
  bone china, 429
  dry-edge, 44–51
  patch-marked, 117–20
Alpine Shepherdess, 158, 286–8, 327, 450, *234*, *270*
The Alpine Shepherds, 161, 391–2, 458, *328*
alumina, 131
Alwyn, Dr, 462
America, 118, 302–3, 360, *249*
Ancaster, Mary, Duchess of, 86
Andromache Weeping over the Ashes of Hector, 160, 252–3, *204*
Angel, 415, 429, 465
Anguier, Michel, 29, 160, 263
animals:
  1770–1810, 141
  bone china, 432–7
  dry-edge models, 32–5
  patch-marked models, 94, 121–5
  transitional models, 55–6
Antique Figure of Justice, 211, 282, *230*
Antique Figure of Peace, 284–5, *232*
Antique Figure of Plenty, 282–4, *231*
Antique Figure of Wisdom, 282, *230*
Antique Seasons, The, 148, 168–70, 322–4, *267*
Apollo, 29, 42, 190, 261, 320, *23*, *265*
Apollo and the Nine Muses, 132, 190–2, *146*
Archers, 415, 429, 463
Architecture, 197
Ariadne, 160
Arinette, 423, *337*
Arithmetic, 197, *151*
Art, Literature and Astrology, 161, 384–5, *322*, *323*
The Arts and Sciences, 16, 17, 154, 197–9, *150–2*
Asia, 118, 302–3, 249, 360, *102*
Askew, Richard, 370
Astrology, 16, 17, *1*
Astronomy, 135, 139, 457
Astronomy and Geometry, 197, *151*
Audran, Claude, 89
Augusta, Princess, 189
Augustus III, King of Poland, 151, 155, 333
Autumn, 16, 31, 44, 45, 63, 64, 72, 73, 93, 118, 120, 140, 169, 170, 192, 202, 221, 267, 270, *28*, *31*, *63*, *103*, *155*, *216*, *218*, *220*
Autumn and Spring, 289
Autumn Candlestick, 80

Bacchus, 160
Bacchus and Ariadne, 293–5, *240–2*
Bacchus Heads, 143
Bacchus with Nymphs on Mount Nysa, 458
Bachelier, Jean-Jacques, 155
Bacon, John, 186, 314, 443–4, 448, 451–2
Bailey, Betty, 417
Bailliu, Pierre de, 160, 233
Baléchou, J.-J., 30
Bamford, James, 362
Banier, Abbé, 180, 196
Banks, Thomas, 444, 451–2
Banks, William, 444
Barlow, William, 444
Baroque, 26, 152, 153
Barr, Mr, 451
Barrett, F. A., 399, 407
Bartolozzi, Francesco, 143, 161, 295, 297, 318, 392, 412
Bartolozzi, Lucia Elizabeth *see* Vestris, Madam
Barton, Richard, 10
bases:
  1770–96, 132–3, *124*
  bone china models, 408
  dry-edge models, 22–3, *7*, *8*
  experimental models, 15–16
  Pale Family models, 58–9
  patch-marked models, 81–3, *72*
  transitional models, 53–4
Basket Boys, 410, 429
Basket Shepherds, 87, 104, *85*
Beewick, T., 161
Belisarius and his Daughter, 376–7, 410, 416, 422, 457, *316*
Bemrose, William, 4, 143, 145–6, 147, 149, 384, 444
Bentley, Thomas, 5, 459
Berling, K., 334
Billy Waters, 412, 418, 463, *343*
Bingley, J., 452
Bird, 25
birds:
  bone china, 437
  dry-edge models, 32
  Pale Family models, 81
  patch-marked models, 94, 125–8
  transitional models, 55
biscuit models, French influence, 155–9
Blackamoor and Negress, 89, 108
Blondeau, 155, 156
Bloor, Robert, 14, 144, 407, 408, 409
Blue Tits, 125, *114*
Boars, 32
bocages, 83, 132–3
Boccaccio, Giovanni, 161, 392
Boitard, 88, 161, 342
Boizot, Louis-Simon, 158
Bolognese Dog, 141
Bolton, John, 25
bone ash, 131, 132
bone china models, 407–37
Boreman, Zachariah, 11
Böttger, Johann Friedrich, 151
Bouchardon, Edmé, 27
Boucher, François, 30, 87, 92, 135, 153, 156, 158, 213, 231, 245, 247, 267, 286, 287, 332–3, 449
Bow factory, 13, 133–4, 156, 257
Bowcock, John, 156
Bower, Richard, 11–12
Boy Crying and Girl Laughing, 330, *272*, *273*
Boy and Girl Dancing a Reel, 158, 201, *153*
Boy and Girl, each with a Dog, 414, 429, 465
Boy and Girl with Flute and Hurdy-gurdy, 174–5, *134*
Boy and Girl with French Horn and Guitar, 173–4, *132*, *133*
Boy and Girl Gathering Flowers, 414, 431
Boy and Girl with Greyhound and Falcon, 431, 465
Boy and Girl as Harlequin and Columbine, 85, 95
Boy and Girl with Macaroni Dog and Cat, 155, 205–6, 368–9, *159*, *307*
Boy and Girl Riding a Dolphin and a Swan, 148, 277, *226*
Boy and Girl in Turkish Costumes, 222–3, *178*
Boy Eating an Apple and Girl Curds-and-Whey, 253, 416, *205*
Boy Holding a Basket, 166
Boy Piping and Girl Dancing with Cymbals, 161, 370–1, *310–12*
Boy Reading a Book and Girl Tatting, 290–1, 354, *237*, *238*
Boy Seated with Cat and Girl with Dog, 229, *182*, *183*
Boy Shepherd and Dancing Shepherdess in Scottish Dress, 69, *52*

Boy Shepherd Piper and Dancing Shepherdess, 28, 38, 62, *21*
Boyer, Robert, 10
Boyle, John, 31
Boyle, Samuel, 31
Boys with Pets, 450
Boys Playing Music, 450
Bradley, Louis, 462
Brandoin, 394
Bricknell, Brian R., 445, 446
Bristol porcelain factory, 205, 214, 252, 267, 407, 460
Britannia, 92, 110, 160, 328–9, 445, *100*, *271*
Bronze, after the antique, of Hermes, *335*
Brooke, Francis, 398
Brown, Mather, 386
Brühl, Count Heinrich von, 17, 221
Brussels, 449
Bull and Cow Suckling a Calf, 121
Bull, Recumbent, 121, *105*
Bullfinches, 94, 126
Bulls, 27, 32
Bulls, Charging, 94, 121
Buntings, 125, *115*
Burke, Thomas, 160, 161, 252, 362
Burrows, Mary, 5, 7
Burton-on-Trent, 447
Bute, Lord, 90
Butts, William, 7

Caffieri, Jean-Jacques, 158
Calliope, 190, *146*
Calliope and Three Naiads, 142
Callot, Jacques, 161, 300, 312, *258–60*
Candlestick group, 64
candlesticks, 79–80, 133
Cantonese Girls, 415, 428, 464
The Capitoline Faun, 160, 376
Caronmeuse, 449
Cars, Laurent, 86
Carter, Thomas, 448
Cat and Dog Candlesticks, 54, 55
Cat with Gold Collar, 416, 432
Catherine II, Empress of Russia, 158
Catherine, Mr, 444
Catholic Church, 94
Cats, 415, 432, 463, *366*
Cats with Prey, 411, 432
Cats Recumbent, 432
Cattle, 411, 415
Caylus, Comte de, 27
Chaffers, William, 3, 25, 451
Chalon, 414
Champion, Eliza, 252
Champion, Richard, 205, 214, 252, 267, 407, 460
Chantilly, 4–5, 89, 155
Charles XII, King of Sweden, 414
Charles Pratt, the Lord Chancellor, 91, 110, 138
Charlotte, Princess, 189
Charlotte, Queen, 147, 189, 394
Charlotte Weeping for Werther, 320–2, *266*
Chatham, Lord, 91, 108, 136, 461, *119*
Cheere, Sir Henry, 445
Cheere, John, 28, 62, 160, 266, 278, 328, 346, 445, 448
Chelsea factory, 4, 10–12, 13, 17, 131, 133–4, 151, 257, 312–13, *198*, *210*
Child with a Basket of Fruit, 184–5, *142*
children, bone china models, 429–31
Children at a Peep-show, 158, 248–9, *201*, *202*
Children Playing Hazard, 158, 247–8, *200*
Children in Turkish Costume, 428
China, 89
Chinaman and Boy, 51, *40*
Chinaman with a Guitar, 30
Chinese Boy Climbing a Creeper-like Tree, 53, 54, 56
Chinese Lady Drummer, 30
Chinese Mother and Child, 31, 51, *39*
Chinese Musicians, 51
Chinoiserie Senses, 30
chinoiseries, 30
Christie, 145
Christie, Messrs, 157
Cibber, Susannah, 84, 95
Clarke, Thomas, 14
Clement XII, Pope, 94
Clifford, Timothy, 250, 258, 311, 384, 398, 444, 446, 454, 455, 457
Clio, 82, 92, 190
Clio and Cupid, 110
Clive, Kitty, 16–17, 18, 156
Coade, Eleanor, 443, 445, 446, 452
Coalports, 415
Cobbler, 28, 40
Cochin, Charles-Nicolas, 247, 249

Cock and Jewel Candlesticks, 133, 135, 141, *122*
Cocker, George, 410, 416
Cockpit Hill, 6
Coffee, Catherine, 445
Coffee, William, 134, 267, 382, 445
Coffee, William John, 366, 399, 405, 406, 415, 445, 446–8, 458
colours:
  1770–96, 133
  bone china models, 408–9
  dry-edge models, 23–6
  Pale Family models, 59–60
  patch-marked models, 83–4
  transitional models, 53
Columbine, 28
Columbine, Harlequin and Punch, 95
Combe, William, 413
Commerce, 197, *151*
Companion Woman Pedlar, 28
Condé, Louis-Henri de Bourbon, Prince de, 4–5, 89
Conway, General Sir Henry Seymour, 91, 108, 135, *91*
A Cook, 154, 243, *195*
Cookworthy, Thomas, 407
Copeland, 150
Copeland, Ronald, 32
Copeland, Alderman William Taylor, 31
Cordier, Nicolas, 160, 279
'Cotton-stem Painter', 60, 453
Cow and Calf, 432, *367*
Cows, Lean, 432
Cows, Lowing, 432
Cox, Alwyn, 412
Cox, Angela, 412, 462
Cox, James, 10
Craven, Babette, 186
crazing, 132, 408
Crested Pheasant, 54, 55, *41*
Crisp, Nicholas, 443
Crucifixion Group, 135, 139, *120*
Cruikshank, George, 412
Cunningham, Allan, 443
Cupid as Bacchus, 332
Cupid and Bacchus Riding, 154
Cupid with Bagpipes, 332
Cupid as a Bewigged Lawyer, 331
Cupid as a Chimney Sweep, 332
Cupid as a Cook, 332
Cupid Disarmed by Euphrosyne, 362–4, 457, *302*
Cupid as a Drummer Boy, 332
Cupid Entreating a Virgin, 401, *336*
Cupid with Euphrosyne, 161
Cupid with a Flail, 332
Cupid and Flora Candlesticks, 358, *297*
Cupid as a Girl with a Hurdy-gurdy, 332, *276*, *277*
Cupid as a Lady's Maid, 331
Cupid with a Magic Lantern, 331
Cupid as a Money-Lender, 332, *275*
Cupid as a Nursemaid, 332
Cupid as Pantaloon, 332
Cupid Riding a Goat and Bacchus on a Panther, 179, *137*
Cupid as a Scullion, 332
Cupid as a Shepherd, 311, 332
Cupid as a Shepherdess, 332
Cupid as a Wounded Soldier, 332
Cupids, Pair of, 304–5, 306, 317, 326, *250*
Cupids in Disguise, 32, 148, 150, 154, 331–4, *274–7*
Cupids Grinding, 410, 429
Cupids Riding Bucks, 154, 289–90, *236*
Cupids Seated with Dog and Falcon, 307–8, *253*, *254*
Cybele, 26, 59, 60
Cybele with a Lion, 29, 42, 63, 73, *67*
Cyfflé, Louis Paul, 161, 376

Daguesant, M., 374
Dance, Nathaniel, 90, 160, 161, 186, 272, *145*
dancers:
  Pale Family models, 65–7
  patch-marked models, 97–100
Dancers, 27, 35, *16*, *17*
Dancing Beribboned Youth, 54, 56, *42*
A Dancing Couple, 154, 182–3, *140*, *141*
Dancing Figures, Pair of, 357–8, 462, *296*
Dancing Girl, 386, 458, *7*
Dancing Group, 145, 231
The Dancing Lesson, 86, 98, *77*
Dancing Shepherdess, 28, 62
Dancing Shepherds, 87, 105, *86*
Dancing Youth, 54
Daullé, Jean, 92
David Garrick as Richard III, 160, 186–8, *144*, *145*

Davies, Thomas, 188
Dawson, Nancy, 356
Deare, John, 448
decorative styles, 1770–96 models, 133–4
Derby, 5
Derby Factory Accounts, 131
Derby Mercury, 6
Derby Museums and Art Gallery, 144
Derby Reporter, 144
Desjardins, Martin, 258
Desplaces, L., 263
Dessert Gardeners, Pair of, 340–1, *283*
deutsche Blumen, 60, 153
Diamond, William, 412
Diana, 60, 81, 265–6, *215*
Diana with a Hunting-dog, 63, 77, 91–2, 110, 224, *92*, *179*
Dickinson, J., 394, 412
Diderot, Denis, 158
Dismal Hound, 94
Dixon, C., 161
Dixon, John, 160, 186, *145*
Doccia, 87
Dr Syntax, 413, 463
Dr Syntax Astride his Horse Grizzle, 422, *350*
Dr Syntax at the Bookseller's, 419
Dr Syntax at York Races, 419, *348*
Dr Syntax Bound by Robbers to a Tree, 422
Dr Syntax Chased by a Bull, 419, *349*
Dr Syntax Crossing a Lake, 419
Dr Syntax Landing at Calais, 413, 422, *351*
Dr Syntax Playing a Violin, 419, *346*
Dr Syntax Reciting in the Greenroom, 419, *347*
Dr Syntax Retiring to Bed, 419, *344*
Dr Syntax Scolding his Landlady, 422
Dr Syntax Seated Sketching, 413, 419, *345*
Dr Syntax Walking, 422
Dr Syntax's Landlady, 422, 463
Dog Orchestra, 415
Dogs and Squirrel Candlestick, 64, 80
Donatello, 332
Dove, 126
Dresden, 151
The Dresden Shepherds, 62, 69, 87, 154, 211–12, 410, *55*, *164*, *165*
drinking cups, 1770–1810 models, 143
Drinkwater, General John, 135, 405–6, 461, *118*
dry-edge models, 6, 15, 21–51
Duck sauce-boats, 143
Ducret, S., 454
Dudley, Martha, 446
Duesbury, Elizabeth, 14
Duesbury, Mary, 8
Duesbury, William I, 3–4, 7–13, 24–5, 53, 58, 131, 133, 134, 148, 157, 159, 443–4, 446, 448, 450, 453, 457
Duesbury, William II, 8, 13, 134, 451
Duesbury, William III, 13, 14
Duesbury and Kean, 13
Duke of Wellington, 413, 422, 463, *356*
Duncan, Admiral Sir Adam, 136, 405, 461
Duquesnoy, François, 156
Duronceray, Marie-Justine, 287
Dusty Bob and African Sal, 412, 417, 463
Dutch Dancers, 86, 97
Duvivier, Mr, 450
Dwarfs, Pair of, 161, 312–13, *258*
Dyck, Anthony Van, 160, 161, 233, 270
Dying Drunk, 414, 416

Earlom, Richard, 161, 189, 444
Earth, 140, 166, 203, *121*, *126*, *157*
Earth and Air, 159, 324, 461
Eastern Lady, 415, 428, 465
Eberlein, Johann Friedrich, 27, 63, 85, 91, 92, 93, 152–3, 154, 155, 221, 223, 224, 226, 257, 302
Edmund Kean as Richard III, 418
Egan, Anne, 8, 12
Egan, Pierce, 412
Egan, Richard, 12
Ehder, Johann Göttlieb, 153
Elephant, Small, 436, 464
Elephant with Mahout, 415, 436, 463
Elephant without Mahout, 409, 415, 436, 464, *373*
El Greco, 153
Elizabeth I, Queen, 351
enamel colours:
- 1770–96, 133
- bone china models, 408–9
- dry-edge models, 23–6
- Pale Family models, 59–60
- patch-marked models, 83–4
- transitional models, 53

Erato, 82, 92
Erato and Cupid, 110

Europa and the Bull, 92, 110, *93*
Europe, 118, 302–3, 360, *249*
Ewe and Ram, 27, 32, *11*
Ewe Suckling a Lamb, 27, 32
experimental Derby models, 5, 15–21

Factory Lists, 144–50
Falconet, Étienne-Maurice, 92, 135, 156, 158, 181, 201, 234, 245–6, 247, 249, 286, 287
Fame and Mercury, 348–50, *291*
Farmer and Wife, 62, 71, *57–60*
Farnese Hercules, 160
Farnsworth, Isaac, 145, 448, 457, 463
Favart, Charles-Simon, 287
Fawkener, Sir Everard, 151
Fearn, Samuel, 14
Feeling, 25, 30–1, 47, 48, 216, *33–5*, *169*
Ferriole, Monsieur, 89
fêtes galantes, 86
Field Marshal Sir Henry Seymour Conway, 90–1, 108, 135, *91*
Finches, 17, 21, 32, 81, 126
Finches, Nesting, 126
Fire, 93, 135, 140, 166, 203, 410, 429, *121*, *158*
Fire and Water, 159, 324, 461
The Five Chinoiserie Senses, 47, *32–5*
The Five Senses, 30, 48, 93, 118, 216, 460, *36–8*, *169–73*
Flambé Musicians, 85
Flora, 161, 393–4, 458, *329*
foliage, 83
Foote, Maria, 412, 417, 465, *337*
foreign personages:
  bone china, 428
  patch-marked models, 108
Fountain Vase, 143, 185
Four Addorsed Blackamoors, 54
The Four Adolescent Seasons, 93, 118–20
The Four Antique Seasons, 93, 118
Four Boys, Group of, 145
Four Boys with Pets, 159, 362, *300*, *301*
Four Boys Playing Music, 159, 361, *299*
The Four Chelsea Seasons, 149, 270, *220*
Four Children Playing Music, 159, 289, *235*
The Four Classical Seasons, 63, 72–3, 93, 118, *63*
The Four Continents, 93
Four Cupids Bird's-nesting, 159, 317–18, *262*
Four Cupids Hunting, 150, 159, 324, 328, 450, *268*
The Four Elements, 50, 93, 135, 140, 159, 166–8, 203–5, 324, 410, 429, 450, 460, *121*, *126*, *127*, *156–8*
Four Figures, Subject Unidentified, 379, *318*
The Four Grotesque Seasons, 202, *154*, *155*
The Four Infant Seasons, 31, 44, 80, 93, 118, 154, 170–1, *27*, *103*, *129*
Four Putti as Seasons, 450
The Four Quarters of the Globe, 93, 117–18, 148, 154, 155, 302–3, 343–4, 360, *102*, *249*, *286*, *298*
The Four Rustic Seasons, 31, 44–5, 73, 192–3, *2–31*, *147*
The Four Seasons, 16, 17–18, 93, 135, 140, 154, 159, 220–1, 226–7, 342, 390–1, *176*, *181*, *285*, *326*, *327*
Four Seated Africans, 89, 108
Fournier, Marie-Anne, 4
Fox, Dr Douglas, 414
Fox, Seated, 94, 121, 436, 464, *107*
Fox Heads, 143
France, influence on soft-paste biscuit models, 155–9
Francis I, King of France, 384
Frankenthal, 86
Frederick Augustus, Duke of York, 394, *330*
Frederick the Great, 153
Frederick George, Prince of Wales, 86
Freemasons, 94
The French Seasons, 159, 267–9, 460, *216–18*
The French Shepherds, 213–14, *167*
Friar's Gate, Derby, 416
Fury Group with Broken Chair, 237–8, *191*

Gaillard, René, 245
Gainsborough, Thomas, 388
Gallant and Lady, 422
Gallant and Lady Attired as Shepherd and Shepherdess, 87, 100, *78*
A Gallant and Lady Candlestick, 79
Gallant and Lady Waltzing, 370, *309*
Gallant Holding a Birdcage, 31
Gallant Taking Snuff, *8*, *9*
Gardener, 59, 140
Gardener Candlesticks, 337–8, *281*
Gardener and Companion, 171–2, 305–6, 364–7, 446, 447, 448, 457, *130*, *251*, *252*, *303–6*

Gardening Group, 140
The Garland Shepherds, 87, 101, 212–13, *166*
Garrick, David, 16, 84, 85, 95, 186–8, 314, 316, *144*, *145*
Gauron, Jacob, 448–9
Gauron, Nicolas-Joseph-François, 11, 134, 157, 159, 165, 168, 204, 267, 448–50
Gear, J. W., 411–12
Gentleman, 54
Gentleman Cellist, 85, 95
Gentleman Flautist, 61, 65, *46*
Gentleman with a Flute and Lady with a Lute, 228
Gentleman and Lady with Dog and Cat, 154, 208–9, *162*
Gentleman Playing a Reed-pipe, 27, 35
Gentleman Reading, 147
Gentleman Seated Caressing a Dog, 56, *43*
Gentleman Violinist, 97
George III, King, 11, 147, 189, 394, 411
George III, 406, 413, 422, 444, 462–3
George IV, King, 189, 394, 452
George IV, 406, 413, 422, 463, *353*
Gérin, Claude-Humbert, 155
Gersulamme Liberata, 233
gilding:
  bone china models, 409
  dry-edge models, 26
  honey-gilding, 26, 84, 409
  mercury gilding, 409
Giles, James, 12, 25
Gilhespy, Brayshaw, 12
Gilpin, William, 413
Giovanni da Bologna, 160, 311
Girl Playing a Guitar, 465
Girl Seated in a Chair, 414–15, 431, 465
Girl-in-a-Swing Factory, 4, 15, 16, 17
Girl-on-a-Horse Factory, 8, 53,
glazes
  1770–96, 131–2
  bone china models, 407–8
  dry-edge models, 21–2
  experimental models, 15
  Pale Family models, 58
  patch-marked models, 81
  transitional models, 53
Goadsby, James, 462
Goat Heads, 143
Goats, 27, 35, *12*, *13*
Goats, Recumbent, 122
Goats, Standing, 122
Godden, Geoffrey, 417
Goethe, Johann Wolfgang von, 320–2
Goldfinches, 126, *116*
Good Morning, 414, 417, 431
Good Night, 414, 417, 431
Gough, 413
Gouyn, Charles, 4
Graham, James, 241
Graham, Dr Thomas, 241
Grape-gatherers, 158, 285–6, 322, 450, *233*
Grape-sellers, 62–3, 72, *62*
Gravant, François, 155
Gravelot, Humbert, 376
Graves, Richard, 322
Gray, 161
Gray, Benjamin, 12
Gray, Thomas, 356
Great Exhibition (1851), 144, 464
Gresley, Sir Nigel, 447
Griffin, Thomas, 413, 462, 464
Griffin Candlestick, 209
Grignion, G., 161, 314, 394
Grimacing Dwarfs, Pair of, 209–10, *163*
Grimaldi, 413
Grimaldi, Joseph, 413
Grimaldi the Clown, 417, 462, *338*
The Grotesque Seasons, 445
Gualtieri and Griselda, 161, 392–3
Guelard, J., 89
Guery, Caroline, 449

Hackwood, 322
Hairdresser Group, 158, 238–9, *192*
Halifax, Lord, 90
Hamburg, 153
Hancock, 408, 413
Hancock, Sampson, 14
Hardenburg, François, 145, 406, 462–3
Hare Heads, 143
Harlequin, 15, 17, 18, 85, *2–4*
Harlequin and Columbine, 27, 35, 61, 65, 154, 300–2, *18*, *47*, *247*, *248*
Harlequin and Punch Candlesticks, 61
Harlequin Candlestick, 66
Harlequin in Motley, 95

Harlequin's Family, 61, 65
Hartington, Charles Stanhope, 4th Earl of, 412
Harvester with a Cornsheaf, *29*
Harvesters, 87, 101
Haslem, John, 14, 31, 87, 143, 144, 158, 406, 410–12, 413, 415, 443, 444, 446–7, 457, 463–4; *The Old Derby China Factory*, 144–6, 149–50
Haymakers, Pair of, 148, 154, 299–300, 344, *245*, *246*, *287*
Hayman, Francis, 16, 85, 161, 314
Hearing, 30, 31, 47, 48, 61, 216, *170*
Heath, Christopher, 7, 11
Heath, John, 3, 6–7, 8, 11, 13
Hebe and Innocence, 415, 429, 464
Henry V, King, 351
Henry Woodward, 15
Henry Woodward as the Fine Gentleman in 'Lethe', 16–17, 18
Henson, John, 14
Heracles Killing the Hydra, 134
Herculaneum, 278
Hill, Joseph, 450
Hobson, A. L., 161
Höchst porcelain factory, 453
Hogg, J., 161, 398
Holland House, 151
Holmes, Charles, 463
Holmes, George, 451, 453
honey-gilding, 26, 84, 409
Hood, Admiral Lord, 136, 405, 406, 461
A Horned Ewe and Ram, Recumbent, 121, *106*
Höroldt, Johann Gregor, 152
Horse, Standing, 436
Hoskin and Oliver, 278
Hoskins and Grant, 279
Hound, Seated, 122, *108*
Hounds, 433, 465, *368*
Howe, Admiral Lord, 149, 161, 386–8, 405, 406, 461, *324*
Hudson, Thomas, 86
Huet, Charles-François, 28
Huet, Christophe, 28, 85, 89, 243
Huet, Jean-Charles, 333
Hughes, Thomas, 7, 451, 453
Huguenots, 4–5, 7
Hulst, 153
Huntsman, 149
Huntsman Flautist and Lady Reclining, 27, 35, *19*
Huntsman and Lady, 87–8, 97, 101, 206–8, *79*, *160*, *161*
Huquier, Gabriel, 30
Hurdy-gurdy Player, 85, 95
Hurter, Henry, 455–6

The Idyllic Musicians, 85, 155, 353–4, *293*, *294*
indianische Blumen, 60, 83, 88–9, 152, 409
Industrious Boy and Girl, 414, 416, 422, 464, *357*
The Infant Bacchus with Nymphs on Mount Nysa, 380, *319*
Inglefield, 10
Inkstands on Cats, 143
Irminger, Jakob, 151
Italian Farmers, 87, 103, *80*, *81*

James Quinn as Sir John Falstaff, 84–5, 95, 161, 314–16, 339, *261*
James, Sarah, 8
japonaiseries, 30
Jason and Medea at the Altar of Diana, 160, 180, 195–6, *149*
Jean-Jacques Rousseau, 135, 138
Jenks, 10
Jewish Pedlars, 88, 106, *88*
Jewitt, Llewellynn, 3, 4, 5, 8, 10, 12, 448, 453
John Drinkwater, 135, 406, 461, *118*
John Liston as Domine Sampson, 412, 418, 464
John Liston as Maw Worm, 412, 418, 465
John Liston as Paul Pry, 416, 418, 464, *339*
John Milton, 345–6, *288*
John Wilkes, MP, *see* Wilkes, John
Johnny Wapstraw and Companion, 145, 366
Johnson, Dr Samuel, 11, 188, 241
Jottrand, M., 458
Joullain, François, 300
Juno, 82, 91
Juno and a Peacock, 110, 265, *94*, *214*
Jupiter, 42, 82, 91
Jupiter and an Eagle, 112, 154, 261–3, *94*, *213*
Justice, 92, 112, 210–11, *95*

Kändler, Johann Joachim, 4, 17, 26, 27, 28, 30, 61, 63, 88, 89, 151–3, 154, 155, 179, 182, 209, 212, 221, 257, 258, 300, 302, 333–4, 368
Kauffmann, Angelica, 143, 160, 161, 252, 295–7, 318, 362, 374, 392, 454, 460

Kean, Edmund, 188, 418
Kean, Michael, 13, 14, 144, 158, 447
Kemble, John Philip, 186–7
Kent, Duke of, 189
Keys, Edward, 406, 413, 415, 463–4
Keys, John, 464
Keys, Samuel, 3, 4
Keys, Samuel (*fils*), 411, 412, 415, 416, 462, 464–5
Keys, Samuel (*père*), 464
King, Charles, 446
King Charles Spaniel, Scratching, 433
King Street factory, 417
Kirchner, Johann Gottlieb, 151–2
Kitty Clive, 15
Kitty Clive as Mrs Riot in 'Lethe', 16–17, 18, *5*
Kneller, Sir Godfrey, 135, 161
Knight, Charles, 374, 398
The Knot in the Cravat, 158, 286, 326–7, 450, *270*

La Rue, Felix de, 156
lace reproduced in porcelain, 157, 173
Lady, 54
Lady and Gentleman, 54
Lady Feeding a Sheep with Hay, 149, 161, 396, 398–9, 447, 458, *333*
Lady Knotting, 147
Lady Playing a Triangle, 85, 95
Lady Riding Side-saddle upon a Prancing Horse, 54, 56, 61
Lady Seated Fondling a Lamb, 56, *43*
Lady Seated Holding a Musical Score, 31, 54–5, 61, 66, *50*
Lady Seated Playing a Mandoline, 58, 61, 66, *49*
Lambs with Sprigs, 463
Lancret, Nicolas, 86, 87, 88
Landlady, 413
Lane, Arthur, 8, 53, 399, 458
Laurence, John, 451
Le Bas, Jacques-Phillipe, 286
Le Prince, 161, 396
Le Vasseur, C., 161
Lead, Leonard, 415
lead glazes, 132
Leda and the Swan, 92, 112
Lefèbre, François, 449
Lefèbre, Jacques, 449
Legros, Pierre, 399
Leopards, 415
Leopards, Prowling, 94, 122, 437, *374*
Lesson in Love, 135, 140, 158
Liberty and Matrimony, 88, 103
Liège, 449
Lion and Lioness, 27, 35, 436, 464, *14*
Liston, John, 411–12, 418, *339*
Literature, 16, 17, 197, *1*, *152*
Littler, William, 8
Locatelli, 452
Lochee, John Charles, 451
Locker, James, 14
Locker, William, 3–4, 14
London Account Book, 7–8, 24
Longdon, 145
Longton Hall, 8, 61, 62, 156, 205, 257, 302
Lord Hood, 405, 406
Lord Rodney, 405, 406
Louis XIV, King of France, 258
Louis XV, King of France, 158
Louis Seize style, 11, 82, 132
Lovers, 63
Lowing Cow, 31, 32
Lück, J. F., 246
Lück, Karl Göttlieb, 191
Lygo, Joseph, 11, 12, 13, 134, 148, 149, 180, 250, 293, 313, 366, 370, 374, 376, 386, 388, 398, 444, 446–7, 448, 451–2, 454–5, 456
Lynch, J. H., 412

MacAlister, Mrs Donald, 4
McArdell, James, 16, 85, 86, 161, 314
Macaulay, Catherine, 160, 238–41, *193*
Mackenna, Severne, 396
Madam Vestris, 412
Madam Vestris as a Bavarian Peasant Woman, 416, 418, *341*, *342*
Madam Vestris as a Broom-Seller, 465
Madonna and Child, 145, 274, *223*
Male Dancer, 61, 65, *45*
Mallet, John, 240
Man and Woman with Milk Churns, 414, 422, *358*
Man and Woman with Milk Pails, 427
Man and Woman Standing beside Hampers, 293, *239*
Man with Flageolet and Drum, 85, 95
Man with Flageolet and Tabor, 85, 95, *73*

Mandoline and Bagpipe Players, 85, 95–7, *74*
Mannerism, 152
Mansion House Dwarfs, 32
Map-seller, 27–8, 40, *22*
Map-seller and Companion, 88, 106, *89*
Marchant, James, 5, 6
Marcolini, Count Camillo, 154
Maria Foote as Arinette, 417, 465, *337*
Marie-Josèphe, Dauphine, 153, 333
marks
  1770–84, 148
  bone china models, 408
  Pale Family models, 59
Marmontel, Jean-François, 287
Mars, 28, 42, 63, 77, 91, 113, 154, 258, *24*, *96*, *97*, *209*
Mars and Venus Candlesticks, 338, *282*
Mason, Thomas, 451
Mason family, 451
Mazeppa, Ivan Stephanovitch, 414
Mazeppa Group, 413–14, 422, 465, *354*
Mead, Mr, 90
Meissen, 9
  influence of, 26, 27, 60, 88–9, 151–5, 411
  marks, 408
Melpomene, 190
Mennecy porcelain factory, 312, 448–9
mercury gilding, 409
Meukin, Ada Isaacs, 413
Mew, Egan, 354
Meyer, Frederick Elias, 27, 31, 61, 93, 153, 154, 170–1, 302
Milton, 62, 67, 110
Milton, John, 148, 160
Minerva, 28, 43, 63, 77, 91, 113, 160, 266, 338–9, 346–7, 445, *96*, *98*, *289*
Minerva Crowning Constancy and Hercules Killing the Hydra, 134, 139, 159, 165–6, 450, *125*
Minton, Thomas, 416
Mintons, 463, 464, 465
Minuet Dancers, 86, 98, *76*
Mire, Noel, 231
modellers, 462–5
modelling
  1770–96, 134
  bone china models, 410
  dry-edge models, 26
  experimental models, 16
  Pale Family models, 60–1
  patch-marked models, 84
  transitional models, 54
models
  1770–96, 134–43
  bone china, 410–37
  dry-edge, 26–51
  experimental, 16–21
  Pale Family, 61–81
  patch-marked models, 84–128
  transitional, 54–6
Monkey with a French Horn, 89
Monkey Musicians, 122, 135, 141, 411, 415, 464
Monkey Orchestra, 415, 431–2, *365*
Monkey Violinist, 89
Monks and Nuns, 148, 254–7, *206–8*
Monnet, Charles, 160, 180, 196, 231
Moor, J. F., 240
Moore, C. F., 160
Mopsorden, 94
Morgan, Thomas, 450
Morning, 457
Mortlidge, John, 451
Moseley, Charles, 16
motifs
  partridge's eye, 60
  star-cross, 60
  see also deutsche Blumen and *indianische Blumen*
Mounteney, Edward, 4
Mountford, John, 462, 464
Muller, J. S., 88, 161, 342
Music, 16, 17, 197, 383, *1*, *150*, *321*
The Music Lesson, 142
Musical Group, 353
Musical Group of Two Figures, 274–6, *224*, *225*
musicians
  dry-edge models, 35
  Pale Family models, 65–7
  patch-marked models, 95–7
mythological models
  1770–1810, 139
  dry-edge, 42–3
  Pale Family, 73–7
  patch-marked, 110–17

Napoleon Bonaparte, 279
Napoleon Bonaparte, 413, 416, 422, 463, *352*

Neal, Henry, 463
Negress, 89
Nelson, Admiral, 463
Neo-Classicism, 11, 132, 154, 346, 455
Neptune, 28–9, 32, 53, 54, 56, 63, *44*
Neptune with a Dolphin, 43, 77, 91, 113, 139, 148, 160, 263–4, 314, 348, *99*, *100*, *290*
Neptune Heads, 143
New Dancers, 61–2, 67
New Hall, 407
New Works, 13, 14
noblesse de robe, 85–6
Noon, 457
North Briton, 90
Nost, John, 445
notables
  1770–1810, 135–8
  bone china models, 422
  Pale Family models, 67
  patch-marked models, 108–10
Nymph Asleep amidst Flowers, 410, 429, 465, *364*

Old Works, 14
Oldfield, Mary, 6
Owl, 126

Painting and Sculpture, 197
Pale Family models, 6, 54, 58–81, 93, 212
Palemon and Lavinia, 161, 372–4, 457, *313*
Panthers, 415
Parian ware, 416–17
Paris Cries, 85, 415, 427, 463
Parker, Richard, 279
Parris, E. T., 144
Parrots, 126, 437, 465
partridge's eye (*œil de perdrix*) motif, 60
paste
  1770–96, 131–2
  bone china models, 407–8
  dry-edge models, 21–2
  experimental models, 15
  Pale Family models, 58
  patch-marked models, 81
  transitional models, 53
Pastoral Group, 134, 145, 168, 326, *128*
Pastoral Group by a Fountain, 148, 177–8, 460, *136*
Pastoral Group with Dog, 230, *184*
Pastoral Group with Dog and Lamb, 158, 231, *185*
pastoral models
  1770–1810, 140
  bone china, 422–8
  dry-edge, 38–40
  Pale Family, 69–73
  patch-marked, 100–5
patch-marked models, 6, 81–128
pâte dure, 158
pâte tendre, 155, 158
Pater, Jean-Baptiste Joseph, 86
Paul Pry, 411–12
Peacock amongst Flowers, 415, 437, 465, *379*
Peacock and Peahen, 94, 128
Peart, Charles, 451–2
Peasant Fiddler and Woman playing a Mandoline, 411, 427
peasant models
  1770–1810, 140
  bone china, 422–8
  dry-edge, 38–40
  Pale Family, 69–73
  patch-marked, 100–5
Pegg, Quaker, 144
Perkins, John, 462
Peter the Great, Czar, 158, 414
Peterinck, François, 159, 464
Phillip, Charles, 161, 270
phosphoric acid, 131
Pigeon sauce-boats, 143
Piggot, 10
Piping Shepherds, 87, 104, *83*, *84*
Pitt, William the elder *see* Chatham, Lord
Planché, André, 4, 5–7, 8, 32, 53, 58
Planché, Jacques, 5
Planché, James, 5
Planché, Paul, 4
Planché, Paul Edmund, 5
Planché, William, 5
Plenty, 320
Pluto and Cerberus, 29, 43, 91, 113, *101*
Poetry and Music, 308–9, *255*, *256*
Pointer, 94, 122, 135, 141, 161, 447, 448
Pompadour, Madame de, 155, 158
Pompeii, 278, 332
Poodle Dog, 415, 433, 464, *369*, *370*
Poole, John, 411
Pope, Alexander, 90, 135, 138, 161, 278

Pope, Bust of, 161
Pratt, Charles, 90, 91, 110, 138
Praxiteles School, 399
prices, 149
Procris and Cephalus, 160, 231–3, *186*
The Proposal, 378, 457, *317*
Prudence and Discretion, 148, 180–2, *139*
The Prudent Mother, 145, 272–3, *222*
Public Advertiser, 9–10
Pug Dog Scratching, 17, 21, *6*
Pug Dogs, 31, 94, 122, 415, 416, 433, 448, *371*
Pug Dogs on Cushions, 411, 433, 464
Pug Dogs, Seated, 122, *109*
Punch Candlestick, 66, *48*
Putti, 59, 63–4, 78, 93, 120, 139, 410, *70*, *104*
Putto Seated Naked beside a Vase, 64, 78

Queen Victoria, 406, 413, 417, 422, 463, *355*
Queen Victoria, Bust of, 422, 465
Quinn, James, 84–5, 314–16, *261*

Rabbit Candlesticks, 54, 56
Rabbits, 415, 437, 465
Raimondi, Marcantonio, 161, 384
Rainer family, 412
Ram and Ewe Suckling a Lamb, 121
Ram with Lambs, 122
Ranelagh Dancers, The, 86, 98, *75*
Ranelagh Gardens, 86
Raphael, 161, 384
Ravenet, 91
Read and Lucas, 409
Red Squirrels, 94, 125, *110*
Reinicke, Peter, 27, 28, 152–3, 154, 243, 300
religious models
  1770–1810, 139
  bone china, 429
  dry-edge, 42–3
  Pale Family, 73–8
Renaldo and Armida, 160, 233, *186*
Reynolds, Frederick, 322
Reynolds, Sir Joshua, 91
Riccoboni, Luigi, 300
Rice, Dennis, 7, 8, 53, 356, 416
Rich, John, 316
Richard II, King, 351
Riedinger, Elias, 27
Ripa, Cesare, 91
Rivet, Thomas, 7
Roberts, 10
Roccatagliata, Nicolo, 332
Rockingham, 411–12, 416, 462
Rococo, 11, 22, 60, 82, 83, 132, 153, 154
Rococo Chinoiserie Candlesticks, 80
Rodney, Admiral George Bridges, 138, 405, 406, 461
Romantic Boy and Girl, 414, 416, 417, 428, 465, *361*
Rose, John, 407
Rossi, John Charles Felix, 180, 185, 250, 293, 388, 452
Rousseau, Bust of, 161
Rousseau, Jean-Jacques, 135, 138, 161, 278
Rowan, Pamela, 32
Rowlandson, Thomas, 413
Royal Academy, 157, 443, 448, 451, 452
Royal Crown Derby Porcelain Company, 14
Royal Family, 134, 138, 161, 189
Royal Society of Arts, 407
Rusconi, 180
The Russian Shepherds, 132, 161, 395–7, 458, *331*
Rustic Carrying Grapes, *31*
Ryland, William Wynne, 297
Rysbrack, M., 160

Sacrifice Figures, Pair of, 160, 179–80, 452, *138*
Sailor and His Lass, 161, 356–7, *295*
St Alkmund's Church, Derby, 5, 6
St Mary's Bridge, 5, 6–7
St Philip, 22, 29–30, 32, 43, 63, 78, *25*, *68*
St Thomas, 22, 29–30, 43, 63, 78, *26*, *69*
Saints and Apostles, 30
Sale Catalogues, 133, 146–7, 149, 157, 411
Salutation Figures, Pair of, 239
Sanders, Thomas, 443
Sansovino, Jacopo, 160, 293
Sartine, Mr, 452
Satyr Heads, 143
Saxony, 151
Scheemakers, Peter, 62, 90, 160, 271, 279, 346, 351, 444, 445
Schimmelmann, Carl Heinrich, 153
Schreiber, Lady Charlotte, 464
Scotin, G., 89
Scotsman and his Lass, 382–3, 447, 448, *320*
screw-holes, 22, *7*

Season Vase, 143
Seated Bagpiper and Lady with a Lute, 352–3, *292*
Seated Bagpipers, 27, 35
Seated Boy and Girl, Each with Flowers, 194, *148*
Seated Boy and Girl with Fruit and Flowers, 154, 173, *131*
Seated Gentleman with Flute and Lady with Lute, 176–7, *135*
Seated Monk and Nun Reading, 154
Seated Musicians with Bagpipes and Guitar, 336–7, *278*
Seated Piper, 397, 458, *332*
'Secondary Bird' painter, 452
Sentimental Lesson, 113
Setter, 415
Setter, Prowling, 433, *372*
Setter, Recumbent, 433, 447, 448
Seven Years War, 153
Sèvres, 60, 83, 92, 133, 135, 153, 156, 158, 408, 409, *199*
Shakespeare, William, 84, 90, 186, 271, 345–6, 351, *288*
Sharp, Samuel, 14
Sheep, 411, 415, 416, 437, 463, 465, *377*
Sheep and Lambs, 463
Sheep Candlesticks, 64, 80, 122
Sheep, Lying Down, 463
Sheep, Recumbent, 122, 437, *375*, *376*
Sheep, Standing, 437
Sheffield, William, 14
Shelton, 407
Shepherd, 32
Shepherd and Shepherdess with Fruit and Flowers, 103, *82*
Shepherd and Shepherdess Playing Flutes, 160, 374–6, 457, *314*, *315*
Shepherd Bagpiper and Lady with a Guitar, 85, 154, 348
Shepherd Playing a Reed-Pipe, 215, *168*
Shepherd with a Dog and Shepherdess with a Lamb, 62, 69, *55*
Shepherd with his Dog, 160, 399, 447, 458, *334*
Shepherdess, 32, *56*
Shepherds, 61
Shepherdson, Charles, 6
Shoe-black Group, 158, 236, *190*
Shoe-maker Group, 158, 235–6, *188*, *189*
Sight, 6, 30–1, 47, 48, 216, *37*, *171*
Singeries, 89, 153
The Singing Lesson, 86, 100
The Singing Shepherds, 104–5, 219–20, 358, *174*, *175*
Singleton, 388
smalt, 81
smear-glazing, 13, 158
Smell, 24, 25, 26, 30, 47, 48, 216, *32*, *36*, *172*
Smith, Constantine, 133, 453
Smith, J., 135, 161
Smith, William, 453
Smollett, Tobias, 316
Snowdon, 10
Soar, 145
Society of Arts, 444
soft paste, last models, 405–6
soft-paste biscuit models, French influences, 155–9
Song Bird, 128
Sonnenschein, Valentin, 454
Spalatra, 278
Spanish Group, 145
Spengler, Jean-Jacques, 13, 134, 135, 149, 158, 366, 370, 374, 376, 380, 384–5, 396, 398, 399, 405, 406, 447, 453–8
Spengler, Johann Jakob Wilhelm, 453, 455
Spode, Josiah, 407
Sportsman and Lady, 59
Sprimont, Nicholas, 4, 10, 131, 133, 151
Spring, 16, 17, 31, 44, 63, 72, 73, 93, 118, 140, 168, 170, 192, 202, 220, 267, 270, *28*, *63*, *64*, *103*, *154*, *216*, *217*
Spring and Autumn, 72, 192–3
Spring and Summer, 62, 72, *61*
Spring and Winter, 226–7, *181*
Spring Candlesticks, 337, *279*, *280*
Squirrels, 411, 416, 437, *378*
Stag and Doe, 432, 465
Stag and Doe at Lodge, 27, 35, 94, 125, 411, 415, 416, 432, *111*, *112*
Stags, 432, 465
Standing Boy and Girl with Fruit and Flowers, 186, *143*
star-cross motif, 60
Steady, Lads, Steady, 414, 427, *359*, *360*
Stean, Ralph, 7
Stephan, Charles, 460

Stephan, Pierre, 134, 157, 159, 166–8, 172, 177, 216, 297, 324, 386, 406, 447, 450, 453, 458–61, *126*, *127*
Stevenson, 14, 408, 413
Stocking-mender Group, 158, 234–5, *187*
Stoke-on-Trent, 416
Stone, Sarah, 4
Stoner, Frank and William, 32
Storer, Hannah, 453
Stothard, Thomas, 398, 456–7
Street Vendors, 31, 84, 156, *28*
street vendors, patch-marked models, 106
Summer, 16, 17, 31, 44, 45, 72, 73, 93, 118, 140, 169, 170, 192, 202, 220, 267, *29*, *63*, *147*, *154*, *216*, *217*
Summer and Autumn, 193, 226–7, *181*
Summer, or Harvester Candlesticks, 63, 80
Swan, 437
Sweetmeat Containers, 78–9, 120, 140, 431
Swinton, 462

Tacca, Pietro, 26
Talbot, Lord, 90
Tallard, J. B., 161
Tancred, Played by David Garrick, 84, 95
Tapp, Major, 8
Tarval, J. H., 135, 161
Tasso, Torquato, 233
Taste, 24, 26, 30, 32, 47, 48, 61, 216, *32*, *37*, *173*
Templeton, Lady Elizabeth, 322
Teniers, David the elder, 31
Terpsichore, 190
theatrical models
  bone china, 417–18
  dry-edge, 35
  experimental, 18
  patch-marked, 95
Thierry, Jean, 92
Thistle Dish, 144
Thomas, Francis, 10
Thomason, James, 14, 144
Thomson, James, 84, 143, 374
Thorpe, A. L., 399, 407
Three Cupids, Group of, 159, 324–6, 450, *269*
Three Figures Learning Music, 244–6, *197*
Three Graces, 457
Three Graces Distressing Cupid, 161, 318, 461, *263*, *264*
The Three Maries, 135
Tigers, 94, 415
Tigers, Prowling, 125, *113*
Tillard, J. B., 396
Time Clipping the Wings of Love, 116, 161, 269–70, 460, *219*
tin oxide, 81, 132
Tithe Pig Group, 88, 105, 161, 341–2, *284*
Titmice, 94, 128
Tomtits, 128
Topers, 88, 103, 409, 414, 416, 427, *359*, *360*
Toppin, Aubrey, 86
Tournai, 157, 159, 449, 458, 462
transitional models, 8, 53–6
Trout Heads, 143
Truchy, 85
Tschirnhaus, Graf Ehrenfried Walther von, 151
Tulip Eggcups, 143
Turk and Levantine Lady, 16, 18
Turk Seated, 415, 428
Turkish Dancers, 63, 79
Turks, 89
Turks Dancing, 108
Turner, Thomas, 462
Twitchett, John, 4–5, 7, 12, 267, 406, 417, 454, 462–3
Two Bacchantes Adorning a Bust of Pan, 161, 297–8, 461, *244*
Two Female Macaronis, 243, *196*
Two Figures Burying a Dead Bird, 369–70, 457, *308*
Two Lovers with a Clown, 54, 61, 66, 85, 95, *51*
Two Philosophers, Busts of, 281, *229*
Two Virgins Awakening Cupid, 161, 295–7, 410, 461, *243*, *363*
Tyrolean Dancers, 85, 98
Tyrolese Singers, 412, 418, *340*

Unfaithful Husband, The, 242–3, *194*
Unidentified Bird, Possibly a Finch, 128
Unidentified Birds, 81, 128, *71*, *117*
Unidentified Yellow and Green Bird, 128

Vain Jackdaw Candlestick, 133, 135, 141, *123*
Vanloo, Carle, 86
Varie Figure Gobbi, 161, 312
vases, 1770–1810, 143
Vases with Best Festoons, 143

Vases with Common Festoons, 143
Vasseur, Charles, 376
Vegetable-seller, 28, 40
ventilation holes
  1770–96 models, 132, *124*
  bone china models, 408
  dry-edge models, 22–3
  experimental models, 15
  Pale Family models, 59
  patch-marked models, *72*
  transitional models, 54
Venus, Chelsea Model, 149
Venus and Cupid, 28, 43, 116, 154, 224–6, 258–60, 97, *180*, *211*
Venus and Cupid Mounted before a Vase, 116–17
Venus and Cupid Seated on a Dolphin, 92, 116, *100*
Venus Standing beside a Dolphin, 92, 116
Vestris, Auguste Armand, 412
Vestris, Madam, 412, 418, 465, *341*, *342*
Vicars, Curates and Wardens, 406, 414, 428, 463, *362*
Victoria, Queen, 144, 394, 413, 422, 463, *355*
Vincennes, 155–6, 409, 449
Violinist, 85
Virgil, Bust of, 160, 277–9, 445, *227*
Virgin Mary, 415, 429, 465
Virgins Awakening Cupid, 454
Vleughels, Nicholas, 86
Vulcan, 117
Vulliamy, Benjamin, 5, 12, 134, 180, 250, 270, 396, 451–2, 454–5
Vulliamy, Justin, 12

War, 93, 117, 135
Warblers, 128
Watch-stand, 31
Water, 23, 30, 50, 135, 140, 166, 203, *121*, *126*, *157*
Water Girl, *124*
Watney, Dr Bernard, 5, 15, 17, 25, 29, 31, 92, 180
Watteau, Antoine, 27, 86, 332
Wedgwood, Josiah, 5, 278, 279, 293, 322, 406, 443, 445, 451, 459–60
Weissenfäls, Duke of, 28, 300
The Welch Tailor and his Family, 120, 154, 221–2, *177*
Wellington, Duke of, 413, 422, 462, 463, *356*
West, Benjamin, 445
Wheatley, Francis, 161, 398
Whitaker, John, 410, 415, 465
Whitaker, Richard, 465
White, Charles, 161, 370–1
Wild Boars, 22, 26, 32, *10*
Wilkes, John, 89–90, 110, 138, 161, 241, 271–2, 460, *91*, *221*
Willems, Joseph, 10, 246
William IV, King, 149, 161, 189, 394, 452, 462, *330*
William Pitt, the Lord Chatham, *see* Chatham, Lord
William Shakespeare, 62, 67, 110, 148, 160, 345–6, 351, *288*
Williams, Sir Charles Hanbury, 151
Williams, Thomas, 9–10, 12
Williamson, F., 4
Wilson, E., 412
Wilson, James, 241
Wilson, Dr Thomas, 241
Winged Time, 160, 267, 311, *257*
Winter, 16, 25, 31, 44, 45, 73, 93, 118, 120, 140, 169, 170, 192, 202, 221, 267, *63*, *65*, *66*, *155*, *216*, *218*
Wirksworth pottery, 458–9
Wolloms, 10
Woman, 59
Woman Asparagus Seller, 427
Woman Holding a Bird's Nest, *30*
Wood, William, 11, 146, 147
Woodpecker, 94, 128
Woodward (pipe maker), 3, 4
Woodward, Henry, 16, 18, 156, 356
Worcester Mice, 415, 436, 464
Worlidge, Thomas, 16
Wright, Joseph, 144, 399, 447

Yates, Catharine, 458
Youth and Girl Seated, 69, *53*, *54*
Youth Standing with Flageolet and Tabor, 62, 67
Youth Standing Playing a Reed-pipe, 62, 67

Zeissig, Johann Elias, 154
Zingara, Bust of, 160, 279–80, *228*
Zoffany, Johann, 147, 161, 189, 444